Understanding Video Games

From Pong to virtual reality, *Understanding Video Games,* 4th Edition, takes video game studies into the next decade of the twenty-first century, highlighting changes in the area, including mobile, social, and casual gaming.

In this new edition of the pioneering text, students learn to assess the major theories used to analyze games, such as ludology and narratology, and gain familiarity with the commercial and organizational aspects of the game industry. Drawing from historical and contemporary examples, the student-friendly text also explores the aesthetics of games, evaluates the cultural position of video games, and considers the potential effects of both violent and "serious" games.

Extensively illustrated and featuring discussion questions, a glossary of key terms, and a detailed video game history timeline, this new edition is an indispensable resource for students, scholars, and teachers interested in examining the ways video games continue to reshape entertainment and society.

Simon Egenfeldt-Nielsen is CEO of the award-winning company Serious Games Interactive and has worked as an assistant professor at the Center for Computer Games Research at the IT University of Copenhagen.

Jonas Heide Smith is head of digital communication at SMK. He has previously taught computer-mediated communication at the University of Copenhagen, the Copenhagen Business School, the IT University of Copenhagen, and Roskilde University.

Susana Pajares Tosca is an associate professor at Roskilde University and is a founding editor of the journal *Game Studies*.

Understanding Video Games

The Essential Introduction

Fourth Edition

**Simon Egenfeldt-Nielsen,
Jonas Heide Smith, and
Susana Pajares Tosca**

Routledge
Taylor & Francis Group
NEW YORK AND LONDON

Fourth edition published 2020
by Routledge
52 Vanderbilt Avenue, New York, NY 10017

and by Routledge
2 Park Square, Milton Park, Abingdon, Oxon, OX14 4RN

Routledge is an imprint of the Taylor & Francis Group, an informa business

First edition published by Routledge 2008
Third edition published by Routledge 2015

Library of Congress Cataloging-in-Publication Data
A catalog record for this book has been requested

ISBN: 978-1-138-36299-4 (hbk)
ISBN: 978-1-138-36305-2 (pbk)
ISBN: 978-0-429-43179-1 (ebk)

Typeset in Warnock Pro
by Apex CoVantage, LLC
Printed and bound by CPI Group (UK) Ltd, Croydon, CR0 4YY

Editor: Erica Wetter
Editorial Assistant: Emma Sherriff
Production Editor: Christopher Taylor
Cover Design: Gareth Toye

Contents

Figures

Tables

Acknowledgments

Knowingly or not, a number of people have helped us write this book, through discussion, comments, or by contagious inspiration. For letting us pick their brains, we are indebted to our ex-colleagues at the Center for Computer Games Research: Espen Aarseth, Troels Folmann, Gonzalo Frasca, Jesper Juul, Anker Helm Jørgensen, Lisbeth Klastrup, Sara Mosberg, Miguel Sicart, and T.L. Taylor. For fast and knowledgeable assistance, we owe thanks to the scholarly subscribers of the Games Network discussion list and to Morten Skovgaard, Thomas Vigild, and Mariann Nederby Madsen.

For encouragement, patience, and love we thank Sidsel Egenfeldt-Nielsen, Marie Louise Bossow Smith, and Martin Selmer.

Introduction

Some years ago, we began the first edition of this book by noting that the world was changing. From the perspective of video games, that may have been a bit mild. In fact, when looking back, 2007 now seems an almost quaint time of comforting stability. Indeed, today we increasingly talk about a society where games and play are ever-present.

Broadly speaking, at that time, commercially ambitious games were multimillion-dollar efforts of Himalayan proportions sold in boxes (or through $11-per-month subscriptions), and the then current generation of **consoles** seemed merely the most recent chapter of a never-ending battle between console manufacturers.

By the time you launched your first angry bird from a creaking slingshot in 2010 or 2011 to exact revenge on unscrupulous, if immobile, green pigs, things looked quite different. Apple's iPhone had (unpredicted by almost everybody) shown itself to be the device that would unlock the potential of mobile games, just as Facebook and other social networks were suddenly becoming heavyweight gaming platforms in their own right. Meanwhile, it was becoming less clear whether the newest generation of consoles would be the latest—or the last. The consoles have proven more resilient than some suspected, but are still struggling to stay relevant in today's still more fragmented gaming landscape despite changing their business model dramatically, bringing in indie developers and embracing online distribution formats. The computing power of television sets has grown and services have popped up that promise to do all the heavy computer lifting and simply stream gaming audiovisuals to you. Despite the promise of these services, the revolution heralded by smart TV and game streaming has still to materialize. But it seems that juggernauts like Apple, Google, and Amazon have

Console: A computer designed for the sole purpose of playing games. Often sold without a keyboard.

far from given up on the power of television for gaming, so new fronts are emerging in the gaming marketplace. To add to the commotion, virtual reality and augmented reality have entered the stage, opening yet another area. The future of the gaming world remains wide open.

Of course, in the much larger cultural scheme of things, ours is a time of impressively sudden, varied, and deep shifts. And our age is one in which technology is often the bellwether of these cultural transitions. From miniscule microchips spring visions of the world that challenge, enthrall, and delight us, intensifying our sense of an ever-expanding world.

At some time in the not-so-distant past, most people were content with being passively entertained. More than happy to comply, writers for the page, for the stage, and for the screen would spin linear yarns of great, and sometimes not-so-great, sophistication; makeup would be applied, locations would be scouted, music would be composed, all to grip the heart and captivate our minds. Today, many are not satisfied with their couch-bound spectator status; today, many insist on a more active role whether through fan culture, e-Sports, game jams, or coding their own indie games.

The remarkable world of digital entertainment we know today all started with a whistling white torpedo sent floating through empty space in an MIT basement in 1961. As the torpedo crashed dramatically into the enemy spacecraft, no horns sounded and no drums shook the ground. This was the first volley in what would be known as *Spacewar!* But beyond the basement, the human race at large paid no notice to the fact that video games had been born.

The conception and subsequent birth were not entirely immaculate. *Spacewar!* was, in fact, shamelessly derivative. Its creators, devoted fans of contemporary science-fiction books, had large-scale visions of converting their passion to the big screen, and *Spacewar!* is reminiscent of many space battle movies. More importantly, *Spacewar!* merely marked the opening line of a new chapter in the larger, millennia-spanning history of games.

Creating and playing games is a basic impulse of *Homo sapiens*. The ancient Greeks, the Vikings, and most likely even our ancient cave-dwelling ancestors had rule-based systems of **play**. These served many purposes, from entertainment to competition to education. But our new, post-*Spacewar!* chapter is remarkable. In the historical blink of an eye, video games have colonized our minds and invaded our screens. From a Boston basement, video games have exploded exponentially—reproducing at an alarming rate, much like the fearful space invaders that inspired so many early games— until they are now everywhere, from tiny mobile phone displays to ostentatious wall-mounted plasma TVs. And although games like the casual mobile game *Angry Birds*, the anti-terrorist, multiplayer *Counter-Strike*, or the role-playing space epic *Mass Effect 3* are indebted to ancient predecessors, games are not what they used to be, either. As the computer has offered up its sublime powers—capable of the impartial processing of even the most complex of rules and the simultaneous dynamic presentation of sound and

Play: Ambiguous term (when contrasted to "games"), often referring to the relatively unstructured, relatively goalless activity of children's (or adults') playful behavior.

graphics—new game forms seem more akin to living, breathing worlds than to backgammon or poker.

It was inevitable that academics would eventually notice. Thus, for the last 15 years, scholars have unleashed traditional theories and methods of analysis with still greater speed—sometimes effortlessly, sometimes more awkwardly—onto the phenomenon of video games. The study of video games has from its humble beginnings in the 1980s accelerated at the same speed as video games themselves become still more mainstream in society. New theories have evolved, coinciding with a growing number of books and websites devoted to the medium and with the ever-growing demand for game design professionals. Since the twin fields of game studies and (video) game design are still in the early phases of construction, and since scholars approach games from widely different paradigms, much of the knowledge is not yet easily mapped—or even findable. Hence the need for this book.

In the following chapters, we aim to provide the reader with a broad understanding of video games and video game studies. We explore what we consider to be the most important developments and the most influential perspectives and discuss the relations between them. We have been greatly helped by the superb enthusiasm with which experienced gamers have begun to document and chronicle the history of the game industry and of the games themselves. This deeply felt devotion to the medium has manifested itself in the publication of impressive books such as J.C. Herz's *Joystick Nation* (1997), Van Burnham's *Supercade* (2001), Liz Faber's *re:play* (1998), and Rusel DeMaria's and Johnny L. Wilson *High Score!* (2002). Comprehensive and extremely useful game documentation projects—like *The International Arcade Museum* (www.arcade-museum.com) and *Moby-Games* (www.mobygames.com)—also serve as crucial information depots for the game scholar.

Such resources nicely complement the publication of thorough and knowledgeable volumes on game design, history, and theory, such as Chris Crawford's now classic *The Art of Computer Game Design* (1982), Espen Aarseth's *Cybertext* (1997), Janet Murray's *Hamlet on the Holodeck* (1997), Richard Rouse's *Game Design: Theory and Practice* (2001), Richard Bartle's *Designing Virtual Worlds* (2003), Andrew Rollings and Dave Morris's *Game Architecture and Design* (2000), Katie Salen and Eric Zimmerman's *Rules of Play* (2004), Jesper Juul's *Half-Real: Video Games between Real Rules and Fictional Worlds* (2005), Ian Bogost's *Persuasive Games* (2007), Tristan Donovan's *Replay* (2010), and Jane McGonigal's *Reality Is Broken* (2011).

Understanding Video Games owes its existence to these predecessors. But needless to say, everything there is to know about games cannot fit snugly into one volume. Even many volumes would be incapable of documenting the astounding growth of the games field. Instead, we refer liberally to original literature and to more comprehensive treatments of many of the issues that we touch upon.

ABOUT THE READER

We have written this book to serve a variety of purposes. Our primary audience is a student of games, perhaps in a program of study anchored within the humanities or the social sciences. He or she is not yet a fully trained games scholar but has an interest in achieving a broad understanding of games. But the comprehensive overview we are striving for should find other beneficiaries as well. Those who are technically oriented or mainly interested in designing games will hopefully find much here to interest them, even if the book does not directly increase their practical skills. Similarly, one of our core assumptions is that any student of games will benefit from at least a passing knowledge of issues not specifically tied to his or her specialty. Understanding how games work and why they look the way they do requires an interdisciplinary approach. We should all, in a perfect world, be equally unafraid of code, aesthetic theory, and social thinking. Finally, we hope that even professional scholars will find useful our attempt to map systematically the pertinent topics in game studies.

STRUCTURE OF THE BOOK

Beyond this introduction, the book is divided into the following chapters:

Chapter 1: *Studying Video Games*: Outlines what it means to study video games, and what major approaches there exist.

Chapter 2: *The Game Industry:* Explores the business side of video games, to provide a basis for understanding large-scale trends in contemporary game design.

Chapter 3: *What Is a Game?*: Introduces the reader to classic and current approaches to the study of games and play, and discusses how to group games meaningfully into specific types or genres.

Chapter 4: *History:* Tells the history of video games, focusing on the development of game form and groundbreaking titles. This history emphasizes the games themselves rather than the game industry or individual designers.

Chapter 5: *Video Game Aesthetics:* Offers a formal description of games in terms of sound, graphics, and use of space and time.

Chapter 6: *Video Games in Culture:* Positions video games in our modern (media) culture and examines the discourses that both surround and permeate the gaming world. It also explores some of the cultural practices of video game players: who they are, why they play games, and how they organize themselves in communities that generate culture inside and outside their games.

Chapter 7: *Narrative:* Recounts the relationship between video games and the art of storytelling, focusing on the role of literary theory in the study of games.

Chapter 8: *Serious Games and Gamification—When Entertainment Is Not Enough:* Introduces the reader to the increasingly important field often referred to as serious games and gamification and discusses topics like "games and learning" and "persuasive games."

Chapter 9: *Video Games and Risks:* Discusses the oft-mentioned and culturally divisive question of whether (or how) playing certain types of games can harm the player.

Discussion questions appear at the end of each chapter. These are designed to stimulate thought and argument on the topics covered and to offer avenues for further reading and research. A Recommended Games section also offers suggestions for games that help to illustrate concepts explored in each chapter. Further Readings are also added to address areas that we find are tangential to the chapter but not always covered in full detail.

THE LARGER QUESTIONS

Many people believe that textbooks should be all-inclusive collections of knowledge on a given topic. This is not an unreasonable ambition, but it can give a false impression of orderliness and can ignore the messy, on-the-ground chaos vital to creative and intellectual advances. Such a perspective implies that most issues within a field are settled and that the scholars all agree; the extent of disagreement within a discipline is ignored. Game studies is a young field. It is a field that has yet to settle, systematically and convincingly, some rather important questions.

One of these is the most basic question of all: "What Is a game?" Game scholars do not agree on this most fundamental issue. If this worries you, take heart—it is a condition common to many fields. Sociologists, for instance, do not all hold identical ideas about what "society" means; media scholars differ in their definition of "medium." In one important sense, of course, the question of what makes up a game is really just a question of definition. We cannot determine empirically or logically what a game is. What we can do, however, is seek a definition appropriate for our questions and be quite explicit about the meaning of "game" when we employ it in important situations.

Another question central to game studies is this: "Why are there games?" Why do we, biological entities capable of creating poetry, climbing mountains, and splitting the atom, spend so much time playing games—especially when playing these games often conflicts with our basic human needs: to sleep, to feed ourselves, to communicate with our spouses? We don't know. Or rather, the question has sparked surprisingly little interest and no consensus exists. However, some answers have been proposed[1] and, not unreasonably, they tend to be rooted in biology. They usually go something like this: the ability to play allows organisms to simulate real-life situations. Through these simulations, the organism can practice important skills in relative safety. The individual with a disposition toward play then has an adaptive advantage over those lacking this disposition; natural selection takes care of the rest. The individual who practices throwing his spear in his spare time stands a better chance of survival when a saber-toothed tiger attacks. Such an answer, though sensible, is not comprehensive. While evolutionary biology, for instance, may explain why there are games, it does not explain very clearly why our games look the way they do. Nor does it explain why people like different games and display such an enormous range of attitudes about the very act of playing games.

Which leads us to the next question: "Why do some people prefer certain games?" Again, we must admit that we cannot answer this with any sort of conviction. In fact, trustworthy statistics documenting such preferences (or documenting whether there is, in fact, variation) are less than abundant.[2] We could speculate that age, gender, social status, religion, or hair color correlates with game preferences, but we would then have to explain why this should be the case. We have lots of ideas but no fully formed theory here. The expanded version of this question is also interesting: do certain types of games appeal to people in certain times or cultures, and, if so, why? Again, we could speculate that there is a correlation between the rise of capitalism and the popularity of certain types of highly competitive games, but what we really need is a coherent theory of why such a relationship should be expected and rigorous testing of specific hypotheses derived from such a theory.

Lastly, there is the question uttered by everyone from pundits to parents: "How do games affect the player?" In this case, there is research but little agreement. The question should not be confused with "Do games affect the player?"—they do. The former question is completely legitimate, but it is also quite difficult to answer (as we shall see in Chapter 9). Some popular variations on this question include: "Do violent games make players violent?" "Do zero-sum games make people less cooperative in real life?" "Can games teach children useful skills?"

These larger themes are woven throughout *Understanding Video Games*, and we attempt to answer some of the questions by synthesizing the work that has been done so far in game studies. But the reader should keep in mind the relative youth of the field. At present, video game studies may have more questions than answers, more doubts than certainties. The rules are still being formed; the orthodoxies have not yet been established. And for the curious researcher, there are many worlds in need of exploration. Of course, this is part of why the field is so thrilling. In other words, the discipline welcomes you; there is much to be done.

NOTES

1. Film scholar Joseph Anderson, in the 1996 book *The Reality of Illusion*, has argued interestingly that play behavior is a biological adaptation. This also explains why we like movies.

2. One source is Kafai, 1998.

Studying Video Games

Grand Theft Auto III: Vice City (2001) took the new millennium by storm

Who Studies Video Games?
How Do You Study Video Games?
Types of Analysis
Schools of Thought

Right at this moment, millions of people around the world are playing video games. One obvious way in which this matters is financial. The rising popularity of games translates into astounding amounts of cash. The game industry is quickly becoming a financial juggernaut. Our research may help make even better games, may help large companies increase their profits, or may offer a critical perspective on the social workings and effects of the game industry. Either way, the very size of the industry justifies our attention. But it isn't just the money that's important.

Video games warrant attention for their cultural and aesthetic elements. The aesthetic developments of game design are intense, constant, and thrilling; this explosive evolution of creative possibility is beginning to influence significantly other types of expression. It is clear by now, after the *Matrix* trilogy, after the *Grand Theft Auto, Uncharted,* and *Red Dead Redemption* games, that movies and games are borrowing from each other's arsenals. For the younger generations, especially, games are crucial to the way they express themselves artistically and, presumably, in the way they conceive of the world. What does it mean, for instance, when a person's self-expression moves away from linear representations, such as books and films, and they find more meaning in interactive, nonlinear systems where outcomes depend on player choices? Maybe it doesn't mean anything. Maybe it means a lot of small changes are happening but no revolution should be expected. And maybe it means that in a decade or two, video games will be so essential to the creation of culture that teenagers will be unable to imagine a world before video games existed. And most likely, perhaps, is some combination of all three scenarios. Regardless, such questions need to be investigated systematically.

WHO STUDIES VIDEO GAMES?

Science is the building upon a foundation of experience, the abandonment of old theories, and the revision of earlier hypotheses. The study of video games is not different, but we still have a fragmented and emerging research field.[1]

Is game research a science in this sense? On the one hand, people who claim to be doing game research clearly do not always live up to the highest standards of the scientific method (true for any field); further, there is even some disagreement about how to actually *do* game research. On the other hand, if we take science to mean the systematic, rigorous, and self-critical production of knowledge, game research *can* and *should* be a scientific discipline.

So who are game researchers? In general, they are professionals predominantly occupied with the study of video games. Undergraduates can now major in video games. PhD programs have emerged. Dedicated journals are available and distinct conferences are held. In the larger academic scale of things, all of this is still new; however, Espen Aarseth, editor of the *Game Studies* journal, noted that "2001 can be seen as the Year One of *Computer Game Studies* as an emerging, viable, international, academic field."[2]

A new generation of researchers considers video games their primary research interest. But the struggle for acceptance and academic credibility can still be considerable. Still looking back just ten years, we now have more credible and respected academic journals dedicated to the study of video games that can provide scholars with the necessary platform for advancing their thinking. The classic *Simulation & Gaming* journal published for the first time more than 40 years ago was at the start of the millennium joined by *Game Studies*. Today we also have several other peer-reviewed journals like *Games and Culture, International Journal of Gaming and Computer-Mediated Simulations, Computer Games Journal*, and *International Journal of Game-Based Learning*.

We study video games, not a phenomenon that epitomizes highbrow cultural expression. While we should acknowledge that our field of research may be frowned upon, we must also avoid any sort of paranoia. If our research is not accepted, we should not comfort ourselves with conspiracy theories nor view other fields as populated by enemies. We should instead raise our internal standards.

A series of very important developments has helped put game studies on the road to becoming a viable field. For instance, the last few decades have witnessed a general rehabilitation of popular culture as a worthy topic of study. Also, many scholars have grown up with video games and see no reason why they should be exempt from enquiry. But more importantly, games have grown highly complex—as has their development—inviting serious attention and creating the need for highly trained game graduates. Over the years, DiGRA as an association has grown with multiple regional chapters.

It has become quite obvious that many fields can contribute to the study of games, and game researchers are an eclectic bunch with a multidisciplinary background. Humanist scholars with film or literature backgrounds constitute a large group, but game research conferences are also attended by social scientists (mostly sociologists), by computer scientists, and, very importantly, by game designers. The presence of the latter group, who are typically not academics, is noteworthy. For the time being at least, there is a relatively close relationship between game researchers and game designers. This may sound obvious but is in fact quite a special situation. In older research fields—such as film and literary studies—the distance between scholars and practitioners can loom large, and it seems at times that the two groups barely speak the same language. This may sometimes seem to be the case in our field as well, but at least both sides are committed to making an effort.

HOW DO YOU STUDY VIDEO GAMES?

To say that there is more than one way to approach video games is to put it mildly. Most researchers, at least at present, choose to adopt methods and approaches from their primary fields. Ethnographers tend to observe players. Those trained in film studies tend to analyze the games themselves and communication scholars tend to analyze interactions between players. There is nothing inherently wrong with this tendency as long as one acknowledges the more general ideal that one should use the methodology best suited to answer the question at hand.

In order to give you a better sense of how to approach games academically, let's examine a few noteworthy studies and discuss the methodological approaches that they represent.

We will start with Dmitri Williams's study of how video games have been represented in US news media over a 30-year period.[3] In order to understand the function of video games in public discourse and the relationship between the portrayal of video games and more general cultural currents, Williams searched the archives of *Time*, *Newsweek* and *US News and World Report*. He analyzed 119 articles, which fit his criteria, and concluded that:

> Consistent with prior new media technologies, video games passed through marked phases of vilification followed by partial redemption. Also consistent with prior media, games served as touchstones for larger struggles within the culture—so much so that perhaps "lightning rod" is a better term.[4]

We should note that Williams tackled not games themselves or even players but rather secondary texts that he subjected to content analysis.

In another study, Nicolas Ducheneaut, Robert J. Moore, and Eric Nickell explored the ways in which *Star Wars Galaxies: An Empire Divided*—a massively multiplayer online game set in George Lucas's *Star Wars* universe—encourages sociability among players.[5] In particular, they were interested in how players interacted in the game's "cantinas"—locations where players could meet and socialize. The observed behavior was analyzed to determine if it conformed to sociologist Ray Oldenburg's notion of "the third place," a term used for informal public places like bars and general stores.

Ducheneaut, Moore, and Nickell chose to combine various methodologies. They began by conducting a "virtual ethnography," that is, they spent time in the field (in the game) systematically observing social interactions in the cantinas. They also videotaped their entire game sessions (with a camera plugged into the graphics card). Finally, they recorded a log of all the interactions that occurred between players as tracked by the game and analyzed it using specially designed software. Among other things, the authors concluded that while the cantinas did not serve as particularly sociable spaces, the entire game, due to more subtle **mechanics** than just these intentionally designed social spaces, was in fact quite sociable.

Mechanics: Ambiguous term often referring to events or actions that the game design allows for; for instance, driving, regaining health, or shooting. May be thought of as the "verbs" of a game, i.e. what the player can do.

Susana Pajares Tosca performed a "close reading" of *Resident Evil Code: Veronica X*,[6] a "survival horror" game, where players have to fight zombies and monsters and solve puzzles in order to escape from an altogether unpleasant island. Tosca's study harnessed the techniques of "reader-response criticism." She employed textual analysis, closely examining the work, looking for noteworthy properties of the game's structure, and teasing out the meaning of the game's story. Tosca's research is primarily concerned with using this specific theoretical toolset to explore the text of the game. Surprisingly, given the number of humanist scholars in the field, this is one of just a few detailed analyses of an individual game title.

Finally, Jesper Juul has pursued the philosophical and ontological foundations of games.[7] His main goals have been to provide a definition of video games that highlights their special properties, and to explore the relationship between video games and traditional games. In order to do this, Juul examined noteworthy former attempts and arrived at a "classical game model" (see Chapter 3), which enumerates the features necessary for an activity to be considered a game. The method employed by Juul is a mixture of logical deduction and induction, laying bare the assumptions, which often go unnoticed when games are discussed or studied.

TYPES OF ANALYSIS

As we have seen, games can be approached from a wide range of academic perspectives and by employing a number of different methodologies. Salen and Zimmerman, in their detailed exploration of game design, suggest that games may be approached with a focus on *rules* (the design of the game), *play* (the human experience of playing the game), or *culture* (the larger contexts engaged with and inhabited by the game).[8] To these three units of analysis we add those of *ontology* and *metrics*, to arrive at these five main perspectives:

1. *The game*: Here, one or more particular games are subjected to analysis. The point is to look at games in themselves and say something about their structure and how they employ certain techniques—of player reward, of player representation in the game world, and so on—to achieve the player experience that the game designer aims for. This is often the type of analysis chosen by those with a background in comparative literature or other aesthetic disciplines.[9]

2. *The players*: Sometimes the activity of playing games is more important than the games themselves. Studies focusing on the players usually wish to explore how players use games as a type of medium or as a social space. Sociologists and ethnographers tend to favor this type of analysis.[10]

3. *The culture*: Moving still further from the games themselves, we can choose to focus on the wider culture that games are part of. Here, we wish to understand how games and gaming interact with wider cultural patterns. For instance, we may be interested in the subcultures that evolve around gaming or in the discourses surrounding gaming, looking at public outrage over violent games as compared to earlier "media panics." Methodologically, such studies often turn to secondary sources like news media or advertising.[11]

4. *Ontology*: Meanwhile, some studies examine the philosophical foundations of games. These studies usually seek to present general statements that apply to all games, and may enable us to understand, for example,

Table 1.1 The five major types of analysis and their characteristics

Type of Analysis	Common Methodologies	Theoretical Inspiration	Common Interest
Game	Textual analysis	Comparative literature, film studies	Design choices, meaning
Player	Observation, interviews, surveys	Sociology, ethnography, cultural studies	Use of games, game communities
Culture	Interviews, textual analysis	Cultural studies, sociology	Games as cultural objects, games as part of the media ecology
Ontology	Philosophical enquiry	Various, e.g. philosophy, cultural history, literary criticism	Logical/philosophical foundations of games and gaming
Metrics	Statistical analysis of logged data	Software development, behavioral psychology	Game design

the relationship between rules, fiction, and the player.[12] Such scholarship builds on logical analysis, which is typically grounded in concrete examples but is not interested in individual titles per se.

5. *Metrics*: Finally, recent years have seen a growing interest in data-driven design research, focusing on "metrics" (i.e. quantitative measures of player behavior). Such studies often examine the relationship between game design and player behavior (or sentiment), for instance, to help developers improve the player experience.[13]

Actual studies, of course, often disrespect such neat reductionism and span multiple categories. The preceding scheme indicates general trends, but we must remember that a certain set of methodologies and a certain set of theories need not always go together.

SCHOOLS OF THOUGHT

To speak of schools of thought within game studies may be an overstatement, as these groupings do not usually self-identify themselves as groups, nor indeed as "schools." Nevertheless, certain perspectives do stand out as particularly stable.

First of all, two research communities currently perform game research on a significant scale. The first of these we can call the "simulation community." Researchers within this group focus on all forms of simulations—including nonelectronic ones—but also consistently study video games. This group is well established and has its own conferences and journals like *Simulation & Gaming*. The second and much newer "video game studies community" sprang into existence around the year 2000; it represents what we refer to as "game studies" in this book. The video game studies community presently revolves around the Digital Games Research Association (DiGRA) and journals like *Game Studies* and *Games and Culture*. Communication and collaboration between the simulation community and the video game studies community is still rare.

Formalism

Within the video game studies community, two general approaches can be identified, though most researchers do not resort solely to one or the other. A "formalist group" tends to use game analysis or ontological analysis. They represent a humanistic approach to media and focus on the works themselves or philosophical questions related to the nature or use of those works. Similar approaches are found in fields such as art or film studies.

Within the formalist group a division sprang up early on, as much was made of the difference between prioritizing *representation* and prioritizing *rules*. These subgroups were known as "narratologists" and "ludologists," respectively (see Chapter 7), and differed in their opinion as to which part of the game product was most worthy of study. Narratologists saw fit to approach games as one might a movie or novel, whereas ludologists, often arguing that **narrative** was a mere trapping, felt that game studies should be the study of systems of rules.

Whereas examples of actual narratologists—people who would claim that narrative was *most* important—are tellingly difficult to find, ludologists were quite vocal. For instance, game designer/thinker Raph Koster claimed that "the stories in most video games serve the same purpose as calling the über-checker a 'king.' It adds interesting shading to the game but the game at its core is unchanged."[14] And game theorist Espen Aarseth claimed that "the dimensions of Lara Croft's body, already analyzed to death by film theorists, are irrelevant to me as a player, because a different-looking body would not make me play differently. When I play, I don't even see her body, but see through it and past it."[15] In other words, the fictional layer—the characters and the plot—is merely an **interface** for the rules, the actual core game.

Situationism

The situationist group is generally interested in analysis of game players or the culture at large. They are not interested in all-encompassing statements that do not take context and variation into account. They search less for general patterns or laws and more for analysis and descriptions of specific events or social practices.

In this camp we often find not just the suggestion that games can fruitfully be studied as socially situated play but also a clear discomfort with the formalist approach. Anthropologist Thomas M. Malaby, for instance, has warned against "concluding from categories" (i.e. formalism), preferring "reasoning from actual experience" (i.e. situationism).[16] In a similar vein, game researchers Ermi and Mäyrä have noted that "if we want to understand what a game is, we need to understand what happens in the act of playing, and we need to understand the player and the experience of **gameplay**."[17]

On the whole, however, game studies have so far been an inclusive field. It is unified by a certain pioneering spirit, and the understanding that the underexplored nature of games leaves room for all those interested. It is also unified in the belief that in order to understand most aspects of video games, you need to play them. So we wholeheartedly encourage you, as someone who wants to understand video games, to seek out video game classics and simply to familiarize yourself with as many genres as possible. Always ask yourself the following questions: Why does this work? Why was it done in this manner? How else might it have been done? And why do players act in this way in this particular game? Love of games is obviously no requirement, but it certainly doesn't hurt when entering the world of game research. And it is to this world that we now turn.

Narrative: A string of connected events making up a story.

Interface: The graphical or textual form of interaction between user and software. Through the interface the user may give commands to the software that are then translated into instructions that the computer can interpret.

Gameplay: Ambiguous term for the total effect of all active game elements. Refers to the holistic game experience and the ability of the game to command the attention of the player.

DISCUSSION QUESTIONS

- There is a move away from linear media (e.g. television) and toward interactive media (e.g. video games and the Internet). What causes this trend? Is it simply that technology offers new forms of interaction with media, or is the move tied to larger societal changes?

- What are the challenges and pitfalls of opening up a whole new field of academic study like video game studies? What considerations should one be aware of when entering territory where very little previous research exists?

- How should students of games whose research focuses on one type of analysis deal with the existence of other types of analysis? Is it necessary, in every case, to address all of the major perspectives on a video game phenomenon? How important is it to play games as a researcher?

FURTHER READINGS

Aarseth, E. (2001). Computer game studies, year one. *Game Studies*, *1*(1).

(Estimated reading time: 8 minutes)

Klabbers, J. (2018). On the architecture of game science. *Simulation and Gaming*, *49*(3), 1–39.

(Estimated reading time: 75 minutes)

NOTES

1. Klabbers, 2018.
2. Aarseth, 2001.
3. Williams, 2003a, 2003b.
4. Williams, 2003b, p. 543.
5. Ducheneaut and Moore, 2004; Ducheneaut, Moore, and Nickell, 2004.
6. Tosca, 2003c.
7. Juul, 2003b.
8. Salen and Zimmerman, 2004.
9. Atkins, 2003; Tosca, 2003c.
10. Kerr, 2003; Taylor, 2003b; Wright, Boria, and Breidenbach, 2002.
11. For example, Consalvo, 2003.
12. Juul, 2003a; Salen and Zimmerman, 2004; Aarseth, 1997.
13. Drachen and Canossa, 2009; Nacke, Ambinder, Canossa, Mandryk, and Stach, 2009.
14. Koster, 2004.
15. Aarseth, 2004.
16. Malaby, 2007.
17. Ermi and Mäyrä, 2005.

2 The Game Industry

E.T. the Extra-Terrestrial (1982) was so unplayable that it managed to capsize the booming game industry in the early 1980s

- The Size of the Game Industry
- The Structure of the Big Game Industry
- The Development Process
- Roles in Game Development

It used to be that most games that drew headlines were not casual products. In the age of the console games during the 1990s and 2000s, the notion of people just developing a game alone or even as a hobby was more a dream of the past than a reality. However, things have changed dramatically, especially in the last five years. The "democratization of game development" that the Danish game technology Unity Technologies used as their slogan has begun to materialize. Profound changes have come about with new gaming platforms, still more elaborate business models, innovative funding opportunities, and incredibly powerful game development tools—all at the fingertips of budding game developers. Whether this trend will continue to grow or become just a footnote in the history of games driven by the profound changes the industry is currently undergoing is still too early to say.

Despite dreams harbored by wistful would-be developers, major video games were not typically made in someone's basement (though in recent years those legendary basements have experienced something of a comeback, especially driven by crowdfunding). Large-scale video games were for many years made by highly trained people working within big companies with real production structures. It is important to consider the mass production of games and the industrial process that makes their production

Hardware: Tangible elements of a computer or console, such as the processor, graphics card, or hard drive (as opposed to software).

possible, since both their aesthetic form and their consumption are influenced by this overarching structure. Current **hardware**, platform ownership, the global economy, competition between publishers, and the goodwill of venture capitalists all influence the games that are available on the market. Still, it is just as important to consider the increasingly powerful alternative to this ecosystem heralded by recent developments in the game industry, especially the introduction of the App Store and Steam's expansion with their Greenlight system in 2012 that is now being replaced with Steam Direct. Today the idea of indie developers getting access to the primary publishing channels seems obvious, but ten years ago, this would have been unthinkable.

Since the medium's inception in the 1960s, the game industry has become still more complex, with specializations, bigger budgets, and new technologies. And yet, during the last decade a countercurrent has represented a startling contrast to "Big Gaming," as independent developers have found it possible to work (and even make a living) outside the standard publishing model—often referred to as indie game developers. Indeed, the standard model has been visibly deflated by inventions such as Apple's App Store, Google Play, and social networks like Facebook, which have proved more than willing to serve as game distribution channels. This is not to mention the even more fragmented ecosystems in Asia, especially China, or the opportunities offered by crowdfunding, where fans on Kickstarter or Indiegogo can fund game projects.

But the means of production and distribution are not the only element to influence the shape of the products. Game designers have to take cultural factors and trends into account if they hope to sell their products successfully. There is an interplay between production and consumption that allows for products that can be both standardized and wildly original. In this chapter, we briefly outline aspects of the industry that game students should be familiar with, to understand both why games are the way they are and how one becomes part of this industry. We also believe that academic research into games becomes more inclusive—and more valuable—when it shows an understanding of the market.

THE SIZE OF THE GAME INDUSTRY

Video games occupy a (pop) cultural niche competing most directly with the movie and music industries for the consumer's time and money, although the so-called serious games space is starting to makes its mark more clearly (see Chapter 8). Cross-industry comparisons are often unfair since business models differ somewhat. For instance, movie business profits comprise box office earnings, DVD sales, rental licenses, and sales to television broadcasters, while the music business has secondary income such as licensing for use in commercials and movies. The video game industry essentially makes money by selling directly to consumers (whether through retail outlets or by downloads), from subscription fees for online games, or indirectly through advertising by consumers clicking on ads on the game page. There are few sources of secondary income, although movies are occasionally based on game licenses. Of course, these examples are based on "software" (i.e. games, music, movies), and if we were to include hardware (game consoles, DVD, CD and MP3 players, etc.), the picture would become even more complicated.

Not just sticking to software, many promising trends in the game industry (such as increases in online subscriptions, the rise of **freemium** games, the proliferation of games for mobile phones and the introduction of AR/VR), means that the games' industry financial revenue is catching up to filmed entertainment: game sales reached $119.2 billion globally in 2018, compared to just above $97 billion for filmed entertainment. In addition, according to IDATE, the expected annual growth rate for games remains high, at 7.7 percent for 2019–2022.[1]

If we zoom in on sales of games, we see that video game revenue is relatively stable in its growth. Earlier notions of the importance of new console generations in driving new growth seem increasingly irrelevant. This development is a consequence of the diminishing overall importance of consoles, apparent in Figure 2.1. Console games are no longer the revenue leaders, despite including hardware revenue; instead, mobile games have taken the lead and are pulling away fast. The new platforms help diversify the game

Freemium: Games (often apps) that you can download for free but for which players then have to pay a fee in order to proceed past a certain point, to eliminate advertising, or to unlock more of the game (for example, new levels or better items).

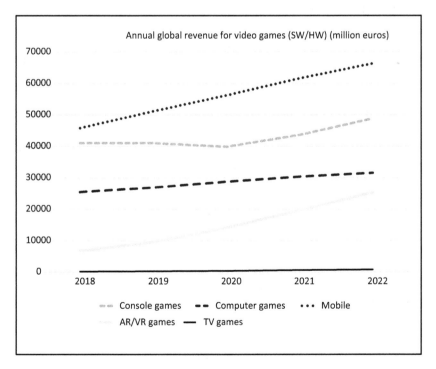

Figure 2.1 Annual global revenue for video games (million euros). The figure shows how the traditional console games and PC games are struggling with declining revenue, whereas mobile games are growing rapidly. (Source: IDATE, 2019)

industry, meaning it is not reliant on blockbuster games to the extent it was ten years ago.

Figure 2.1 also shows that PC games are relatively marginal, in financial terms, compared to mobile and console games. However, the PC is an important platform for indie games and online games, and it handles some important game types requiring more complex controls—especially **strategy games**—almost exclusively; thus, it should not in any way be discounted as a platform. It is also worth remembering that PC games have traditionally been more prone to illegal copying than console games—for this reason the PC is in fact a more popular platform than sales data suggest. Finally, there is a massive number of more or less free games for mobile and PC, which obviously do not feature in sales statistics. The introduction of smart TVs has never really materialized as a gaming platform. AR/VR has already gotten off to a way better start, but it is still way behind the more established platforms for games.

Looking at broader developmental trends, the game industry experienced strong growth throughout the 1990s and 2000s. Although the financial crisis starting in 2007 also eventually hit video games, the industry has increasingly defied the so-called console cycles. Previously, the market had operated in distinct cycles: the release of a new generation of console led to a burst of revenue from the sales of games designed for the new machines. Revenues would then slowly decrease, prompting console manufacturers to release new machines, typically within five years. Within each cycle, the most popular machines would often be engaged in "console battles," as each company would tout the strengths of its newest model. Currently, some are beginning to speculate about whether consoles will continue in their current form. Even if consoles do not disappear, they may have longer cycles and less impact on the industry.

Interestingly, the major console manufacturers—Sony, Nintendo, Microsoft, Sega, and Atari—have never really made money on the console hardware itself.[2] The profit is in the games, as console game developers pay license fees to console manufacturers. As a result, the battle revolves around getting the largest consumer base in the three major markets: the United States, Japan, and Europe. A large consumer base ensures large game sales, which then encourages developers to make new games for a specific platform.

Until the seventh-generation console cycle, Sony led the market with their PlayStation 1 and 2, although they were challenged by the Xbox from Microsoft. Still, it was Nintendo's Wii that, after the failure of GameCube, took the lead, to most analysts' surprise. Instead, Xbox 360 and PlayStation 3 fought hard for the close second place.[3] In the latest console generation Microsoft came off to the best start, but then Sony pulled away from Microsoft and Nintendo. Xbox One and Switch are struggling to keep up, as Table 2.1 shows. PlayStation has historically appealed more to the hardcore gamers, and many nonhardcore gamers are abandoning the consoles in favor of the vast mobile alternatives, which may explain why PS4 is in the lead. With

Strategy games: Games focusing on the ability to deal with dynamic priorities, typically in a context of resource shortage. Strategy games may be divided into **real-time strategy games** and **turn-based strategy games**.

Table 2.1 Lifetime sales of major consoles. The table shows that PS4 has taken the clear lead with Nintendo and Microsoft locked in a tight fight for second place.

Console Sales—millions of units sold (2018)[4]	
Sony PS4	94.2
MS Xbox One	40
Nintendo Switch	32.72

Switch, Nintendo tried to repeat the earlier success by introducing a different kind of creative vision for a console platform, where you could create your own hardware controls.

The market leader used to be able to influence publishers, distributors, and retailers, directing their focus to a particular console and thus making life increasingly difficult for competitors. But the sheer size of console gaming, and of video gaming more generally, makes the market highly lucrative and tempting, all but ensuring constant rivalry. For instance, *Madden NFL*—which has a new version released each year—sold more than 99 million copies in the United States alone from 2001 to 2013.[5] One of the most talked-about games in the last 15 years has been the mostly PC-based *The Sims* series. *The Sims* sold more than 125 million copies between its release in 2000 and 2010,[6] and the PC version was the bestselling PC game in North America in 2000, 2001, 2002, and 2003. More recently, by the end of 2014 indie title *Minecraft* had secured sales of more than 17.5 million copies,[7] but with more than 100 million downloads, leading the way for a major acquisition by Microsoft at $2.5 billion in late 2014.[8] Despite the impressive sales of the more classic game franchises, the mobile space is also challenging the status quo with huge successes from companies like King (*Candy Crush Saga*), Supercell (*Clash of Clans* and *Hay Day*) and Rovio (*Angry Birds*). Thus, even if entering the market may seem difficult, potential sales are impressive enough to ensure competition.

Indeed, the challenge increasingly seems to be that the competition is too fierce. With entry barriers like the cost of game engines and distribution platforms vaporizing, many hopeful indie developers enter the market only to hit the wall of obscurity. Rising acquisition costs make the situation even more difficult. With (Free to Play) business models getting a strong foothold, it almost seems harder to make it as a game developer compared to just a few years back. Now you need to master the dark arts of monetization design on a much more ingrained level and be able to sustain your game after development for a much longer time before it turns a profit. Smaller developers, through reduced salary, cannot easily carry this cost in addition to the numerous out-of-pocket costs associated with development and marketing (for example, in ads). As such, the game industry is in a strange flux. On the one hand, it has never been easier to make a game and get it out, but the chances of making a dent in the universe has, relatively speaking, maybe

Engine: The basic code that defines the relation between game objects and determines the limits of graphics and sound.

never been lower. You disappear in obscurity and on top of that the dream of the long tail seems distant. Many believed that with digital distribution channels it would be easy to have a much higher number of games to choose from (the long tail), but ultimately what has happened is that nobody can find these games. So even if the game market grows, this is not to the benefit of all developers but primarily to the benefit of market leaders.

This may have been the reason why crowd-funding platforms like Kickstarter and Indiegogo have from the start been very popular, connecting developers desperate to make what they love, a huge potential jackpot if you get to the top, and fans cheering on the next new interesting titles. What you get may be a lot of great games but also even more extreme competition from people trying to push their way forward with what is ultimately free cash from fans. In such an environment it is hardly a surprise that new distribution platforms have received a lot of attention, in recent years especially.

OnLive tried to set the stage early but, after valiantly struggling to gain momentum, closed business mid-2015. However, this is likely not the end of streaming but rather the start, as the major players like Google, Amazon, Microsoft, Verizon, Sony, and EA are increasingly looking to streaming, which has vast advantages like reducing hardware cost (thereby extending the player base), fighting piracy, increasing profit per player, providing ongoing updates, continuous tracking, and the superior business model of in-app and subscription neatly tying into it.

THE STRUCTURE OF THE BIG GAME INDUSTRY

Since the 1990s the game industry has consolidated and evolved more standardized and professional structures for developing new products. Companies have been acquiring one another and forming strategic alliances, all to handle the increasing demands of game production. More powerful hardware and a continuous arms race between game developers have resulted in larger production teams, increased development costs, and tougher competition. However, as the budgets and teams grew, a counterreaction started in the indie movement, where small teams would develop simpler games on their own. As the game industry has fragmented in the last few years, a larger variation in development teams has become apparent.

AAA: The term used for video games with the highest development budgets, e.g. the *Grand Theft Auto* and *Assassin's Creed* series.

MS-DOS: A nongraphical operating system developed by Microsoft that was dominant before Windows.

Large-scale commercial games are often referred to as "AAA titles" ("triple-A titles"), and they are still the major force in the industry. It is not unusual for such a game to involve 100 or more specialized experts, each focusing on different aspects of sound, programming, animation, graphics, marketing, game design, and production. In this light, productions of the late 1980s can seem quaint by today's standards. The **MS-DOS** version of the 1989 hit game *SimCity*, for example, lists a fairly small number of contributors, with a total of 20 (including people receiving "special thanks").[9] Compare this to the extensive and much more differentiated credits for *Halo 2*, produced in 2004, which lists more than 80 people.[10] *Call of Duty: Modern Warfare 2* from late 2009 listed more than 200 people in the credits, underlining the accelerating complexity of the game.[11] *Grand Theft Auto 5*, released in 2013, allegedly became the most expensive game to date, with a production budget of $265 million, and over 500 people in the credits.[12]

But, as mentioned, AAA titles are not the only games out there. The push toward even larger budgets has initiated a strong countertrend: the growth of independent games. Low-budget games produced outside the system of big publishers have in the last few years become a truly mainstream phenomenon through the growth of online and mobile games. This "casual" market is regarded with much enthusiasm by the game developer community, which sees inflated productions as a potential threat to creativity and innovation in the industry.

To take an example, Introversion Software's *Darwinia* from 2005 (in which the player must help eradicate a virus from a simulated world, partly by ordering around little units created by the inventor Dr. Sepulveda) gained respect from many quarters by making creative use of limited resources and by taking an irreverent approach to traditional genre divisions. As such they became one of the first successful proponents for the indie game developer movement. This development model was replicated with even greater success by Danish game developer Playdead in 2010, with the bestselling *Limbo* (see also Chapter 4), in which the player guides a small boy through a hostile black-and-white world. The aforementioned Swedish sandbox game *Minecraft* took home three awards from the Game Choice Awards in 2010 and continues to be vastly influential in redefining the conception of games in 2015.

As traditional retail distribution channels continue to be weakened and new online channels take over, the chances are that the current fragmentation of the game industry will continue. Today the standard has become that development teams vary in size depending on what business model and platform they target. Today we have small teams for the App Store, medium-size teams for Facebook, large teams for online games, and huge teams in the AAA space—but even within these platforms, variation and composition of the team is significant. Returning to the larger scale of mainstream game publishing, we can see how specialization and increased complexity have resulted in differentiation. The industry presently comprises the following elements.

The hardware manufacturer makes the console or the component necessary to play the game on a PC (for example, a graphics card, made by a producer like NVIDIA). The game developer makes the game. Small developers usually need a separate publisher and distributor (similar to the book business), while big companies perform all these functions in-house.

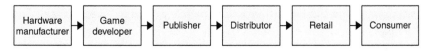

Figure 2.2 The value chain of the game industry

For example, *Rez*—a critically acclaimed abstract shooter game, released in 2001—was developed by UGA and distributed by Sega, while for the acclaimed city builder *SimCity* Maxis took on both roles. The games are then stored by distributors in their warehouses, before being sold to retailers (like your local Walmart) and eventually to consumers. Increasingly, games can also be purchased for download, which is changing the role of the distributor and publisher and entirely cutting off the retail link.

Typically, the publisher is seen as the pivotal component of the industry. Publishers buy projects from independent developers (i.e. companies that are not owned by or affiliated with a publisher) or have in-house game development sections, and may at any time be searching for independent developers to acquire. To a certain extent, however, publishers are challenged by the strong hardware manufacturers, whose influence can be felt throughout the industry (in the form of demands for exclusive titles that can only be released for one console, for instance). Furthermore, various ways of making money from online gaming are emerging as serious alternatives to the standard model of game production. Thus, the dominant model of game production described above is under transformation. Although the preceding description refers to the classic AAA business ecosystem, this also holds true for the new marketplaces like mobile, albeit with less stringency. For example, Apple has become both the hardware manufacturer and distributor—and even in some cases the publisher.

The game industry is often compared with the movie and music industries: all three share high production and marketing costs as well as a similar reliance on blockbusters. The rule of thumb is that 90 percent of revenue in the game industry is generated by the top 10 percent of titles. These figures resemble those of the movie industry, where box office revenues have been increasing in direct proportion to larger marketing budgets and production costs.

For some years the transformation away from AAA, especially with Facebook and the App Store, was heralded as a way to change the rules of the game. But it seems that the transformation only offset the marketplace for

Table 2.2 Major companies' revenue. The table shows that a lot of the revenue within games is going to nongame companies that have entered the market.

Company	Country	Revenue (millions $)
1. Tencent	China	19,733
2. Sony	Japan	14,218
3. Microsoft	USA	9,754
4. Apple	USA	9,453
5. Activision-Blizzard	USA	6,892
6. Google	USA	6,497
7. NetEase	China	6,177
8. Electronic Arts	USA	5,294
9. Nintendo	Japan	4,288
10. Bandai Namco	Japan	2,741

Source: Newzoo, 2018.

some years, as we now see that the new marketplaces are dominated by a limited number of companies.

Console versions sell for upwards of $60, although the price varies between countries, and has become more varied over the years as the consoles have also introduced online services. Typically, this sum is divided among the various players in the industry as follows: for each copy sold, the retailer gets about $12, the console manufacturer gets $12, and the distributor, the publisher, and the developer split the remaining $36. PC games are cheaper, but the revenue is split in much the same fashion. The price difference between console and PC games reflects the fact that console game developers must pay license fees to console manufacturers, and also that PC games are the easiest to copy illegally, thus the price must be low enough to deter some of this piracy.

By 2010, development budgets for AAA titles had soared to between $18 and $28 million[13] or more, and a typical production schedule can take anywhere from 18 to 36 months. And development is only part of the budget, as marketing can cost in the range of $1 to $30 million per title. However, with the latest console cycle the budgets have risen yet again to as high as $60 million, with development schedules creeping upwards. Indirect evidence also points to skyrocketing marketing budgets that can be as high as two to three times the development budget in AAA.[14] In the new marketplaces on mobile we also see the so-called CPI (cost per acquisition).[15,16] In general, these numbers are climbing, particularly as improved hardware creates consumer demand for more complex products, which in turn requires more elaborate input from more and more specialists (and the accompanying marketing savvy to make people want it). However, the biggest concerns are probably rather the increased marketing expenditure in an increasingly competitive marketplace.

Of course, publishers also release game titles that do not qualify for the AAA label, but that are still far more complex productions than the "independent games" discussed above. Such games may have development budgets ranging from $0.6 million to $5 million, and similarly smaller marketing budgets in the $0.2 million range. These titles take 12 to 18 months to develop, and console versions usually sell for considerably less.

"Value titles" have even shorter development times—usually between five and six months—and have limited budgets hovering around $200,000 to $300,000. Hence, the marketing spend is also quite limited, at about $40,000, and retail prices are set somewhere between $20 and $30 depending on the platform. Interestingly, in the last ten years, value titles have been increasing in number and quality alongside the growing availability of middleware tools—software tool sets that assist the developer in one or more areas of development and that can compete with the tools used for developing more high-profile titles.

The video game industry used to be clearly dominated by AAA titles, which are the ones you would see in store windows, the blockbuster titles like *Grand Theft Auto, Red Dead Redemption, Call of Duty,* or *World of*

Warcraft. Today, however, numerous other platforms exist, and we are on the horizon to see the fragmentation continue, although it is too early to say where the next disruption will come from—one good guess is virtual reality where Oculus Rift continues to spawn hype as it was acquired by Facebook in early 2014.[13]

THE DEVELOPMENT PROCESS

As mentioned previously, the development time of video games varies depending on the range and ambition of the project. AAA titles will usually have the longest development cycles and involve the most detail, but almost all productions will go through a conceptual phase, a design phase, a production phase, and a testing phase. These steps are outlined in the following.[17]

The Conceptual Phase

First, the game concept is formulated, in just a few pages, in order to convey the core idea of the game and various features, such as platform and sometimes concept art. Next, the designer creates a game proposal that functions (hopefully) to attract funding and to plan the actual production. It is much more detailed than the game concept, covering market analysis, technical issues, and budget projections, as well as audiovisual style and descriptions of how the game would actually feel to play.

The Design Phase

If all goes well, the game concept and game proposal provide the basis for further descriptions of the game's specifications. Although not always kept separate, the game designers now describe, in great detail, the functional and technical specifications. The former provides concrete details about features and how the player will interact with the game while the latter specifies how to achieve the desired design on a technical level. Together these specifications, sometimes referred to as the design document, may take up as much as several hundred pages, depending on the scope of the project. AAA titles require very extensive documentation, while small independent productions need much less. A design document consists of text, illustrations, mockups, concept drawings, and other details, such as lists of objects in the game. It is a living document that is updated constantly as development advances. A decade ago, the design document might have been enough to get a publisher on board. But in a sign of how competitive/demanding/ruthless the industry has become, few investors today will give the green light to a project based on the design document only; most developers now need to produce "demo versions" of the games where the main features are already visible, and even playable to a certain extent. The few exceptions to this requirement are cases where the publishers have commissioned the game, or where the parties have a long-standing relationship.[14]

Based on the design document, the game developer makes a decision regarding the game **engine**. The (game) engine is the software, which provides the basic architecture of the game but not the concrete content. For instance, a first-person-shooter engine will specify the basics of first-person-shooters (a player has one **player character**, the game world is seen from the player character's perspective, there can be other characters in the world, etc.) but not the details of how player characters must look or the structure of the actual levels in the game. Thus, a game engine is loosely comparable to a word processor, which enables an author to write words of her choosing, or to a theater with props, which enables a director to stage plays without building everything from scratch. More specifically, the game engine handles the artificial intelligence (how computer-controlled units act), the audiovisuals, and the physics (e.g. the effect of bumping into walls, and the effects of gravity). The developers may choose to build their own engine, but often a license is acquired to use a generic third-party engine. Popular commercially available game engines include the Unreal Engine, originally developed for the *Unreal* series but later forming the basis of games such as *Tom Clancy's Splinter Cell, Mass Effect 2*, and *Batman: Arkham City*. Another engine is Unity3D, increasingly favored by casual game developers of projects like *Limbo*, mentioned earlier.

> **Player character (PC):** In-game character controlled by a human player.

Apart from the game engine, developers make use of general third-party software tools to handle elements, which are imported into the engine, such as music or textures (graphical elements to be "stuck" onto elements like buildings). Many third-party tools are used in the game industry, but on the graphics side, software packages such as Maya and 3D Studio Max are often used for 3D objects, while Photoshop is used for 2D.

Having made choices regarding game features, engine, and other tools, the next step is usually the creation of a working prototype—a fragment of the game that shows off its main features (and in advanced versions may even be playable). The aim is to give developers, marketers, investors, and others a feel for the game, and to ensure that the core game design works and is worth pursuing further. The prototype is also used by developers to secure further funding from publishers.

Production and Testing Phases

Armed with design document and prototype, the developers start the production proper. As one may guess, the design document only completely and effortlessly guides the production in a hypothetical perfect world. In practice, developers stumble onto unforeseen challenges and are sometimes forced (by funding issues, changes in the competitive situation, etc.) to change game elements during production.

The actual production of the game involves the writing of the game's code and the creation of different elements such as graphics and sound. This process takes several months and is done in specialized groups (in the case of large productions). When the separate elements have been individually made, they are linked together to form the alpha version of the game. The alpha version is the first version—alpha being the first letter of the Greek alphabet. It contains all main elements for a playable game but lacks fine tuning and polishing. It is therefore only used internally to test for technical errors (bugs) and for issues concerning ease of use and playability: a game must be as easy as possible to use (i.e. have high usability) but must also of course be fun and appropriately challenging to play (i.e. it must have high playability and be attractive to play). Typically, this testing reveals a number of problems, which are then addressed before the production of the beta version. The beta version is used for "real-world testing," typically by inviting a number of beta testers (ideally gamers as close to the target audience as possible) to play the game for an extended period and report on any problems or give suggestions. Typically, beta testers are not paid for their efforts but may receive a free copy of the game or other benefits. Apart from these core functions of beta testing, the process may also work to inspire interest and to recruit "ambassadors" who will promote the game to other gamers by word of mouth.

Based on input from the beta testing, final changes and corrections are made to the game and, if all goes well, the "gold master"—the first actual release of the game—follows soon after. What this means to the developer depends on the game type. Before the mid-1990s, a gold master could mean the developer turning entirely to other projects. Today, however, many game productions lead directly into the production of a sequel or the production of an add-on package. And for large-scale online games, like MMOGs, the very concept of a gold master has little meaning, as the sometimes-gargantuan challenge of providing customer support and ensuring stability still lies ahead when the game is officially launched. Also, Internet proliferation has led many developers (particularly PC game developers) to rely on the ability subsequently to provide "patches," which must be downloaded and which fix or tweak aspects of the game. This phenomenon does inspire some disgruntlement, as paying customers are arguably used as testers, but the ability to observe widespread actual use may also reveal subtle issues that are difficult, if not downright impossible, to detect under test conditions.

ROLES IN GAME DEVELOPMENT

Accomplishing the massive undertaking described earlier—especially in the creation of a large-scale game—requires five areas of expertise: design, art, programming, project management, and testing.[18] Different companies use different titles for the same functions, but the following brief description gives an overview of some of the competencies involved.

The game designer is considered the most prominent contributor, similar to a movie director. A game designer outlines the vision and describes the game in detail. Though this may seem like a very creative process, more often the designer's focus is to facilitate new ideas and continuously manage a game's identity, especially in the case of long-term franchises such as the *FIFA* series. Depending on the size of the production, other participants may have the roles of interface designer (who handles the user interface), level designer (who creates detailed levels for the game, which usually involves the programming of entire areas in 3D), and so forth.

The graphics for the game are created by graphic artists. Some specialize in 3D while others focus on the 2D material. They work with sub-specialists like animators, modelers, texture artists, and character animators. Being a graphic artist typically requires a background in art and a deep knowledge of common game industry tools such as Maya and Photoshop. Specialist artists are often overseen by lead artists and, at a higher level, by art directors.

Programmers are the ones who put everything together and turn the individual elements into a playable game. A typical large-scale game production can have a team of around 25 programmers who focus on different aspects of the game. Engine and tools programmers create the backbone of the game. The networking programmer is especially important in multiplayer games, for which he or she sets up the client-server architecture, writes basic protocols, and deals with online gaming issues like latency (the critically important period of time it takes for the computers involved to communicate data) and security. The artificial intelligence programmer is responsible for the behavior of **game objects** (or characters) that need to respond sensibly to the player's actions (by chasing the player character, for example, or devising counter-strategies). Other programmers will be focused on various aspects of graphics and audio. Increasingly, programmers are managed by a lead person who supervises productions and coordinates with other parts of the project.

Game object: A distinct entity in a game world, such as a character, a sword, or a car. Does not refer to things like background graphics, sounds, interface details, etc.

Finally, game productions are overseen and managed by a producer. The producer functions as a project manager, keeping the project on schedule and on budget, while also ensuring that the production team has sufficient and appropriate resources.

All of this may give the impression that AAA game development is a hugely complex, specialized, and time-consuming process, sometimes resembling assembly work more than creative work—which would be exactly right. The continuous increase in production size may well explain some of the apparent interest in creating and sharing more formalized conceptual tools for game design and development, underscored by the large number of recent books on these topics. With this many people, and this much money involved, one simply cannot be bogged down by misunderstanding emanating from imprecise terminology and lack of clear responsibilities. The drive for more mature management is strengthened by the outcry in the developer community in recent years against the unacceptable working conditions in some studios during development, where 70-hour work weeks were not unusual. This was seen especially during the so-called crunch, when a game needed to be shipped no matter what. The uproar over such working conditions[19] is a sign of the maturing industry. According to the IGDA (the International Game Developers Association),[20] it is important to maintain quality of life in general, and it also makes good business sense to keep experience in the field rather than people burning out.

Of course, unwieldy and financially risky productions have also—as mentioned earlier in this chapter—paved the way for a counter-movement toward more manageable (and sometimes more creative and satisfying) productions, as in the case of "indie gaming." Thus, we have recently seen and will most likely continue to see two parallel themes in game development: increasing AAA budgets on one side, and increasing interest in alternatives to the full-scale model on the other. The best opportunities for huge revenues still reside firmly on the AAA side, but with continued calls for more focus on creativity and artistic courage, smaller scale development will seem increasingly attractive to many.

DISCUSSION QUESTIONS

- Marketing materials for games and consoles have changed considerably over the years. Find video game ads from the past and present—in print or online—and discuss the development of advertising themes and messages in your examples.

- What does the success of the Nintendo Wii, PlayStation 4, Microsoft Kinect, and the new fascination with Oculus Rift tell us about player preferences and likely future developments in the game industry? Discuss this in relation to three key concepts: gameplay, visual quality, and game interface.

- What are the risks and benefits of inviting large numbers of beta testers to test a not-yet-completed game? Why do developers still see this as a vital part of development?

- What do the latest statistics on global video game sales tell us about developments in the industry? What role will mobile gaming play? What does the future for PC and console gaming hold?

RECOMMENDED GAMES

Minecraft—The game that became the symbol for indie games, and ultimately turned to what many indie considers the dark side: Microsoft.

Angry Birds—The game that defined the success of the new mobile platform through a brilliant simplicity, built a huge brand spreading to other media, and heralded the rise of the Finnish game industry.

FURTHER READINGS

Taylor, H. (2018, May 11). The era of "break-out indie success" is long dead. *Gamesindustry.biz*.

(Estimated reading time: 8 minutes)

NOTES

1. PwC, 2014.
2. See, for example, Williams, 2002.
3. Snow, 2007.
4. Dedicated video games sales units, 31 December 2018, www.nintendo.co.jp/ir/en/finance/hard_soft/index.html.

   Sony Consolidated Historical Data 2016–2018, 1 February 2019, Sony Investor Relations.

   Chapman, T. Xbox One Total Lifetime Sales Pass 40 Million Milestone, 13 December 2018, https://screenrant.com/xbox-one-lifetime-sales-total-microsoft/
5. Video Game Sales Wiki, 2011.
6. Takahashi, 2010.
7. Minecraft, 2015.
8. Microsoft, 2014.
9. MobyGames, 2007a.
10. MobyGames, 2007b.
11. MobyGames, 2007c.
12. Scotsman, 2014.
13. Crossley, 2010.
14. Kotaku, 2014.
15. Mobiledevmemo, 2014.
16. Forbes, 2014.
17. Based on Tim Ryan's article "The Anatomy of a Design Document"; see Ryan, 1999a, 1999b.
18. Mencher, 2003.
19. Frauenheim, 2004.
20. IGDA, undated.

3

What Is a Game?

General Models for Understanding Games

The Issue of Genre

Tic-tac-toe illustrates the concept of a game at its simplest level

Are poker and *Assassin's Creed* examples of the same phenomenon? The playing situation could hardly be more different. Poker is inherently multi-player and is governed by abstract rules not justified by any fictive world—a full house beats two pairs, aces are higher than jacks. Meanwhile, *Assassin's Creed* is a single-player, stealth-based fighting game that takes place in colorful historical settings, the rules of which mimic those of the physical world (see Figure 3.1). These two games are so different that it might be hard to see how they both belong to the same category.

Nevertheless, there are similarities. For instance, in both games the player faces opposition—albeit from wildly different "foes"—and has his or her choices evaluated by the rules of the game.

In this chapter, we dig beneath the surface to examine what games are made of. We will introduce influential theoretical approaches, and their respective models. By discussing the (admittedly rare) "classics" of game studies, we aim to show the different ways in which games have been theorized. We will be returning to these perspectives throughout the book. We also introduce a genre system that we shall use to distinguish between different types of games.

Figure 3.1 Assassin's Creed: Unity (2014). One of the most successful new franchises in the later years.

GENERAL MODELS FOR UNDERSTANDING GAMES

In daily life, we tend to define games informally; the general public, and even most serious gamers, don't require formal criteria in order to enjoy their games. For students of games, however, definitions are essential. Understanding the way games work and how they differ from other types of entertainment helps us choose the appropriate methods to analyze video games. If we are not specific, we run the risk of using terminology and models inappropriate to our discussion, or we risk blindness to the bias of our perspective. For instance, if we consider games to be stories, we will focus on rather different things than if we consider games to be drama, or systems, or types of play. The challenge here is not so much to find the correct perspective but rather to be aware of and explicit about the assumptions we make.

Our criteria for what makes a game can have another serious consequence. Defining anything is a highly political project. Define games as "narrative" and the research grants are likely to end up with departments devoted to film or literature studies. Define games as a subcultural teenage phenomenon and studies of games are less likely to be funded by ministries of culture, to reach the pages of the "serious" press, or to be available in public or research libraries. In other words, definitions are tremendously important, and not just for academic reasons (see also the discussion of genre systems in the next section).

Ludwig Wittgenstein and the Problem of Games

German philosopher Ludwig Wittgenstein (1889–1951) could not think of a common definition that would include all "games." Wittgenstein, in his *Philosophical Investigations*, famously argued that there was no common

feature of the objects that we call games, and
that we could hope for nothing more than
"family resemblances." Wittgenstein looked at
a number of activities traditionally referred to
as games, including chess, tic-tac-toe (otherwise known as noughts and crosses), tennis,
and ring-around-the-rosy. While some of these
have elements of luck while others require skill,
he notes that "we see a complicated network of

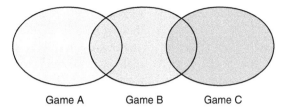

Figure 3.2 Family resemblances. Illustrates the fragmented
nature of what we commonly refer to as games.

similarities overlapping and criss-crossing: sometimes overall similarities,
sometimes similarities of detail."[1] According to Wittgenstein's definition of
family resemblances, while Game A shares features with Game B and Game
B shares features with Game C, Game A and Game C need not share any
features, as illustrated in Figure 3.2.

We must realize that Wittgenstein was not really interested in games
per se but used his analysis as an element of the larger project presented in
his *Philosophical Investigations*. Nevertheless, in our context, there are two
problems with Wittgenstein's analysis. First, he does not really try to find
the common feature that he claims does not exist. He merely offers a few
examples and notes how they do not share certain (more or less random)
features. Second, Wittgenstein's analysis rests on a peculiarity of language.
German, like English, does not distinguish between formal games and the
informal games that children play; ring-around-the-rosy and chess are both
"ein Spiel" (a game) in German. But this is not the case in Scandinavian
languages, for instance. In Danish the word "spil" refers to formal games
(including video games), while the noun "leg" refers to informal playful
activity like playing house. Thus, Wittgenstein's argument may be quite language specific, and we should not be led by his analysis to believe that games
necessarily escape sensible definition.

Johan Huizinga and the Magic Circle

Historically, games have been severely undertheorized. However, in the
mid-twentieth century a few writers did look more closely at games than
others (including Wittgenstein) had done. In 1938 Johan Huizinga, a Dutch
scholar whose PhD dissertation focused on the clown figure in Sanskrit
drama, published a homage to play entitled *Homo Ludens*,[2] which underscored the importance of play in culture. This study, whose title translates
roughly as "Man the Player," re-evaluates the status of play in cultures that
have historically treated it as inferior to work and other "serious" activities.
Despite his approach, Huizinga has little to say on defining or understanding games. He does, however, make the important and much-cited observation that games construct a "magic circle" which separates the game from
the outside world.[3] Playing a game, in this view, means setting oneself apart
from the outside world, and surrendering to a system that has no effect on
anything that lies beyond the circle. When you begin a game of chess, for

example, you are submitting to a formally defined experience with rules that are clearly distinct from those we follow outside this special activity. The chess rules make sense in themselves and are only important within their particular context. Thus, arguably, the chess players construct (or enter into) a magic circle to engage in an activity cut off from the outside world.

Huizinga's vision of games has merit but also clear problems. First of all, it is perhaps too closely tied to an ideological agenda. Huizinga's intention was to praise the act of play, and in his effort to protect play—from what he saw as the destructive influence of the Protestant work ethic and a Western culture that prized seriousness over fun—he may well have overstated his case. Games are special contexts where particular rules apply, but we can apply this definition to a wide array of utterly different activities: work, family life, university classes, weddings, the nightlife of a big city. All of these situations are governed by special rules and norms that do not always—indeed, could not always—apply in other contexts. Games, then, are not entirely different from the remainder of our lives, and should not necessarily be treated as an aberration.

As we criticize Huizinga's philosophy, we must acknowledge that the modern game researcher's agenda may in fact be ideological too. For instance, economist and **virtual world** theorist Edward Castronova has echoed Huizinga's point:

Virtual world: Multiplayer (or multiuser) system presented as having a large-scale geography. May be divided into game worlds and social worlds, the latter having no objectives or goals.

> As meaning seeps into these play spaces, their status as play spaces will erode. As their status as play spaces erodes, the laws and expectations and norms of contemporary Earth society will increasingly dominate the atmosphere. When Earth's cultures dominate, the game will be over; the fantasy will be punctured; the illusion will be ended for good.[4]

Castronova acknowledges that no bulletproof philosophical argument can be made to support the idea of games as a completely separate sphere of human existence. He is arguing instead that all of us, as gamers and as societies, should attempt to erect or uphold such barriers if we want game worlds to retain their unique appeal.

Apart from the ideological dimension of Huizinga's argument, we should consider whether it is really true that games do not extend into other spheres of life. Although the conflicts within a game—between you and that stubborn enemy nation, for example—do not usually extend directly into other parts of your life, games do have real-world consequences. We can easily name a small number:

- *Games require time*: Games affect our lives by substituting for other possible activities, from watching television to reading a book to sleeping.
- *Games affect our moods*: Games can make us feel satisfied, or enraged, or thrilled. These and a plethora of other emotions can easily carry into other activities.
- *Games are communication media*: Games may communicate ideas and values. For instance, a strategy game may teach us how complex systems

like cities or warring nation states work. Or advertising in a game may brand a certain product in our minds.

- *Games affect our behavior*: Games may make us do things that we would not otherwise have done. For instance, the American military have used the game *America's Army* as an (allegedly efficient) recruitment tool.[5]
- *Games may directly affect the outside world*: Activities that occur in a game may have concrete effects in "real" life. For instance, objects acquired in game worlds are sold for real money on trading websites like eBay, blurring the boundary between the two domains.

All of these aspects of gaming belie the myth that the magic circle truly separates games from the outside world. Thus in game studies today, magic circle arguments are often treated with suspicion or seen as primarily applicable on a strictly formalist level of analysis—as when one brackets other aspects of a game to study its design closely (so speaking as if a game could be separated entirely from the outside world).

The notion remains crucial and widely used, as we can see in the influential writings of Chris Crawford,[6] and Katie Salen and Eric Zimmerman.[7] More recently, however, controversy has arisen over this issue, as a few researchers have rejected the validity of the magic circle model and the usefulness of its application to game studies. In her 2009 article, revealingly named "There Is No Magic Circle,"[8] Mia Consalvo claims that we cannot understand games from a purely formalist point of view, one that sees them as mainly rule-based activities. The idea of the magic circle "emphasizes form at the cost of function, without attention to the context of actual gameplay." She points to her own work, and that of researchers like T. L. Taylor, Thomas Malaby, and Constance Steinkuehler, as an example of giving attention to the context in which games are played. This reveals underlying tensions and social contexts that we wouldn't see just by thinking of the rules of gameplay, therefore:

> we cannot say that games are magic circles, where the ordinary rules of life do not apply. Of course they apply, but in addition to, in competition with, other rules and in relation to multiple contexts, across varying cultures, and into different groups, legal situations, and homes.[9]

In the same vein, Thomas Malaby also refuses to see games as only objects: "Every game is an ongoing process. As it is played, it always contains the potential for generating new practices and new meanings, possibly refiguring the game itself."[10]

On the other side of the table, one of the identified formalists, Jesper Juul, insists that the process/contingency researchers have misunderstood the magic circle idea. He admits that the metaphor might be confusing, but it is not exclusive of other approaches. He proposes that we look at games as existing within three frames: the inner layer as goal orientation, the second layer as experience, and the third as a social context. Paying attention to the inner layer (the rules) doesn't mean that we reject the others. He puts it like this:

> every game action can therefore be evaluated according to three different considerations, with the desire to win being only one of three considerations. We cannot generalize about the relative weight of these considerations as players have individual understandings of how important it is to win vs. how important it is to keep the game interesting vs. how important it is to manage the social situation. Some players believe that friends should help friends in a game, and some players believe otherwise. Does this disprove the existence of a magic circle? No, but it shows us what the magic circle is.[11]

Roger Caillois and the Sociology of Play

French philosopher Roger Caillois has articulated a more specific vision of the nature of games than Huizinga's magic circle. In his 1958 work *Man, Play, and Games*, Caillois stressed four essential qualities of play: that it must be performed voluntarily, is uncertain, is unproductive, and consists of make-believe. He also famously divided games into four categories, according to their dominant features. The categories are: *agôn* (competition), *alea* (chance), *mimicry* (imitation), and *ilinx* (vertigo). Additionally, he argued that all games exist on a continuum between *paidia* (playfulness) and *ludus* (formal, rule-based game behavior).

Adventure games: Games focusing on puzzle-solving within a narrative framework. These games typically demand strict, logical thought.

- *Agôn* (competition): In play of this type, competition is central, and skill determines whether the player is successful or not. This includes hide-and-seek, chess, physical sports, and most video games within the action genre.
- *Alea* (chance): Here, chance is the most important parameter for the play experience. Chance decides who wins a lottery or a dice game. Most video games have an element of chance and randomness, although some classic **adventure games** are entirely linear and lack this quality.
- *Mimicry* (imitation): Here the important play experience centers on being someone else, the ability to take on the role of a vampire, sibling, clown, or pilot. Winning is not usually an important part of this play form, which is often found in traditional role-playing games and adventure video games.
- *Ilinx* (vertigo): This play form offers the chance to experience a pleasurable sensation, often through physical activities like riding a roller coaster or carousel. In video games, it is found most vividly in racing games like *Stunt Car Racer* and *Super Monkey Ball*.

When describing a particular game, these features can be combined to form complex play forms such as *mimicry-agôn-ilinx*. *Super Monkey Ball*, for example, is a video game where the player controls a monkey (*mimicry*), who competes against other players (*agôn*), and who drives fast around various tracks, and sometimes over the side and into the abyss (*ilinx*). These

	Agôn (Competition)	Alea (Chance)	Mimicry (Imitation)	Ilinx (Vertigo)
Paidia ↑	Racing ⎫ not Wrestling ⎬ regulated etc. ⎭ Athletics	Counting-out rhymes Heads or tails	Children's imitations Games of illusion Tag, Arms Masks, Disguises	Children "whirling" Horseback riding Swinging Waltzing
Tumult Agitation Immoderate laughter				
Kite-flying Solitaire Patience Crossword puzzles	Boxing, Billiards Fencing, Checkers Football, Chess Contests, Sports in general	Betting Roulette Simple, complex, and continuing lotteries	 Theater, Spectacles in general	Volador Traveling carnivals Skiing Mountain climbing Tightrope walking
↓ *Ludus*				

Figure 3.3 Caillois's classification of games. The figure shows Caillois's classification of games that is quite contested, as it seems hard to fit any game into one of the genres[12]

different categories of play can be further analyzed on the spectrum between *paidia* and *ludus*. Figure 3.3 illustrates the relation between *paidia/ludus* and the four play categories.

In a *paidia* activity, one is not bound by rigid rules. *Ludus*, by contrast, refers to systems with formalized rules like chess, soccer, or backgammon. Although winning or losing is not anathema to *paidia*, these goals are not always present; who wins is much more a matter of negotiation between the players than something decided by specific rules. In *ludus* play forms, there are rules that must be adhered to, and winning is a result of meeting these specific conditions. In the new field of video game studies, Caillois's categories have been widely cited, but his formulation has its critics. Game scholar Jesper Juul, for one, does not find Caillois's categories very useful in describing video games:

> Although it is commonly used, we find Caillois' categorization to be extraordinarily problematic. The individual categories can in many cases be useful, but their selection and the distinction between them are very hard to justify: while the distinction between paidia and ludus is more or less correct on a formal level, the idea that they would be opposite ends of a spectrum on an experiential level stems from the misunderstanding that rules are strictly limitations, and that the player can do nothing more complex than what the rules explicitly specify.[13]

While perhaps immediately appealing, these four game types seem somewhat arbitrary and don't always help distinguish between individual games. Take, for instance, the soccer game *FIFA 12*. The game is competitive, has elements of chance (at least from the players' perspective), and simulates a sport, thus placing it in three of Caillois's four categories. His claim that "sports in general" belong solely to *agôn* does not seem enlightening in relation to video games.[14]

In addition, you may have noticed that the distinction between *paidia* and *ludus* is somewhat similar to the common distinction between *play* (as in "children in play") and *game* (as in "they sat down to play a game"). While a very useful distinction, it is usually best not to think of them as entirely separate. Play—even in the loose-knit form of *paidia*—will always have *ludus* elements, since even free-form play has some rules. When children play in the sandbox, they still have to—as their parents insist—"play by the rules." These rules may be implicit, or may even be flexible, but they function as guidelines nevertheless. Sandbox activity will often be "about" building the biggest, tallest, or prettiest sand creation. Most children will also be aware of the social rules that one should not take sand from the other children's sandcastles, step on them, or steal others' designs and claim to be the inventor. These rules, although unspoken, shape the entire experience of being in the sandbox with others.

Forms of play with stronger *ludus* elements, in contrast, have precise rules and a quantifiable outcome. However, even *ludus* experiences contain room for interpretation, alteration of the rules, and some actions that are not covered by the rules. In chess, a standard rule states that once you have moved a piece the move is binding; an even stricter variant states that you must move a piece even if you have only touched it. But in casual play, the strictness with which this rule is enforced varies greatly. This may seem like a minor detail, but chess is arguably the strictest *ludus* game and an oft-cited archetype of this more severe end of the gaming spectrum.

We should note that video games differ from traditional games in the sense that their rules are enforced by the computer—rather than a gullible younger sibling or a tender-hearted older relative—and thus not open to the same type of negotiation possible in traditional board games like chess. Nevertheless, the overlap between *ludus* and *paidia* is also found in video games. One must consider video games both as rule systems and as more open-ended universes. In a game like *Microsoft Flight Simulator*, for example, the player is engaged in *paidia* when just flying around, but when he chooses to go on a mission, the experience takes on a greater element of *ludus*. Modern video games in particular often let the player choose between trying to achieve the goals and simply roaming the game world.

And while it is true that we cannot negotiate with our computers, we are often not competing solely against a program. Gamers don't hesitate to discuss, often fiercely, the rules of a video game, and a fundamental element of playing a video game is discovering the rules about how it is played. Both before and during play, as anyone who has ever played a video game with a friend knows, it is common to try and figure out "which rules apply." It has been suggested that over time rules inevitably become less ambiguous, and that this makes games suitable for a computer platform, where, in order to work, the computer requires that rules be unambiguous.[15] This theory, of course, hinges on our perception of rules. In multiplayer games, the negotiation of rules is often part of play, and players and developers may continuously add new rules (on various levels) to the game universe.[16] For instance, players of the **real-time strategy game** *Age of Empires II* would often spend time trying collectively to define legitimate strategies before starting a battle on Valve's online gaming system Steam.

Real-time strategy game: Strategy game in which the action is played out continuously, without breaks (as opposed to **turn-based strategy games**).

	Agôn (competition)	Alea (Chance)	Mimicry (imitation)	Ilinx (vertigo)
Paidia (loose)	StarCraft		Minecraft	Johann Sebastian Joust
	DOTA2		Goat Simulator	B.U.T.T.O.N
Ludus (rules)	Forza Motorsport	Slotomania	The Sims	Dance Dance Revolution
	Tekken	Big Fish Casino	Nintendogs	Wii Sports

Figure 3.4 Video game examples put into Caillois's classification of games. Finding examples for each genre turns out to be quite difficult

More specifically, a certain video game type tends to encourage free-form play over strict adherence to rules and single-minded attempts to fulfill game goals. In this book, we call such games "process oriented" (and deal with them in detail later in this chapter). An example is *SimCity*, in which the player indirectly controls the development of a city without any clear end goal.

If we try to play along with Caillois's classification (see Figure 3.4), it becomes clear that it is difficult to constrain almost any video game to one of the categories. It seems that the classification only to quite a limited extent captures the important elements that we intuitively use to categorize games as similar or dissimilar. In general it seems that the *paidia* types of games for many years lived a quiet life in the video games industry but have now come into fashion, all the way from the omnipresent indie hit *Minecraft* to the massive AAA game *Grand Theft Auto* and the more obscure surprise hit *Goat Simulator*. We also see that the category *ilinx*, which most gamers would have written off just five years ago, is now coming into play with new interfaces that extend the game experience beyond the screen. Experimental games like *Johann Sebastian Joust*, where you play by attuning your body to a piece of Bach music, is much more physical and sensorial then past games, although we have seen something similar in the past with the original Japanese smash hit *Dance Dance Revolution*.

Marshall McLuhan and Games as Cultural Reflections

Both Huizinga and Caillois agree that games are entirely separate from the outside world. Others, however, see games as reflections of culture, and claim that a culture's most popular games can even reveal its core values. One major proponent of this position is Canadian media theorist Marshall McLuhan, referred to by some of his 1960s contemporaries as "the oracle of the electronic age." In a brief chapter of his book *Understanding Media*, McLuhan loosely defines games:

> Games are popular art, collective, social *reactions* to the main drive or action of any culture. Games, like institutions, are extensions of social man

and of the body politic, as technologies are extensions of the animal organism. Both games and technologies are counter-irritants or ways of adjusting to the stress that occur in any social group. Games are dramatic models of our psychological lives providing release of particular tensions.[17]

Here, McLuhan makes two claims: the first is that game forms are tied to the culture in which they exist, and thus reveal its nature; the second is that games release tension. An example of the first claim, from McLuhan's own discussion, is that American football is gaining in popularity at the expense of baseball because football is "nonpositional." Any player can take any position during play. Baseball, where players fulfill specific positions, represents industrial society, while football agrees "very well with the new needs of decentralized team play in the electric age."[18] He also claims that the reason why Russians, surprisingly, like "individualist" games like ice hockey and soccer (clearly representing a problem for his theory) is that these games have an "exotic and Utopian quality" for people still considered "tribal." Although there may be some general truth to McLuhan's claim, he undermines himself somewhat by explaining away problems in such an offhand manner.

McLuhan's second argument, that games release tension, is also not entirely obvious. Games, and in particular multiplayer games, can obviously provoke both anger and frustration. Beyond this, the general idea of "catharsis" (Greek for cleansing) through games is not backed up by much empirical data. The same is true of McLuhan's claim that "we enjoy those games most that mimic other situations in our work and social lives." If we look hard enough we can find similarities between most things, but we are equally likely to find examples from our list of favorite games that make this claim sound hollow.

More generally, the idea of games as reflections of cultural themes remains an interesting but underexplored idea.

Gregory Bateson and Play as Communication

In games, we are perfectly willing to accept the presence of orcs even if we would strenuously deny their real-world existence. We may even hold a series of assumptions regarding game orcs who have not even been encountered; they are likely to be evil, not to appreciate beauty, and generally to be bad company.

The British anthropologist Gregory Bateson's theory on meta-communication helps us understand why we accept such fictions as meaningful. Meta-communication means communication about communication, and refers to the wealth of cues we transmit and receive about how statements or actions should be interpreted. In conversation, for instance, we use body language and tone of voice to tell the other party how seriously a statement should be taken. In play, we also communicate (through numerous, often subconscious, means) that what we are doing is not to be taken at face value: we are not fighting but playing at fighting. We, as animals with higher cognitive functions, are able to appreciate that an action has different meanings within different contexts, and we come to learn this through play. As we mature, we expand the ability to meta-communicate into other areas of life and are perfectly capable of interpreting fiction (adequately meta-communicated to be fiction) in a different light than we would shine on reality.

Some recent games, known as **alternate reality games**, have challenged our ability to know and maintain the frame of play even more than traditional games. In *Majestic*, for example, part of the game consists of using real websites, fax numbers, and email addresses in order to uncover a conspiracy; the player becomes an investigator collaborating with other "real-life" players, all chasing increasingly complex clues. As play progresses, the line between what is within the video game and what is outside blurs. Huizinga would say that the magic circle is challenged, and Bateson might see increasingly subtle forms of meta-communication.

It is worth noting that alternative reality games have not achieved widespread popularity, perhaps indicating that most players are not particularly interested in playing with the very boundaries of what constitutes a game.

Alternate reality games: A game genre that mixes the game world with reality, so the boundaries become blurred—for example, using real websites as part of the game.

Brian Sutton-Smith and Games as Play

Since the 1970s, educationist Brian Sutton-Smith has been a significant force in establishing games and play as a legitimate area of research through papers, anthologies, and conferences. Sutton-Smith never fails to stress the multifaceted nature of games, noting that "a game is what we decide it should be; that our definition will have an arbitrary character depending on our purpose."[19] According to Sutton-Smith, the variety and widespread presence of games in many cultures should not be interpreted as proof that games are inevitably a part of every culture. Rather, games emerge as societies mature and develop more advanced political and social organizations. Games reflect the evolution of a society: the more complex a social system, the more advanced its games.

Sutton-Smith sees a game as finite, fixed, and goal-oriented. He defines games as "an exercise of voluntary control systems in which there is an opposition between forces, confined by a procedure and rules in order to produce a disequilibrial outcome."[20] This definition is quite broad but necessarily so, given the multifaceted nature of games. Games come in very different forms, ranging from social games, to solitary games, physical games, and theoretical games. *Monopoly* is a system with rules and procedures for working out a final state—one victorious player. Each individual player tries to establish dominance by making the right moves. In soccer, players interact with each other within teams to score a greater number of goals than the opposing team.

Although Sutton-Smith has refused to give a one-line definition of play, the complexity of the challenge has not prevented others from trying, as we will see in the following sections. In fact, it seems that almost every well-known philosopher has theorized on play. For example, German philosopher Friedrich Nietzsche said that "two different things wanteth the true man: danger and diversion. Therefore wanteth he woman, as the most dangerous plaything."[21] Psychoanalyst C.G. Jung refers to the creative aspect of play: "The creation of something new is not accomplished by the intellect but by the play instinct acting from inner necessity. The creative mind plays with the objects it loves."[22]

George Herbert Mead and Role Training

Social psychologist George Herbert Mead considered play to be an important ingredient in what he called the process of the genesis of the self. According to Mead, who wrote his influential work, *Mind, Self, and Society* in 1934, a self arises through a learning process in which children understand and eventually come to master normal human social activity. Social activity is all about communication, where humans use a shared system of symbols to exchange ideas with each other. Play and games, also being symbolic, are for Mead a clear precursor to adult communication.

His definition of play is mainly what others have called "make-believe," in which children pretend to be one thing or another and play a role: a mother, a policeman, or an adventurer, for example. This is different from the way animals play, in that children deliberately take on another role and build a temporary self by using the symbols that indicate that role. This kind of play is usually limited to one role at a time, even though children can change from one role to another very quickly. The essential difference between this kind of play and organized games is that in games, the player has to "take the attitude of everyone else involved in that game, and that these different roles must have a definite relationship to each other."[23] This means that the player needs to be conscious about the other players' roles at all times, something that is facilitated by the rules of the game. Rules are "the set of responses which a particular attitude calls out."[24] So to go from play to game requires the individual to integrate himself into a higher level of group organization.

For Mead, an individual can only obtain his unity of self when he has internalized this "generalized other," that is, the attitude of the whole community. Games are excellent mirrors of the way that people organize themselves, where all actions are related to each other in an organic way that can be understood by learning the rules. Children experiment with many different kinds of social organizations as they grow up. The exercise of learning to belong, of learning different roles and rules, allows their personality to develop.

Henry Jenkins and the Art of the Game

An influential cultural view of the nature of video games has been presented by a professor of comparative media studies, Henry Jenkins.[25] Jenkins argues that video games are a new form of popular art, and game designers the artists of our century. His work is inspired by cultural critic Gilbert Seldes, who in his book *The Seven Lively Arts*[26] argued that the most important American contributions to the world of art were to be found in popular culture formats like the comic strip and jazz music. Although some of these cultural forms have today acquired a certain cultural respectability, Seldes's focus on popular aesthetics instead of on the "great arts" was rather revolutionary in the mid-twentieth century.

For Seldes, the "lively arts" are mainly kinetic—that is, they seek to move people emotionally rather than to appeal to the intellect as the classical arts do. Popular artists, Jenkins explains, explore new directions and new media:

> Cinema and other popular arts were to be celebrated, Seldes insisted, because they were so deeply embedded in everyday life, because they were democratic arts embraced by average citizens. Through streamlined styling and syncopated rhythms, they captured the vitality of contemporary urban experience.[27]

For Jenkins, video games are the worthy heirs of this trend:

> Games represent a new lively art, one as appropriate for the digital age as those earlier media were for the machine age. They open up new aesthetic experiences and transform the computer screen into a realm of experimentation and innovation that is broadly accessible.[28]

Jenkins reminds us that a lot of the social prejudice leveled against video games today has clear parallels with the reactions against the cinema in Seldes's time, for example, the vitriol leveled against the depiction of violence and sex.

He nevertheless acknowledges that many games are "banal, formulaic and predictable," following well-known recipes instead of innovating. Economic constraints are not a valid explanation for their aesthetic conservatism, as this doesn't prevent artists in other media, such as film, from delivering good products. (However, we must not forget that video game technology changes so dramatically every few months that designers spend a lot of time catching up instead of exploring the medium aesthetically.) Jenkins argues that games are an art form still in its infancy, but some games with advanced **aesthetics** already suggest that the form can provoke strong emotions. Video games have also already given us such memorable characters as Sonic the Hedgehog and *Super Mario Bros.*'s Mario and Luigi.

In order to understand how key developmental moments come about in video games, we need to understand them as a medium. For Jenkins, games are about player control, and the best experiences arise when players perceive that their intervention has a spectacular influence on the game, such as when a *Civilization V* player understands that her carefully planned strategy ensured her narrow but crucial victory over a warring neighbor nation.

The games Jenkins admires are those that offer players the opportunity to do things that were not possible before. For example, in *Black & White* players are gods whose every decision has moral consequences and affects the balance of good and evil in the game world.

Jenkins talks of play as a performance, where a person's interaction with a game facilitates a kind of immersion unknown in other media. In order to

Aesthetics (of a video game): All aspects of a video game that are experienced by the player, whether directly (such as audio and graphics) or indirectly (such as rules). (Note that **aesthetics** is an ambiguous term used in many ways across disciplines.)

facilitate the player's sense of extreme control over the game he is in—vital to Jenkins's vision of a successful game—the design and aesthetics of the game are crucial. Even more than cinema, games make use of "expressive amplification," a process in which the impact of specific actions is exaggerated so that the player feels increased pleasure at executing these actions. In Jenkins's view, the artistic potential of video games will be met when designers concentrate on exploring the aesthetics of action instead of trying to imitate other media.

Formal Definitions

Thinkers like Huizinga and McLuhan, as well as many others, have used games primarily in the pursuit of other questions, and are not solely concerned with creating a "formal" definition of a game. Others, however, have tried to define games in their own right. Game historian David Parlett, for instance, suggests that a game—in the sense used in this book—has two defining components: *ends* and *means*.[29] *Ends* refers to the notion that a game is a contest, with a goal that only one player or team can achieve. Thus, to Parlett, a game always has a winner. *Means* refers to the game equipment and rules. Parlett's definition is obviously both strict and broad. Many of the phenomena that we label here as games in fact do not qualify according to Parlett's concept of a game as something that can be won, and by only one player or team.

Parlett writes mostly on nonelectronic games and this focus shows. Process-oriented single-player video games, for example, cannot be won in the sense that poker can be won. The 1983 classic *Elite* is a game where the player explores deep space; part of the game's brilliance, which has been copied by more recent games, is that it has no fixed endpoint, no single goal. But as a result it would be excluded by Parlett's strict definition. The same goes for persistent (i.e. those that are always available and never reset to the initial state) multiplayer games like *World of Warcraft* (a fantasy role-playing universe in which players can complete **quests** alone or collaborate with characters controlled by other players); these games do not end, and in principle all players can reach the highest level. At the same time, Parlett's definition is usefully broad, since it includes activities that we would not normally consider games—auctions, for instance, and certain types of democratic elections.

Quest: A mission in a game, structuring action for the player.

A more elaborate definition is proposed by philosopher Bernard Suits in his book *Grasshopper: Games, Life, and Utopia*. He writes:

> To play a game is to engage in activity directed towards bringing about a specific state of affairs, using only means permitted by rules, and where the rules prohibit more efficient in favour of less efficient means, and where such rules are accepted just because they make possible such activity.[30]

Importantly, Suits stresses that game rules are inhibiting, and favor "less efficient means." It is a highly compelling, though counterintuitive, model: that to enjoy ourselves we in fact seek out rigid and restrictive structures.

Like most one-sentence truths, however, it has limitations. Think of the board game *Monopoly*. The most efficient way of moving around the board would be to just move your car as you please, without bothering about dice, cards, and other formalities. But of course *Monopoly* isn't really about driving at all. The game is about amassing wealth and ruining opponents. One very efficient way to do this would be just to roll the dice and hand out play money according to the rolls. A simple roll of the dice would decide the winner and the loser. Clearly, this would be a less than thrilling experience; we appreciate the difficulty of making money in the game, and our appreciation is evidence in favor of Suits's definition.

However, we should also stress that *Monopoly* could be far more difficult than it is. "Less efficient" certainly should not be interpreted as "least efficient," since it would appear that what makes *Monopoly* fun is not so much extreme difficulty but rather its appealing goal—which is really quite simple—and the set of well-balanced rules we follow to try and achieve that goal. The *Monopoly* rules create excitement not just by being more difficult than our minimalist one-dice-decides-all version. The game system introduces an element of skill and encourages us to use strategy while still maintaining the importance of chance, thus keeping alive, if only barely, the hope of recovery from unfortunate situations. What is crucial—at least for our *Monopoly* example—is a particular combination of rules and chance; the rules-as-limitations concept is powerful but is not without its problems.

While Suits and Parlett are not specifically interested in video games, others have put forth definitions that clearly take into account the rise of electronic entertainment. The first writer to seriously and systematically address such issues was game designer Chris Crawford. In 1982—several years ahead of the crowd—Crawford published *The Art of Computer Game Design*, an exploration of how to understand games and their relation to players. Crawford's book boldly attempts to "address the fundamental aspects of video games to achieve a conclusion that will withstand the ravages of time and change."[31] Crawford does not offer any one-line definition but rather names four features that are common to all video games: representation, interaction, conflict, and safety.

1. *Representation* refers to games being about something else; or as he writes, a game "subjectively represents a subset of reality."[32] Games model external situations—a baseball game, for example—but they are not actually part of these situations. Crawford stresses that most games, in fact, do not attempt to be truly faithful simulations; hence their representation is "subjective."

2. *Interaction*, according to Crawford, is crucial to games' appeal. The player must be able to influence the world of the game and get meaningful responses to his actions, so that he feels engaged with the game.

3. *Conflict* is the idea that a game has a goal that is blocked by obstacles, whether human or electronic. Conflict can be "direct or indirect, violent or nonviolent, but it is always present in every game."[33]

4. *Safety* refers to the fact that the conflicts in a game do not carry the same consequences as those same conflicts in the real world. For instance, losing a war game may be humiliating, infuriating, and even costly, but it does not mean that your actual home is destroyed. Thus, although games can have consequences, Crawford considers them safe ways of experiencing real situations.

Of these characteristics, representation and safety stand out as the most debatable. Crawford ties the former to the idea that games are systems, but in this regard, *representation* is an odd term to use. We can have a system that is not a representation in any ordinary sense of the word. Many games do not represent real-life situations: the gold-coin-filled worlds of *Super Mario Bros.*, for example, or the endless array of puzzle games like *Tetris*. Crawford argues that while these games do not represent any objective phenomenon, they nevertheless represent something to the player: "the player does perceive the game to represent something from his private fantasy world."[34] Thus, the player can perceive the game action as meaningful even though it makes no reference to the outside world.

As for safety, it implies that games operate inside the "magic circle" discussed previously in this chapter—that game events are without direct real-world consequences. Crawford's position, however, is more nuanced than that of Huizinga and Caillois (he agrees that there are consequences; they just aren't direct), and so he doesn't invite the criticism leveled at "strong" magic circle thinking.

More than 20 years after Crawford's pioneering book, game scholars have recently picked up the challenge of defining games. Their work is notable for its commitment to engage seriously with what has come before. Of the resulting definitions, two are particularly useful.

The first was suggested in 2003 by game theorists Katie Salen and Eric Zimmerman, in their book *Rules of Play*: A game is a system in which players engage in an artificial conflict, defined by rules, that results in a quantifiable outcome.[35] The second definition comes from theorist Jesper Juul:

> A game is a rule-based formal system with a variable and quantifiable outcome, where different outcomes are assigned different values, the player exerts effort in order to influence the outcome, the player feels attached to the outcome, and the consequences of the activity are optional and negotiable.[36]

These definitions look quite similar, and they are both very thoughtful. They both stress that games are systems and have quantifiable outcomes. The most obvious difference, perhaps, is that Salen and Zimmerman's description of "an artificial conflict" returns us to the idea of the magic circle, whereas Juul is concerned less with the nature of the conflict and more with describing the player. Salen and Zimmerman's definition is brief and elegant, but it is not exclusive to games. Depending on how we read "artificial conflict" it might, for instance, include university exams. Here, the student is engaged in a conflict (to outdo her fellow students, to prove wrong her skeptical teacher, or to overcome the "challenge" of the situation), this conflict is defined by rules (the university's laws and regulations), and it results in a quantifiable outcome (her grade). The conflict is artificial in the sense that the exam situation takes place within a magic circle, with a variety of rules that do not really apply outside. (We should note that the conflict is not, however, artificial in Crawford's sense; it is not a representation of a real-life situation.)

Juul's definition, on the other hand, gets around this particular objection by stipulating that the consequences be optional and negotiable. His definition is interesting for its inclusion of the player in the equation; a game in Juul's terms depends on the player's attitude toward the activity. Of course, this may invite objections. Inevitably, for example, there will be players who neither exert much effort in their games nor feel particularly attached to the outcome; but we would not want to exclude such a person's game of poker—much less *the game of poker*—from the "game" category.

Juul's definition is an attempt to tease out the criteria that we intuitively use to differentiate games from nongames. To this end, he offers a model that shows our often implicit reasons for calling something a game (see Figure 3.5).

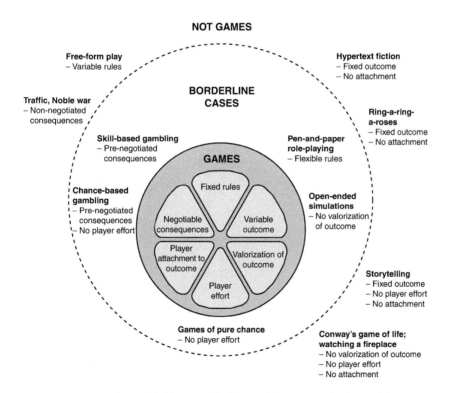

Figure 3.5 Jesper Juul's model of how standard game definitions work. The model captures the fragmented and double nature of games by offering a more flexible classification. (Source: Juul, 2003a, p. 11)

Juul refers to this as the "classic game model," based on his observation that certain modern video games in fact do not comply with the criteria that have traditionally been part of game definitions. The six inner slices in the model represent the classic criteria. The level labeled "borderline cases" includes phenomena that only marginally qualify as games in terms of the classic model. For instance, pen-and-paper role-playing games do not always have fixed rules. The third level holds activities that plainly fall outside the classical model—"storytelling," for example, which has a fixed outcome, requires no effort by the player (in this case the listener) and that, according to Juul, requires no attachment. By contrast, a video game like *Lemmings*, in which the player is faced with unambiguous goals, where the rules are fixed, and the outcome is not prescribed, falls squarely within the "classic" model of games.

For every game like *Lemmings*, as Juul insists, we could probably find another example of a video game that proves Juul's observation about video games not fitting the "classic" criteria. In massively multiplayer **online role-playing games** like *World of Warcraft*, for example, players can set their own goals and there is no one way to win. The criteria also don't apply to wide-open gamespaces like that of *Grand Theft Auto: Vice City*, where players can be so distracted from their missions by the vibrant city simulation that they may not ever complete the game's plot. Even certain older video games do not fit into the classic model. In *Little Computer People*, released in 1985, the player interacts with a character that performs various tasks—based on the player's treatment—as a sort of virtual pet. The program, which was of course marketed as a game, does not meet the

Online role-playing games: Game type in which players (typically several thousand of them) act simultaneously in the same server-based world. Users normally pay a monthly fee and connect through their Internet account. An online role-playing game is a graphically illustrated MUD. This type of game is often termed a MMORPG (massively multiplayer online role-playing game).

Figure 3.6 Little Computer People (1985): One of the famous early examples of a borderline game that has later become so popular with games like *Grand Theft Auto*

"valorization of outcome" criterion of Juul's model, and would therefore be classified as a borderline case.

At a glance, perhaps, the attempts to provide formal definitions discussed above may appear to be relatively abstract exercises with few real-world implications. But they are important, since they help us refine our thinking on what constitutes a game and thereby address subconscious biases, and since they help us clarify whether the conclusions we reach are unique to games or perhaps apply to other media as well. If, for instance, we study the effects of games on learning we would do well to reflect on whether a measured effect is due to audiovisual representation (an aspect shared by other media) or to the fact that players interact with a rule system and thus "experience" its **dynamics** (which is not the case with books, movies, or television, for instance).

> **Dynamics:** The processes and events in a game that are generated by the relationships between rules, game world physics, player input, etc.

Our point here is that it is more important to acknowledge and specify one's own definition than it is to try to decide on the "correct" one. However, based on this discussion we see that there is a good deal of overlap between the definitions proposed.

First, they are focused on games as rule systems and are unconcerned with matters of representation. In other words, audiovisual feedback is not a requirement, and the definitions say nothing about digital computation and thus are definitions of *games* and not merely video games. One of the shared requirements that is most useful in distinguishing games from other activities is the notion that events or actions should be evaluated, for instance, by the game assigning points to the player. Essentially, this means that a game has goals somehow specified by the game design. It is not enough that a person has a goal (say, finding a specific street address) for something to be a game; the experience must be designed. But nor is it enough that an experience is designed. Virtual worlds like *Second Life*, for instance, are designed but have no specific goals and thus would fall outside most of the definitions discussed. Of course, designed experiences with goals does not work as a definition either (since, again, it would include university exams). It is the additional characteristic, like feedback or goals, that an activity must display to be a game, which in fact seems to cause disagreement and which is therefore all the more worthwhile to consider in one's efforts to understand games.

Having discussed formal definitions, which are the results of attempts to understand games, we turn now to definitions that—quite intentionally— are less rigorous but that also serve a different purpose, as tools for actual game design.

Pragmatic Definitions

The "formal" definitions discussed above aim to be as consistent and precise as possible. They are not tools for the creation of new games. Rather they can be compared to philosophies of language; they may be truly insightful without ever making anyone a better communicator.

Another type of definition, labeled here as "pragmatic," has the opposite characteristics—it is meant as a tool for action and not as a philosophically bulletproof concept.

Perhaps the most famous recent game definition, famous enough to make it into most design books and onto the T-shirt of many a gamer, is that of game designer Sid Meier: "A game is a series of interesting choices."[37] In contrast to formal definitions, Meier's is less rigorous, much more casual, and perhaps intentionally simplistic. Probably we actually need to amend it slightly if it is to make sense. Surely something does not cease to be a game if the choices are uninteresting? That merely makes it a bad game. So Sid Meier should be read as saying "a good game is a series of interesting choices." By stressing that choices must be interesting, Meier is pointing out (or claiming) that cases where one option is clearly better than others or where one's choice does not affect how the game plays out are not particularly engaging to the player.

For example, in *Civilization V* (designed by Meier himself) the player must constantly choose whether to spend resources on research, diplomatic standing, or armament. At any given time, the player has clues about which choice is likely to be most sensible, but there is no single correct choice. The element of chance is ever present, and the player's choices invariably depend on what she thinks the enemy is doing.

Action games: Games focusing on speed and physical drama that make high demands on the player's reflexes and coordination skills.

From a critical perspective, Meier's statement is very useful for thinking about strategy games but less appropriate for **action games**. In *Super Mario Bros.* (Figure 3.7), you have no choice but to jump to a certain platform, or down a particular pipe. The choice is not interesting in itself; the activity, however, may still increase your heart rate, since the outcome depends completely on your skill. Improving your abilities and finding the correct solution to Mario's problems make the game interesting, but there is no interesting choice as such.[38] In classic adventure games like *Blade Runner*, there may be only one correct choice and there may not even be any physical skill involved, but the investigation process can still feel exciting. Meier's definition is thus helpful, and wonderfully pithy but not really sufficient.

A simple, yet highly useful, pragmatic way of modeling games emerged out of several workshops held at the Game Developers Conference in California between 2001 and 2004. The "MDA model," developed by Robin Hunicke, Marc LeBlanc, and Robert

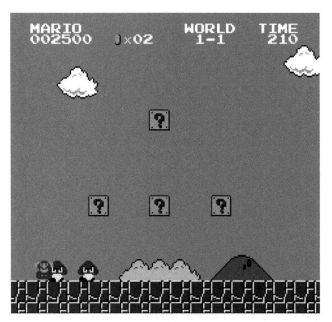

Figure 3.7 Super Mario Bros. (1985) doesn't really fit with the idea of interesting choices as a core element in videos games

Zubek, seeks to divide games into three separate dimensions: mechanics, dynamics, and aesthetics.[39]

Mechanics are the rules and basic code of a game. It is not what we see or hear while we play a game. Rather, "mechanics" refers to the vast amount of information that goes into constructing the world of the game—the series of algorithms, for example, that determines the reaction pattern of a computer-controlled character.

Dynamics is the way the game actually plays based on the mechanics. It is the events that actually occur, or can occur, during the course of the game as experienced by the player. For instance, the game mechanics may contain complicated algorithms by which the behavior patterns of an enemy soldier are determined in a probabilistic fashion, while the player is merely presented with a dangerous foe hiding behind a tree and opening fire. Dynamics are functions of the mechanics, but they may also be surprising, as complex processes interact in ways that cannot always be predicted. For instance, certain mechanics of the narrative-based shooter *Deus Ex* were flexible enough that a player could complete missions in ways not predicted by the game's designers (as we describe further in Chapter 5, under the heading of "**Emergence**").

Aesthetics covers the favorable emotional responses evoked in the player as he or she interacts with the game. Hunicke, LeBlanc, and Zubek list the elements that attract us to games:

1. Sensation (game as sense-pleasure)
2. Fantasy (game as make-believe)
3. Narrative (game as drama)
4. Challenge (game as obstacle course)
5. Fellowship (game as social framework)
6. Discovery (game as uncharted territory)
7. Expression (game as self-discovery)
8. Submission (game as pastime)

Emergence: (1) The phenomenon whereby a complex, interesting, high-level function is produced as a result of combining simple, low-level mechanisms in simple ways. (2) The phenomenon whereby a system is designed according to certain principles, but interesting properties arise that are not included in the goals of the designer.

A game will usually offer some of these pleasures but not all of them. *Tetris*, for instance, emphasizes challenge, submission, and perhaps sensation but does not offer narrative or expression. *Grand Theft Auto: Vice City*, on the other hand, affords most of the pleasures with the exception of fellowship. The categories should not be seen as "objective" as they depend on interpretation and the context in which the game is played. For instance, we can interpret both *Tetris* and *Grand Theft Auto* as providing a social framework, and we can imagine a player expressing herself through *Tetris* by modifying the game[40] and designing new background images.

The MDA model is a very useful tool for understanding—and discussing—the way games work. Although admittedly simplistic, it offers a decent distinction between the various elements of a game, and highlights the ways in which games are systems rather than linear, pre-determined structures like novels, movies, or television programs. However, MDA has limitations. It is more of a designer's tool than a satisfying account of how gameplay actually works. Powerful parts of the gaming experience—everything from the context in which we play a game, to the culture that frames the game, to its intended or unintended links to other games, or movies, or texts—fall outside the model's ambit. For instance, a teenager playing *Grand Theft Auto: Vice City* might enjoy the game's anti-establishment attitude, and might relish participating in the violent acts that have caused such media uproar. This pleasure does not strictly emerge from the game mechanics, though there is a clear connection. Further, the model is centered on the rules of a game, and except for the aesthetic category of "sensation"—which alludes to the pleasure brought about by a game's audiovisuals—MDA all but ignores the expressive side of the game.

Though their definitions are not perfect, Sid Meier and the developers of the MDA model offer two of the most prominent pragmatic definitions of a video game, thus providing useful "tools for thought," helpful in inspiring game design work.

THE ISSUE OF GENRE

In both popular and academic literature on games the concept of genre tends to play a role. Observations may pertain only to certain game types and thus many game scholars and journalists find it hugely useful to establish systems for categorizing games.

Existing genre systems are based on a variety of criteria. Rigorous attempts to define mutually exclusive genres are rare but can be found in Mark J. P. Wolf's *The Medium of the Video Game*[41] and in work by Espen Aarseth aimed at producing multidimensional genre systems.[42]

Wolf, a media theorist, discusses the relevance of various approaches to defining genre in other media. These approaches generally focus on representational, surface phenomena—what we actually see on the screen—but according to Wolf, **interactivity** is more important in video games as it "is an essential part of every game's structure and a more appropriate way of examining and defining video game genres."[43] Wolf's notion of interactivity is closely linked to a game's goals:

> In a video game, there is almost always a definite objective that the player strives to complete . . . and in doing so very specific interactions are used. Thus the intention—of the player-character at least—is often clear, and can be analyzed as a part of the game.[44]

However, Wolf then goes on to outline 43 distinct genres, many of which are only vaguely linked to his own interactivity criterion—from abstract to board games, and from educational games to sports. Thus, despite Wolf's

Interactivity: A term used in many fields but typically as a measure of user influence. The higher the degree of interactivity, the more influence the user has on the form and course of a media product.

reasonable discussion, we end up with a list of genres based on no discernible system of categorization.

Game theorist Espen Aarseth considers it unproductive to define a genre based on one variable (such as theme), as this is likely to have major overlaps (e.g. games that are about shooting and flying) or tell us nothing very interesting. Instead, he suggests that video games should be evaluated based on a series of variables. From this perspective we could decide on a game's genre by rating it in relation to each of the variables selected. This approach has the advantage of categorizing every possible game that could be conceived. The drawback of this system is that it is of limited practical use.

Less formally, popular magazines and websites often have their own—more or less idiosyncratic—way of dealing with genres. Gamespot.com, a major games website, divides games into more than 30 genres of varying specificity (one genre is "action," another is "baseball"). While useful for the purposes of the website, these genres are obviously not derived from any standard principle. For instance, "driving" implies a game's theme while "action" implies a more fundamental characteristic.

Philosophically speaking, the large number of genre systems exists because there is no objective way to measure the differences between two things. An example: two books will share many characteristics (e.g. they have pages and they can be carried) but also have many differences (e.g. the covers look different, they have different titles, they don't weigh the same, and they don't have the same content). But there is no objective way of determining which similarities or differences are the most important.

The same goes for people. How different are human beings from one another? The answer is all in your perspective. Anthropologists and other students of culture may tend toward "very different," while biologists might lean toward "very similar." Neither group is right or wrong. Similarly, no one can prove that it is better to focus on differences rather than similarities, or vice versa.

Genres, then, are arbitrary. They are analytical constructs imposed on a group of objects in order to discuss the complexity of their individual differences in a meaningful way. But are genres just categories with no bearing on reality? No—the conventions of each genre create expectations. Take movies. When you watch a romantic comedy, you expect the movie to follow certain conventions and ignore others—you expect the man and woman to kiss and make up, and you are confident that a crazed murderer will not jump out from the bushes and kill them. When watching a slasher movie, you might have the opposite expectations. Perhaps more importantly, producers make movies that conform to established genres. Box office receipts may indicate that war epics do well financially, and this may influence a producer's decision to approve the next World War II movie instead of a teen comedy.

How exactly one chooses to split the cake and divide up games may be a largely arbitrary decision, but some methods are more consistent than others. One way to ensure consistency is to use genre labels based on the same criterion. An example of the reverse is revealing: an inconsistent genre system might consist of girl games, home-computer games, racing games, and sports games. This system is not useful, as a particular title could easily fall into all four categories.

In this book, we propose a genre system based on a game's criteria for success. We ask: "What does it take to succeed in the game?" To explore this concept, let's look at two games that are quite different: the ever-popular *Tetris*, and *Myst* (a narrative adventure where the player has to explore a mysterious world and investigate the disappearance of certain characters). To succeed in *Tetris* you need fast reflexes and decent hand-eye coordination. To succeed in *Myst* you need puzzle-solving skills and deductive logic. These criteria for success are quite different. So rather than focus on criteria like theme or narrative, the system we're proposing focuses directly on a feature important to games: goals, and how to achieve them.

Another example that further illustrates this distinction is a comparison of the two soccer-themed games, *FIFA 12* and *Championship Manager 2011*. In *FIFA 12*, the players must wiggle their **joystick**s in order to outscore each other. In *Championship Manager 2011*, the player takes on the role of soccer coach, and concentrates on high-level strategy rather than playing in the matches. Thus, while both are "about" soccer, we do not consider them to be in the same genre.

Two types of game pose a challenge to our system: single-player and multiplayer role-playing games. The first problem is that these two types of role-playing games are, in fact, quite different from each other. Single-player games such as *Dragon Age: Origins* (a fantasy-themed game where the

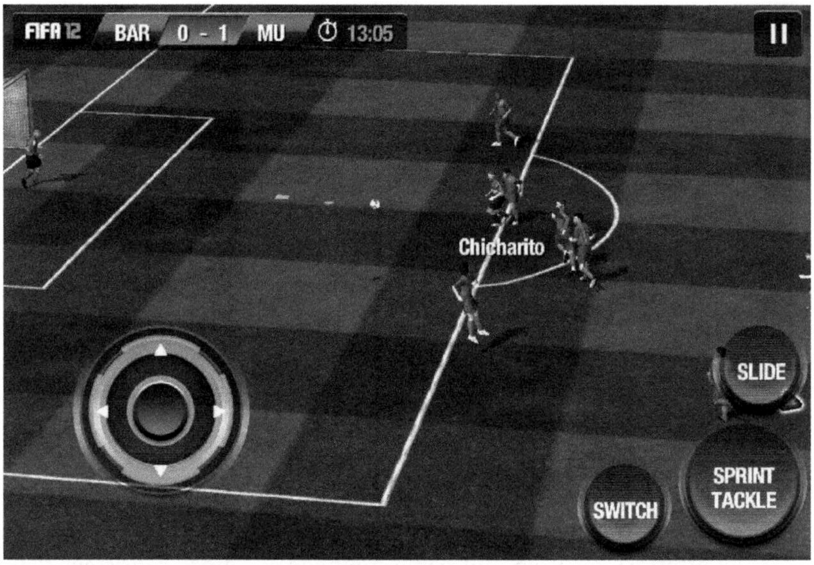

Joystick: A type of **controller**. The player chooses "direction" by manipulating a stick (as in a fighter airplane).

Figure 3.8 In *FIFA 12* (2011), you play soccer by using a joystick to score goals

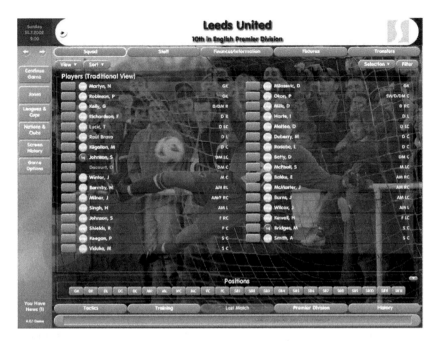

Figure 3.9 In *Championship Manager 4* (2003), you play soccer by setting the right strategy

player controls multiple characters) demand strategic skills and include puzzle solving, while online multiplayer games such as *World of Warcraft* (where thousands of players can act in the same fantasy-themed world simultaneously) do not have very explicit goals and do not generally contain puzzles, but do require social skills for dealing and collaborating with the other players. The second challenge to our system is that certain games (e.g. *World of Warcraft*) cannot be so readily categorized based on criteria for success because they are not obviously goal-oriented (or at least they invite players to set their own goals to a large degree). We recognize these problems as weaknesses of our genre system, and choose to group single-player role-playing games with strategy games, and to place games with vague goals (or no goals) in the special category of "process-oriented games." We describe the four genres in our system below.

Action Games

To some, the action game is the archetypical video game. Action games are often intense and usually involve fighting or some kind of physical drama. *Pac-Man* is an action game, as is the shooter *Red Dead Redemption* and the racing game *MotorStorm: Apocalypse*. What ties these games together is that their criterion for success is motor skill and hand-eye coordination. In classical **arcade** action games, the player mostly had to coordinate the movement of the on-screen character and did not have to worry about what the correct choice might be (one simply and obviously had to jump an

Arcade: Public gaming facility offering computer games (arcade games). Arcades were highly popular in the early 1980s. A game would typically begin when the player inserted the equivalent of a US quarter. Action games were especially well suited to arcades.

approaching barrel at the right time, for instance). In more complex titles like the 2003 platform game *Prince of Persia: The Sands of Time*, the player must still perform challenging feats of coordination but must also put effort into figuring out how to solve the game's spatial puzzles (each challenge must be analyzed to arrive at a solution and subsequently solved in practice by a sequence of jumps, climbs, etc.).

Adventure Games

Adventure games are characterized by requiring deep thinking and great patience. These skills are employed to participate in, or uncover, narratives that are often based on detective story templates. Typically, the player is represented by an individual character involved in a plot of mystery or exploration, and faces puzzles of various kinds. Quite often, adventure games are entirely devoid of fighting and of action sequences; sometimes they even lack the risk of the main character dying. To succeed the player must exhibit skills of logic and deduction. Examples of the genre, in its pure form, include *Adventure* (from 1976), *Maniac Mansion* (from 1987), and *Dreamfall: The Longest Journey* (from 2006). We also include single-player role-playing games under this heading, although we acknowledge that they have strong strategy elements. Examples of this subgenre include *Ultima*, *Wizardry*, and *Baldur's Gate*.

Strategy Games

Occupying a space somewhere between action and adventure games, we find the strategy genre. The most common form is perhaps a game of war, but rather than the player being on the battlefield (typical of the action genre), she takes on the distant role of general. Variations on the general role can include anything from mayor to deity. The conflict is often represented on a map that resembles classic board games, and which illustrates anything from a whole continent to an urban street.

Two important subgenres exist: real-time strategy and turn-based strategy. Real-time strategy games do not pause between turns but rather play out in real time or, perhaps more appropriately, continuous time (since a single game session may span thousands of years in the game world's internal chronology). As a result, they resemble action games, in that the player's score is dependent on fast reactions and skillful manipulation of mouse and keyboard. To win, the player must carefully balance large numbers of interdependent variables, paying careful attention to signals of other players' choices and strategies. Despite their action component, these games are strategic, since understanding the ways in which priorities and perceptions interplay over time is ultimately more important than speed with the mouse. Examples of real-time strategy games include *Dune II*, *Warcraft*, and *Warhammer 40,000: Dawn of War*. In the other subgenre, turn-based strategy, the action stops while players make their choices, following classic board games such as chess or *Risk*. Examples include *Balance of Power, Civilization*, and *Warlords*.

Process-Oriented Games

Though winning seems an essential element of games, a (growing) breed of software exists at the edges of this definition of a game. Instead of giving the player one or more goals, process-oriented games provide the player with a system to play with. These products receive the "game" label not so much for staging conflict or competition but because they are made for entertainment purposes; they could fit the definition of a toy rather than of an actual game. Think of populating and watching an aquarium as opposed to playing chess.

There are two main approaches to the design of process-oriented games. In one type the player is a character exploring and manipulating a dynamic and ever-changing world. Another type puts the player in charge of more fundamental variables, such as taxation levels or elements influencing an ecosystem.

Process-oriented games lack any standard or consistent criterion for success, although each game encourages certain types of play: most players will want to build a large city in *SimCity*, or try to reach higher levels in *World of Warcraft*. A few other examples include *Elite, The Sims*, and *Zoo Tycoon*.

A subgroup of process-oriented games try their best to mimic concrete, real-world experiences, such as driving a car or flying an airplane. These are often referred to as **simulation games**.

While many action games do flout ever-greater levels of realism, simulation games go further than action games, and reproduce minor details even at the expense of immediate gratification. The obstacle in these games need not be any external enemy; it is often the challenge of mastering the complexities of the interface. The challenge of a flight simulator, for example, is learning the details of getting a passenger plane off the ground. By this definition, games such as *SimCity* or *SimEarth* are not simulation games, since they do not try to simulate a concrete experience or strive to replicate minute details. Examples of simulation games include *Flight Simulator 2002, Microsoft Train Simulator*, and *Sub Battle Simulator*.

Simulation games: Games focusing on realism. Typically they make heavy demands on the player's ability to understand and remember complex principles and relations.

The four game genres are summarized in Table 3.1. We will be referring to them throughout the remainder of this book.

Table 3.1 The characteristics of the four genres. The table shows a genre classification based on the key actions and success criteria to win the game.

	Action games	*Adventure games*	*Strategy games*	*Process-oriented games*
Typical action	Battle	Mystery solving	Build nation in competition with others	(Varies)
Criterion of success	Fast reflexes	Logic ability	Analyzing interdependent variables	Ambiguous

DISCUSSION QUESTIONS

- Consider Marshall McLuhan's idea of games as cultural reflections, and discuss how well it applies to sports or other games that are popular in your area.

- Game and media critic Henry Jenkins has argued that game designers should "concentrate on exploring the aesthetics of action instead of trying to imitate other media." Do you agree with this statement? Why, or why not? Consider several recent video games and discuss their design in terms of this issue.

- Using data available online, find out what the current best-selling games are. Discuss to what extent these titles borrow from movies, whether in terms of form or content. Could any of these titles function as movies or do they only really function as games?

- Take a look at the different genre classifications systems, and try to categorize ten random best-selling games into each of the systems. Do you think the classification systems are appropriate? Consider whether genres are useful at all, and if so why? Can you use each classification system for different things?

RECOMMENDED GAMES

Myst—The game that for many defined the modern adventure game with its magical and engaging world.

FIFA 2012—One of the strongest sports brands in the game industry that shows the core of an action game.

Age of Empires—Demonstrates the real-time strategy game that is among the most popular genres on the PC platform.

Civilization II—Has become the archetype for turn-based strategy that despite its smaller appeal is still a strong niche genre.

The Sims—Redefined what a game could be and what target groups could be reached through something that was barely a game.

SimCity—Probably the first game to truly show the potential of sandbox gameplay.

Microsoft Flight Simulator—If you talk simulation games, this is it. With its absurd realism, it has been claimed to be capable of teaching you to fly a real plane.

FURTHER READINGS

Hunicke, R., LeBlanc, M., & Zubek, R. (2004). *MDA: A formal approach to game design and game research.*

(Estimated reading time: 15 minutes)

Apperley, T. (2006). Genre and game studies: Toward a critical approach to video game genres. *Simulation & Gaming, 37*(1), pp. 6–23.

(Estimated reading time: 38 minutes)

NOTES

1. Wittgenstein, 1967, §67.
2. Huizinga, 2000.
3. Huizinga in fact merely uses the concept as an example of how a game can be delimited in relation to the outside world. Within game studies, however, the term has come to refer to the more general idea that games take place within special spaces set aside from the outside world.
4. Castronova, 2004, p. 7.
5. Singer, 2009.
6. Crawford, 1982.
7. Salen and Zimmerman, 2004.
8. Consalvo, 2009.
9. Consalvo, 2009, p. 411.
10. Malaby, 2007, p. 102.
11. Juul, 2008, p. 61.
12. See also Caillois, 2011; Juul, 2003a, p. 11.
13. Juul, 2003a, p. 11.
14. See also Juul, 2003a.
15. Juul, 2003a.
16. Newman, 2004.
17. McLuhan, 1964, pp. 208–209.
18. McLuhan, 1964, p. 212.
19. Avedon and Sutton-Smith, 1971, p. 7.
20. Avedon and Sutton-Smith, 1971, p. 7.
21. Nietzsche, 2005, p. 80.
22. Jung, 1928, p. 107.
23. Mead, 1967, p. 152.
24. Mead, 1967, p. 152.
25. Jenkins, 2005.
26. Seldes, 1957.
27. Jenkins, 2005, p. 177.
28. Jenkins, 2005, p. 177.
29. Parlett, 1999.
30. Suits, 1978, p. 34.
31. Crawford, 1982, p. 1.
32. Crawford, 1982, p. 7.
33. Crawford, 1982, p. 14.
34. Crawford, 1982, p. 8.
35. Salen and Zimmerman, 2004, p. 80.
36. Juul, 2003b, p. 35.
37. See also Rollings and Morris, 2000, p. 61.
38. Smith, 2006b, pp. 65–66.
39. Hunicke, LeBlanc, and Zubek, 2004.
40. Wolf, 2001.
41. Wolf, 2001.
42. Aarseth, 1997; Aarseth, Sunnanå, and Smedstad, 2003.
43. Wolf, 2001, p. 114.
44. Wolf, 2001, p. 115.

Chapter 4

History

Spacewar! (1962) is considered by some the first video game to show the potential of the new medium and was developed in 1961–1962 at MIT

The history of video games, as we have seen, may have begun with the launching of a tiny white torpedo in an MIT basement. However, while the three creators of the torpedo launch—more on them later—did inspire many a programmer of the time, they were of course standing on the shoulders of giants.

A BRIEF PRE-HISTORY OF VIDEO GAMES

In fact, the history of *video games* is merely the latest chapter in the fascinating and much lengthier history of *games*. If we hope to come anywhere near the roots of this history, we must travel several thousand miles southeast from Cambridge, Massachusetts, and some 4,600 years back in time. This will place us in ancient Egypt during the Third Dynasty (2686–2613 BC); here we should be able to observe people playing the game of Senet. As far as scholars can surmise, Senet was a game of skill and chance not unlike present-day backgammon. Some speculate that Senet's status changed over time, from a purely recreational pastime to an activity with potent symbolism and religious significance. But even more remarkable is that, in a culture and an era utterly foreign from our own, we find a form of game that maintains its appeal four millennia later. Even with the omnipresence of computers today, and their astoundingly complex technological possibilities, we still choose to play old-fashioned board games that ancient Egyptians would have quite an easy time learning.

Around the time of Senet, although somewhat to the east, Mesopotamians played what is known as the Royal Game of Ur, an elaborate board game with an element of chance determined by dice. Although games at various times may have served ritual functions, it is clear that they also served the functions familiar to us—to entertain, to delight, and to create social interactions.

Nor were these two games alone. The Oriental game of Go has been played since at least 200 BC. Dice have been used as a game of chance from the seventh century BC, about 1,400 years prior to the first mention—in a Persian romance—of chess. This period also marks the beginning of the Olympic Games in Greece (the first documented games were held in 776 BC). Like board games, sports are activities carefully framed by rules, assigning scores to the performance of participants. The Olympic Games, then, like early known board and dice games, are testament to a fundamental human tendency: we create games. Indeed, we even adapt most nonrecreational activities into games. Only think of how many nongame activities we have appropriated from our own lives—or the lives of those people we dream of being—to make into games: we run and swim; we shoot and sail and fly.

At the time of the first documented Olympics, there existed a version of chess called *chaturanga*, a Sanskrit term referring to a battle formation. While not identical to present-day chess, *chaturanga* ranks as an undisputed ancestor; one particular piece, like the king, was all-important to victory, and different pieces were endowed with different powers. A plethora of *chaturanga* derivations existed, since rules diverged between regions. The game traveled widely, and by the tenth century had arrived in Europe and Africa in the luggage of Arab travelers. Only in the late fifteenth century can we see the rules of chess undergo a process of standardization. At this time, card games—which had been known in Europe for two centuries—were given standardized card suits. Analogous to the history of Senet, playing cards took on symbolic or mystic functions in the mid-eighteenth century, as they were employed in the service of fortune-telling.

The idea of using board games to simulate actual real-world activities—as opposed to merely drawing upon them for symbolism—flourished in the wake of the *Kriegsspiel*, developed in 1824 by a Prussian lieutenant, Georg von Reisswitz.[1] This strategy game, in which players were offered a range of complex situations, became popular with Prussian army personnel. Decidedly more peaceful was *The Mansion of Happiness*, released in 1843, the first commercially produced game in the United States. The board game offered a beautifully simplistic vision of the world, where good deeds were rewarded and bad deeds punished.

The Mansion of Happiness, however, will lie forever in the shadow of that singular international success story, *Monopoly*. Published in the mid-1930s by Parker Brothers, it was based on an earlier board game, *The Landlord's Game*, and a number of its derivatives but achieved a fame unknown to its predecessors. Perhaps anticipating much of the second half of the twentieth century, *Monopoly* makes no pretense of lauding in-game niceties. The game, which has sold more than 200 million copies worldwide, combines chance and strategic thinking as players vie for domination of a fictional world of real estate.[2] To the seeming delight of 12-year-olds everywhere, the game rewards nothing as much as bold capitalist perseverance, and is a fascinating example of how games can reflect cultural values or trends. Its success also helped establish the board game as a foundational activity for family and friends, young and old alike.

In the aftermath of World War II, electronic games were struggling toward life in circuits of various types, but the launch of the tiny white torpedo was still a long way off. The 1950s, however, saw the publication of numerous strategic war games, including the still influential *Risk* and *Diplomacy*. While the complex rules of the *Kriegsspiel* do live on in many of these war games, it is worth noting that *Diplomacy* relies on the most minimal of rule sets. As players battle for domination of World War I Europe, negotiation and interpersonal scheming come to the fore, thus creating a layered, Machiavellian experience out of the simplest of rules.

By the mid-twentieth century commercially produced games were an established part of cultures around the globe, in myriad manifestations: we played games of chance, games of war and strategy, and games that simulated still more aspects of the rest of our lives. One development that cannot go unmentioned (even if it did not technically come before video games) is pen-and-paper role-playing games (RPGs). These did not develop in a cultural vacuum (few things do) but rather were the result of a remarkable convergence of popular trends and interests in the early 1970s. The 1960s had seen the commercial proliferation of war games, tabletop games of strategy where maps, dice, and figures were used to simulate battles, allowing players to recreate historical conflicts. And in 1954, worldwide publication of J.R.R. Tolkien's *The Lord of the Rings* altered the landscape of literature and introduced the world to the fantasy genre. A host of authors followed suit, recreating worlds from the medieval to the mythical, stocked with magic, dragons, and heroes. These derivations, though never attaining the popularity of Tolkien's epic, catered to the many hungry readers and fostered a community of fantasy fans that continues to thrive today.

Both war games and fantasy literature found a primary audience among teenage males, so it was perhaps only a question of time before the two genres merged. Soon after, fantasy-themed war games appeared, where elves and orcs replaced the armies of European empires. In fact, the mother of all role-playing games, *Dungeons & Dragons*, was directly based on a fantasy war game called *Chainmail*. Created by Dave Arneson and Gary Gygax, *Dungeons & Dragons* was commercially launched in 1974. Despite a slow start, it was selling 7,000 copies a month by 1979, spawning a multitude of sequels and inspiring untold numbers of gamers to become game designers. The game's complex rules seemed to be a magnet for budding designers, who adapted them in countless ways to create their own fantasy worlds.

In the medieval world of *Dungeons & Dragons* (first edition), a player chose to be either a warrior, wizard, thief, cleric, halfling, dwarf, or elf. Groups of players, seated around a dining room table or huddled in a basement, conducted their adventures in hostile dungeons and castles, battling monsters and trying to accumulate treasure and "experience points." The game revolved around a "dungeon master," who conducted the adventure and interpreted the rules for the rest of the players. Play occurred (and still occurs) through a lot of talking: the dungeon master described the imaginary scenes the players were encountering, and controlled the endless monsters and dragons and other nonplaying characters; the players, in turn, would state what actions their characters would take. The result of a player's action was then decided by a roll of the (often many-sided) dice; the result of each roll was interpreted in accordance with what was agreed in rulebooks.

For example, the dungeon master might describe a scene in which an unknown hunch-backed, troll-like creature approaches my dwarf warrior. My options are to attack or to run; I decide on the former, and roll a dice, one with 20 sides, to decide whether I hit the creature, based on my dwarf's abilities and skills. The dungeon master consults our rulebook, and can see that I do hit the creature. I then roll again to see how much damage I cause, adjusted for my abilities and any spells in play. The creature then gets an attack on me, for which the dungeon master rolls the dice. He misses and I get another attack and hit the foul creature, slaying it. I then get experience points based on the difficulty of the opponent, which in time will bring my dwarf to a higher and more powerful level.

The materials necessary to play were remarkably simple: the book of rules, sheets that describe the abilities and proficiencies of each character, and often maps and figures to create a visual representation of the adventure. Interestingly, these tools remain the basic setup for all role-playing games, although contemporary ones insist more on character interpretation, dialogue, and storytelling more generally, whereas older games are more centered on the accumulation of points and treasure.

After *Dungeons & Dragons*, role-playing games seemed to grow like weeds. Some aimed to simplify complex rules while maintaining a fantasy setting, like 1976's *Runequest*. Set in a fictional world during the Bronze Age, its rules have been praised as the beginning of modern role-playing. Others introduced new settings and universes, such as the successful science-fiction game *Traveller*, from 1977. However, by the end of the 1970s there was widespread concern about the hobby of role-playing, as the news media connected cases of youth suicide or criminal behavior to role-playing games. The general public did not always appreciate a pastime that encouraged young people to sit in their living rooms and discuss the finer points of medieval weaponry and slaughtering monsters, all with a passion that struck more than a few parents as morbid and unhealthy. Especially within religious circles, role-playing games were lamented for being blasphemous. Not surprisingly, video games have become embroiled in nearly identical controversies. Despite the flare-up of cultural controversy—and in some cases, no doubt, because of such controversy—the hobby continued to mature, with the arrival of new kinds of games, rule systems, and universes. The following list gives a small sample of the diversity of role-playing games in the recent past:

- *Call of Cthulhu*, 1981. Reproducing the universe of H. P. Lovecraft, this was a game of investigation under the constant threat of insanity. Here, emphasis was usually put on character enactment rather than fulfillment of particular goals.
- *GURPS* (Generic Universal Role-Playing System), 1984. Rather than offering a specific universe, this was simply a rule system that could be adapted to any scenario. It offered great freedom to creative game masters and players, and made it easier than ever for amateur game designers to create their own worlds.
- *Toon* and *Paranoia*, both from 1984. Both of these easy-to-learn games relied on humor, marking another alternative to goal-fulfillment in the traditional sense (of slaying monsters, recovering treasure, etc.).
- *Cyberpunk*, 1988. Though the subgenre of science fiction already had an established cult following, *Cyberpunk* was a remarkably popular sci-fi RPG.
- *Vampire*, 1991. With its simple rules and its emphasis on storytelling, this game changed the hobby by introducing more serious themes and continued an emphasis on narrative over rules and goals.

If we look at sales, we can safely say that computer role-playing games have eclipsed their tabletop counterparts. It is also no coincidence that in the list above the most recent truly noteworthy tabletop RPG is over two decades old. The appeal of RPGs, at least to new audiences, seems to have waned. Nevertheless, their influence is clear, as computer RPGs are often based on this early generation of role-playing games: characters grow by accumulating "experience points," which are often acquired by fighting and picking up treasure; similarly, many games revolve around simple missions (also called quests) where a player's ability to hack and slash is all-important, and the more subtle skills of role-playing—telling a convincing story, for example, or negotiating with other players—are optional. Incorporating more player-centered storytelling on the computer has been difficult, due to the absence of a human game master and the standardization required by video games. Historically, as we'll see below, tabletop role-playing games have inspired two types of video games: the text adventures initiated by *Adventure* (1976) and *Zork* (1980), and the multiplayer **MUDs** and their graphical

MUD (multiuser dungeon): A system for virtual role-playing. Can be conceived of as a thematically charged chat room with a focus on role-playing. Certain types—so-called MOOs (MUD, object-oriented)—operate with objects that the players/users can interact with (and sometimes alter or create). Many online role-playing games are direct descendants of MUDs.

descendants. Text adventures have evolved into graphic adventure games (and later hybrids such as action-adventure games), and early digital multi-player role-playing games have grown into today's huge graphic worlds of the **MMORPG**s.

Video games, then, have a long and varied pre-history. The preceding examples hardly scratch the surface. But it should be clear that video games are a result of the evolution and reconstitution of various elements of games going back several thousand years. Video games let us experiment with chance and probability, and partake in complex strategic interaction, and allow us to simulate things that cannot (or that we do not wish to see) happen in real life. They do so by tapping into our desire for spectacle and our thought-provoking willingness to submit ourselves to strange and arbitrary rules for the sake of entertainment.

DOES HISTORY MATTER?

History, unfortunately, does not fall into convenient categories. Any historical account must leave out substantially more than it includes and these choices are always subject to debate. Since the purpose of this chapter is to give an overview of video games themselves, we choose here to downplay important issues of hardware, business, and individual achievement.

The account is structured by decade, each one beginning with an introduction describing cultural and technological events significant to the development of video games. Following this brief overview, the games themselves are described by genre.

First, however, we may want to ask: "Does history matter?" Have not video games progressed so far that comparison with 20-year-old forebears—which can already seem hopelessly out of date, even a little absurd—becomes highly suspect, or merely irrelevant? We do not believe that the game student needs to be a walking encyclopedia of historical game arcana. It is also clear that for many research projects game history is of little importance—if one studies how teenagers today use *World of Warcraft*, it is not essential to know how their parents played *Pac-Man*. But to understand the wider significance of contemporary games—from their aesthetics to their technology to their cultural influence—one must often look to history for explanations. Indeed, history has a habit of repeating itself.

Today's dominant game types, while technically enhanced, often take their design cues from quite early games. For instance, the 2010 game *Starcraft II: Wings of Liberty*, while employing advanced 3D graphics, was structurally tied to the pioneer real-time strategy title *Dune II* from 1992. Indeed, it could be argued that many potential design paths are simply not options for today's designers, because real-time strategy fans have become accustomed to the conventions established by titles released a decade ago. Similarly, an MMORPG (massively multiplayer online role-playing game) like *World of Warcraft* from 2004 builds liberally on its text-based predecessors—all the way back to *MUD* from 1978—copying such conventions as corpse retrieval and leveling, and largely copying the player-to-player communication interface from these much earlier games.

The cultural position video games occupy today is difficult to understand without a sense of how games were initially conceived and marketed. Similarly, the serious gaming student will be helped by a sense of how games, through various historical phases, have moved between public and more private spheres (e.g. from arcades to home computers). For these and so many other reasons, history does matter, and can only enrich our understanding of video games and the world they've created.

A HISTORY OF VIDEO GAMES

Somewhere in the preceding pages we left a tiny white torpedo hanging in empty space. Before returning to its impact, we need to address more directly the question, "What came first?" This is another of those trick questions that we have plagued the reader with a few times already. No trumpets sounded at the birth of video games, and so we must choose what constitutes the beginning. As we look for games emerging from the primordial soup, a few events that cannot be ignored breach the surface. As early as 1949, researchers at the University of Cambridge (UK) were operating the Electronic Delay Storage Automatic Calculator (EDSAC), one of the very first stored-program computers in the world. Back then a stored program was a revolution; today we merely know it as any program stored on a hard drive. Only three years later, PhD student A. S. Douglas, as part of his research project, programmed and ran a computerized EDSAC version of tic-tac-toe named *Noughts and Crosses*. This single-player experience, where you competed against the computer's simple reasoning, was groundbreaking but had limited influence on the outside world since the EDSAC was a unique machine.[3]

Another important event took place in the Brookhaven National Laboratory, Long Island. The local public, nerves frayed by the recent deployment of nuclear weapons in Japan, was anxious about the lab's cutting-edge research in nuclear physics. And as taxpayers funding this expensive computer equipment, they were unimpressed by the huge mainframes, lacking any displays, that just stood there seemingly doing nothing. In 1958, Brookhaven employee William Higinbotham thought of a way to generate more community interest in the lab: a tennis game. He developed *Tennis For Two*, a very basic game where visitors had to decide the angle of a ball and push a button at the right time. While certainly an electronic game, it ran on analog equipment: an oscilloscope. This precursor of the far more lauded *Pong* even introduced the idea of separate control equipment—what would eventually become joysticks. Accounts of the time agree that the game was a huge success among lab visitors.[4]

This brings us back to Cambridge, Massachusetts. In 1961, three MIT employees divided their time between reading a series of pulp science-fiction novels by cereal chemist Edward E. Smith, watching B movies from

Asia, and working. The three men, Steven Russel, Wayne Wittanen, and J. M. Graetz, fantasized about bringing Smith's *Skylark* novels to the big screen. Now, much like Brookhaven, guests at MIT's annual visitors' day were less than impressed with the low hum of mainframes, and the three were enlisted to create demonstration programs that would capture the minds of visitors. In a humorous and oft-quoted article,[5] Graetz describes how this demand led to the development of steadily more interactive programs ranging from *Bouncing Ball* (which was just that), *Mouse in the Maze* (in which a mouse would traverse a user-designed labyrinth), *HAX* (a kaleidoscope based on user settings), and *Tic-Tac-Toe* (where the player could make textual input that then generated textual output).

Though interesting, such programs did not truly captivate users, whose part in the process was obviously minor. This, and the procurement of the user-friendly DEC PDP-1 computer, led to the development of *Spacewar!*, up and running in February of 1962. The game was based on the three men's dreams of how their favorite sci-fi books might be adapted as movies. It featured two spaceships named Wedge and Needle, each manned by a player, who were engaged in galactic warfare. The possibilities were quite simple. Each ship could fire torpedoes at the other, turn, and increase or decrease thrust.

As previous examples make clear, *Spacewar!* was far from the first video game. However, claiming that things started with *Spacewar!*, as some have done, is not entirely unjustified. Here is a game that is truly novel and relies on the actual capabilities of the computer. Also, *Spacewar!*'s adherence to programming standards (as opposed to games that were directly bound to unique machines) would serve as direct inspiration for later game development.

The game was a runaway success. Its inventors did not consider it commercially interesting and simply let it spread across North America at its own pace. Over the next few years, several updated versions were created. These involved more strategy—through adding features like a star, which created a gravity pull on the ships, and the possibility of hyperjumps—thus adding chance to the rule-governed universe, as well as mainly aesthetic touches such as real constellations in the background.[6] The result was a single, simple game that had an enormous influence on early programmers.

Perhaps due in part to the availability and popularity of *Spacewar!*, little else related to video games happened in the 1960s. One innovation, however, stands out. In 1966, television engineer Ralph H. Baer pondered a novel usage for the 80 million television sets then installed in North American homes. Why not use these sets to play games? With this thought he laid the basic circuits for what would become the video game console. By 1967 he had a working prototype that plugged into an ordinary antenna terminal to display the pretentiously named game *Fox and Hounds* (it could just as well have been called "Spot and Spot"). The player navigated his "fox" to try and capture the "hounds." Baer and his employer were pleased, and the project was continued. New technologies would soon enable users to play a light-sensitive shooting game, as well as *Firefighter*, in which the player tried to prevent the TV screen from turning red by rapidly pumping a single fire (or, in this case, "water") button.[7] With the bold addition of a third "character" (or object, such as a ball), Baer's team was even capable of sports games, most obviously ping-pong. In 1968, they had a saleable console but encountered serious resistance from TV manufacturers. Through a combination of stubbornness and luck, they finally landed a deal with Magnavox. Nothing would come of this, however, until well into the next decade.

Almost all the games mentioned here belong to the action genre. Early video game designers may have preferred this genre because of its immediate appeal to players without detailed instructions and without the need for advanced audiovisuals.

THE 1970S

Whereas previous decades had seen only small-scale beginnings, the 1970s saw the video games phenomenon grow explosively. The 1970s marked the birth of video games as an industry, and paved the way for gaming consoles much like the ones we use today. Most importantly, perhaps, the 1970s established video games as a cultural phenomenon to be reckoned with (**arcade games** featured in movies as early as 1973, for example, in the US movie *The Last Detail*). And during these years the subculture of gamers was born. Those gamers, mostly young men, would gather in the newly created arcades, large rooms both wondrous and dank, that housed this new, cutting-edge digital entertainment.

Arcade game: Game played on dedicated "arcade" machines. The player inserts coins to play and a game is typically quite brief.

The most important producer of video games was Atari. Electrical engineer Nolan Bushnell had quickly perceived the financial possibilities inherent in *Spacewar!* It was obvious to him (although not to many others) that people would pay money to play such games in the right setting. Around 1970 the technology to realize this ambition was becoming available. The result was *Computer Space*, the world's first proper arcade game, and very much inspired by the original *Spacewar!* While not particularly successful, it paved the way for *Pong*, which would soon rocket Bushnell's new company, Atari, into the video game stratosphere. While the company earned about $3 million in 1973, only two years later that figure had risen to $40 million. In 1976, the company was bought up by Warner Communications; heavy-handed changes in the previously informal work environment upset a number of employees, not least Bushnell, who left in 1978. This would be the first of many conflicts between the often laid-back culture of game creators and the very different atmosphere of corporate America. With successful consoles and games, however, Atari continued to thrive, and in 1979 gross income rose to $200 million.

Video games in the 1970s also entered the home. Ralph Baer's arrangement with TV manufacturer Magnavox spawned the Odyssey console in 1972. The system was heavily hyped, with Magnavox marketing the promise of nuclear family fun for only $100. Some potential buyers, however, were confused, since Magnavox hinted that the system required one of the company's own TV sets to work. A total of about 200,000 Odysseys were sold.

In the same vein, Atari went domestic in 1975 with Home-Pong, a highly successful one-game-only console. More technologically interesting was the Channel F console, which hit the market in 1976 and was the first console to use plug-in cartridges containing individual games. Previously consoles were shipped with one or more built-in titles, which the player chose by flipping switches or inserting cards that held the appropriate settings. During its four-year lifespan, 21 games were published for the Channel F. Atari soon followed suit with the Atari Video Computer System (the Atari 2600), which would remain successful well into the next decade.

Two other events that would have substantial bearing on gaming occurred in those years. On a technological level, few inventions rival the microprocessor in importance. Invented in 1972, and commercially interesting a few years later, the new technology of the microprocessor would heavily influence not only arcade games and consoles but also the personal computers about to make their entrance. Perhaps equally important for gaming culture, as we have mentioned, was the publication of the pen-and-paper role-playing game *Dungeons & Dragons* in 1973. As noted, *D&D* introduced players to procedural (as opposed to goal-oriented) fantasy world role-playing, and would share a (sub)cultural niche with video games for a long time, appealing to the very same subset of young, predominantly male players.[8]

Action Games

The world's first arcade game was a failure. Inspired (heavily) by *Spacewar!*, Nolan Bushnell drew many wrong conclusions from the game's design and certainly failed to appreciate the desires of his audience. He was not producing a game for dedicated computer scientists but rather for crowded, smoke-filled bars and the technologically innocent. Not surprisingly, *Computer Space* did poorly. The game's graphics resembled *Spacewar!*, but the game was single-player and featured a spaceship battling against two UFOs. In addition, the game controls were hard to master, creating a learning curve too steep for new players who were unfamiliar with the very concept of video games. Bushnell, however, learned his lesson and learned it well. His follow-up product, *Pong*, single-handedly launched the video game as an industry. Released in 1972, its success was massive. Whereas the first version of *Computer Space* had been single-player, *Pong* was multiplayer at its heart. Further, the complex controls of the space battle were sacrificed for simple paddles, and the rules were summarized in a single line, "Avoid missing ball for high score," offering a Zen-like exercise in simplicity. As in previous games, the player's perspective was detached and omniscient. All objects in the game—two white paddles, one ever-bouncing ball—were contained within a single screen.

Arguably, *Pong* was itself highly derivative and the slew of *Pong* clones that followed, in arcades as well as in homes, relativizes any claim that copying proven games is in any way a modern phenomenon. In 1973, Atari followed up on the success with a two-player race through space, appropriately entitled *Space Race*. Each player navigated a spaceship through a meteor field in order to reach the top of the screen. Again we see a very simple, competitive two-player game formula, which served as a template for so many early game successes.

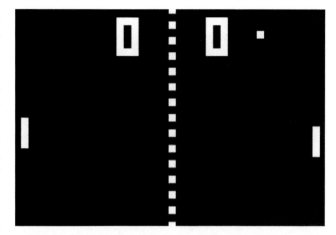

Figure 4.1 *Pong* (1972) is considered the midwife of the commercial video game industry

Marking a return to the shootout theme of *Spacewar!*, players in 1974's *Tank* would attempt to shoot each other in a mine-strewn black and white maze. Much the same concept, although with restricted horizontal movement and different obstacles, made *Gun Fight* a success in 1975. The perspective remained centered while two players took on the roles of Wild West gunslingers.

The year after would see more dramatic developments. On the level of design, Atari's *Night Driver* from 1976 was one of the first games to challenge the dominant third-person, one-screen perspective. This driving game was among the first to employ a first-person perspective, placing the player directly behind the wheel, so to speak. In addition, the game world only gradually revealed itself to the player as the road curved ahead to the horizon. While not a standard case of scrolling, the effect was very similar.

Figure 4.2 *Night Driver* (1976) introduces first-person perspective to the arcade

This design development cannot be taken lightly. It was suddenly clear that the third-person omnipresent viewpoint was not the only possibility. Drawing comparisons with another modern form of expression, this is not dissimilar to movie makers' "discovery" of the moving camera and the point-of-view shot.

Later that same year, however, another game would more loudly draw attention to itself. *Death Race* marks the end of innocence for arcade games and the beginning of a long-standing tradition of public outrage and worry over the morality of games and their players. *Death Race* centered on two

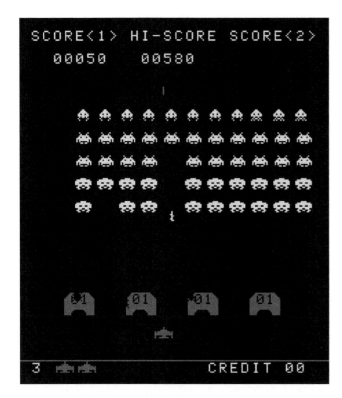

Figure 4.3 Space Invaders (1978) is remembered fondly by many people and a cultural icon for video games

cars running over stick-figure people who, when hit, turned into crosses. However, the crude graphics allowed for the possibility that the stick-figure people were "gremlins" (as the developers insisted) and thus not technically alive. Much controversy ensued. Thus was born the concept of the video game as public spectacle, and as a symbol of cultural ailment, developments that continue to this day.

Though not revolutionary in any obvious way, two action games published toward the end of the decade would become benchmarks for later design and earn their seats in any unofficial game history hall of fame. The first of these was *Space Invaders* from 1978. This single-player game upholds the most basic video game conventions—on the surface it is even comparable to *Computer Space*. However, the controls were much simpler than those of its forebear, and the gameplay compelling. The player controlled a tank moving horizontally at the bottom of the screen. The objective was to shoot down a formation of aliens slowly approaching, while utilizing four shields to create tactical advantage. If the aliens shot the player or reached the bottom of the screen, a life would be lost. Repelling one wave of attackers brought forth a new armada, this one moving slightly faster. The explosive success of *Space Invaders* did much to draw games out of the dimly lit arcades and into the fluorescent light of diners, shopping malls, and convenience stores around the United States.

Though it had a smaller cultural impact, Atari's 1979 hit *Asteroids* made even more money than *Space Invaders*. *Asteroids*, too, focused on gameplay over fancy graphics—although the stylized and incredibly simple visual components are noteworthy for their trance-like qualities. This effect was to some degree a consequence of early **vector graphics**, first seen in 1977 in *Space Wars*, and already used by Atari with some success earlier in 1979 in *Lunar Lander*.

Vector graphics: Graphics defined and generated on the basis of mathematical statements, meaning the perspective becomes flexible.

In *Asteroids*, a single-player game, a lonely spaceship had to fight its way through an asteroid belt visited by the occasional enemy flying saucer. Shooting an asteroid would split it into many pieces that then each had to be destroyed. The legacy of *Spacewar!* is obvious in the wraparound, seemingly never-ending space, and the feel of gravity's tug on the ship.

The *Spacewar!* template was highly visible here, and even in the more varied appearances of many successes to follow, not least of which was the first true color arcade game, *Galaxian*, from 1979. Considering these triumphs, we can conclude that, although various design experiments were conducted during the decade, action games didn't evolve much beyond the beautifully simple standards set by *Spacewar!* 18 years before.

Adventure Games

Although it might have seemed so at the time, not all games in the 1970s were action games. There were plenty of reasons to try different approaches to game design. Action games held limited possibilities for storytelling, and basically appealed to people who enjoyed games that challenged motor skills. The more contemplatively minded might not be thrilled by fire-button thumping and a reliance on good reflexes. And some designers most likely lacked the skill or resources to actually produce a state-of-the-art action game. For these and no doubt for other reasons, text adventure games started showing up on mainframes in the early 1970s, and a few years later would be easily and enthusiastically ported to personal computers.

The founding father, arguably, was *Hunt the Wumpus*, written by Gregory Yob in 1972. This simple construction placed the player in an underground cave system plagued by the presence of a clearly evil wumpus—a subterranean monster—with little interest in peaceful dialogue. The player, using only written commands, typed in his intention of either moving or shooting. Through the purely textual interface, the game would give hints as to the location of pits, bats, and the monster itself. No graphics meant modest demands on the player's hardware; the program was light, easy to understand, and addictive to more than a few people in whose imaginations the evil wumpus sprang to life.

More influential on game design was *Adventure*,[9] originally constructed by programmer William Crowther around 1972 and then expanded and improved by Don Woods at Stanford to be widely distributed in 1976. *Adventure* combined Crowther's interests in cave exploration, fantasy roleplaying, and programming. The purely textual game led the player through a world full of events, objects, and creatures, each with their own properties. The player would write his commands in "natural language," typically as a combination of verb and noun (for example, "examine building"), and the program would offer a result. Thus, the beginning of the game could read:

> At End of Road
> You are standing at the end of a road before a small brick building.
>> Around you is a forest. A small stream flows out of the building and
>> down a gully.
> [Player input] *Examine building*
> It's a small brick building. It seems to be a well house.

Traveling through the textual world, the player would encounter small puzzles and creatures, armed only with a series of simple commands to interact

Figure 4.4 Mystery House (1990) set a new standard for the graphics in the early adventure games

with them. *Adventure* was distributed for free over the ARPANET, a rudimentary precursor to today's Internet.

At the same time as free distribution was widespread, video games were beginning to make money, and *Adventure*'s successor, *Zork*, was considered a commercial opportunity almost from its inception. Designed by a group of MIT students, the game was more ambitious and in some ways technically superior to its recent ancestor. Spurred on by the game's popularity among their fellow students, the designers founded Infocom to handle the production and distribution.[10] Nevertheless, the first *Zork* game did travel widely across the ARPANET, although the game's code was partially obscured to prevent other designers from copying features directly.

Both *Adventure* and *Zork*, of course, were heavily influenced by the era's fascination with Tolkien and the growing popularity of fantasy role-playing. *Dungeons & Dragons*, more perhaps than later role-playing games, held obvious appeal to the technically interested; hand-drawn paper maps of dense dungeons and foreboding forests were pored over by *D&D* and *Zork* players alike. In early adventure games, as in early tabletop RPGs, the game experience was centered more on puzzles or logic than on narrative. Playing *Zork* involved not only solving puzzles within the game but also guessing what written commands the game's input interpreter could comprehend. Although the focus on logic and puzzles fascinated many, these themes would be downplayed throughout the next decade. Beginning the trend toward narrative was Ken and Roberta Williams's *Mystery House*, published in 1979 for the Apple II. While the game structure didn't rival *Zork*'s, *Mystery House* sported crude graphics to enhance the player's experience. Based on the success of *Mystery House*, the two authors went on to found On-Line Systems, which would soon become Sierra Online, a company that would strongly define the genre in the decade to come.

Strategy Games

Several games of the 1970s circulated as ideas or snippets of code; multiple designers might expand on these, so a game could exist in multiple incarnations at any given time. One such game was *Hamurabi* (occasionally spelled *Hammurabi*, and sometimes known as *Kingdom*). In this text-based game, the player was a ruler managing a nation's resources. With each command, the player would have to balance his country's various resources and also attend to popular opinion. More complex and more influential was Walter

Bright's *Empire*, from 1978, in which the player attempted to conquer an unexplored world using a series of military units. Another game of the same name, written by Peter S. Langston, was a yet more complex multiplayer game with a notable economic system. Compared to action and adventure games, strategy games did not undergo dramatic development in this decade, perhaps because they already had a considerable history (in terms of board games) which was mostly built upon and adapted to video game format.

Process-Oriented Games

Looking to digitize the role-playing experience, others went in somewhat different, and less commercial, directions than the makers of *Zork*. At Essex University in the last years of the decade, Roy Trubshaw and Richard Bartle were working on a system called *MUD*. The *Multi-User Dungeon* was essentially a multiplayer version of the *Adventure/Zork* template. Users would connect to the game, which ran on a server (i.e. a central machine that players could connect to via their own machines), and could then interact with the objects in the system as well as with other players. The world of the game, which would continue cyclically for a considerable period and then reset to the initial state, incorporated the actions of every player, and quickly became far more dynamic and unpredictable than the static worlds of single-player adventure games. *MUD*, which would turn into the label for the whole subgenre, was a success, albeit a local one since only a few people had network access at the time. Its influence, however, would be wide-ranging and is clearly detectable in the massively multiplayer online role-playing games (such as *EverQuest* and *Star Wars Galaxies*) to come. Before these, however, a wide range of *MUD* manifestations would serve as the playing ground for many hobbyists and academics through the 1980s and early 1990s.

THE 1980S

The 1980s were marked by rapid technological progress, a number of novel approaches to game design, and the proliferation of personal computers. The decade was also marked by what is sometimes called the Great Videogame Crash of 1983. Though dramatic and sudden, the "crash" was actually the result of a combination of factors. In the first third of the decade, the industry exploded and everything seemed promising. By 1983 one in four American homes housed a game console. Game sales had more than tripled (to $3.2 billion) from the previous year and there were few, if any, alarm bells ringing. One potential—though ignored—warning was the 1981 Atari 2600 adaptation of the arcade smash hit *Pac-Man*. The adaptation was legendarily poor, with very few of the aspects that made the original so popular. Following up on this artistic (if not commercial) disaster, Atari released *E.T. the Extra-Terrestrial* that same year, a game so poorly designed and so rushed through production that it became one of the biggest flops of the industry. The failure was underlined by Atari dumping and destroying huge numbers of *E.T.* cartridges in the New Mexico desert.[11]

Atari, though controlling two-thirds of the industry, then attempted to stifle third-party competitors by taking them to court, arguing that independent development for Atari machines should be illegal. Bushnell's old company lost, which led to an explosion of third-party publishers, and the market was soon flooded with huge numbers of games of uneven quality.

The final, and perhaps largest, nail in the coffin was home computers. In the early years of the decade, a variety of personal computers became available at prices that could compete with the game-dedicated consoles. As consumers realized the potential of home computers, and the growing number of games sold on 3.5-inch floppy disks, there was little reason for acquiring consoles that were less versatile. The Apple II—produced in 1977 by former Atari employee Steve Jobs—supported a large catalog of games. For price-conscious gamers, Commodore's VIC-20 was a big success at under $300, as was its more powerful younger brother, the Commodore 64.

In very little time the console industry virtually ceased to exist (Atari itself avoided bankruptcy but never regained its strength). Investors grew wary of anything video game–related, and it would be another two years before the Japanese company Nintendo kick-started the console business once again. In 1986 they released their Nintendo Entertainment System (NES) in the United States, a version of the Famicom (short for "family computer") which had already done very well in Japan.

By the end of the decade Nintendo had assumed the crown as the most successful console manufacturer, emphasizing their victory with the success of their handheld GameBoy (launched in 1989), which outperformed Atari's handheld Lynx released that same year.

Action Games

Before 1983's "crash," Atari released action games at a brisk pace. Following up on their earlier successes with vector graphics, *Battlezone* (1980) put the player inside a tank fighting other tanks in what today looks like an abstract landscape of geometrical shapes. The game was so successful—and was considered so realistic—that the US Army commissioned a special version for training purposes. This collaboration between Atari and the US Army continues to shape present-day debate about the military's use of games.

The same year saw the release of yet another space shooter, although this one was less faithful to the original mechanics of *Spacewar!* In *Defender*, the player protected small, inanimate humanoids from aliens who swooped down to the planet's surface, picked up a humanoid and carried him to the top of the screen, where he would transform into a mutant alien. The player had use of a laser, a number of "smartbombs," which would destroy all aliens on-screen, and could also hyperjump to a different part of the screen (a

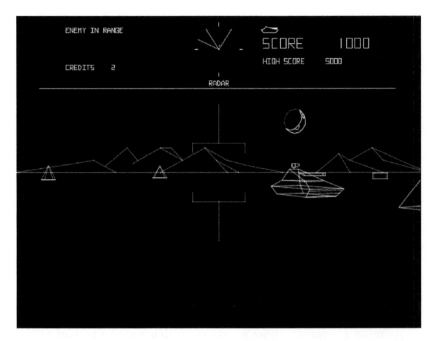

Figure 4.5 *Battlezone* (1980) became one of the first games to mark the military's use of commercial off-the-shelf video games for training

feature well known since a late iteration of *Spacewar!*). Whereas *Spacewar!* employed a wraparound space made famous by *Pac-Man*, *Defender* used a different version of the same concept. The scrolling game world was circular; going far enough in one direction would place you back in your original position without any apparent relocation of your spaceship. Helpful in the battle was a radar illustrating your position in the game world. While a few years before an arcade game had been considered successful if 15,000 cabinets were sold, *Defender* approached sales of 60,000.[12]

The thirst for space shooters must have seemed insatiable. Building on the *Space Invaders* theme, *Gorf*, from 1981, was the first arcade game to offer (somewhat) different levels; it also introduced the concept of battling a big bad something at the end of each level—in this case the Gorfian mother ship. Other small innovations included a flickering force shield that would slowly be destroyed by enemy fire, the

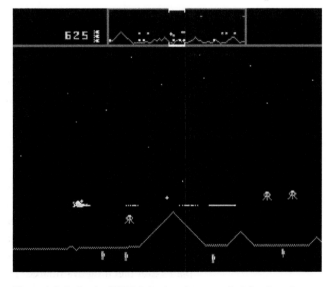

Figure 4.6 *Defender* (1980) introduced a new principle where the game world would circularly scroll, which became very successful

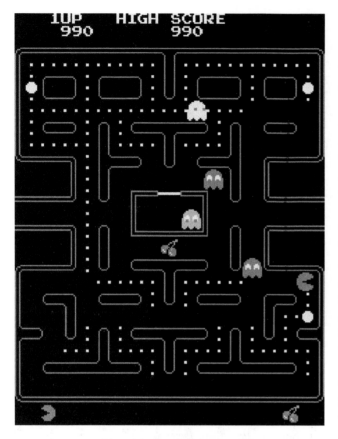

Figure 4.7 *Pac-Man* (1980) became hugely successful and one of the first games to successfully create a character that became a well-known brand

limited vertical movement of the player's ship, and the ability to shoot only one torpedo at a time (shooting another before the first exploded would cause the previous torpedo to disappear).

After 1980, however, the dominance of *Space Invaders* clones began to be eaten away. *Pac-Man*, deliberately cartoonish and quite simple to play, was a remarkable success in Japan and was then exported to the United States. Originally called *Puckman*—considered too tempting for English-speaking vandals—*Pac-Man* was the name of a small, pizza-like wedge that had to gobble up a maze of small dots and floating fruit, while alternately avoiding and (with the help of "power-ups") attacking the four ghosts that stalked the gamespace.

As in the earliest games, the player was omniscient and the game was confined to one screen. Thus, although technological advancements were numerous, many successes of the early 1980s were quite conservative. *Pac-Man* was revolutionary, though, in one essential aspect. Unlike all previous game hits, this one had an identifiable main character. *Pac-Man* was quickly licensed to appear on merchandise—from towels to T-shirts—at no extra cost to Namco, the game's developer, or Bally/Midway, the US distributor. Like cartoon characters, Pac-Man did not develop a Hollywood ego, nor did he demand a cut of the licensing income. The game and the Pac-Man character were popular enough to warrant an ABC-TV show (*The Pac-Man Show*) and a slew of clones, copies, and sequels. Of these, *Ms. Pac-Man* was the most important, and became a large success in its own right. Another sequel, *Pac-Land*, transported the adventurous wedge into a side-scrolling world where he had to navigate a series of platforms and obstacles.

This piece of the Pac-Man universe exemplifies several important trends in arcade games, particularly the triumph of so-called platform games, as we'll see later. With over 300,000 units sold,[13] *Pac-Man* is considered the best-selling arcade game of all time, and with the astounding success of character-based cuteness it seriously challenged the powerful sci-fi templates that had long dominated the industry.

Alongside the dominant single-screen game, these years witnessed the beginning of the "platform game," as mentioned. The game that launched this subgenre was *Space Panic*, from 1980, in which the player controlled an astronaut who climbed ladders and dug holes to combat enemy aliens.

On a superficial level at least, Nintendo's highly successful arcade game *Donkey Kong* from 1981 (before Nintendo's console successes) drew obvious inspiration from *Space Panic*. Mario, a heavyset and conspicuously mustached plumber, had to move from the bottom of the screen to the top by navigating a series of ladders and obstacles, all to rescue his fiancée from the clutches of a large gorilla. The game launched designer Shigeru Miyamoto's career, and would be the cornerstone of Nintendo's coming success in America.

Mario returned, along with his brother Luigi, in 1983's *Mario Bros.*, where they did some actual plumbing. In this nonscrolling platform game, the brothers were out to combat the turtles and other beasts thriving in poorly maintained pipes. Each player could bump his head into the floor below a turtle, flipping it onto its back, and the plumbers could then kill the turtle by running into it.

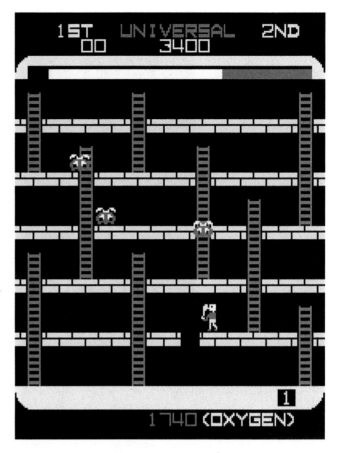

Figure 4.8 *Space Panic* (1980) may not be that well-known, but it invented the popular platform game mechanics

The game's revolutionary possibility—for players to cooperate against a common foe—had been introduced the year before in *Joust*, and would be used to great effect in 1985 in *Gauntlet*. In *Gauntlet*, up to four players could cooperate in ridding a dungeon of monsters. The four characters—a warrior, an elf, a wizard, and a Valkyrie—each had different abilities, betraying the concept's roots in pen-and-paper role-playing. The game in fact earned Atari a patent, confirming the company's invention of "multiplayer, multi-character cooperative play video game with independent player entry and departure."[14]

Mario Bros. was followed by *Super Mario Bros.* in 1985—which, like *Pac-Land*, scrolled horizontally—in which Mario and Luigi fought to rescue the Mushroom Princess from the evil turtles. This time around, enemies could also be killed by landing on top of them. This version kept a crucial feature of the original—that the player had to decelerate before turning around, even though the ground did not appear to be slippery. This particular mechanism was in turn a legacy of the original space shooters, from *Spacewar!* to *Asteroids*.

As the decade continued, platform games became a staple of the action genre, with notable examples being *Elevator Action* (1983), *Impossible*

Figure 4.9 Gauntlet (Commodore 64 version) (1985), one of the first successful multiplayer games that Atari earned a patent for

Figure 4.10 Moon Patrol (1982) introduced scrolling background layers that created the illusion of depth

Mission (1984), *Wonder Boy* (1986), *Rainbow Islands* (1987), *The New Zealand Story* (1988), *Ghosts 'n Goblins* (1985), *Prince of Persia* (1989), and *Sonic the Hedgehog* (1991). These introduced a variety of gaming elements—like the need to time your jumps between platforms, to name one of many—which would be standard for years to come.

Sideways scrolling and jumping could also be combined with classical space battle themes, as seen in *Moon Patrol*, from 1982. Here the player drove a purple vehicle across a futuristic lunar landscape while fighting alien spaceships above and avoiding holes and rocks (some of which could be blasted away). The game featured "parallax scrolling," in which background layers passed across the screen at different speeds to create the illusion of depth.

By the early 1980s, driving—particularly race cars—had been a popular electronic pastime for several years. Building upon successful games such as *Sprint 2* (from 1978) and the first-person driving games that followed the success of *Night Driver*, *Pole Position* swept through arcades in 1982. The player raced a car around a circuit, competing against other cars and the clock. Rather than a bird's-eye view, the perspective of the game was from behind the car, which of course constitutes the first of many variations on the first-person driving game.

The intensity and intuitive controls of racing games helped ensure the popularity of this subgenre, along with a string of commercial successes: *Pole Position* was followed by games such as *Pitstop* in 1983, the split-screen, two-player sequel *Pitstop II* one year later, the stylish *Out Run* in 1986, the motorbike racer *Hang-On* (1985), the fast-paced *Lotus Esprit Turbo Challenge* (1990), and the *Test Drive* series that stretched from 1987 to 1999. (Later games, such as the *Need for Speed* series, starting in 1994, and the *Gran Turismo* series, first published in 1997, ensured that driving would remain among the most popular electronic simulations of "real-life" activities.) Other racing games focused less on realism and more on abstract or cartoonish aesthetics, such as *Bump'n'Jump* from 1982, *Spy Hunter* from 1983, *Super Cars II* from 1991, and *Mario Kart* from 1992.

Another subgenre that burst onto the scene in the early 1980s was sports games. While individual sports had been simulated many times, a new breed inspired by the 1984 Olympic Games offered the player a variety of disciplines. Following the arcade game *Track & Field* from 1983, Activision published *Decathlon* for the Commodore 64 that same year. The Commodore 64 soon boasted Epyx's Games series, inaugurated with *Summer Games* in 1984 and followed by *Summer Games II, Winter Games, World Games*, the highly popular *California Games*, and others.

Figure 4.11 Summer Games II (Commodore 64) (1984), one of the prime examples of the increasing popularity of sports games

TOP 008900
1UP 000600

H

L

ENEMY
PLANE
▸=20

FUEL ▮▯▮▯▮▯▮▯▮▯▮▯▮▯▮▯▮▯▮▯▮▯▮▯▮   F
                    © SEGA 1982

Figure 4.12 Zaxxon (1982), the first game to introduce the successful isometric perspective in video games

Isometric perspective:
Also referred to as 2.5D because it tries to mimic the 3D effect. However, although it may look like 3D, the objects are drawn (and are viewable) from only one perspective.

Shooting games continued to evolve. A noteworthy experiment with form was *Zaxxon* from 1982, which introduced the **"isometric"** perspective. In *Zaxxon*, the scrolling game world is watched from above but at an angle; as the player flies through a heavily guarded enemy fortress, the spaceship's altitude and horizontal position is crucial for survival, making the isometric perspective integral to the game. This perspective was rarely used in action games, with a few notable exceptions like *Blue Max* (1983) for the Commodore 64 and 1985's *Paperboy*. More consistently popular in shooters was the standard third-person perspective on a scrolling screen, with games more or less equally divided between a vertical scroll—*Xevious* (1982) and *1942* (1984) are prominent examples—and a horizontal scroll—*Scramble* (1981) and *Blood Money* (1989).

Although cooperative games were quite successful, and sports and other simulation games began to reshape the industry, the classic one-on-one fighting game—with obvious echoes of *Spacewar!* and *Gun Fight*—was still very much alive in the 1980s. *Karate Champ* from 1984, for example, was the first two-player karate game. Each level was set in a new arena, a visual convention that would be followed for decades. Similar fighting games following in the mid-1980s include the single-player game *Yie Ar Kung-Fu* (1985), *International Karate +* (1987), and *Street Fighter* (1987), as well as later games from *Mortal Kombat* (1992) to *Tekken* (1994) to *SoulCalibur* (1998).

The cooperative versions of these "beat' em up" games typically featured horizontal scroll. One illustrative example is *Double Dragon*, from 1987, in which Billy and Jimmy Lee battled a host of street-fighting thugs to save Billy's girlfriend. In an obvious parallel to early moviemaking, the archetypal rescue-the-damsel-in-distress story line was widely used in 1980s games, including *Donkey Kong* (1981) and *Super Mario Bros.* (1985). *Double Dragon*, however, was not a feel-good buddy game: players were able to hurt each other (accidentally or not) and at the end had to fight over who got the girl (a feature evident in later strategy games, where victory is handed to the "last man standing").

Strategy Games

Games requiring careful analysis and strategic thinking are obviously ill-suited to noisy arcades, where games rarely last more than a few minutes.

However, with the triumphant entry of home computers, games of strategy found an obvious home, and an eager audience.

Strategy games in the 1980s were, to a large degree, direct adaptations of board games or largely inspired by their cardboard brethren. As is still the case today, the genre consisted mainly of wargames (although there were important exceptions). The distributor SSI dominated the market in board-game-inspired wargames. *Kampfgruppe* (1985), *Gettysburg: The Turning Point* (1986), *Storm Across Europe* (1989), and the fantasy-oriented *Sword of Aragon* (1989) all expanded (or just copied) the board game formula without adding revolutionary new elements.

In 1987, Walter Bright and Mark Baldwin published an updated version of *Empire* (originally from 1978). As in the original, the player began with few resources and explored the game world to find, and hopefully defeat, enemy nations. Although now considered a war game classic, Bright had serious problems finding a willing publisher. One publisher, MicroProse, rejected the game because they were looking for action-oriented "real-time" strategy simulations. Bröderbund did not find the story original enough nor the graphics advanced enough, and Epyx did not consider it appropriate for their favored platform, the Commodore 64. When released by Interstel, however, the game did prove highly successful.[15]

Several war games experimented with diplomacy and political maneuvering. In 1985, *Balance of Power* addressed the acute Cold War tension of the era. The player assumed the role of a superpower leader trying to win

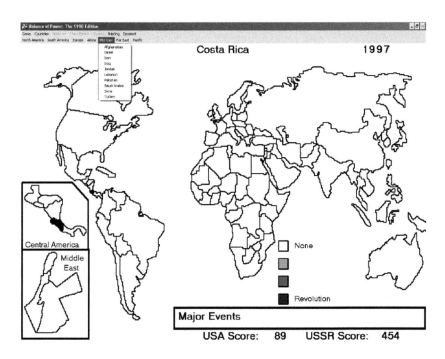

Figure 4.13 Balance of Power (1990 version) (1990) set new standards for the realism and depth of strategy games

the world over to his side without fatally provoking his opponent (either the computer or a second player) into a nuclear attack. The entire nail-biting experience was made possible by nothing more than graphics of a world map; this economical design approach has underlined the game's status as a classic. Although strategy game interfaces were adapting to the point-and-click era and graphics were becoming more detailed, the genre has traditionally relied very little on the impressive visuals seen in other genres.

A small breed of strategy games took the pillars of the genre—the poring over battle maps, the consideration of endless interdependent variables—less seriously. The French game *North and South* (1989), for example, was blatantly cartoonish and focused less on maps and more on utilizing the full audiovisual potential of the Commodore Amiga. The game, based on the comic book series *Les Tuniques Bleues*, was set during the American Civil War and would alternate between a strategic level and action sequences. The latter would unfold once the player made the strategic decision to attack a fort or board a moving train.

Equally colorful but more satirical was *Nuclear War* from 1989, which caricatured real-world political leaders and their simple-minded responses to nuclear threat. Most hardcore strategy gamers were unimpressed: the jokes overrode attention to gameplay, as the computer opponent was capable of only very simple strategies, and the consequences of the game's choices often seemed random.

North and South was not the only game to mix strategy with action sequences. The developer Cinemaware was especially prolific with this hybrid strategy, seen in late 1980s games such as *Defender of the Crown* (1986), *King of Chicago* (1987), and *Lords of the Rising Sun* (1989). The first of these, remade in 2003, featured groundbreaking graphics and cast the player as a post–Robin Hood British lord vying for control of the country. With limited strategy components and a reliance on action sequences, which seemed to imply that strategy alone couldn't keep players entertained, these hybrid games never found universal acceptance among hardcore strategy gamers.

One game that did effectively combine strategy and action was *Herzog Zwei*, released in 1989 for the Sega Genesis (known in Europe as the Sega Megadrive), a strong competitor to Nintendo in the console business at this time, with the Genesis marketed as a cooler and more adult-oriented machine than the Nintendo Entertainment System. In *Herzog Zwei* the player defends and expands his territory while managing resources and creating various military units. In an important departure from all other strategy games (and their board-game predecessors), players competed without taking turns. In other words, players made choices simultaneously and without interruption (as they would in any action game like *Pong*). *Herzog Zwei* thus qualifies as the first real-time strategy game, a subgenre that would prove both hardy and prolific in the decade to come.

Two other highly important strategy games helped end the decade with a flurry of creative activity. One of these was Bullfrog's *Populous* from 1989,

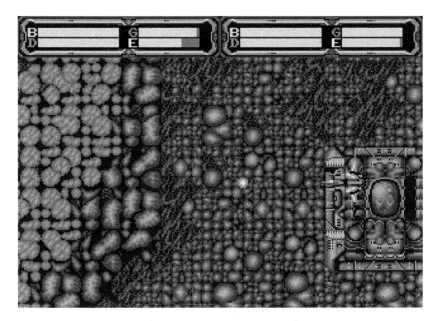

Figure 4.14 *Herzog Zwei* was the first real-time strategy game

which combined the real-time concept with an isometric perspective (this would later become a standard combination for the subgenre). The game positioned the player as a deity thriving on worship and capable of godly deeds of wonder and destruction.

The second noteworthy entry from the end of the 1980s was the legendary *SimCity* from 1989. Although it featured many strategy elements, it was the culmination of the decade-long merging of the strategy and process-oriented genres, and will be discussed in the "Process-Oriented Games" section later in this chapter.

As the 1980s came to a close, the strategy genre looked radically different than it had a mere ten years earlier. These games experienced an adolescence-like explosion, moving in a short period from an almost total reliance on text and crude graphics to a wide range of gaming experiences that pushed against the very boundaries of the genre. Strategy game designers had dutifully explored the possibilities offered by board games, and seemed ready to burst into new arenas. Spurred on by the enormous promise of the home computer, the possibilities were endless, though two phenomena stood out, and would continue to alter the genre: real-time strategy and the influence of process-oriented games.

Adventure Games

Throughout the 1980s, multiuser dungeon games (or MUDs) would remain constrained by the lack of networked computers; meanwhile, however, *Zork* and its many offspring would find happy new lives in the rapid proliferation of home computers. The adventure world offered something fundamentally new, and both the technical and the popular press displayed great interest. In 1980, Infocom designer P. David Lebling described *Zork* in *Byte* magazine as not a video game but a "CFS (computerized fantasy simulation) game," defining it as "a new art form: the computerized storybook." He was simultaneously skeptical that *Zork* could be enhanced by the use of graphics: "the player's imagination probably has a more detailed picture of the Great Underground Empire than could ever be drawn."[16]

The connection to literature, and the player's storytelling imagination praised by Lebling, was essential to ensuring the cultural acceptance of the genre. In what is likely one of the first reviews of video games in its august pages, the *New York Times Book Review* in 1983 described Infocom's *Deadline* as "more like a genre of fiction than a game." Infocom has been a major pioneer in such games, which have been called 'participatory novels,' **'interactive fiction'** and 'participa-stories.'[17] The hesitant use of the label of "game" is both intriguing and revealing, as it demonstrates how different the text-reliant adventure games seemed from their arcade shooter contemporaries.

Infocom continued to cultivate their literary image, and many adventure game designers thought of themselves as different—and perhaps more sophisticated—than other game designers. A distinct image, of course, had marketing advantages: "old media," like the *New York Times*, might be more interested in a new "art form" than just another video game; and computer owners who didn't consider themselves gamers might be more willing to try a game sold as "interactive fiction." Similarly, early filmmakers sought to enhance the legitimacy of their medium by associating it with already admired forms of expression, particularly classical theater. But marketing concerns aside, adventure games were highly innovative (though stubbornly bound to a pure textual interface), and Infocom led the genre for most of the decade.

The aforementioned *Deadline* was the genre's most significant follow-up to the foundational success of *Zork*. Moving the adventure genre out of Tolkienesque dungeons, *Deadline* drew on the whodunit standards of mystery novels and movies, as the player negotiated a New England colonial estate to solve the murder (or was it suicide?) of Marshall Robner. *The Witness*, also from 1983, drew upon many of the same principles, as the player had only 12 hours to solve the crime story. The same concept was recycled in 1984's *Suspect*, in which the player must defend herself against false murder charges.

Dungeons and detectives were complemented by science fiction plots in *Planetfall* (1983) and *Stationfall* (1987). Of these, *Planetfall* is best remembered, as it featured the robot Floyd, one of the industry's first examples of a convincing and dramatically important character who was not a player. (At one point in the game, Floyd would even sacrifice its life for that of the player.)

Other adventure designers, in contrast to Lebling, didn't believe that the player's imagination—weaving visions entirely from text—was crucial to

Interactive fiction: Contested label for types of fiction based on high user participation. Normally the term refers to computer-based types of fiction, but role-playing games such as *Dungeons & Dragons* and special forms of paper-based literature may also deserve the label "interactive." (Sometimes used to refer solely to text adventure games.)

the genre. In 1980, Sierra Online had already introduced the possibility of a graphics-based adventure game with *Mystery House*. This was followed in 1981 with *Ulysses and the Golden Fleece*, set in ancient Greece and featuring color graphics illustrating the player's situation.

So far, however, the nascent use of graphics had merely described events and locations within the games. These static images could not be manipulated, but this would change dramatically in 1983 with *King's Quest*. Here, the player assumed the role of Sir Graham, traveling the magical land of Daventry in search of three treasures. Graham was represented by an on-screen **avatar** who could interact with nearby objects—which had of course been common in other game genres since the birth of gaming. The player, however, could still only interact with the game via text, and still had to guess the correct combinations of words in order to create the necessary commands. Graphic innovation, however small, was rewarded, and the *King's Quest* series became a steady success, with new installments as recently as 1998 (and ongoing talk of remakes and continuation).

Avatar: Graphical representation of the user in an online forum, especially a role-playing game.

Fueled by this development, Sierra released *Space Quest: The Sarien Encounter* in 1986. Its unlikely hero, Roger Wilco, had survived an alien attack by napping in his janitor's closet, and now had to set things right. The humorous tone struck a chord with many softcore gamers and the *Space Quest* series lived on until 1995 (with constant rumors of more games being developed since then).

Among gamers not traditionally drawn to the genre, Sierra's best-known games may be the *Leisure Suit Larry* series (based on *SoftPorn* from 1981). Larry is an ambitiously dressed and balding wannabe, a ladies' man

Figure 4.15 King's Quest I: Quest for the Crown (2004 remake by Anonymous Game Developers Interactive) introduces the idea of an avatar in adventure games, so the player can move around on the screen to interact with objects

anti-hero who seeks love in a world of pretense, smooth surfaces, and low comedy. *Leisure Suit Larry in the Land of the Lounge Lizards*, the first of the series, seemed a commercial failure when released in 1987, but word of mouth made it a slow-build best-seller as well as an informal classic. The third installment, *Leisure Suit Larry 3: Passionate Patti in Pursuit of the Pulsating Pectorals* from 1989, added a novel twist as the player alternated between controlling Larry and his (ex-)girlfriend Patty.

Through the first half of the decade, the literary Infocom and the less purist Sierra dominated the genre. However, a development was on the horizon that would do more than add pictures to the stories. In 1987, an alternative was found to the gamer's endless search for the right combination of words, long the frustration of text adventures, as Lucasfilm Games (later known as LucasArts) released the humorous horror story *Maniac Mansion*.

In addition to requiring the player to switch between teenage protagonists, the game introduced the point-and-click interface to the genre. Instead of typing commands, the player would be offered a series of verbs that could be combined with graphical elements in the game by use of mouse or joystick. The player was more constrained than in text adventure games with large vocabularies but no longer had the aggravation of having to guess the right word combinations. The creators of 1990's *Loom*, which used the interface style introduced in *Maniac Mansion*, explained: "[We] think you like to spend your time involved in the story, not typing in synonyms until you stumble upon the computer's word for a certain object."[18]

Building on the template, Lucasfilm Games soon released the equally witty *Zak McKracken and the Alien Mindbenders*, and followed with *Indiana*

Figure 4.16 Maniac Mansion (2004 remake by LucasFan Games) (2004) introduced the point-and-click interface to the adventure genre

Jones and The Last Crusade in 1989. The latter saw the guest appearance of Chuck the Plant, an unusable object from *Maniac Mansion*, and introduced the phrase "I'm selling these fine leather jackets," which would resonate through later LucasArts games. These intertextual mini-jokes served to reward fans for their loyalty. But more important than this cleverness, the point-and-click interface proved massively appealing, and soon textual interaction was on the decline. A new breed of adventure game was born, and would prosper until midway through the next decade.

Meanwhile, the role-playing branch of adventure games was also blossoming. Throughout the 1980s, these games remained loyal to Tolkienesque fantasy and were the genre's most obvious heirs to the *Dungeons & Dragons* legacy, focusing on large explorable worlds and relying on the concepts of hit points, skill levels, trade, and random encounters far more than the games produced by Infocom, Sierra, and LucasArts.[19] Especially toward the end of the decade, RPGs also replicated the concept of the adventuring party, in contrast to the genre's previous reliance on the single protagonist.

Designer Richard Garriot began the decade with *Akalabeth*, which he followed later in 1981 with *Ultima*. Launching a series that would continue until 1999, *Ultima* offered a bird's-eye-view perspective on the simple graphics that made up the world of Sosaria. Other series soon followed. *Wizardry: Proving Grounds of the Mad Overlord* featured first-person dungeon exploration in 3D vector graphics and inspired a large number of sequels. *Tales of the Unknown, Volume I: The Bard's Tale*, from 1985, colorfully mixed 2D and 3D graphics (two sequels followed). We should also note that RPGs were not confined to home computers. In 1987 Nintendo fans could enjoy (the misleadingly named) *Final Fantasy*, which kicked off a series that would proliferate across platforms for at least the next two decades.

Although not dissimilar in structure to standard adventure games, the openness of computer RPGs would assure them a very different fate in the decade to come.

Process-Oriented Games

Much like adventure and **turn-based strategy games**, process-oriented games were unthinkable in a fast-paced arcade but seemed made for home computers. Indeed, quick and intense arcade-like experiences are usually anathema to process-oriented games, many striving for realism, while some focus more on recreating the physical experience of dealing with a real-world system—and pay less attention to the game's accessibility or how much fun it is, or even to whether it has a clear victory condition.

Of course, it wasn't only process-oriented games, which strove for some sort of realism. One arcade game lauded for its faithful representation of reality was *Battlezone*. While the 1980 game does simulate a battle tank, it focuses on shooting and the complex controls of the actual vehicles are downplayed. This was not so in many process-oriented home computer games. In the case of the *Microsoft Flight Simulator* series, which had a

Turn-based strategy games: Strategy games divided into "turns," as in board games (and as opposed to real-time strategy games). Typically a player moves all his or her units, then the next player moves all their units, and so on.

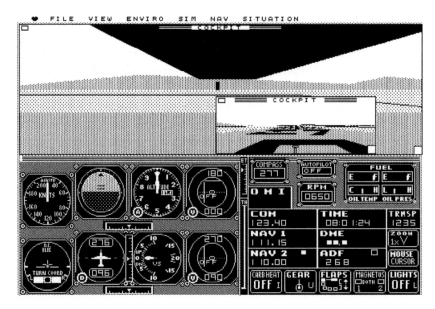

Figure 4.17 Microsoft Flight Simulator (1986 Mac version) (1986) set new standards for the realism of simulation games

remarkable 24-year run from 1982 to 2006, the manual for the first game was adamant that "Microsoft Flight Simulator is a highly accurate simulation of flight in a single-engine aircraft. Its working instruments, panoramic out-the-window graphics view and real-time flight conditions will give you the excitement of flying in a real plane." It also stressed that "Flight Simulator gives you full use of the flight instruments and controls. This instrumentation is so accurate that it meets the FAA regulations (part 91.33) for day and night, visual and instrument flight conditions."[20]

The game had a steep learning curve, as players had slowly to familiarize themselves with the complex controls, and succeed in a long flight across fairly monotonous land in order to land at the next airport.

Other process games added action elements to broaden their appeal. Sierra's *3-D Helicopter Simulator* saw itself as "computerized flight training with realistic action!" as it put the player in control of the McDonnell Douglas "Apache" military helicopter. The 1987 game was also significant as the first to introduce head-to-head multiplayer combat, via the then impressive technology of a telephone modem.

With the exception of flight simulators, many "vehicle" games had optional action modes. You didn't have to engage with the action elements but rather could choose to, according to your liking. Submarine simulations such as *688 Attack Sub* from 1989 and *Sub Battle Simulator* from 1987 took clever advantage of limited processing power. The murky, vague graphics enhanced the feeling of paranoia from being in a confined space underwater; just as in the depths of the ocean, there was often very little to see while playing this game, and the player's limited perception of the surrounding world added to the anxiety.

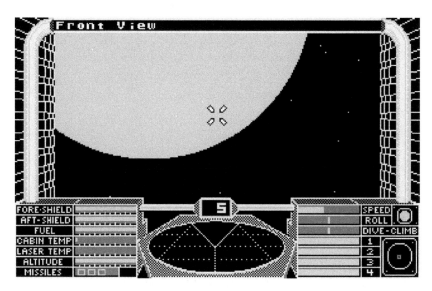

Figure 4.18 Elite (DOS version) (1985) was a successful open-ended world sporting some of the earliest 3D polygon graphics that would later become an industry standard

One landmark game combined strategy and action more seamlessly than many contemporary genre hybrids—the 1984 space merchant classic *Elite*. One of the first home video games with **polygon** 3D graphics, *Elite* also sported a pompous (if technically simple) *2001*-style classical soundtrack. The player was plopped into a huge universe (seemingly constructed at random) with a modest spaceship and limited cash. From these humble beginnings the player had to engage with the worlds around her, using some combination of trade, smuggling, bounty hunting, and quest-solving. Approaching a floating, three-dimensional, semi-abstract space station at low speed was an experience unparalleled in game history. With no story line or set goal, the game created a unique sense of vastness and unlimited opportunity, and was among the most revolutionary home video games of the time.

Polygon: Geometric figure; a closed-plane figure bounded by straight lines. 3D graphics usually consist of polygons and are therefore not dependent upon a fixed perspective.

The idea of open-ended games lacking clear conditions for victory slowly caught on. One innovative game, which offered a dynamic world (although it did have a goal and could, in fact, end), was *Sid Meier's Pirates!* from 1987. As an aspiring pirate, the player traveled the Caribbean in search of treasure and fame. You could follow various plot strands, with their resulting ebb and flow of alliances, which created the impression of being just one person in an evolving world.

Despite their landmark innovations, the fame of *Elite* and *Sid Meier's Pirates!* pales next to *SimCity*, designed by legendary game designer Will Wright. In this 1989 game, the player assumed the role of mayor and managed a city that would grow or diminish almost organically in response to the player's choices on everything from zoning and construction to taxation. Angry citizens might protest and leave the city, while a content populace

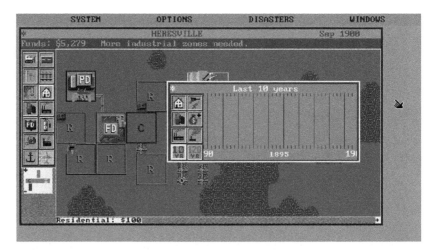

Figure 4.19 SimCity (DOS) (1989) heralded a new genre of open-ended complex builder games

would settle down, have more children, and generate more income. Since all parts of the game's world interacted, a fairly small number of game settings and variables would elicit complex behavior from the system. Aside from this complexity, the design of course draws upon the *Hamurabi* legacy (see the previous section) of managing a world, though the popularity of *SimCity* would influence not just the design of future games but the role of the entire industry.

Meanwhile, various MUDs had descended from the original, and some manifestations of the genre belonged more to the process-oriented category than their adventure relatives. Of these, *Habitat* stood out, applying the Lucasfilm ethos of moving away from text and toward cartoonish graphics. Launched in 1985 for the Commodore 64, its players logged in via modem and encountered a graphical world full of social interaction and quests. The concept was very ambitious, and players encountered equally difficult technical and social challenges.[21] Though plagued by these problems, many of the lessons learned (as well as the actual features used) inspired "social worlds" for years to come, including *There.com* (which initially closed in 2010, only to reopen in 2012) and *Second Life*, both launched in 2003.

By the end of the 1980s a great deal had happened. Many genres and subgenres had solidified into formats still going strong today (perhaps most evident is the case of single-player RPGs). Also, the console-based business had fallen from legendary pre-1983/1984 heights, against most predictions, only to resurface within a few years to coexist with home computer gaming. Video gaming itself had become a staple of pop culture, which most children—and sometimes, indirectly, their parents—had experienced, and worried voices had been raised about the influence of gaming on young minds.

At the end of the decade game production was also quite a different undertaking than it had been in earlier days, as increasingly powerful hardware formed the backdrop of an audiovisual arms race and necessarily more complex game production processes. The latter would continue as a key industry trend into the 1990s and beyond.

THE 1990S

Though during the last decade of the twentieth century most video games relied upon already established genres and conventions, a few developments were truly significant. In the technology arena, the personal computer (by now universally referred to as the "PC") awoke fully as a hardcore gaming platform, due to major advances in sound and graphics hardware. A well-equipped PC rivaled the audiovisuals of all but the very newest consoles at any given moment. In addition, the spread of network technology and the rise of the Internet created both explosive growth and broad diffusion, which would change both the experience of playing a video game and the game design templates themselves. Meanwhile, the commercial introduction of the CD-ROM as a software storage medium simultaneously destroyed the floppy disk and swiftly increased the size of a typical game. And in the realm of graphics, by the decade's end 3D polygon graphics would replace two-dimensional graphics as the industry standard. By 1990, text input interfaces were only seen in marginal examples of the adventure genre and in MUDs (although home computer games usually rely on a combination of keyboard and mouse).

In terms of genre, the classical adventure game would start a long decline in the late 1990s, and action games would be forever marked by the arrival of the first-person shooter template around 1993. More generally, the four genres, as we have described them here, began to challenge their own boundaries. Toward the last third of the decade, hybrid games became the norm instead of the exception. Action games would employ strategy elements, strategy games would lean toward action (most notably in the prolific subgenre of real-time strategy), and adventure games would continue to spice up their puzzle-solving with action sequences.

As for consoles, the Nintendo Entertainment System (NES) still dominated at the end of the 1980s but began to encounter unprecedented competition from Sega's Genesis. Nintendo, which used gray plastic cartridges for storage, had succeeded partly through tight control over game production, to avoid flooding the market with low-quality games. Sticking to cartridges, however, meant costly products and harsh publishing rules regarding content and quality, and made life difficult for many developers. Further, as Nintendo strove to maintain their machine's family-friendly image, Sega in contrast portrayed their own console as cool and radical (embodied in the early 1990s slogan, "Sega does what Nintendon't"). The same strategy would also be used by upstart video game producer Sony, as their 1994 PlayStation outclassed the Sega Saturn and two years later continued to sell well against the Nintendo 64 (which was also troubled by Nintendo's loyalty to cartridges). Sega in 1999 did well with their Dreamcast console (the first to be designed for online play), although within just a few years the competition became too strong, and they changed strategy to developing game titles only.

The growth of local area network technology (computers close to each other sharing a network) across the globe and the emergence of the World Wide Web created perfect conditions for multiplayer gaming. The wiring of the world also to some extent meant the return of the arcade—now in the form of gaming cafés (more pervasive in some countries than others). Whereas home computers had isolated players in some ways, network technology brought them back together.

Action Games

The action genre displayed limited creativity and originality at the decade's outset. In 1992, however, change appeared in the shape of *Wolfenstein 3D*. The game, based on an earlier 2D game, was the original first-person shooter (although it was preceded two months earlier by *Ultima Underworld: The Stygian Abyss*, the first modern-looking 3D action game with a first-person perspective). In *Wolfenstein 3D*, the player was a lonely soldier invading a Nazi castle; the game world was seen solely through the eyes of the protagonist. Although the player could move freely in the game world, the graphics were not technically 3D, since they consisted of 2D objects and not of three-dimensional polygonal shapes.

Though popular, the game could not prepare the world for 1993's *Doom*. Here, the player assumed the role of a lone, no-nonsense soldier defending the universe from the unfortunate, and seemingly unceasing, onslaught of the hordes of Hell. Since such creatures are not known to engage in

Figure 4.20 Wolfenstein 3D (1992) was the first game to herald the still immensely popular first-person shooter genre

constructive dialogue, the player was required to use varied weaponry to send them all back where they came from.

As with *Wolfenstein 3D*, the developers at id Software released the first version of *Doom* as shareware, meaning it was available for free on the Internet. The game's server was quickly and persistently overloaded.[22] And, as with the former game, *Doom* was easily modified, creating intense interest among serious and casual game designers alike; altered versions of the game thrived on online bulletin boards and as separately marketed productions (which required the original to play).

Its striking difference from mainstream action titles, as well as its creative and efficient use of sound and graphics, was enough to ensure *Doom*'s fame. However, it also became one of the earliest mainstream games to make good use of local area network technology, as players could fight head-to-head in the slime-ridden hallways.

Doom made a huge impact on action games from the mid-1990s onwards. *Doom II* (1994) updated the original's success. *Heretic* (1994) used the *Doom* setup for fantasy purposes. *Quake* (1996) embellished the concept with true 3D graphics. *Unreal* (1998) introduced more story elements, while *Half-Life* (1998) played successfully with alien/conspiracy pop culture themes.

A subset of the now ubiquitous first-person shooter—the tactical shooter—arrived in 1998 with *Delta Force*, which relied more fundamentally on multiplayer gaming and required cooperation and coordination skills.

A subgenre born into great popularity in the previous decade—the platform game—converged in 1996 with adventure structures and 3D graphics in *Tomb Raider*. This action-paced archeological expedition also represented

Figure 4.21 Doom (1993) showed the true potential of shareware and showed the way for **modding**

Mod (modification): A piece of software that modifies the appearance and/or rules of an existing game. Mods are often made and published by enthusiastic players.

a very different merger, between the video game industry and pop culture, as it introduced one of gaming's most famous virtual personalities, adventuress Lara Croft.

In "The first real 3D interactive exploratory adventure," as the game claimed, the player guided Lara, scantily dressed and wearing her two trademark guns, as she hunted through temples and jungle levels to find a lost artifact. While competently designed, the Lara Croft personality (and indeed appearance) was far more important for the popularity of these games. Lara became a symbol of cool, appearing in lifestyle magazines and throughout the media landscape; she was both a favorite icon of the era's girl power movements and an academic object of desire for cultural studies of various persuasions. By all accounts, Lara paved the way for other female game protagonists, such as Jill of the *Resident Evil* series and the female prisoner and protagonist in *Unreal*. The limited creativity of the game and its sequels eventually diminished its cultural relevance but not before it provided the basis for one of the most commercially successful game adaptations for cinema, first 2001's *Lara Croft: Tomb Raider* and then the follow-up *Lara Croft Tomb Raider: The Cradle of Life* two years later.

Controller: The hardware through which the player sends his or her input to the game, typically a "pad" with a number of buttons that can be mapped to perform various functions depending on the game.

Sometimes, of course, one does not need to be creative to make an impact. Violence will quite often do the trick. This was one of the principles behind the one-on-one fighting game *Mortal Kombat* from 1992 (which we will return to later). The game looked like many other action titles but was distinguished by features that horrified many and delighted more than a few: each character had a number of "fatality moves," and with a few dexterous moves on the **controller**, your defeated opponent could be killed in various gruesome ways. The parental and media outrage that followed

Figure 4.22 Mortal Kombat (DOS version) (1992) with its violence content single-handedly cleared the way for rating of video games in United States

would become the driving force behind the US Videogame Rating Act of 1994, which forced the industry into establishing a system for rating games.

Another game that fueled the same fears was *Carmageddon* (1997), which built heavily on standard racing templates, and used mechanics reminiscent of *Death Race* but offered far more lifelike casualties.

Aside from this, subgenres such as racing games thrived during this decade but did not make any noteworthy conceptual changes. And while action games did make use of the increased storage capacity represented by CD-ROMs, this change was quite gradual, and its fruits would not truly be seen until the following decade.

Adventure Games

Continuing their innovative approach to interface design, LucasArts in 1990 published the intriguing *Loom*, in which puzzles were solved by the use of magic created by music (notes were selected with the mouse to construct brief musical snippets with various effects). That same year they released an adventure game classic, *The Secret of Monkey Island*. The game, a pirate parody stuffed with pop culture references, obviously needed sword fighting. So what could one do if one doesn't want actual action sequences? LucasArts introduced us to "insult sword fights," where the player dueled using a series of proposed insults that had to outclass her opponent's taunts.

A big splash was made by the 1993 arrival of *The 7th Guest*, a haunted house story that was one of the first games to utilize the storage capacity of the CD-ROM medium. The game in no way challenged the boundaries of the adventure genre, but it was technically ambitious as its graphics were digitized film clips populated by real actors. This was impressive to many but bought at the price of limited flexibility in terms of player actions. The game also began a tendency toward marketing games by their size, notably followed by Sierra's *Phantasmagoria* (1995), which also starred real-life actors and spanned seven CDs.

The genre's technical evolution is also embodied in Sierra's *Gabriel Knight* series, featuring the decade-long investigations into the occult of "shadow hunter" Gabriel Knight. In the first game, *Gabriel Knight: Sins of the Fathers*, from 1993, all graphics were 2D and hand drawn in the style of *King's Quest* from a decade earlier. The sequel, 1995's *The Beast Within: A Gabriel Knight Mystery*, leaped forward to use digitized film on background photos, and the last game—*Gabriel Knight 3: Blood of the Sacred, Blood of the Damned*, from 1999—mixed several types of graphics but relied mostly on the 3D polygon mode. These changes are indicative of adventure game design in the 1990s. As designers began to utilize the increased capacities of CD-ROMs, and as possibilities for three-dimensional graphics grew, the look of adventure games became far more complex, and mesmerizing. The genre's most famous development was the digitized "interactive movie" experiences of the middle of the decade; games like *Ripper* (1996), *Phantasmagoria*, and the second *Gabriel Knight* installment flirted heavily with Hollywood, often using popular screen actors as the basis of the game's characters, and designing the game using classical cinema conventions.

Before all of this, however, *Myst* happened. Released in 1993, *Myst*'s strong narrative and atmospheric world made it one of the most famous and best-selling home computer games ever. Its appeal to the literary-minded is obvious: in addition to the thematic focus on books and reading, the ability to wander through this world offered an altogether meditative experience. The game was taken seriously by the media, and widely reviewed in the literature sections of newspapers and elsewhere.

Myst, like the decade's other adventure games, did have one large problem. It was decidedly single-player, and since it was based on tightly woven narratives that didn't allow for much (if any) unexpected interference, it couldn't take advantage of the explosion of network technology in the second half of the decade. Though plenty of successful adventure titles were released during the 1990s—*Alone in the Dark* (1992), *Day of the Tentacle* (1993), and *Under a Killing Moon* (1994) are a few of the others—the genre in its classical form was struggling for air.

Role-playing games, on the other hand, let nothing stand in their way. SSI kicked off the decade with a series of games based directly on *Advanced Dungeons & Dragons*[23] rules and game worlds. While some, such as *Champions of Krynn* (1990), were classic *Ultima*-style games (using the isometric perspective), others, such as *Eye of the Beholder* (1990), in which the player traversed dungeons fighting monsters in real time, employed the first-person perspective. Other, older series were continued alongside stand-alone games; most of these, like *Darklands* (1992), were based on standard RPG conventions.

A few other adventure games deserve individual note. Complexity and creativity were beautifully merged in the post-apocalyptic *Fallout* from 1997, and in 1999's philosophical amnesia thriller *Planescape: Torment*. As was the norm throughout the decade, these games used the isometric perspective, probably because it affords a clear sense of space in combat situations while keeping the player close to the protagonists. While not structurally innovative, *Baldur's Gate* from 1998 set many new adventure standards because of its impressive size and the extraordinary freedom of choice within the game, as the player decided whether and how to complete quests and engage with the world's many subplots.

Many continued to appreciate the virtues of this game type, even if it did not truly adapt well to multiplayer play.

Strategy Games

At the start of the 1990s real-time-strategy games had just blinked into existence. With *Dune II: The Building of a Dynasty* (1992) this subgenre would find a form so powerful that today's games are merely more complex variations. Later games include *WarCraft: Orcs and Humans* (1994), *Command & Conquer* (1995), *Age of Empires* (1997), and *StarCraft* (1998). These

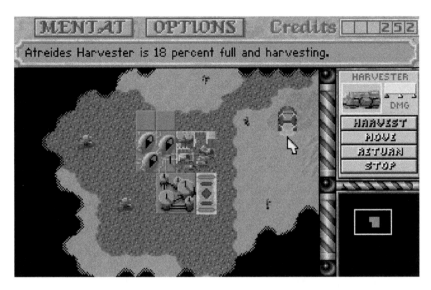

Figure 4.23 Dune II (1992) started the reign of the real-time strategy games that became wildly popular in the 1990s

games differ in their speed and complexity but typically focus on eradicating the enemy while building up an economy based on one or more resources (spice in *Dune II*, for example, and food, wood, stone, and gold in *Age of Empires*).

And unlike their adventure cousins, real-time strategy games adapted smoothly to the new possibilities of network technology, becoming hugely popular for online or LAN play. In LAN play, you typically sit together in the same location, and are connected through the local area network (LAN) as opposed to online play, where you connect through the Internet. In theory, a LAN can extend throughout a large area (e.g. a campus), but often it is related to playing at home, at a net café, or LAN party. At a LAN party, hundreds of gamers gather to play together—often for up to several days. As the complexity of these networked worlds has grown, various features have been introduced to help players keep track of their nations. But in an interesting choice, real-time-strategy (unlike almost all other games) remained a 2D pastime; only in the following decade would they experiment with polygons. The basic gameplay of most of this subgenre, however, remains much like that of *Dune II*.

Turn-based strategy games, however, did anything but roll over and die. *Warlords*, for example, was a popular 1990 game that allowed up to eight people to compete on the same computer. It was quickly overshadowed the following year by Sid Meier's *Civilization*, which was an international smash hit. The player chose from among a series of historical civilizations to lead toward glory. The game's fame arose not because of its features but from the way it combines familiar gaming elements in highly entertaining ways, creating a wide range of playing styles and strategies.

Figure 4.24 Sid Meier's *Civilization* (1991) marked the birth of the strongest franchise among turn-based strategy games

Adding various elements and a new theme to the subgenre, 1993's *Master of Orion* dropped the player into a galactic battlefield, where he had to command a race for domination of the universe. From the same publisher, MicroProse, came *UFO: Enemy Unknown* (1994), in which the player desperately defended Earth from alien invasion. The game offered two distinct modes: on the "Geoscape" level, the player managed and deployed assets, while on the "Battlescape" level the player fought the aliens in turn-based combat with an isometric perspective.

Process-Oriented Games

Though the standard adventure games like *Myst* didn't take advantage of the newly wired gaming world, other entries—which existed between the adventure and process-oriented genres—did adapt to the demand for multiplayer experiences. Certainly, *Ultima Online* from 1997—the first mainstream large-scale, persistent[24] online game world—did look much like its single-player brethren. The game built on the foundation of 1985's *Habitat* but also on the semi-successful *Meridian 59* from 1996, which (not unjustifiably) had introduced itself as "The First-Ever Internet-Based 3D MUD."

Ultima Online, like the MUDs, invited players to create characters and explore a universe of adventure housed in servers around the globe. As opposed to most MUD creators, however, Origin—the developer of *Ultima Online*—had a serious business plan. Players would buy the game box, including the client software, and also pay a $10 monthly subscription fee to play. The game, not quite as pretty as its offline contemporaries, used the isometric perspective and a highly complex character and skill system.

Ultima Online, much to the surprise of most observers, had 100,000 paying subscribers within the first year. Ten dollars multiplied 100,000 times is, of course, a substantial sum, and other developers followed suit. Problems quickly arose, however. Origin quickly learned the difference between friendly, bug-tolerant MUD users and paying customers, as a group of disgruntled players filed a lawsuit against the distributor for negligence, breach of contract, and intentional misrepresentation. The case was settled out of court but offered the first look at the brave new world—and the many accompanying problems—faced by the makers of such technologically innovative games.

THE 2OOOS

At the turn of the millennium things were relatively stable. By and large, games were produced by organized developers who depended heavily on publishers who in turn looked favorably upon tried-and-tested formats.

On the PC, multiplayer shooters thrived, and for those who enjoy gunning down their friends with sophisticated weaponry (maybe even in space), this was certainly the time. *Unreal Tournament* and *Quake III: Arena*, published in 1999, offered all of this and more (and for console owners, *Medal of Honor* offered more story-driven shooter thrills on the PlayStation 1).

Following hot on the heels of *Ultima Online*'s success, two similar-themed MMOGs had opened in 1999. *EverQuest* and *Asheron's Call*, both 3D and somewhat less complex than *Ultima*, gave further indication that MMOGs were a new development to be reckoned with.

Meanwhile, production costs were soaring. Sony's PlayStation 2 launched in March 2000 and was followed by Microsoft's Xbox and Nintendo's Game-Cube the following year. Rapidly increasing hardware capability created the possibility of ever-more technically ambitious games, and when the Play-Station 3, the Xbox 360, and Nintendo's Wii were announced mid-decade there was widespread worry that Hollywood-scale budgets would stifle creativity and lead to a numbing cascade of sequels and semi-identical formats.[25]

Worried game designers for a while looked hopefully to the notion of **user-generated content**. Will Wright, perhaps the most widely respected game designer alive, fed the dream as he announced (at a packed keynote at the Game Developers Conference in 2005) how the upcoming *Spore* would cleverly let player-created creatures enter a pool of content that would then populate other players' games. An intriguing alternative to the classic single-player/multiplayer dichotomy.

User-generated content: The idea that you can empower players to seamlessly generate new content to a game continuously to keep the game fresh.

While *Spore* (eventually released in 2008) was quite successful, hopes for a user-generated future were largely unmet. The trend never affected the mainstream significantly, perhaps because the complexities involved in fact tend to overshadow any gains from outsourced content production.

Rather, the revolution came in three other shapes. One was the massive change in distribution infrastructure arising from increased Internet bandwidth and connectivity, heralded of course by the rise of MMOGs at the end of the previous decade. That games had to come in cardboard boxes and provide many weeks' worth of entertainment suddenly seemed less obvious, as creative developers could (in some circumstances) bypass publishers entirely or contribute to much more versatile collections of downloadable games.

Casual games: Games with a modest learning curve and that require little time investment in order to be enjoyed, such as a brief online card game.

Another significant change was the sudden rise of **casual games**. Browser-based tile-matching game *Bejeweled* had entranced web users from as early as 2001, but the trend only became glaringly obvious with Nintendo's surprise move in November 2006, known as the Wii. While Sony and Microsoft were locked in a war of high-flying technical specifications, the Wii was technologically underwhelming in almost every sense. With virtually the same technical specification as its predecessor the GameCube, the Wii seemed only to bring its motion sensor technology to the table. But Nintendo also managed to appeal to a nonhardcore audience and suddenly it seemed (for a while at least) as if the technologically superior rivals were the dinosaurs.

All three consoles performed quite strongly, with the initially quite expensive PS3 (launched one year after the Xbox 360) selling the fewest total units worldwide. However, eliminating the head start of the Xbox 360 from the equation, the two consoles were almost equally popular. In 2013, the PS3 had sold more than 80 million units,[26] while Xbox 360 surpassed this in 2014, with 84 million sold.[27] Finally, Nintendo topped this one year later, reporting 104 million Wiis sold as of early 2015.[28] As discussed in Chapter 2, in the last console generation PlayStation 4 came off to the best start, with Wii U and Xbox One in close competition for second place.

The last radical change of the 2000s was mobile. From the early days of the decade, mobile gaming had been the subject of hopeful aspiration. Global mobile phone penetration was increasing rapidly and tiny computers in people's pockets promised whole new markets. For years, however, the reality was quite a mess. With widely varying specifications, very few standards, and inelegant modes of software distribution, developers had to release their games in several hundred versions (at least in principle) to cover the market. And often consumers were neither exposed to new games nor knew how to install them. For years, console-like devices like PlayStation Portable (PSP) and Nintendo DS (and later 3DS) brought some stability to the mobile games space but were shuttered by an innovation from Steve Jobs of Apple.

An epically successful alternative appeared almost overnight in 2007, in the shape of Apple's iPhone. With advanced audiovisual capabilities, diverse interface options (due to the touch-sensitive screen), and built-in distribution of new apps (the "App Store" was launched in mid-2008), the iPhone rapidly became a hotbed for mobile game development. A clear alternative to the existing publishing system, the boost to mobile game design also presented something of an outlet for those despairing of big-budget conservatism.

Alongside these major changes, and in hindsight, more gradual developments are also visible.

With production teams growing ever larger, the need for professionalism and the ability to transfer skills between projects became crucial to the game industry. Thus, designers began—on an unprecedented scale—to share their hard-earned experience and merge their vocabularies.

The growing breadth and depth of gaming knowledge coincided with the steady growth of university programs on game design. The start of the twenty-first century also marked the explosive birth of video games as an academic object of study. For some time considered unworthy of critical analysis, video games were now working their way into academia with journals like *Game Studies* and *Games and Culture*, and in the diverse scholarship presented at conferences like the biannual conference of the Digital Games Research Association (DiGRA).

At a broad level, the business of video games was booming. Global sales tripled between 2000 and 2009, with North American sales making up about half of the global total of around $40 billion.[29] Consoles were the center of attention but PC gaming remained relevant. While only 16.6 percent of games were sold for the PC in the United States in 2005 (down 27 percent from 2001), the PC remained popular for genres like MMOGs and real-time strategy games. Also, piracy may explain the decreasing commercial importance of the PC, as it is much easier to copy and distribute PC games than console games. Access to pirated games may mean, in fact, that the PC as a platform is more popular than game sales would imply.

Action Games

The offspring of *Doom* lived on. First-person shooters remained popular throughout the decade. Early on, PC screens formed the battlefield of a noticeable number of team-based tactical shooters. *Delta Force* (1998) was still popular and was joined by *Return to Castle Wolfenstein* in 2001 and *Battlefield 1942* in 2002. The popularity of these games pales, however, in comparison with that of the long-lived shooter phenomenon known as *Counter-Strike* (1999), in which a terrorist team would fight anti-terrorists. Originally a humble modification of *Half-Life*, the game came to epitomize team-based shooters throughout the decade and was the game most commonly used for large-scale competitive play.

Shooters were not as dominant on consoles. Until, that is, Microsoft decided to accompany the launch of their first console, the Xbox, in 2001 with that of *Halo: Combat Evolved* (followed by *Halo 2* in 2004). *Halo* was a story-driven first-person shooter in a science fiction setting, in which two players could cooperate in slaying the alien hordes. The game was almost universally praised, was sold alongside every other Xbox, inspired comic books and fan fiction, and was most clearly a well-chosen exclusive console launch title. Since one obvious disadvantage of the Xbox was its release without an existing game library (in contrast to the PlayStation 2, which could run existing PlayStation games), the success of *Halo* in all probability did much to ensure the console's acceptance.

Figure 4.25 Halo (PC version) (2001) brought first-person shooters to the consoles and ensured Xbox a good launch

With 2003's *Max Payne II: The Fall of Max Payne*, shooters began exploring their interactive environments in earnest. With increasingly advanced engines, objects in most game worlds—from barrels to tables—would now be programmed to interact with other objects (or characters) in realistic, often unpredictable, ways. Whereas *Max Payne II* may have pioneered the feel of a "living" world, this vibrancy felt more integrated with the gameplay in releases like *Far Cry* (2004) and *Half-Life 2* (2004).

The continued success of consoles, more often than not remaining offline till later in the decade, had the consequence of encouraging single-player formats. One sign of this constraint was the continued growth of "survival horror" games, the most famous being the *Silent Hill* series (whose first game was released in 1999) and the *Resident Evil* series (launched in 1996). These games, which pit a single player against a creepy, often zombie-ridden, environment, need only relatively simple controls. Thus, while powerful hardware allowed players to enter immersive, open worlds of free exploration, there was a demonstrable trend toward more controlled, narrative experiences. The *Resident Evil* games, in their linearity, underline this, as does the consistently best-selling *Call of Duty* series (which from 2003 offered World War II missions, and later on more modern settings) and, with the next generation of consoles, the tightly scripted Indiana Jones-esque antics of the *Uncharted* series.

Apart from *Halo*, other games (often of the action persuasion) have appeared exclusively on one platform, and indeed such limited distribution of attractive titles has done much to decide the fate of consoles. Next to *Halo*'s cosmic drama was the driving game *Project Gotham Racing* (2001), also on the Xbox, and around the same time Nintendo's GameCube was graced by the exclusive presences of *Metroid Prime* (2002) and *The Legend of Zelda* series (originally begun on the NES in 1986). Nintendo also offered a bold alternative to the decade's barrage of violence with the 2001 release of *Super Monkey Ball* for the GameCube. Hardly a game that could be accused of drawing on the easy cliché, *Super Monkey Ball* let four players guide a monkey inside a ball through colorful obstacles. The game highlighted the difference between Nintendo's and Microsoft's approaches, as the former stressed casual, lighthearted play and the latter tended toward hardcore game formats. *Super Monkey Ball* also embodied the growing popularity of nonrealistic, (mostly) nonviolent games, as suitable for group play at a party as for the solitary gamer.

But, with the exception of *Halo*, these games do not compare with Sony's coup in acquiring *Grand Theft Auto III* (2001), and its offspring *Grand Theft Auto: Vice City* (2002), and all the way up through *Grand Theft Auto V* (2003). *Vice City*, in particular, which started humbly as an expansion pack,[30] has reached legendary status on two very different fronts. The game's questionable moral code has made it a favorite target of those who protest against media violence, and the original version has been banned in several countries. The protagonist is a gangster who undertakes various shady assignments and acquires funds in rather unethical ways (the most infamous of which is having sex with a prostitute and robbing her afterwards). Had this been the game's only claim to fame, however, it would have been little different from controversial titles like *Death Race* and *Mortal Kombat*. But to many, *Vice City* is also an astounding piece of game design. It reaches new levels of openness, allowing the player unprecedented use of the objects in the game world, and also displays a coolness of style alien to many games, as it parodied (or paid homage to, depending on your interpretation) cheesy police fiction of the 1980s. Thus, the game to cause the loudest outcry in recent time also became America's best-selling console game of 2002,[31] with two characteristics the game has maintained over the years—best-selling and highly controversial.[32] Indeed, *Grand Theft Auto V*, the series' latest installment, continues to spark huge controversy, and was pulled from retail in Target Australia after it faced a petition of 45,000 online signatures demanding the game to be pulled from the shelves for its depiction of violence against women.[33]

Of course, both the *Halo* and the *Grand Theft Auto* series, despite their elegance and many innovative elements, adhere to tradition in the sense that they are hugely expensive productions of massive scope, sold at premium prices in cardboard boxes. MMOGs and browser-based games had shown that alternatives existed, and the playful multiplayer fun of *Super Monkey Ball* as well as the party-friendly motor challenge of *Dance Dance Revolution* (a game in which players would take turns reproducing dance steps on a touch-sensitive floor mat, released in the United States for consoles in 1999) had driven home the fact that nonhardcore concepts could gain traction. Yet few were prepared for the sudden popularity bestowed by 2005 Christmas-season shoppers on the PS2 game *Guitar Hero*. *Guitar Hero* was developed by Harmonix, a small company with a long history of resounding failures and a few minor hits under its belt. The game shipped with a guitar-shaped controller with which the player would try to hit the right notes at the right time. Sufficient accuracy, and the on-screen rock guitarist would faithfully render the memorable riffs of such hard rock classics as Joan Jett and the Blackhearts' "I Love Rock and Roll" and Deep Purple's "Smoke on the Water." Receiving almost unanimous praise from reviewers, the game sold more than 1.5 million copies, was followed by a long list of sequels, and inspired the original developers to work on the *Rock Band* series (begun in 2007).

The thundering success of *Guitar Hero* perhaps made the instant appeal of Nintendo's "casual" Wii console, launched in 2006, less of a shock. Clearly a new, casual market had opened up, populated by people without decades of gaming experience, without the time or patience to learn complicated multibutton control schemes, or who simply wanted quick bursts of less demanding entertainment. The Wii's motion-controlled sports games offered exactly that, as they were somewhat self-explanatory (for tennis, simply move the controller as you would a racket, etc.).

The motion controller was well suited for game elements where you would move, and less precise for pointing at menu options, so Wii game design showed a very strong preference for the action genre.

While music games and the Wii console had unmistakably demonstrated the existence of a market for casual games, these were still fairly massive productions—there was nothing casual about the development side. As mentioned in the section introduction, the launch of the iPhone torpedoed many supposed truths about game development and in many ways undercut the existing system. With the iPhone, many developers, frustrated with what they saw as the heavy-handed conservatism of big publishers, caught a whiff of freedom. And suddenly the dream of making it big by merit and creativity (and from your own garage) no longer seemed a thing of the past.

Well-known brands (in such titles as *Silent Hill: The Escape* and *Metal Gear Solid Touch*, both from 2009) were ported for the iPhone. But much more modest titles, harking back to the "golden" days of arcade gaming, made their way to the top of the App Store charts. In *iCopter* (2009), the player pilots a helicopter through a treacherous cave, the only available control being pressing the screen to increase thrust. Another 2009 release was notable for alerting many to the fact that the ground beneath traditional game development was shaking. Adam Saltsman self-published *Canabalt*, in which a businessman runs and jumps across the rooftops of a city crumbling under what seems to be an alien invasion. Nothing is made of this backstory, however, and the player is allowed only one action: to jump, which must be timed accurately to avoid tumbling to an unpleasant death (to start the game over). The game (actually a port of a browser-based hit) sold 770,000 copies in its first week on the App Store[34] and inspired other hit games like the following year's (much more irreverently silly) *Robot Unicorn Attack*.

While casual formats brought freshness and experimental joy, and reached new audiences, AAA titles did not exactly cease to appear. The shooter *BioShock* (2007) placed the plane-crashed protagonist in a fictional underwater dystopia to grapple with the remains of a failed socio-technical experiment. The original story line, told through atmospheric steampunk aesthetics, attracted wide praise. The *New York Times* even exclaimed that *BioShock* could "hold its head high among the best games ever made."[35]

Other similarly story-intensive blockbusters emphasized that hardcore gaming certainly wasn't going away. *Uncharted: Drake's Fortune* (2007) and its sequels *Uncharted 2: Among Thieves* (2009) and *Uncharted 3: Drake's Deception* (2011) were high-production-value updates of the action adventure format (harking back to the heyday of one Lara Croft). Also in 2007, *Assassin's Creed* wowed console and PC audiences with its detailed animation and convincing recreation of twelfth-century city life, and has since grown into Ubisoft's best-selling franchise.

Adventure Games

In sharp contrast to the obvious importance of the action genre in the decade, classical adventure games struggled for life. The struggles, however, were sometimes quite heroic. Third-person sci-fi story *The Longest Journey*, which featured the female protagonist April Ryan, was lauded as a worthy example of the genre when released in 1999. The same critical praise was accorded *Syberia* two years later, a game that also used colorful pre-rendered backgrounds and limited 3D modeling. This somewhat nostalgic form was not dominant, however, as witnessed by 2003's *Broken Sword: The Sleeping Dragon*, which featured a free-perspective 3D world.

Meanwhile, the great milestones of the adventure game genre were being remade, often by fans, resulting in graphically updated versions of *King's Quest* (remade in 2001), *Maniac Mansion* (2004), *The Secret of Monkey Island* (2009), and others. Such remakes showcase the affection that many fans bestow on the classics but do not seem to have delivered sufficient interest for developers to brush off these traditional formats.

Single-player role-playing games continued to thrive, mostly in the form established in previous decades. A notable exception was 2002's *Neverwinter Nights*, widely praised for offering a player the chance to act as game master, similar to the days of *D&D* play around dining room tables (in truth, *Vampire: The Masquerade—Redemption* introduced the feature first, two years previously). In both games, the game master could control various aspects of the game's scenario as it unfolded. *Neverwinter Nights* was sold with an invitation and accompanying software from the game's ambitious developer for the players to create their own adventures and share them with the user community. *Star Wars: Knights of the Old Republic* did nothing this innovative when released in 2003, but it did introduce true 3D graphics to the RPG subgenre and was almost universally heralded as one of the best of the (many) games based on the Star Wars license.

With *The Elder Scrolls IV: Oblivion* (2006) the subgenre further embraced the open-world experience, as the player could explore the expansive land of Cyrodiil, taking on missions without necessarily paying much attention to the story line. And with *Dragon Age: Origins* (2009) the *D&D*-style, party-based (i.e. multiprotagonist) role-playing game proved still to be an exceptionally popular format.

Strategy Games

One strategy game that stands out from the early days of the decade is Lionhead Studios' *Black & White*, from notable game designer Peter Molyneux. The game caused a stir in 2001 due to its novel design, and initially received rave reviews, although it later made number one of GameSpy.com's list of "25 most overrated games of all time."[36] No one, however, denies that the game was innovative. In a parallel to *Populous* from 1989, the player assumes the role of a deity and is given a nation and a magical creature, which develops its own personality and knowledge based on how it is treated by the player. At the same time, the player's choices affect how his subjects perceive him, leading to various possibilities and constraints.

Real-time strategy games, early in the decade, embraced 3D graphics, as illustrated by the 2002 releases *Warcraft III: Reign of Chaos* and *Age of Mythology*. Also, games such as *Warhammer 40,000: Dawn of War* (2004) upped the tempo significantly, placing less emphasis on the careful construction of one's home base.

Broadly speaking, little else has changed in the genre, although gameplay experiments have been tried such as the "home city" feature of *Age of Empires III* (2005) and the somewhat alternative experience offered by *Warcraft III*, which included role-playing elements and focused on small battalions as opposed to massive armies.

Meanwhile, some turn-based series experimented with multiplayer modes, for example, *Sid Meier's Civilization III: Play the World* from 2002. Another breed of turn-based strategy game catered to those wargamers eager for complex and credible simulations of specific epochs or conflicts. Among the industry's best examples of this level of intricacy are the *Europa Universalis* games (2000–2013) and *Hearts of Iron* from 2002.

Quite a different branch sprang from the real-time strategy tree with the sudden influx of "tower defense" games. In this subgenre, the player carefully places (or equips, or upgrades) stationary towers that must eliminate the enemy before the forces of evil can move from one point of the screen to another. Arguably tower defense games had existed in various forms for decades, but with debuting game designer Paul Preece's Flash browser game *Desktop Tower Defense*, from 2007, the format seemed to solidify.

This subgenre also worked well on small screens, as testified to by the popularity of iPhone games *Fieldrunners* (2008), *TapDefense* (2008), and *Plants vs. Zombies* (2010; originally a PC/Mac game).

Another 2008 iPhone strategy game turned quite a few heads, as it strode to the top of the App Store charts to rake in earnings for its one-man developing team.[37] *iShoot* was essentially an update of the classic MS-DOS shareware title *Scorched Earth* (1991), in which two tanks capable of limited pre-fire movement attempt to eliminate each other with a wide assortment of (quite differently priced) weaponry. Low-powered shells come cheap while serious investment can add spectacularly lethal artillery to the player's arsenal. While *iShoot* built on this solid foundation (which had already inspired the *Worms* series of games from 1995 on), developer Ethan Nicholas also made the game visually thrilling, with colorful background graphics and smooth animations. The story of Nicholas being able to comfortably quit his day job as substantial checks from Apple started appearing in his mailbox was one to inspire many would-be developers.

The feeling, lost for many years, that individuals or small development teams could actually strike it big in the games world had been rekindled. This idea would receive a monumental boost in the final days of the decade with the out-of-the-blue release of the almost unprecedentedly successful *Angry Birds*. The game's impact was felt in the following decade, and we'll discuss it in the next section.

Process-Oriented Games

Mid-decade, developer interest in massively multiplayer online games skyrocketed, and a startling number of titles were known to be in development at the same time.

The most ambitious Western titles in the decade's early years were Funcom's science fiction themed *Anarchy Online* (2001), Vivendi's *Dark Age of Camelot* (2001), and Sony's *Star Wars Galaxies* (2003). Of these, *Anarchy Online* faced tremendous technical trouble at launch, while *Dark Age of Camelot* is often described as something of a miracle in terms of flawless launches of ambitious online games.[38] None of these titles rebelled against the standards established by *EverQuest* and others, although variety in the specific mechanics did lead to somewhat different game experiences.

With *Asheron's Call* (1999), *EverQuest* (1999), and *Dark Age of Camelot* all exploring classical fantasy RPG territory (with levels, quests, corpse retrieval, etc.) many believed that the fantasy niche was sated. But they were proven wrong by Blizzard's extraordinarily successful *World of Warcraft* in 2004. With little that was radically new, *World of Warcraft* geared its dynamics toward more casual play and quickly attracted more than twice as many users as *EverQuest*—until then the most popular Western MMORPG—had ever had.[39] In the years following, *World of Warcraft* came to epitomize the mainstream MMORPG and has remained highly popular since launch (although subscription growth has slowed in the 2010s).

MMO (Massively Multiplayer Online): See **Online role-playing games**.

It is curious that **MMOGs** have been mostly confined to their region of origin. As a general rule, Western games have enjoyed very limited success in Asia, and vice versa. In Asia, the game *Lineage: The Bloodpledge* (1998) drew players in numbers that surpassed even the most successful Western MMOGs to come before *World of Warcraft* (although differences in how subscriptions work make comparisons difficult). The graphics were two-dimensional, not unlike those of *Ultima Online*, and the game focused on battle. Other Asian MMORPG successes include Gravity Corporation's *Ragnarok Online*, a graphically stylized 2002 release, *Final Fantasy XI* from 2003, and *Lineage*'s successor *Lineage II: The Chaotic Chronicle* from 2004. The pattern of geographical isolation was challenged successfully by *World of Warcraft* and similarly fantasy-themed *Aion* (released in Korea in 2008 and in other regions the year after).

It is clear that the MMORPG genre quickly solidified around conventions harking back to the days of MUDs and thus to classical RPGs (fantasy settings, level progression, skill trees, etc.).

The website MMOData.net, which collected statistics on MMOGs subscriptions, estimated the total number of MMOGs subscriptions to have peaked at a little above 22 million in 2011 (up from a select few in the mid-1990s). At the end of 2013 it had declined to 18 million subscribers.[40]

Microtransaction: A payment exchanged for virtual/in-game services, often used in otherwise free-to-play games (and a staple in freemium titles).

More recently, revenue for MMOs has been gained less in subscriber fees and more via in-game **microtransactions**—that is, players spending real money on virtual goods or extra services. Table 4.1 shows the highest-revenue MMOGs games in terms of in-game spending, as of 2014. It is telling that Asian titles (especially from Korea) are especially well positioned, taking almost half the chart.

Apart from MMOGs, noncompetitive vehicle simulators remained an important niche in the process-oriented genre in the early part of the decade. Microsoft continued to publish reality-faithful simulators, like the 2001 *Microsoft Train Simulator*. Here, the player controlled various train types and was able to operate everything from brakes and horns to windshield

Table 4.1 Top subscription-based MMO titles by revenue (2014) (YTD)[41]

		Revenue ($ million, YTD)	Worldwide market share
1	*League of Legends*	946	11.9
2	*CrossFire*	897	11.2
3	*Dungeon Fighter Online*	891	11.2
4	*World of Warcraft*	728	9.1
5	*World of Tanks*	369	4.6
6	*MapleStory*	240	3
7	*Lineage*	178	2.2
8	*Counter-Strike Online*	148	1.9
9	*DOTA 2*	136	1.7
10	*Hearthstone: Heroes of Warcraft*	114	1.4

wipers. To ensure realistic representation, Microsoft teamed up with actual railroad operators, with the sole aim of mimicking the experience of actually running a train. But the fact that Microsoft has offered no official update to its long-running *Flight Simulator* franchise since 2006 speaks of a sub-genre about to sunset. Though sporadic efforts are made (such as *Euro Truck Simulator* from 2008), the market for strongly realistic games seems to have declined even as audiovisuals have in fact reached a level of sophistication resembling reality.

THE 2010S AND BEYOND

By the turn of the decade, three new trends had snuck into many game developer conversations: the "distribution revolution" (retail sale of cardboard boxes seemed less than cutting-edge), the rise of "social games" (games piggybacking on social networks spread virally), and the body as interface (the classic controller, with its legion of buttons, had come under attack).

To start with distribution, the classical model of developers working for publishers who reach retail shelves through distributors now seems something of an anachronism. Apple offers easy distribution of games for its devices through its App Store (taking 30 percent of sales, significantly less than publisher and distributor would take in the old model) with no need—or indeed use—for physical objects. As for consoles, both Microsoft and Sony have well-established "app stores" of their own, offering complete (though often small-scale) games for convenient download. And for PC and Mac gamers, platforms such as Steam offer direct purchase, data storage, downloadable content (DLC), and other community features. Obviously this has led to some reshuffling of power, as publishers and—most evidently—distributors have had to reexamine their business models. Traditional publishers have been busy catching up what they lose in retail in downloadable content.[42] Indeed, EA in their latest quarter posted that DLC made up 41 percent of the revenue.[43]

Meanwhile, independent game development has flourished and the platforms mentioned (along with the web itself) is awash with experimental titles that often challenge conventions and seek to push at the boundaries of the medium itself. An example of an independently developed game that did very well commercially, yet most likely would not have been made in the "old world," was Playdead's award show darling *Limbo* (2010). In this eerie black-and-white platformer, a nameless boy traverses a threatening underworld in search of his sister, notably without common game trappings like energy bars or points. Premiering exclusively on Xbox Live, the game broke even within weeks, selling 300,000 downloads in a month,[44] and competed for awards with the biggest of AAA titles. With the Playdead team being accused of taking many commercially unwise decisions along the way (and yet scoring big), *Limbo* was quickly made a poster child for indie game development. Indie gaming continues to grow with the entry barriers disappearing, and can now be said to be mainstream. As such, the traditional perception of indie developers as a few random guys with a good idea making it big is getting further and further from the truth.[45]

Game developers themselves have also had cause to pause and take stock. In 2009 a new breed of games had appeared, one that used ever-more popular social networks (principally Facebook) as their method of distribution. The first to make an audible splash was Zynga's *Mafia Wars* (2008), in which players built criminal empires by recruiting new players to work for them, by performing various tasks and by eliminating underworld rivals. While the game boasted around 45 million new accounts per month in the summer of 2010, the number of monthly active users was down to 500,000 in the fall of 2014, vividly illustrating the hardships Zynga started to faced soon after their hyped initial public offering (IPO) in 2011.

By that time, however, Zynga had bigger fish to fry, in the form of the genre-defining *FarmVille* (2009), in which players managed farms for points, being able to buy various upgrades via micropayments. In early 2010 *FarmVille* counted almost 30 million active users.[46] To maintain this success, *FarmVille 2* was launched in 2012 (and by 2013 had over 40 million users[47]), and in 2014 also hit the App Store as *FarmVille 2: Country Escape* to much acclaim, keeping it consistently within the top-grossing games on the App Store.

As millions worked their virtual farms, others were dismayed. The *New York Times*, in an August 2010 editorial, felt that "It is a touch dismaying that social gaming is a world where players are festooned with gratuitous awards, sold trinkets for hard cash, and reap rewards for dragging in their friends."[48] And in the game world itself, criticism mounted, with game scholar and commentator Ian Bogost noting that

> We've never before seen this kind of deliberate unconcern for the aesthetics of the experience. . . . They don't really care about the longevity of the form or the experience. That sort of attitude is the sort of thing you usually hear about from oil companies or pharmaceuticals. You don't really hear about it in arts and entertainment.[49]

Ethics aside, social games of the *FarmVille* variety are usually defined (following Jon Radoff) by their asynchronous gameplay (players needn't log on at the same time), by leveraging the players' social network, by having no winning conditions (often there is just constant progression), and by having a virtual currency, often one that can be bought for real-life money.[50]

The vocal disparagement of social games, and indeed the feeling that gold-diggers were unethically exploiting the game format with meritless superficiality, was one that would soon find a new target.

Not long after social games had enraged a certain breed of developers, another, equally infuriating trend appeared on the scene, under the heading of **gamification**. While arguably an old phenomenon, it was game developer Jesse Schell's February 2010 presentation "Design Outside the Box," in which he spoke of a near future in which many mundane actions (such as

Gamification: The act of inserting game mechanics into a product, site, or service to make it more engaging.

brushing one's teeth) had been turned into games, that kicked off the debate in earnest (see Chapter 8).

In parallel with gamification, a change took place that affected mainstream game design itself. On the heels of the shockingly successful Wii and *Guitar Hero*'s nonstandard controllers, both Microsoft and Sony joined the post-controller fray in 2010 with so-called natural user interfaces. With its many arbitrary symbols and hardcore connotations, the standard console controller was seen by some as a relic of a forgettable past. Breaking with this tradition, Microsoft launched its Kinect system under the heading "You are the controller." Kinect, which uses webcam-style technology to detect the player's movements, was an instant success with both consumers and most reviewers.

Selling less aggressively, Sony's Move system combined a webcam (the "eye") with a movement-sensitive controller (reminiscent of the Wii controller). While not employing the player's body itself as the controller, the aim was to make the control scheme seem far more intuitive and less like a memory test (Sony's slightly excessive tagline was, "This changes everything"). The use of augmented reality is still seeing interest but hasn't yet managed to become mainstream. Oculus Rift—quite symptomatic for this era—blew the world away through crowdfunding via Kickstarter in 2012, and was later acquired by Facebook in 2014. Google projects like Google Glass and the more recent Google Cardboard smartphone mount have also helped to encourage this trend hinting at the future background of virtual and augmented reality. However, the other big players in this space have not taken long to launch their counterattacks, most notably Project Morpheus from Sony and Microsoft's HoloLens.

While "natural interfaces" are an interesting development that may in time affect game design more radically, at this point it seems to offer mostly complementary pleasures. Far from all big game launches cater to these new control schemes, and rather than causing a revolution, natural interfaces will likely continue to coexist with the hard-to-kill hardcore AAA format.

As for concrete games, the decade kicked off with a flurry of airborne resentment. In *Angry Birds* (2009), from Finnish developer Rovio Mobile, green pigs have made off with a nest full of bird eggs and the bereaved fowl are not amused. Armed with varying arsenals of differently colored birds, each type with its own characteristics, the player fires the birds one by one in a parabolic arc from a slingshot, with the aim of striking all pigs in sight. The defensive structures of the pigs must often be carefully destabilized, making play increasingly puzzle-like as the game progresses. This curious cocktail became a runaway iOS success, and was ported to a range of other platforms (and a shocking array of merchandise) as the *Angry Birds* fever caught on, with a total of two billion downloads in 2014, and as many monthly active users as Twitter.[51]

What made *Angry Birds* an iconic mobile game? The game's mechanics themselves were not new and it is difficult to explain its success in simple terms. But *Angry Birds* stands out as a highly appealing audiovisual experience, which combines elegant core gameplay with a pleasing design, resulting in a game that is attractive to interact with while also providing continuous intellectual stimulation. It also has a cast of characters residing comfortably in the borderland between cuteness and utter madness.

Other independently produced titles, such as the compelling tile-matching game *Drop7* (2009), the helter-skelter stunt motorcycle escapades of *Trials HD* (2009), and the aforementioned, curiously entertaining low-res construction-plus-zombies combo of *Minecraft* (2011), have also impressed, and from its release in 2012 *Candy Crush Saga* has established dominance in its genre, only outshined by Finnish game company SuperCell, which dominated the charts of the app scene with the launch of *Hay Day* (2012), *Clash of Clans* (2012), and *Boom Beach* (2013), leading some to believe that the AAA era was about to end. But big studios begged to differ, as their blockbusters (while often modeled closely on tried-and-true prequels) impressed all but the most jaded of indie fans. Thus, games like *Call of Duty: Advanced Warfare* (2014), *Civilization: Beyond Earth* (2014), *Assassin's Creed Unity* (2014), and *Grand Theft Auto 5* (2013) launched to general applause.

Pokemon Go in 2016 showed the potential of the new mixed realities by becoming a plague that caused car accidents as people ventured into streets to catch the latest virtual creature. *Pokemon Go* (2016) arguably became the first mainstream successful augmented reality game, and estimates set its total revenue at almost \$2 billion.[52]

Just one year later, *Fortnite* (2017) proved that the classic first-person shooter genre was not dead and could be re-invented. Borrowing heavily from

Figure 4.26 Angry Birds (2009), with its simple gameplay, appealing visuals, and strong character design, became a synonym for the booming App Store

PlayerUnknown's Battlegrounds (2017) it popularized the so-called battle royal genre, a last-man-standing game. Here you constantly fight for survival while scavenging, exploring, building, and fighting your way to the top.

PERSPECTIVES

Where are video games going? The history of the medium teaches us one unmistakable lesson: even the intelligentsia of the games world habitually see their predictions shot to pieces. No, games have not (by and large) become gradually more like movies; no, multiplayer games have not swept single-player games aside; no, natural interfaces have not killed the controller; no, AAA games have not withered and died in the face of indie creativity; no, games have not shed all narrative ambitions to embrace their "core" gameness.

A telling example of this failure to predict even the near future was game design guru Will Wright's 2002 MMOGs *The Sims Online*, a game almost unanimously thought to be surefire gold when unleashed upon the gaming public. Instead a modest subscriber base was disappointed from the very beginning, reviewers were unimpressed with core mechanics and graphics, and the game never found any substantial following (it was ultimately shut down in 2008). Indeed, the entire MMOGs format—at one point thought to represent an instant goldmine opportunity—plateaued some years back in terms of player interest, losing ground fast to new free-to-play alternatives.

All of this just to say: predictions in the game world are likely to be the butt of ridicule a few years down the road. Yet we'll risk pointing to a handful of likely developments.

First, hassle-free distribution (via app stores, etc.) and the demands of radically different screen sizes will further boost experimentation. Developers, free to follow nonconventional ideas, will play with game design norms and will thus playfully illustrate the "language" of game design, a process that will enable many to see game design as an art form. We can also see interfaces as a constant arena for experimentation. For examples of such experimentation, look online for smaller, creative games like *The I of It* (2011), *Digital: A Love Story* (2010), *Don't Starve* (2013), and *A Story About My Uncle* (2014), or dig into the tons of short-form on Twine, such as Zoe Quinn's *Depression Quest* (2013).

Second, while "gamification" in various forms may continue to spark controversy, the analytic and theoretical work of game designers will further serve to identify game elements that can be applied regardless of platform. Games, and games elements, will slide naturally into contexts far removed from dedicated console gaming—contexts such as advertising, education, and interaction design in the broadest sense.

Third, the game business will demand its share of cultural attention. As the medium (and the "language" of game design) matures further, games will increasingly demand to be treated on par with older media. This will intensify debates over legal definitions (e.g. the extent to which games are protected speech) and over government funding, particularly in regions with a strong tradition of state funding of the arts. "Why are authors and filmmakers so much more worthy of support?" some game developers will ask, and politicians will be under growing pressure to provide coherent answers.

The ability to maneuver in this changing world of games, to evaluate new trends, and ultimately to design worthwhile and innovative games is contingent on understanding what has gone before, how we got to where we are, and how to avoid oft-repeated mistakes. In a nutshell: it's an ability which depends on understanding the history of video games.

DISCUSSION QUESTIONS

- Many game types have analog predecessors, but massively multiplayer games arguably bear only faint resemblance to previous media forms. From what other areas or fields may one borrow inspiration for the design of MMORPGs? Discuss examples of MMORPGs that seem to draw inspiration from other media.

- From a publisher's perspective, what are the pros and cons of having one's game labeled "controversial," "violent," or even "morally depraved"?

- In the future, which games will be the most popular—games incorporating more sophisticated or less sophisticated storytelling than is the norm today? Why?

- To what extent does the development of the games medium mirror the history of the development of other forms of expression?

RECOMMENDED GAMES

A trip down memory lane to experience a few of the defining games throughout the last 50 years—this may require a bit of fiddling with a DOS emulator, but it is well worth the time investment, as you will find numerous gems in the treasury.

DOSBox is a tool that allows you to emulate a lot of old games. To get started, install DOSBox. Make sure you find the right operating system (usually Mac OS X or Windows). You can also choose a front end to make it easier to use DOSBox. We recommend Boxer for Mac OS X and D-Fend-Reloaded for Windows, which are currently the most used.

Be aware that currently the legal status of many old games is in limbo. So even if you can find them on numerous abandonware sites this does not make the titles legal to share and download. In recent years the site www.gog.com has become a great way to get your hands on these old classics, albeit a lot of especially older DOS games are not offered.

CLASSICS TO PLAY BEFORE YOU DIE

Space War—one of the first games to successfully deploy multiplayer back in the early 1960s.

Space Invaders—probably the first really successful arcade game to eat your hard-earned coins.

Pac-Man—The game that changed cheese forever, and the first truly successful game brand.

Hunt the Wumpus—The first adventure game, which shows indeed how far we have come in terms of graphics, interface, and gameplay.

Hamurabi—one of the first strategy games, and one that is truly difficult to play, with a text-based input and scarce explanation of what the game was.

Pole Position—The first game to herald the future success of racing games. With its revolutionary graphics it became a big hit, inspiring numerous successors.

Double Dragon—One of the first side-scrolling arcade fighting games to rise to prominence.

Defender of the Crown—One of the first strategy games to open the genre to the masses, with its fantastic graphics and casual gameplay.

King's Quest—A defining game in the adventure game genre. Although it was not the most innovative within the genre, it was one of the first to really get it right.

The Secret of Monkey Island—Probably the funniest game in game history, which changed the perception of what an adventure game could be.

World of Warcraft—The massively multiplayer game that for many years set the standard for the genre.

FURTHER READINGS

Ashcraft, B. (2016, December 27). The 31 most important Japanese games ever made. *Kotaku*.

(Estimated reading time: 12 minutes)

Consolazio. D. (2018, October 8). The history of esports. *Hotspawn*.

(Estimated reading time: 8 minutes)

Virtual Reality Society. History of virtual reality.

(Estimated reading time: 9 minutes)

NOTES

1. See Leeson, 2005.
2. Hasbro, 2006.
3. An EDSAC emulator for various operating systems is available at www.dcs.warwick.ac.uk/~edsac/.
4. For more information, see Hunter, 2000.
5. Graetz, 1981.
6. Java emulation available at http://spacewar.oversigma.com/.
7. Burnham, 2003.
8. Fine, 2002.
9. Sometimes referred to as *Advent* or *Colossal Cave*.
10. For the history of Infocom, see Briceno et al., 2000.
11. DeMaria and Wilson, 2002.
12. Hunter, 2000.
13. Novak, 2007.
14. Morrison, 2005.
15. DeMaria and Wilson, 2002.
16. Lebling, 1980.
17. Rothstein, 1983.
18. Lucasfilm Games, 1990.
19. The one notable exception is Sierra's 1982 publication of the RPG *Ultima II: Revenge of the Enchantress*.
20. Microsoft Game Studios, 1982.
21. Morningstar and Farmer, 2003.
22. King and Borland, 2003.
23. A version of *Dungeons & Dragons* published in parallel and featuring more player options and more sophisticated rules.
24. A "persistent" game world is one that lives on when any individual player logs off. Such a world may be either fully persistent (i.e. keep evolving as long as the game exists) or reset with intervals, the latter being a rarity for modern virtual worlds.
25. Many who imagined a mythically pure past were mistaken, however. We need only recall the number of *Pong* clones that flooded the market at the birth of arcade gaming to realize that the industry, in all of its stages, has always tried to ride the wave of success.
26. www.prnewswire.com/news-releases/playstation3-sales-reach-80-million-units-worldwide-230771611.html.
27. www.gamespot.com/articles/e3-2014-399-xbox-one-out-now-xbox-360-sales-rise-to-84-million/1100–6420231/.
28. www.nintendo.co.jp/ir/library/historical_data/pdf/consolidated_sales_e1412.pdf.
29. Video Game Sales Wiki, undated.
30. Expansion packs are quite widespread in the game industry, and are usually small sequels to popular games that sell at lower prices than the original game. Often expansion packs require the original game but provide more characters, levels, or scenarios, which extend the lifespan of the original games.
31. IDSA, 2003.
32. www.gameinformer.com/b/news/archive/2015/03/07/learn-about-grand-theft-auto-39-s-controversial-history.aspx.
33. www.mirror.co.uk/lifestyle/staying-in/video-games/gta-5-torture-row-teachers-2278689 and https://news.yahoo.com/gta-5-violence-against-women-132100049.html.
34. Boyer, 2009.
35. Schiesel, 2007c.
36. GameSpy.com, 2003.
37. Chen, 2009.
38. Bartle, 2003.
39. Woodcock, 2006.
40. MMOData.net. The website is now shut down but archives of the site and its data are available at MMOData.net.dk.
41. http://venturebeat.com/2014/10/23/the-10-highest-grossing-online-pc-games-in-2014-hearthstone-dota-2-cant-compete-with-league-of-legends/.
42. www.pcgamer.com/electronic-arts-hopes-to-hit-1-billion-in-dlc-revenues-this-year/.
43. www.forbes.com/sites/greatspeculations/2014/01/30/electronic-arts-misses-revenue-guidance-but-expands-margins-through-digital-growth/.
44. Sheffield, 2010.

45. www.gameacademy.com/the-indie-revolution/.
46. Cashmore, 2010.
47. http://techcrunch.com/2013/01/04/zynga-farmville-2/.
48. *New York Times*, 2010.
49. Jamison, 2010.
50. Radoff, 2011.
51. www.vg247.com/2014/01/22/angry-birds-downloaded-2-billion-times-has-as-many-maus-as-twitter/.
52. Valentine, 2018.

5 Video Game Aesthetics

Rules
Geography and Representation
Number of Players
Games Without Boundaries

Heavy Rain (2010) won the hearts of critics and a number of awards for its artistic and dramatic appeal

We have already tried to reach an understanding of what games are—to give a sense of the formal qualities that we can use to decide what constitutes a game. In this chapter, we will look more closely at how to understand major game features like interactivity, rules, and **gamespace**.

By "aesthetics" we are referring to all aspects of video games that are experienced by the player, whether directly (such as audio and graphics) or indirectly (such as rules). Thus, importantly, aesthetics as used here is not limited to how a game looks or sounds but is more broadly related to how it plays, as a function of the various design choices of the developers. Or to put it differently, Chapter 3 was about describing games as a phenomenon in contrast to other phenomena, whereas this chapter is about describing the elements that actually make up games.

Gamespace: The entire space (or world, or universe) presented by a game.

- *Rules*: These defined limitations determine what you (and other characters in the game) can and cannot do, and which actions or events increase or decrease the score. In chess, for example, there is a rule that one cannot place one's own king in a position of check. In the snowboarding game *SSX 3*, there is a rule that a certain aerial maneuver gives the player a particular number of points.

- *Geography and representation*: Like the cardboard playing surface of a traditional board game, a video game's geography "physically" blocks certain actions (generally, you cannot pass through walls), while allowing others (you may be able to jump from one platform to another). The world of a video game is typically represented to the player by means of graphics and sound. Within the realm of representation there is an enormous variety of design possibilities. For instance, graphics may be two- or three-dimensional, sound may be realistic or cartoonish, and the perspective may be isometric or first-person.
- *Number of players:* In terms of design and development single-player games differ greatly from multiplayer games. In the former, computer-controlled opponents—or the environment itself—must respond entertainingly to the player's actions, while in the latter designers must ensure level playing fields, efficient communication features, and so forth.

On a very abstract level, these three elements could be independent of one another. One set of rules, for example, could be attached to a variety of game representations (we could have a game of *Star Wars* chess, which in fact we do). But, as we shall see, the choices regarding one of these elements tend in practice to shape the others.

The issue of narrative and setting is not mentioned here, since it will be dealt with separately in Chapter 7.

RULES

Recall, if you can, the 1983 blockbuster film *WarGames*. The characters played by Matthew Broderick and Ally Sheedy have come amazingly close to destroying the world—all by playing a video game. As an out-of-control military supercomputer ticks down to an imminent nuclear war, they race to reach the one man who may be able to help them, Dr. Steven Falken. Reluctant to help, Falken instead lectures them on game design. "Did you ever play tic-tac-toe?" he asks Sheedy. She answers yes but adds that she doesn't play it anymore because it is a boring game and always ends in a tie. Falken agrees: "There's no way you can win." As most of us realize at around age six, Falken is right. Unless one player makes a mistake—or is too young to grasp the structure of the game—tic-tac-toe will always end in a draw.

The savvy Broderick realizes the beauty of Falken's simple lesson, and proceeds to save the world by forcing the nuke-enabled runaway computer to play repeated games of tic-tac-toe. The goal is to teach the computer that a nuclear war between the superpowers cannot be won. In the nick of time the computer catches on and proclaims: "Strange game, the only winning move is not to play."[1]

Although deliciously dramatic, the movie's logic is hardly flawless. Strictly speaking, one does not, of course, win tic-tac-toe by not playing it. The perfect analogy would require either a cost or a disadvantage to playing the game in the first place (in the movie's plot, for example, the disadvantage would be analogous to the cost of engaging in a nuclear war). Nor is it obvious why the computer should generalize its newfound understanding of tic-tac-toe to the Cold War as a whole, when it has played hosts of other games where one side actually can win. Nevertheless, the film demonstrates how tic-tac-toe, despite its design "flaw," is a compelling example of the functions of a game's rules.

Let's look at the incredibly simple, mundane rules of this paradigmatic nonelectronic game. In Katie Salen and Eric Zimmerman's formulation,[2] they are:

1. Play occurs on a three-by-three grid of nine empty squares.
2. Two players alternate marking empty squares, the first player marking Xs and the second player marking Os.
3. If one player places three of the same marks in a row, that player wins.
4. If the spaces are all filled and there is no winner, the game ends in a draw.

Most of us would agree that these are indeed the rules of tic-tac-toe. However, these rules alone do not guide the way we play the game. Stephen Sniderman reminds us, for example, that in standard tic-tac-toe rules, as stated above, "nothing has been said about time. Is there a time limit between moves? Normally, we both 'understand' that there is, and we both 'know' that our moves should be made within a 'reasonable' time, say 20 seconds."[3] If you realize that you have made a mistake and will lose on the other player's next turn, nothing in the four basic rules would seem to prevent you from actually never making your move, thus halting the game forever. But as Sniderman puts it:

> Anybody who seriously resorted to such a tactic would be considered childish or unsportsmanlike or socially undesirable and would probably not be asked to play in the future. This behavior seems to violate some fundamental but rarely stated principle of the game without any of us ever having to discuss it.[4]

The implication, as Salen and Zimmerman underline, is that it is not possible to state all the rules that apply to most nonelectronic games. Video games, however, are somewhat different in this regard. A game of *Microsoft Solitaire* on a Windows computer has fewer unstated rules than our paper-and-pencil game of tic-tac-toe, since everything taking place within that game must have been made possible (and legal) by the game code. Nevertheless, you could of course choose to avoid the embarrassment of quitting a hopeless game by cutting the power to the computer.

What, then, is the relationship between a game and its rules?

In a very important sense, a game *is* its rules.[5] Rules, arguably, are the most defining characteristic of games; they are the element shared by everything we usually understand as a game, and are the element that sets games apart from linear media such as novels or movies. (A novel, for example, has its own geography, its own representation—text—and its own narrative and setting.) An important feature of rules is that they are not tied to one particular type of material; in other words, they are transmedial.[6] Thus, the game of chess does not rely on black and white pieces moving about on a physical game board. It is possible, as many die-hard Lucas fans know, to play chess using pieces representing Star Wars characters; it is just as possible to have real geographical features function as a board, and have people function as the pieces, or to have the whole thing taken care of by a computer. Thus, no matter how and where you choose to represent the chess conflict, as long as you follow the rules, you are still playing chess.

If we accept the limited definition that a game is its rules, then all games are transmedial. Of course, this does not mean that the rules of a game can be transferred into anything that someone has classified as a medium. You cannot play chess on or through a movie (although a movie can tell the story of chess, or can depict a specific chess match). The transmedial nature of games simply tells us that although a game cannot be played through any medium, a game is not tied to a specific medium.

Do you agree with the above concept? If not, perhaps you are envisioning a game of chess played using various types of Barbie dolls in a forest divided into grids—such a game would feel extremely different, no doubt, from a classical chess match with its elegant, almost minimalist, setup. In other words, you might feel that the context of the game is crucial to determining the experience of a game. You would be absolutely right, of course. But here we need to distinguish between the *formal* and the *phenomenological* levels of a game. As Salen and Zimmerman put it: "the formal system of a game, the game considered as a set of rules, is not the experience of the game."[7] Context is clearly important to any player, but when analyzing games we must sometimes bracket this acknowledgment in order to discuss how games are alike or different in terms of their more basic aesthetics.

A Definition of Rules

Science fiction author and game critic Orson Scott Card has said:

> Remember, gamewrights, the power and beauty of the art of gamemaking is that you and the player collaborate to create the final story. Every freedom that you can give to the player is an artistic victory. And every needless boundary in your game should feel to you like failure.[8]

Card's declaration will make immediate sense to many gamers and certainly has merit as a piece of game design advice. But if we believe that interactivity is central to the enjoyment of a game, does it follow that enjoyment is closely linked to player freedom? Not necessarily. Stephen Sniderman notes that "to play a game is to pursue that game's object while adhering (more or less) to its constraints."[9] Similarly, Salen and Zimmerman are adamant that one of the essential qualities of rules is that they limit player action.[10]

Many may instinctively think of rules as bad, or constraining, or a burden. We seek to fight against rules, to find ways around them. But we would do better to acknowledge that rules are an essential component of a game. These limits on our freedom as players are actually what give a shape and a drive to the playing of the game; they are what challenge us in the game world, they are what enable us to feel satisfaction when we win. Perhaps what we should hope for is not no rules at all but rules that limit player freedom in entertaining ways.

To be more formal, we can say that *a rule is an imperative governing the interaction of game objects and the possible outcome of this interaction.*

Types of Rules

Despite the brevity of the definition above, it can be difficult in practice to determine which aspects of games belong under the heading of rules. Helpfully, a number of authors have specified different types of rules. Game designer/scholar Gonzalo Frasca, for example, has proposed a dualism of rules: *ludus* rules relate to the conditions by which a player wins, and *paidia* rules refer to game procedures (such as "pawns move one square at a time" in chess).[11] As you've probably guessed, both terms are borrowed from Roger Caillois, who used them in a slightly different sense (see Chapter 3). For a more formal approach, we can turn to Jesper Juul's three levels of rules:[12]

1. *Game state rules*: These rules cover the basic aspects of the game state (i.e. the exact condition at any point in time of all game elements).
2. *Outcome valorization rules*: These rules define which outcomes are considered positive and which outcomes are considered negative.
3. *Information rules*: These rules determine what information the player receives during play about the game state.

As with Frasca, we find a distinction between rules that determine processes, and rules that relate to the outcome of the game. Juul's third category allows us to consider another important aspect of game systems: the amount of information that the player is given about the state of the entire game. To Juul, the player of *Pac-Man* has perfect (or complete)[13] information—he can see the entire screen and cannot be surprised by any new information; a *StarCraft II: Wings of Liberty* player, immersed in a world bursting with unexpected occurrences, is in a quite different position.

However, we must add that while the amount of information given may be clear, its significance may not be. One piece of information may support multiple interpretations of the game state. Imagine, for instance, that a player of *Age of Empires II: The Age of Kings* comes upon a nearly depleted and abandoned goldmine. What does this tell him about the game state? Technically, it tells him only that there is a nearly depleted mine at certain coordinates. But it may also lend credence to one or several additional hypotheses, such as "Player B has mined gold here but was disturbed and is apparently too busy or too rich to mine the remaining gold." Thus, the information that a player actually understands can be quite different from the information that they receive.[14]

A rather different typology is suggested by Katie Salen and Eric Zimmerman. They too have three rule types:

1. *Operational rules*: These are what one would typically describe as the rules of a game. In a combination of Juul's "game state" and "outcome valorization" rules, they govern both a game's processes and its conditions for victory.
2. *Constitutive rules*: These are the underlying formal structures of a game that define its basic dynamics. For instance, some games (were one to disregard their presentational aspects) may be reduced to core logical/mathematical problems.
3. *Implicit rules*: These are all the unwritten rules that we take for granted when playing a game.

These three levels describe well the rules of nondigital games. For video games beyond a certain level of complexity (say, anything more advanced than *Tetris*), this typology is still useful but works less well in practice. The concept of constitutive rules, for example, is not often applicable; it is not easy nor necessarily meaningful to describe *Halo: Reach*—a game of vast complexity—in terms of underlying formal structures.

One is free to employ whichever typology is the most useful. But in writing this book, we have found it most useful to merely distinguish between two types of rules, along the lines of Frasca's proposal. The first type, what we call "interplay rules," determines the relationships and the properties of elements in a game. These correspond to the physical laws of the gamespace. They determine what can be done and, combined with player input, what happens. The second type, "evaluation rules," decide which occurrences are rewarded and which are punished. For instance, in *Super Mario Bros.*, one interplay rule states that Mario will jump to a certain height when a player presses the "A" button on their controller; one evaluation rule is that killing enemies by landing on them gives you points.

Gameplay

The term "gameplay" is often used but rarely defined. As commonly employed, it refers to the game dynamics, or more simply, "how it feels to play a game." Although this feeling is influenced by a game's audio and visual aspects, gameplay is usually considered a consequence of the game's rules rather than its "representation" (which we'll discuss in the following section). Using this basic definition, we can say that the gameplay of chess is deliberative, while the gameplay of *Burnout Crash!* is frantic and easily accessible. In line with this usual use of the term, we will define gameplay as *the game dynamics emerging from the interplay between rules and game geography*.[15] These dynamics may be entertaining, or not, and they may be more or less predictable. Let us look at some examples. In *Super Monkey Ball*, the rules and geography combine to ensure that the game will be hectic and competitive and fast-paced. *Star Craft II: Wings of Liberty*, on the other hand, contains many potentially successful strategies, and, depending on the aggregate choices of the players involved, a game can be quite hectic or far more deliberative and defense-oriented.

In part, this variety in gameplay stems from the different conflicts staged by the two games. In the racing subgame of *Super Monkey Ball*, each player largely plays against the game system (even though it may not feel that way); the actions of the other players are mostly irrelevant, because your main concern is to get the monkey through the level as fast as possible. *Star Craft II*, on the other hand, provides a more chess-like geography for what is essentially a conflict between players.

Game Balance[16]

With very few exceptions, game designers attempt to achieve "balance" in every game. Essentially, this means that winning a game should be a function of player skill plus any element of randomness or luck that the game employs but should be unrelated to the game's initial conditions. In chess, for example, if black began the game with three more knights than white, the game would not be balanced. We should note that balance can exist both within the game itself (called "in-game balance") and between players ("player-player balance"). But sometimes the term also refers to a designer's attempt to balance various strategies and game units (such as soldier types) against each other in interesting ways. In a real-time strategy game, even if both sides had this option (so that the game was technically fair), it shouldn't always be best simply to concentrate on one particular unit type or strategy.

Staying with real-time strategy games, we can see how difficult it can be to achieve balance. Since each player can typically choose among various races or civilizations—each with different strengths and weaknesses—the developers must plan carefully and test meticulously to ensure that all potential interactions are balanced; further, these interactions must remain fair even across the different types of maps available, and regardless of whatever ingenious strategies players bring to the game. Examples of failure in balance are not difficult to find. In 1994's *Warcraft: Orcs and Humans*, for instance, the orc player producing warlock units will almost always win.[17] Similarly, in *Age of Empires II: The Age of Kings*, some civilizations were often considered too strong compared to others, and players often agreed not to choose these overpowerful civilizations (until a game patch fixed the issue).

One classic way of achieving in-game balance is the use of transitive relationships. The principle is well known to anyone familiar with the hand game rock-paper-scissors (Figure 5.1).

Rock-paper-scissors has only three strategies available to the player. But the success or failure of choosing rock, paper, or scissors depends entirely

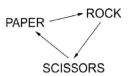

Figure 5.1 Rock-paper-scissors shows the classic principle underlying many strategy games

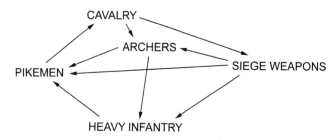

Figure 5.2 Selected unit relationships in *Age of Empires: Age of Kings* (1999). It is fundamentally the same as rock-paper-scissors but vastly more complex

on what the other player chooses; and, just as importantly, no strategy is inherently better than any of the others. For *Age of Empires II*, we can plot a simplified relationship between the game units (the types of soldiers, etc., that a player can create and use), as shown in Figure 5.2.

As we follow the arrows, we can see that the cavalry is very effective against archers and siege weapons but vulnerable to pikemen. Adding to the complexity, each of these characters (or units) has a production cost (it requires a certain amount of wood to build heavy infantry, for example, and a different amount of gold) and a production time (e.g. siege weapons take longer to build than footmen). These factors are further influenced by the specific map being used (on maps with few forests, units requiring wood are effectively more expensive to build), as well as the civilization chosen by the player (each civilization has particular advantages, such as special units). In other words, achieving in-game balance is quite complex.

When considering game balance, the field of economic game theory is helpful. Game theory is a discipline (or perhaps more accurately a set of techniques) that originates in economics, and uses the terminology of games in order to model situations of strategic interaction.[18] Of particular interest here is the concept of the Nash equilibrium (and the related concept of dominant strategies). Simply put, a game has an equilibrium state if playing a particular set of strategies produces a situation where no player can benefit from changing his strategy (assuming that the strategies used by the other player or players also remain constant). Players tend to gravitate toward this equilibrium and, once there, no one will budge (because there is no incentive to do so). In certain real-life situations this is very useful (everybody gravitates toward driving either on the left or on the right side of the road), but it is a problem for game design, because such a game will tend to be played in the same way every time. The related term "dominant strategy" refers to a strategy that is simply the best one to choose, regardless of what the other player or players are expected to do. The existence of such a strategy usually saps the game of the potential for choice, thus making it boring.

Economic game theory, while not originally intended as a tool for video game development, is highly useful for grasping the dynamics of how different rules create different player relationships. Concerned as it is with choice, it helps us (whether we are designers or analysts) understand balance and the related concept of strategy. Thus, the reader interested in these issues is encouraged to seek out (economic) game theory literature, even if it is not directly tailored toward video game analysis.

GEOGRAPHY AND REPRESENTATION

The splendid sunsets of today's massively multiplayer online role-playing games seem only distantly related to the primitive (if groundbreaking) two-color visuals of *Spacewar!* This section provides an account of the various strategies of geography and representation employed by game designers.

Obviously, the way the game world is laid out is related to the way it looks. If you're roaming a three-dimensional city and the way ahead is blocked, you will typically notice something large in front of you (as opposed to just suddenly being stopped by an invisible barrier). But there is also a difference between geography and representation. In the 1982 arcade game *Moon Patrol*, the player patrols a lunar surface for aliens, while futuristic buildings scroll by in the background. These buildings have no direct in-game effect; for instance, they don't block the player's movement or provide cover. They are simply there for the visual effect. Similarly, the "splendid sunsets" referred to above have no direct bearing on the player's possibilities. They mostly add to the atmosphere, provide a sense of realism, and generally make the game world seem alive.

Game students and scholars who focus closely on rules run the risk of reducing audiovisuals to the category of surface phenomena. Graphics, in particular, are sometimes treated as mere window dressing, eye candy providing an enticing way of interacting with the actual game beneath. As we shall see, that view is much too simple, as graphic types have different properties and afford different gameplay styles. Also, a graphical style may ideally be chosen for its ability to support the game mechanics, but in the real world the causal arrow is sometimes reversed, as graphics determine the mechanics. For instance, if a game designer starts out with a preference for a certain graphical style, this preference is likely to influence the kind of game she will make.

Imagine, for instance, a game designer who has access to graphical tools developed for a first-person shooter. All other things being equal, she is unlikely to produce a real-time strategy game. Similarly, if she sets out to make a real-time strategy game, she may debate whether to incorporate 2D or 3D graphics, but she is likely to choose a third-person perspective.

Geography, representation, and gameplay are interrelated. To see this more clearly, let us look at the way in which games have developed over the years. Concerns over the relative merits of 2D and 3D game engines were not pressing on the minds of the *Spacewar!* developers in the early 1960s. Working under severe hardware constraints, they were forced to limit the number of on-screen objects and to limit the details of these objects. Nothing, however, forced them to create the game's puzzling wraparound space, which ensured that a spaceship leaving the right edge of the screen would materialize on the left. It would be odd, yes, to have the ships crash against the screen edges (space is supposed to be infinite, after all), but there is certainly no logic demanding that the ships make this odd and unexplained transition to another position in space. Although hardware was important, this was one of many design choices, with profound implications for the gameplay of this and many other games to follow.

We see the action of *Spacewar!* from an abstract position—rather than from the perspective of one of the game's protagonists—so we can say that the game employs a third-person perspective. The alternative to this would be a first-person perspective, in which the player sees the game from her character's perspective, as is the case in first-person shooters.

The galactic shoot-out takes place on a single plane, in which the spaceships can move in any of the cardinal directions but not down or up away from the plane. This is equivalent to a space battle carried out on a game board—lacking any depth—and is of course not realistic in any way. Thus, we say that the graphics are two-dimensional. The action takes place on a simple coordinate plane and the position of an object can be described using only two coordinates (see Figure 5.3). This is as opposed to three-dimensional graphics, which also have depth, much like the physical world.

Spacewar! was a competitive two-player game where the players (typically) were watching the same screen; thus it would be difficult to have the perspective move to follow one of the players. The *Spacewar!* world therefore did not scroll. "Scroll" refers to the movement (usually horizontal) of the perspective to follow the action, somewhat like the gradual unrolling of the contents of a paper scroll, or a camera on a track that rolls along beside a scene.

Multiplayer one-display games that scroll have typically been cooperative action games like *Golden Axe, Gauntlet,* or *Double Dragon,* in which it is to players' advantage to move in synchrony. Thus, *Spacewar!'s* nonscrolling perspective may have been a function of gameplay details but another choice made by the designers, one not required by the logic of the game or its technological constraints, is the game's off-screen space. Because the playing field wraps around to meet itself, *Spacewar!* technically has no off-screen space. Thus, the players can see all the objects in the game at all times, and do not have to worry about anything lying beyond the screen. Again, hardware limitations might have played a role, but this design choice also suggests the pervasive influence of classical board games. In chess, *Stratego* and *Risk,* for example, nothing exists beyond the board.

Though *Spacewar!* is simple, the types of choices faced by its designers are similar to those faced in later and more complex game productions. Figure 5.4 is a table of basic

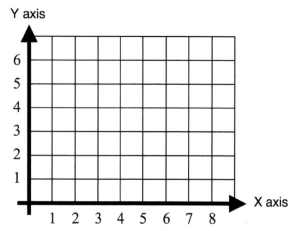

Figure 5.3 Two-dimensional graphics mean that the game action is limited to a simple coordinate system

Perspective	First person			Third person		
Dimensions	Two			Three		
Space type	Torus		Abstract		Free	
Off-screen Space	Dynamic		Static		None	
Scroll	Vertical	Horizontal		Free		None
Exploration	Forced		Free		None	

Figure 5.4 Basic graphical/spatial game characteristics. The figure does not indicate any relationship in the columns

geographical and representational characteristics that we shall use to distinguish between aesthetic strategies in games, followed by a detailed description of each.

Perspective

Excluding text-based games and abstract puzzle games (in which perspective is irrelevant), all video games employ either a first- or a third-person perspective (or the ability to toggle back and forth between the two). In addition, games can also employ either an isometric perspective (similar to an architect's sketch of a building) or a top-down perspective (also known as a bird's-eye perspective).

In the first-person perspective, we see the game action from the point of view of the protagonist—it is as if the player himself is experiencing the action. In the third-person perspective, the player watches whatever it is that he controls, which can be an on-screen object (a character, a vehicle), a number of objects (an army of soldiers, a group of villagers), or various settings (such as tax rates or city zoning). In the case of games like *SimCity*, the player is not even directly represented in the game world, suggesting that we can enjoy interacting with a system without the need (so obviously present in narrative film, for instance) to identify with actual characters. If we consider video games as an extension (or variation) of classical board games, we won't be surprised here. Card games, dice games, or board games such as mancala or backgammon are engrossing without any human-like representation of the player.

What is more surprising is that video games seem to work equally well in both the first and third-person perspectives. Nor is there any indisputable difference between the experience of playing the two. It is easy to assume that the first-person perspective offers a unique, visceral, and hectic experience, but this is belied by the blood-pumping enthusiasm that many players have brought and still bring to even the simplest of third-person action games (like *Spacewar!*).

One general statement we can make, however, is that genres and subgenres (as discussed in Chapter 3) consistently adhere to one or very few perspectives. For instance, real-time strategy games always employ the third-person perspective. The same holds for turn-based strategy games and for most action games, which require the careful coordination of physical activities by different players. We can imagine the difficulty, for example, of maneuvering for the vine swinging and pyramid climbing of archaeological adventuress Lara Croft while seeing the game world through her eyes.[19] In comparison, almost all modern action games that revolve around shooting are tellingly referred to as first-person shooters; it would be hard to imagine these in the third person. Multiplayer third-person shooters, however, are far less unlikely than a first-person strategy game. The reason for this is that strategy games do not have single protagonists, making such a design experiment rather meaningless.[20]

One subgenre not clearly linked to either perspective is role-playing games (whether single- or multiplayer). Throughout the subgenre's history, both perspectives have been used. In *The Elder Scrolls III: Morrowind*, where the player assumes the role of a single character, she is mainly offered a first-person perspective of events (but can shift to third person). In *Baldur's Gate II: Shadows of Amn*, where the player is responsible for the well-being of an entire party of adventurers, the player must content herself with a third-person perspective. Similarly, MMORPGs usually "prefer" the first-person perspective but always offer a multitude of different perspectives.

Some other games seek the best of both perspectival worlds: they avoid the strict first-person perspective (seeing through the character's eyes) in favor of a point of view placed very close to the object controlled by the player.

As we follow the historical evolution of video game design, it is clear that a strict division between first- and third-person perspectives becomes less helpful; rather, we should discuss a game's point of perception[21]—the point from which the player perceives the gamespace. Importantly, a game may offer varied, often overlapping, points of perception. Real-time strategy games, for instance, offer maps of the entire gamespace that coexist with the standard view chosen by the player.

What makes the difference is often the distance of the point of view from the game action. In *Half-Life 2*, the point of perception is that of the player character, which shows only a very limited portion of the game world as a whole. This ensures very limited knowledge and a frantic, nonstrategic approach to problem-solving. *Baldur's Gate II: Shadows of Amn*, on the other hand, uses the so-called isometric perspective.

The isometric perspective is a technique normally used in architectural drawings, as a method for presenting three-dimensional objects in a two-dimensional form. Technically speaking, the angles between the projection of the three axes (X, Y, and Z) are all 120° and there is no vanishing point as seen in the second *SimCity* game (Figure 5.5). The isometric perspective is not necessarily more effective or engaging than a top-down perspective, but it does allow for a less abstract perception of the gamespace. We can

Figure 5.5 SimCity 2000 (1993) demonstrates the isometric perspective

see this by comparing the top-down perspective of the first *SimCity* game (Figure 4.19) with the sequel *SimCity 2000* (Figure 5.5).

Two early uses of the isometric perspective were the 1982 arcade space action game *Zaxxon* and the 1984 ZX Spectrum game *Knight Lore*, in which a werewolf roamed a magical castle in the hopes of lifting the curse upon him. Notable later games to employ the isometric perspective include *Paperboy* (1985), *Diablo* (1996), and *The Sims* (2000). Today, the perspective is a staple of the real-time strategy subgenre, although early examples—such as *Dune II* and *Warcraft*—in fact used a top-down perspective. Role-playing games with a third-person perspective (such as *Baldur's Gate* or *Lineage: The Bloodpledge*) also always use the isometric perspective, probably because it facilitates identification with on-screen characters and simultaneously allows for a strategic understanding of the gamespace.

Perspective is of great importance in game design, since it directly shapes how we perceive the game world and how close we can get to its characters and objects (and whether we can even relate to individual characters at all).

Dimensions

Although we shall soon discover gray areas, in essence all computer graphics are either two-dimensional or three-dimensional (not to be confused with "3D projection," discussed later). We have already seen examples of both, but now is the time to be more specific.

Two-dimensional graphics are somewhat comparable to paintings. They are created in computer applications like Adobe Photoshop, originally designed to facilitate drawing, sketching, and image processing. They can be printed on paper without losing essential qualities (unlike 3D graphics which, if printed, would obviously no longer be rotatable, etc.).

Elements of a 2D image may consist of either vector graphics or raster graphics (to name the most important possibilities). Vector graphics are geometric models described as mathematical statements. Thus, they can be turned, twisted, rotated, and resized without any loss of quality. Raster graphics (or bitmap graphics), on the other hand, are rectangular maps of pixels (points of color), each pixel endowed with a color value. When thousands or millions of these individual pixels are grouped together, they create a comprehensible image. Raster graphics are used to transfer photographs from a digital camera onto your computer screen and cannot be resized—at least not upwards—without obvious quality issues.

Three-dimensional graphics are fundamentally different: they add the Z-axis, and 3D graphics objects thus become spatial (see Figure 5.6).

Also, the computer will typically store 3D objects as models (see Figure 5.7), which can then be rendered wherever appropriate in a game, for instance, as running right next to the player character with sunlight illuminating one side. Such on-the-fly rendering can be computationally demanding and thus gaming has tended to drive hardware development.

There are creative ways of achieving 3D-like effects using 2D graphics, to create a feeling of depth without the complexity and cost of real 3D, or simply because it fits the designer's aesthetic purpose. Designers most often use the isometric perspective in this way, as discussed earlier. *Sim-City 2000* (Figure 5.5) uses 2D graphics but attains depth by using the isometric perspective.[22] *Wolfenstein 3D*, the first modern-looking first-person shooter, uses a first-person perspective but "fakes" a three-dimensional effect by use of 2D models (see Figure 4.22). Simply put, the enemy soldiers are merely bitmap figures scaled to match their distance from the player's point of view (a visual trick quite obvious if you look for it). These enemy soldiers have no backs—so it's fortunate that they always face the player. A related technique—known as "parallax scrolling"—provides an image with depth by moving layers at different speeds. Thus, objects "close" to the player move faster than more distant objects. This technique is used in *Moon Patrol*, *Shadow of the Beast*, and *Canabalt*, for instance. Since two-dimensional processes can be used to fake three-dimensionality, distinguishing between whether graphics are technically 2D or 3D is not vital for our discussion of game form. Thus, in this book we categorize

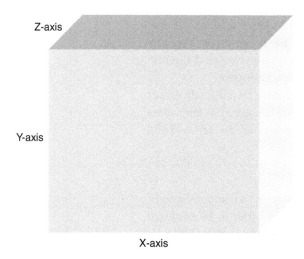

Figure 5.6 In games with three-dimensional graphics, the gamespace can be thought of as the inside of a box

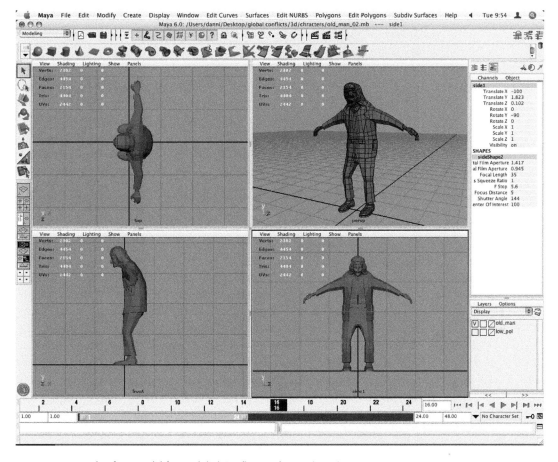

Figure 5.7 Example of 3D model from *Global Conflicts: Palestine* (2007)

as 3D any game that allows for movement in three dimensions—that is, up and down, and into the gamespace.

What, we might ask, is the relationship between a game's perspective and the number of dimensions it uses? Since 3D can be faked using 2D, there seem to be none. While there are no rules about this relationship, nearly all games follow similar standards. A game with third-person perspective can exist in two dimensions or three. But it is hard to imagine a first-person game that does not use (or at least fake) three dimensions. Again, we see how aesthetic aspects that are technically only loosely related tend to be tied together in practice. Creative game design tends to happen through appreciating the existence of such conventions and considering how one may innovatively challenge them.

At this point, it is worth addressing a potential confusion. As most large-scale games have adopted 3D graphics, the term **3D games** is increasingly reserved for games that offer "3D projection." These games can make game objects appear to float between the player and the screen, an experience similar to that of watching a 3D movie. Technically, this can be achieved by

3D games: Refers to gamespaces modeled in three dimensions, or to three-dimensional projection, in which the player's eyes are "tricked" into perceiving depth in the image.

various methods,[23] but it always involves sending a slightly different image to each of the player's eyes (the difference between what is seen by each eye is one reason our brains perceive depth in the real world).[24] The PlayStation 3 (PS3) introduced 3D projection in the spring of 2010, and games like *Gran Turismo 5*, *MotorStorm: Pacific Rift*, and *Top Spin 4* soon started appearing with differing types of 3D integration. Nintendo made headlines with the early 2011 release of their Nintendo 3DS, a version of the best-selling handheld device offering a 3D experience without the use of special glasses. While early sales were decent, 3D games have not, at the time of writing, taken off conclusively (similar to television with 3D capabilities).

As for 3D games themselves, they have not tended to differ greatly from their 2D versions, although much emphasis has been placed on long objects protruding from the screen.

Space Type

Most nonabstract games of recent vintage occur in a "lifelike" space, comparable to that illustrated in Figure 5.6. But early games like *Spacewar!*, as we have seen, used 2D graphics and had a somewhat idiosyncratic gamespace. When the player-controlled spaceships left the gamespace at one side, they immediately appeared on the opposite side. This gamespace by its nature is abstract. Another interpretation, however, is that the gamespace was in fact circular, or torus-shaped (see Figure 5.8). Thus, going far enough in one direction lands the players back at their starting point.

The *Spacewar!* approach to gamespace was copied by many later games, such as *Pac-Man* and the arcade hit *Defender* (see Figure 4.6). In *Defender*, for no obvious reason, the player navigates a torus (possibly the alien-ridden planet is extremely small and the player merely circles it). This approach has fallen out of fashion in recent decades, as the technological capabilities of game platforms have increased exponentially—and perhaps, in turn, a player's desire for a more "realistic" gamespace to navigate.

And yet modern games, which typically let the player roam more freely, do not allow immediate access to the entire gamespace. We have already discussed how most games limit vertical movement and most also divide the gamespace "box" into various levels that the action may move between.

An important element of space is the basic size of the gamespace. Early games, like *Spacewar!* and *Pong*, were limited simply by what one screen could hold. But soon games (such as *Night Driver* and *Bump'n'Jump*) started transcending the one-screen gamespace. At least three alternative approaches emerged early on (along with a number

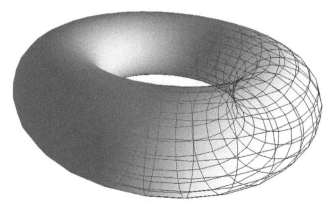

Figure 5.8 The torus illustrates the looping space in some games

of combinations): unconnected levels, zone-based multiscreen spaces, and seamless multiscreen spaces.

In games with unconnected levels, when a level is cleared the player character is merely transported to a different place; there is not necessarily an implication that the two places are physically connected. Examples of this approach include *Pac-Man* and *Bomb Jack*.

In the case of zone-based multiscreen spaces, the player character exits through one side of the screen and the perspective then jumps to show the player character on the other side of the next screen. For instance, reaching the right side of the screen, the perspective skips to show the player standing on the left side of the next screen, facing right (the implication is that the perspective has moved, not the player character). This type of space was popular with many early graphical adventure games, such as Warren Robbinett's *Adventure*, from 1978.

Finally, seamless multiscreen spaces use a scrolling perspective, so the player gradually reveals the gamespace as he moves. This is the case in games like *Ghosts 'n Goblins, Time Pilot,* and *Super Mario Bros.*

The space type has clear consequences for gameplay. With a one-screen gamespace, all of the objects in a game are usually visible at all times. When all elements are visible, a player may concentrate all resources on that which is known. The player doesn't need to save energy for unexpected situations or use precious mental capacity to plan for various contingencies. The same holds true for games with unconnected levels, although when these levels are linked in terms of the game's goals the player may still have to worry about getting hold of objects needed at a future level, for example, or conserving energy for the final showdown. In seamless multiscreen spaces, quite the opposite is true. Here, projections of what might come must inform the player's choices. In the racing game *Bump'n'Jump*, for instance, the player has to consider what the odds are that various obstacles (such as pools of water) may be looming ahead, and then play accordingly.

Off-Screen Space

The concept of off-screen space originates in cinema. If a movie scene shows two people meeting in an office and the soundtrack contains the sound of traffic in the street below, then that street is part of the scene's off-screen space. In video games, there are two distinct types of off-screen space. We can refer to them as "passive" and "active." In passive off-screen space nothing really happens. This is the case in a game like *Spy Hunter*. The player controls a weapons-laden car as it barrels down an unfolding road, shooting enemy vehicles. We know that the gamespace is larger than what fits in any one screen, and as the road scrolls past we encounter enemies appearing from both below and above. But when they are not visible on the screen, the other vehicles are irrelevant; their behavior and accompanying fate is processed by the game only when they are on-screen. The off-screen space, then, is passive: logically it exists, but nothing happens out there.

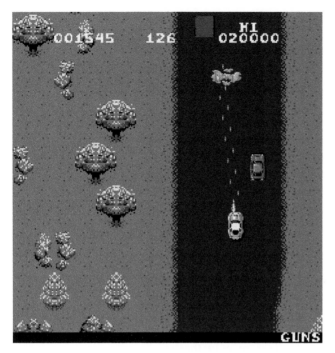

Figure 5.9 Spy Hunter (1983) demonstrates well the off-screen space that you know is in front of you but you can't yet see

This is not the case for games in certain other genres. Since real-time strategy games rely heavily on active off-screen space, let's take a look at one representative example—*Warhammer 40,000: Dawn of War*.

As the player's budding warlord lays the foundations of his glorious fortifications on one side of the gamespace, other characters (controlled by additional players or the computer) are doing the same in unseen areas of the game's world. What happens beyond the frame inevitably affects the course of the game. Thus, the off-screen space here is radically different from that of *Spy Hunter*. It is dynamic, living, or active.

The extreme approach to active off-screen space is of course that of MMORPGs, in which the player at any one time experiences only a miniscule portion of the gamespace. In addition, in MMORPGs the game is processed even when the player is not even present in the game world—also referred to as the world being "persistent"—and plays even when the player is not active.

Modern games tend toward more active off-screen space, whereas almost all arcade games had passive off-screen space; but the distinctions are not always clear-cut. Take, for instance, *Grand Theft Auto V*. While often applauded for its "breathing" game world and the openness of its gameplay, *GTA V* is not, in fact, a living simulation of an entire city. At any given moment, objects that are not directly related to the player character (those that are very close or on the screen, or being tracked by the player's radar) are not being processed by the game. As an example: the player hijacks the car of a poor city dweller—the victim does not then (for example) lose his job, become a criminal, and pose a danger to the player in dark alleys. Instead, he or she just disappears when the player character has reached a certain distance from the crime scene. Similarly, a dramatic car crash does not slow down traffic in other places in the city, or leave nearby streets unguarded by police. A similarly partial approach to off-screen space is found in virtually all recent action games, such as *Red Dead Redemption* and *BioShock*. The rarity of an active off-screen world in action games is in sharp contrast to the abundance of life that happens off-screen in MMORPGs and real-time strategy games, and reflects the different priorities of these genres. The former prize the intensity of conflict above all else—the bigger world is quite peripheral—whereas the satisfaction of MMORPGs and real-time strategy games lies in figuring out the ramifications of the endless possibilities of human (and nonhuman) interaction.

Scroll

As we have seen, "scroll" refers to the gradual unveiling of gamespace. A game can scroll horizontally, vertically, or freely, meaning both vertically and horizontally; or not at all. In scrolling games, the perspective is typically centered on the player character. The concept is not usually applied to first-person games, which do not have an "implied camera" tracking the game action.

Horizontal scroll was common in many arcade games of the 1970s and 1980s. Often, the player character would fight his way from left to right, by either battling or avoiding opponents. Examples of early horizontal scroll abound: *Defender* (1980), *Scramble* (1981), *Kung-Fu Master* (1984), *Ghosts 'n Goblins* (1985), and *Wonder Boy* (1986).

Vertical scroll was slightly less common in early games but could be found in both personal combat-style games and aircraft shooters. Examples include *Spy Hunter* (1983), *1942* (1984), *Commando* (1985), and *Rainbow Islands* (1987). Some arcade games scrolled both ways. Certain games, such as *Time Pilot*, scrolled freely (within the gamespace), while in others, such as *Gauntlet*, movement was constrained by walls or other features.

In the main, it seems that platform games (where the player must jump between platforms) work best with horizontal scroll, one of very few exceptions being *Rainbow Islands*, which did not set an influential precedent (although later games like *New Super Mario Bros.* and *Limbo* include sections of vertical movement).

Scroll is typically only used in the context of 2D graphics, since 3D gamespaces are not usually gradually revealed in the same paper scroll-like manner.

Exploration

In a given game, is the player free to explore the gamespace at her own pace? Or are there constraints—a ticking clock, to name one obvious example? Most arcade games employ the latter principle. Arcade games make more money the more often they're played, so a moving perspective that literally pushes the player forward quickly became the standard. This variation of scroll we call "forced exploration." In the vertically scrolling *Rainbow Islands* mentioned previously, the bottom of the screen slowly filled with water, forcing the player upward. Forced exploration was even more common in vehicle-based shooters, like *1942* or *Scramble*, where the forward propulsion of the airplane (or spaceship) forced the player to keep moving. In sharp contrast, gameplay time is not an issue on consoles or home computers. Here, with the exception of certain flight games, exploration tends to be unforced, and the player is free to navigate as quickly or as slowly as he desires.

Having examined how space is created and used in video games, we turn now to an equally important feature: time.

Time

Time in a video game is also an aesthetic aspect—that is, something experienced by the player. It is also largely under the control of the designer, who may adjust many aspects of time, for example, whether or not it can be sped up during trivial tasks (such as traveling).

Compared to the interest in gamespace, research on the issue of time in games is limited.[25] While time has been a very important topic in literary and film studies, especially from a structural perspective, it draws little attention in game studies. But as Jesper Juul suggests,[26] looking at game temporality can help us understand how different game genres are influenced by different aesthetic conventions, and can even shed some light on the historical development of the industry. If we look at the beginnings of game history, coin-operated arcade machines offered a distinct sense of time compared to today's games: as mentioned previously, arcade games were fast-paced and designed for short playing sessions, in order to maximize the dropping of coins into that bottomless slot. With the arrival of PC games, designers found a very different set of parameters, which allowed for longer playing sessions and encouraged "slow" genres such as adventure games (although such games had been pioneered on earlier machines).

Inspired by concepts of discourse and story time, and how they create a sense of narrative, Juul proposes that we distinguish between play time (the "real" time a player spends playing a game) and event time (the time that passes in the game world during this game). These two concepts apply only to games that project a fictional world; in abstract games, the concept of event time does not make much sense. The relationship (or "mapping") between these two "times" is, Juul suggests, highly variable. For example, in action games such as *Quake* or *Unreal Tournament*, play time and event time are equal, which means that every action the player takes (moving with the mouse, or shooting a bad guy) immediately affects the world inside the game. In this case, we say that the game happens in real time. By contrast, strategy and process-oriented games often compress event time so that action can span across years and even centuries, and a few hours of play can make or destroy civilizations. For example, in *SimCity*, we might play for two minutes of real time (play time), and two years could pass on the game world clock (event time). In some of these games the player can adjust the event time according to their desired speed (typically quicker if they are experienced players and slower if they are still learning how the game works).

Cut-scene: Dramatically important sequence, often displayed without the interaction of the player. The scene is typically shown to motivate a shift in the "plot" of the game and displayed outside of the game engine.

Games that contain **cut-scenes** represent an interesting anomaly: the relation between play time and event time is interrupted, while at the same time cut-scenes contribute to the construction of event time (for example, by showing what happened in an span of five years). Another interruption of play time in many contemporary games is simply a consequence of technology: the player has to pause—for a few seconds or a few minutes—while the console loads the game's many levels. Some game designers consider the inevitable wait a negative player experience. Juul calls these interruptions of play time "violations." A prime violation, in Juul's opinion, is the much-discussed possibility of saving games. Does the ability to return to a game later on ruin the aesthetic experience of playing? Is it a necessary evil in order to complete difficult games, or is it simply a design feature that can be both used and abused? This is an aesthetic debate among designers, and not one with an obvious answer.

The distinction between play time and event time points to how players understand the mapping between their actions and the game's fictional world, but it does not tell us a lot about the gameplay itself, since in principle every game is played in real time. Even slow adventure games offer an immediate connection between player action (clicking a mouse, for example) and events in the game world (character movement, dialogue, decision-making). The significant difference between play and event time, then, is actually in pace. Think of the reaction speed that different games require of players, and the fact that every genre has conventions of pace and speed that the player must learn to be successful. For example, many of the early (and also abstract) arcade games are about learning to react on time to the same challenges again and again, so that players become quick enough to complete each level.

Time becomes even more significant when we realize that we already categorize several types of games based on how they use time aesthetically. Turn-based games, sports games, and multiplayer action games are all founded upon the particular way that time passes. An even more extreme example is MMORPGs, where a huge time investment is required by the player in order to build a character skilled enough to truly explore the game. Many intriguing questions about time in video games have not yet been explored in detail. Time, however, is such a basic human tool for understanding our place in the world that it continues to be a significant (if subconscious) tool for game designers. Further study of time's many ramifications should only increase our understanding of the building blocks of a video game's design.

Graphical Style

In the previous pages we have glimpsed the variety of elements that a designer must decide between—from perspective to space type to the way time progresses—each of which has obvious implications for gameplay. But designers must also decide on graphical style—how the game should express itself visually. For instance, *Warcraft III* and *Rise of Nations* are both real-time strategy games and share a number of design elements; but to the player they feel rather different, in large part because of their divergent graphical expressions. *Warcraft III* copies a cartoonish graphical style, and makes no pretense of realism, while *Rise of Nations* portrays characters and buildings in a mostly realistic manner.[27] Game scholar Aki Järvinen[28] has identified three graphical styles that have dominated video game design since its inception: photorealism, caricaturism, and abstractionism. We will discuss the three styles briefly in turn.

Photorealism

All media and art forms have at one time or another been employed in the service of realistic representation. In painting, for instance, it was common at least until the mid-nineteenth century for artists to attempt as faithful as possible a rendering of reality on the canvas (the subjects, of course, could be imaginary or fictitious, but the style was realistic). Starting in the 1860s the French impressionists Manet, Renoir, Monet, and others dramatically challenged the dominant style by attending to subjective, fleeting moments (an idea that seems quite conservative, of course, compared to what came after). In the 1960s, following multiple schools of abstraction, came photo-realism: a style of painting that tried to mimic photographs. Computer graphics have similarly been unable to resist the lure of the "real." We could argue that video games have attempted to depict reality from their beginnings but were long hampered by insufficient technology. A dominant branch of video game graphics development has craved improved hardware able to process more and more details. Nowhere in video games has such an attempt been more obvious than in the "interactive movies" of the early to mid-1990s (see Chapter 4). Believed by many at the time to be the culmination of games' search for realistic graphical expression, these adventure games typically saw Hollywood actors performing pre-filmed action sequences in filmed environments. Illustrative examples include *The 7th Guest, Ripper, The Beast Within: A Gabriel Knight Mystery*, and *Under a Killing Moon*.

Photorealism has given birth to two subcategories: televisualism and illusionism. The former is a graphical style that attempts faithfully to mimic the aesthetics of television, usually in the form of sports. Such games mimic multicamera productions and use sports TV features such as instant replay. These games copy an evolved form of representation clearly suited to the sport at hand (though not necessarily optimal for a game in terms of control or identification).

Games taking the route of illusionism use photorealistic graphics in the service of nonrealistic content. A science fiction game may attempt to present aliens and unearthly machinery in a fashion that seems lifelike, even though the objects presented have no real-life counterparts. For instance, the looming metallic tripods of *Half-Life 2* seem to move with menacing realism, although the player has no real-life experience of such monstrosities.

Caricaturism

Long a favorite of political cartoonists, caricatures attempt to present the essence of a person or object by exaggerating the most prominent features. In recent years, a few games have taken this approach, often achieving the feeling of a cartoon.

Despite their departure from reality, and their similarity to cartoons, these games are not always intended for younger audiences. Many games based on caricaturism are gripping, which belies the notion that immersion is intimately linked to realism in any direct sense. *Doodle Jump* and the *Crash Bandicoot* games take a caricaturist approach, as do the *Zelda* and *Jet Set Radio* games.

Doodle Jump was in fact part of a strong trend in mobile casual games in which for a time game designers would aim for a pronounced "sketch aesthetics," a whimsical style invoking the creative process, sometimes making the game look like a draft. This style was employed in games such as *Line Rider* in 2006, *Jelly Car* in 2008, and *Max and the Magic Marker* in 2010 (and some years before, in 1999, in *Vib-Ribbon*).

We can make a few generalizations about the relationship between graphical style and genre. With exceptions like the realistic play of *Jet Set Radio*, caricaturist games are mostly unrealistic (or semi-abstract) in their gameplay. Thus, most platform games fall within this category. Other sub genres—such as **3D shooters** and racing games—cling tightly to photo-realism. But many genres resist graphical categories, and contain games in a range of graphical styles. In the case of real-time strategy games, for instance, games such as *Rise of Nations* or *Command & Conquer: Generals* are photorealistic, while *Warcraft III: Reign of Chaos* is caricaturist.

3D shooter: Action games in which the action is seen through the eyes of the protagonist and where the graphics are three-dimensional (and often constructed of polygons). Synonym: first-person shooter (**FPS**).

Abstractionism

Our third category is a visual style that does not try to represent people or real-life objects. Though rarely seen in commercial titles, it is far from unimportant in the industry's continuous experiments with game form. At heart, abstractionism can be said to be "about" form.[29] A prime example

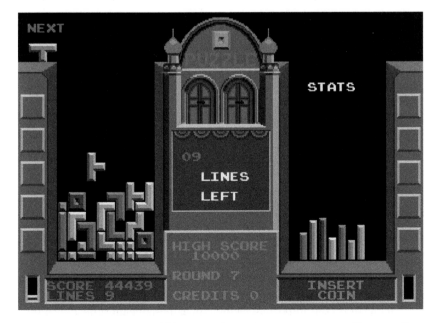

Figure 5.10 Tetris (1987) is world famous with numerous permutations and is among the most successful abstract games

here is the legendary Soviet smash hit *Tetris*, which began its worldwide reign in the mid-1980s.

Long before *Tetris*, however, there was 1981's *Qix*, in which the player draws rectangular shapes while avoiding Qix and Sparx, the game's abstract, line-drawn enemies.[30] The same year, and more famously, there was *Tempest*, in which a yellow, three-dimensional crab-creature valiantly defended a barely delineated world from strange abstract beasts that continually emerged from a tunnel. More recently, abstractionism saw a brief resurgence of interest with the courageous *Rez*, a rhythm-based shooter game in which the player traverses a psychedelic gamespace populated by colorful shapes and figures. While scoring big with critics and the experimentally minded, *Rez* was less of a commercial success.[31] The game's lack of influence led Aki Järvinen to worry that "abstractionism might end up as a marginal [footnote] in the history, and future, of an audiovisual cultural form also known as computer and video games."[32]

The overarching problem with abstract games, not surprisingly, is that they are hard to market. It is difficult to create hype purely around a game's mechanics (as opposed to its amazing story, or its sexy lead character) and next to impossible to make money on merchandise (not to mention movie rights), while a trailer of an abstract game is unlikely to wow the marketers and buyers at game fairs. Equally important is the fact that contemporary games seem to attach increasing importance to narrative; just as film and literature have proven over time, despite ongoing murmurs of experimentation, humans seem ineluctably drawn to the simplest form of all—the story. But while AAA titles will rarely be fully abstract, mobile gaming has breathed life into tile matching and *Tetris*-like puzzle games, and so abstractionism thrives in your pocket with titles such as *Drop7, Glow Puzzle*, and *Blue Block*.

Game Audio

Think about your favorite game. Now try to describe what it sounds like. Unless you are unusually analytical about your video games, you will likely be (a) unable to remember the sound and music clearly or (b) unable to analyze the sound design in any detail. When we want to approach game sound systematically, we face two problems. One is a broad, and embarrassing, tradition of ignoring the audio side of audiovisual media. In film studies, for instance, sound has received extremely limited attention relative to its importance to the experience of a movie.[33] The second problem is that we are generally not taught how to describe the qualities of sound. In fact, our common vocabulary does not even include many terms that can be used to differentiate sound types. This causes a problem for interaction designers—professionals who design interfaces in the widest sense—who want users to state their sound preferences or comment on sound design. To comment systematically on this important element of games, one must become familiar with a complex language ("transparent," "narrow," and "full," for example, are adjectives used to describe sounds).

The sound landscape in video games may be understood by applying the following categories:

- *Vocalization*: This refers to the voices of characters in a game (including voice-over speech and other off-screen elements).
- *Sound effects*: These are sounds made by in-game objects (for instance, the sound of a gun being fired).
- *Ambient effects*: These are nonspecific sounds contributing to the game atmosphere (a bird calling, the distant sound of machinery).
- *Music*: This is the soundtrack to the game. Music is usually used to add to the atmosphere of the game (or set the mood) but can also be directly tied to the game world.[34] In the *Grand Theft Auto* series, for example, the soundtrack is provided by car radios.

Whether we notice or not, music and sound play a truly important role in game design. Modern game credits often list several people responsible for various aspects of sound, and game audio today requires the collaboration of a number of specialized professionals. But it wasn't always so. In the very beginning, games did not have sound at all. In the 1970s it became possible and practical to store and play sound files. Some systems could play actual sound recordings while others used MIDI-like formats (in the MIDI format, a sound file is simply a series of references to sounds that are then played back by the sound card, analogous to a sheet of musical notation, which requires instruments, players, and interpretation to actually make sound).

By 1980, game designers still faced severe limitations on sound design. Whether stored directly or in a MIDI file, game sound typically consisted of a few basic sounds or rhythms complemented by various event sounds that would be played when a certain condition was fulfilled. For instance, in *Pac-Man* a brief introductory jingle gives way to an ambulance-like sound that plays throughout the game. On top of this layer of sound, the characteristic munching sound is triggered each time Pac-Man eats a dot. Distinct event sounds are triggered, when you eat a ghost, for example, or when a "dead" ghost (if you will) returns to the ghost headquarters. When Pac-Man is killed, another jingle is heard. Whereas the introductory jingle ascends in pitch, the death jingle mimics an object spiraling downwards, or the sound a ball makes when bouncing to a standstill. The audio of *Pac-Man* is obviously context dependent. However, it is also very simple. The sounds themselves are rudimentary, and they do not influence each other or vary according to secondary conditions.

Another good example of the creative use of primitive audio was *Asteroids*. A heart-like beat would slowly increase in intensity over time. Exploding missiles made pleasant thumping sounds, and the abstract majesty of the gameplay was suddenly interrupted by the shrill alarm sound of alien spaceships. The only other sounds were the thrust noise of the protagonist spaceship and the explosions of asteroids breaking into smaller parts.

In the 1990s, most storage constraints fell away (at least for PC games). Thus, the size of the sound files became less important. The epic multivoice choir scores of *Phantasmagoria* from 1995 and its contemporaries testify to this development. However, for all platforms (each of which dedicated different amounts of resources to sound processing) processor speed was a serious constraint on developing fully dynamic game soundtracks. Thus, while epic compositions could be played back, very little on-the-fly processing could be done. For instance, the designer of a survival horror game might want the tempo of a tune to increase as the monsters get closer. In this case, the processor would have to calculate the physical relationships between the characters and shift the audio playback accordingly. In another case, our designer might want sound effects to reflect present game conditions, like the altered pitch of a car as it speeds through a tunnel. As the speed of console and PC processors has caught up with storage capacity, more and more dynamic sound processing has become feasible.

As illustrated by the preceding examples, today's games use sound to do far more than simply reflect the action on screen. Ongoing developments mean that sound effects in contemporary games can also be affected by:

- *The environment*: For instance, the size of the location, the material of the walls, the characteristics of the carrying medium (air, water, etc.), and the weather conditions.
- *Spatiality*: Sounds are situated in space. Thus, the sound of a monster 30 yards to the left and concealed by trees is different from the sound of the same monster 1 yard behind you.
- *Physics*: The sound may be affected by relative movement (it may mimic Doppler shift, etc.).

Although technically challenging, these advancements merely mean that game designers strive for a realism similar to that of a movie soundtrack. While describing the rules of sound generation is quite different from adding sound effects to a movie in post-production, the principle is not hard to grasp, and we will discuss this development in the following section.

The Quest for Dynamic Music Generation

Much as a video game narrative is not predetermined but generated dynamically based on the actions of the players, so auto-generated music is music created (from fragments of various size) to match present game conditions. While presenting a considerable challenge, we should remember that some forms of pre-electronic music—like jazz—are at their heart improvisational; likewise, live music is often adapted to local conditions. Also, as with system-generated narrative, system-generated music is rather an old idea. A famous example, celebrated during the Romantic era of literature (in the decades around 1800), is the Aeolian harp. The Aeolian harp consists of a sounding board with strings attached lengthwise across two bridges.

Depending on how the strings are tuned, music (of a sort) is created when the wind blows across the strings.

Video game designers typically want the music to adapt to the present circumstances of the game. There are two important aspects to this. First, a single piece of music can be modified to fit changing conditions. Say a certain tune is attached to a nonplayer character (**NPC**). The tune might then be altered to reflect the protagonist's relation to the character, or the character's state of health, or both. If the NPC has turned from enemy to friend but is badly wounded, the tune might be played in a desperate (or perhaps mournful) tempo.

NPC (nonplayer character): Any character in a game not controlled by the player.

But the designer might not be content to merely play back a piece of music when some single condition is fulfilled. In more open-ended games, sound designers attempt a much more dynamic soundtrack by describing more basic relationships and principles. Certain music files, for instance, may be split into various sections and looped for various periods of time. Specific conditions—anything from the protagonist's state of health to the type of on-screen action—may combine to inform the game what music is most appropriate; similarly, built-in rules may tell the game how and when to shift from one composition to another.

This is not dynamic music generation, strictly speaking (it is merely rule-based playback of pre-composed music). Asking the computer to generate music itself, we encounter what has been called "the computer music problem."[35] Whereas today it is a comparatively straightforward task to instruct a computer to process rules and analyze large amounts of data, we are not very good at formalizing creative and high-quality music performance and composition (if indeed this can be formalized at all). Thus, we are incapable of telling a computer how to go about composing good music.

The Function of Sound and Music in Games

Sound and music are essential to enhancing the gaming experience. They do so mainly by informing the player about the state of the game world and by cuing emotions that enhance the immersiveness of the game. Music, in particular, can have a visceral link to our emotions, and when used effectively can evoke feelings from excitement, to melancholy, to desperation. Certain kinds of music seem to have nearly universal emotional associations: high tempo music, for example, cuing activity and outward-directed feelings. Most traditional or conventional music, in fact, uses tempi that lie within the normal heart rate range for adults. The cues offered by other pieces of music, however, can vary widely depending on context. The grand strains of a classical orchestra, for example, have long been used by filmmakers to connote an epic narrative; the sound of a lone saxophone, meanwhile, might connote the mournful loneliness of a big city.

In a designer's many uses of sound, we must note that the aim is not realism in the strict sense. What sound design should achieve, apart from increasing a player's sense of immersion, is the feeling of realism.[36] In the case of video games, this feeling of realism actually requires randomization. As sound designer Marty O'Donnell says, "the biggest tip off to the listener that something is artificial is when the crow always caws just after the leaf rustles and before the frog croaks every thirty seconds or so."[37] Thus, generating a sense of realism is not just a question of faithfully reproducing the sounds of actual objects (such as gunshots). It is a more complicated question of creating an aural world that mirrors the complexity of the visual one.

We shouldn't be surprised to discover the source of many game audio conventions. In the cinema—and the many video games that follow suit— sound and music are used as the glue that ties together different shots. Thus, the image may change dramatically, but because of the continuous sound (and use of editing conventions), the sense of continuity is not broken. Apart from the continuous music, "sound bridges" also prepare the viewer for a change in perspective by actually starting up the sound of a new shot before the image of the old is replaced. In games that use cinematic aesthetics, the role of sound is just as essential as it is in a movie. For instance, the survival horror game *Resident Evil 4* has a very memorable sound design, in which the destruction of monstrous enemies is accompanied by detailed (and gruesome) sounds. Anyone playing a game such as *Resident Evil 4* can observe just how much atmosphere careful use of audio can add to the game experience.

Audio as Mechanic

In the lyrical point-and-click adventure game *Loom*, from 1990, young Bobbin Threadbare passes through a magical land armed only with a magical distaff capable of producing music. The player, essentially solving puzzles within the framework of the C-major scale, must cast spells by reproducing sequences of notes.

In *Loom*, music is not mere ambience but rather a core gameplay-related element. Related experiments followed, but a broad movement did not begin until the mid-2000s, when dancing games were joined by music games like *Guitar Hero*, *Donkey Konga*, *Rock Band*, and *SingStar* (in turn somewhat inspired by the PlayStation 1 (PS1) game *PaRappa the Rapper* from 1996). In these titles, music creation is the core mechanic, as players (typically) attempt to hit the right notes at the right times. Graphically, "music games" tend to be cartoonish, and the visuals serve mostly to display the required notes and so forth, and to display clear feedback on the player's performance.

Music games have also made names for themselves on the iPhone, perhaps because of the touchscreen lending itself so well to rhythm tapping. Key titles include *Tap Tap Revenge* and its many sequels, in which the player taps balls at the right moment to make music; *Rhythm Racer*, in which the player races in pursuit of "power spheres" which keep the music playing; and the *Riddim Ribbon* games, where the player creates remixes by steering a ball along a track.

Also on the iPhone, a more radical experiment appeared in late 2010 with *Papa Sangre*. Here the player, transported to a land of the dead where eyes

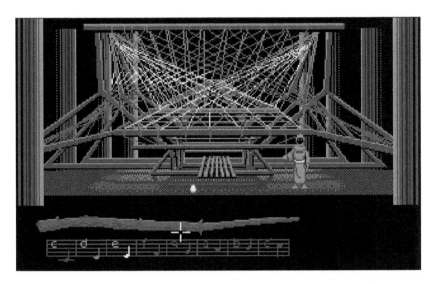

Figure 5.11 *Loom* (1990) was an early example of how music can be used as core gameplay

are of no use, must navigate the castle of Papa Sangre solely through audial clues about the surroundings. The screen shows a minimalist interface, and essentially this is a game that tries to demonstrate the power and potential of audio.

Emergence

Emergence is a phenomenon whereby the interaction of simple principles on one level creates complex results on another, higher level.[38] Certain species of ants, for instance, doing no more than acting on their simple, genetically determined dispositions, will create towering mounds of sand that look like the results of a very careful design. Similarly, flocks of birds moving in complex and seemingly coordinated patterns are no more than the emergent result of each bird following basic "rules" of behavior. One compelling example of emergence in simulations is John Conway's famous *Game of Life* from 1970, a simple simulation of population dynamics in which very basic relationships create interesting patterns.[39]

In game design (as in so many other fields), the concept has been in vogue for some years. Here, "emergence" refers to the fact that game dynamics (in the sense of the mechanics-dynamics-aesthetics design model; see Chapter 3) may arise without being planned for. The archetypical example is taken from 2000's *Deus Ex*. The game's lead designer, Harvey Smith, describes how:

> Some clever players figured out that they could attach a proximity mine to the wall and hop up onto it (because it was physically solid and therefore became a small ledge, essentially). So then these players would attach a second mine a bit higher, hop up onto the proximity mine, reach back

and remove the first proximity mine, replace it higher on the wall, hop up one step higher, and then repeat, thus climbing any wall in the game, escaping our carefully predefined boundaries.[40]

Here, the rules of the game (in the broad sense) interact to create possibilities that the designers themselves had not predicted. Such emergent possibilities have increased recently, due to the increasingly advanced physics engines in modern games and a strong focus on making game worlds feel more alive.

The concept of emergence, while fascinating, is not in itself new. Returning to the example of chess: simple rules combine to create a (practically) infinite set of possibilities, so that not even a grand master can know for certain how a game will progress (although it gets increasingly easy to predict as the game goes on).

Another way to look at emergence (and its opposite) is to consider games in terms of their degree of openness. This can be thought of in a number of ways. For instance, certain games are world-centered as opposed to protagonist-centered. In the case of the former, the game is a world with its own active laws of physics, and here things occur without the protagonist necessarily being involved (generally in the active off-screen space).

In protagonist-centered games, however, the entire game system revolves around the protagonist; nothing noteworthy takes place beyond the radius of the protagonist's action. In her humorous account of US video game culture, *Joystick Nation*, game journalist J.C. Herz referred to the former approach as the "Old Testament approach to game design," emphasizing that the designer here creates the basic material and the basic rules (analogous to the laws of nature). This she contrasted with the "'Pirates of the Caribbean' syndrome, where you feel like you're on some kind of monorail through the game."[41]

Another, and more precise, distinction was made by Jesper Juul, who described games as being on a continuum between two basic structures: "emergence" (as described above) and "progression."[42] Emergence, to Juul, is "the primordial game structure, where a game is specified as a small number of rules that combine and yield large numbers of game variations."[43] In progression games, on the other hand, "the player has to perform a predefined set of actions to complete the game."[44] Clear-cut specimens of the latter include adventure games such as *Myst* (1993) and *Gabriel Knight 3* (1999). Juul stresses that the progression form of gaming is practically unique to video games, since most board games, card games, and other forms of entertainment remain interesting precisely because their few rules offer many potential outcomes.

NUMBER OF PLAYERS

In terms of player experience, and in terms of game design, an important difference is that between single-player and multiplayer games. The discussion here is kept brief, as many issues concerning social interaction between players are addressed in Chapter 6.

The differences between single-player and multiplayer games affect a number of game elements, from artificial intelligence to the importance of communication features and the issue of cheating in games. But before we tackle those issues, let's start with a simpler task. Can you name one nonelectronic game that only requires one player?

Chances are you eventually thought of solitaire. But other answers are few and far between. In recent years there have come new nonelectronic games that can be played with a single-player, like *Arkham Horror*. Still, there are strikingly few nonelectronic games that do not require the presence of several players. Video games thus represent something of an anomaly in gaming—which historically and culturally has been a fundamentally social pastime. As witnessed in Chapter 4, the history of video games is full of titles that pit man or woman (singular) against machine.

Many video games today are designed with options for solo play and multiplay. *Doom III*, for instance, features an elaborate single-player campaign, but it also contains two multiplayer modes, which emphasize either collaboration or take-no-prisoners mutual destruction. Thus, the single- and multiplayer game forms are not fundamentally at odds, but they do contain some important differences.

This design choice can affect the form of the game. Single-player games often function as obstacle courses (*Half-Life, Donkey Kong, Pikmin*) or procedural systems (*SimCity, Sid Meier's Pirates, Railroad Tycoon*). Multiplayer games, by contrast, can be thought of as playing fields, as in team sports, that is spaces endowed with rules and structural features to create an interesting competitive experience (*FIFA 12, Tekken, Warcraft II*). Most progression games, in Juul's sense, are single-player games, since progression games are typically player-centered.[45]

Single-player games usually require what game designers refer to as artificial intelligence (**AI**). Such systems do not constitute attempts to create anything as complex as human intelligence but rather consist of virtual entities endowed with response patterns enabling them to respond flexibly and with *apparent* intelligence to game conditions (and particularly the actions of the player). The behavior of one's soccer opponents in the *FIFA* series is an example of game entities that may seem to know exactly what they're doing while being guided by relatively simple rules of behavior. In action games, in particular, the "intelligence" of enemy nonplayer characters has improved remarkably since the mid-1990s.

AI (artificial intelligence): Often used to describe the behavior patterns of computer opponents.

For certain genres, the computer's "intelligence" is crucial. Success in real-time strategy games, for instance, is far easier if the player can trick a gullible computer-controlled enemy. In general, computer-controlled players in such games employ a very limited number of strategies and are unable to learn from their own mistakes. Thus experienced human players will often have very little trouble beating even the highest level of computer-controlled resistance (unless the AI "cheats" by gathering resources unnaturally fast, for instance).

Designers of multiplayer games, on the other hand, do not have to worry about AI, as their players face other gamers who are (often) smarter than even the most advanced of AIs. On the other hand, multiplayer games face crucial balance issues that single-player games don't. To be enjoyable, the playing field must be truly level (without being boring), as in shooter levels, which cannot merely look the same from the starting point of both teams. And if the game features a variety of characters, each needs to have its own unique features but none can be innately superior to all others, since that would spoil the fun.

The biggest challenge for developers of multiplayer games, however, may be to facilitate constructive social interaction between (sometimes) large numbers of players. In *Spacewar!*, the social dynamics of the game world were limited—you physically met, played one or more rounds, and that was that. Today, large multiplayer spaces (with players usually not in the same physical location) are social systems that invite both cooperation and conflict.

GAMES WITHOUT BOUNDARIES

Finally, a new form of games has emerged in the past decade that is not only inspired by other cultural forms but that also operates within their codes and parameters to create a meta-form of gaming. This new kind of experience has been called "pervasive gaming," "alternate reality gaming," or even "cross-media gaming." The concept is derived from the idea of ubiquitous computing, which emphasizes that computers are omnipresent in our society, and control even the smallest aspects of our everyday lives. *Majestic* (2001) is perhaps the best-known example of these pervasive games, which may begin in your computer but then use other media to exist beyond the screen. For example, a player of a pervasive game is walking through her town and gets a message on her mobile phone; she is warned (thanks to location technology) that a player from the game's enemy faction is in the same square. The two players can then choose to "battle," using their mobile phones to send their attacks; afterwards they can each go home to check the number of points their team has earned during the day, communicate with other players, and then decide their next strategies. In this case, the game uses video games and mobile phones as tools, while the physical location of players also plays an important role.

However, the aspect of pervasive gaming that has so far been most intriguing for researchers relates to the game's ability to "mix" with the real life of players; these games not only happen at any time during the day (including the players' working hours) but also use the same daily communication devices. In a mixed-reality game, players can get phone calls, emails, or faxes from characters in the game, see messages related to the game in the screen titles of films or television programs, and search for information on game-based websites that look just like real websites. For example, in the game *Enter the Matrix* (2003), launched alongside the cinema release of *The Matrix Reloaded*, players could start by visiting what looked like the authentic corporate website of Metacortex,[46] where the main character, Neo, worked. From there, they could investigate further and uncover dark secrets.

The most successful of early pervasive games has been *The Beast*, released alongside Steven Spielberg's film *AI* (2001), where thousands of players followed clues buried in the film trailers, Internet sites, and even newspapers, trying to uncover a murder conspiracy. This player community thrived online, where information was exchanged in many forms across countries and languages. Speculation was made into an art. Jane McGonigal, a game researcher who has worked extensively on this kind of game, has reported how a group of *The Beast* players, the Cloudmakers, treated the very real events of 9/11 as if they were part of the conspiracy in the game, and talked about "solving" 9/11. Though these players might seem delusional, McGonigal explores their sense of **agency**, and how new social networks emerge where people can engage in different kinds of social action.

Agency: The player's ability to influence the game world through their decisions and actions.

Although quite different in application, the notion that games (or elements of games) can move smoothly beyond the screen is echoed in the more mainstream principles of "gamification," which we'll discuss in Chapter 8, on "Serious Games."

DISCUSSION QUESTIONS

- In what sense are game rules like real-life laws of nature?
- What are the dangers of discussing a game only in terms of its rules?
- It seems that most games are very concretely tied to the physical world (few games are entirely abstract). Although game developers can control the game world physics entirely, they often use real-world, Earth-like principles of gravity, avatar forms, and so forth. Why do you think this is?
- What game genres, in your opinion, benefit from using 3D graphics instead of 2D graphics? Discuss using examples of past and present games.

RECOMMENDED GAMES

Tic-tac-toe—Shows just how simple a game is at its core, and how difficult it is to keep it simple and balanced.

Rock-paper-scissors—The fundamentals of gameplay demonstrated with utmost simplicity.

FURTHER READINGS

Taylor, A. (2013, March 28). How to make a video game for the blind. *Popular Mechanics*.

(Estimated reading time: 5 minutes)

Mandal, S. (2013, April). Brief introduction of virtual reality and its challenges. *International Journal of Scientific & Engineering Research*, 4(4).

(Estimated reading time: 21 minutes)

NOTES

1. Badham, 1983.
2. Salen and Zimmerman, 2004, p. 128.
3. Sniderman, 1999, p. 2.
4. Sniderman, 1999, p. 2.
5. The reader is encouraged to consult Jesper Juul's *"Half-Real: Video Games Between Real Rules and Fictional Worlds"* (Juul, 2003a) and Katie Salen and Eric Zimmerman's *Rules of Play: Game Design Fundamentals* (Salen & Zimmerman, 2004) for details and more elaborate arguments.
6. Juul, 2003a.
7. Salen and Zimmerman, 2004, p. 120.
8. Friedman, 1995.
9. Sniderman, 1999, p. 2.
10. Salen and Zimmerman, 2004.
11. Frasca, 2001a, p. 9.
12. Juul, 2003a, pp. 66–67.
13. The concepts of perfect and complete information derive from the field of mathematical game theory, in which they refer to slightly different things. Technically, perfect information means that all events having passed prior to one's next move are known while complete information means that players know the entire gamespace and the goals of all other players. See Smith, 2006b.
14. Some prefer to distinguish between "data" and "information," where "data" is the input that actually reaches the senses while "information" implies interpretation.
15. This comes very close to the meaning of "dynamics" in the MDA model (see Chapter 3).
16. The reader interested in game balance is advised to consult also Rollings and Morris's *Game Architecture and Design* (Rollings and Morris, 2004) and Rollings and Adams's *Andrew Rollings and Ernest Adams on Game Design* (Rollings and Adams, 2003).
17. Rollings and Adams, 2003, p. 247.
18. Smith, 2006a.
19. Though hardly impossible. The main point here is that such a design choice would be unlikely.
20. Obviously, not all games let themselves be defined so strictly. In Bullfrog's *Dungeon Keeper*, for instance, the strategic third-person view was substituted during battle scenes for a first-person sequence, as the player (taking on the role of evil dungeon keeper) assumed control of an individual minion.
21. Järvinen, 2002.
22. Note that an isometric perspective can also be used alongside 3D graphics—as demonstrated, for instance, in *Age of Mythology*.
23. See Walton, 2010.
24. Walton, 2010.
25. But see Juul, 2004; Rau, 2001.
26. Juul, 2004.
27. While the graphical style may lean toward realism, the gameplay itself

does not. For instance, armies and cities are somewhat arbitrarily symbolized by a few buildings or units.

28. Järvinen, 2002.
29. Järvinen, 2002, p. 123.
30. A design copied by cell phone manufacturers under names such as *Erix*.
31. Hawkins, 2005.
32. Järvinen, 2002, p. 124.
33. It is telling that Richard Rouse's otherwise recommendable book *Game Design: Theory and Practice* (2001) does not dedicate one single subsection to audio.
34. In movies, sound originating from the fictive world is usually labeled "diegetic" while sound effects or music that do not have an in-movie source are labeled "non-diegetic."
35. Weir, 2000.
36. As it is put in the movie *Demolition Man*: "This isn't the Wild West. The Wild West wasn't even the Wild West." If we saw real footage from the old West we might not find it realistic, since our concept of the time is mostly constructed by Hollywood. For a list of semi-realistic movie sound clichés, many of that are accepted as realistic, see www.filmsound.org/cliche/. In a video game context, see Hämäläinen, 2002.
37. O'Donnell, 2002.
38. Holland, 1998; Johnson, 2001.
39. See, for instance, www.bitstorm. org/gameoflife/.
40. Smith, 2001.
41. Herz, 1997, p. 154.
42. Juul, 2002.
43. Juul, 2002, p. 324.
44. Juul, 2002, p. 324.
45. But since arcade games are (or were) never process oriented, we see cooperative multi-player games of the progression type in this format (e.g. *Golden Axe* and *Double Dragon*).
46. www.metacortechs.com.

6 Video Games in Culture

The Cultural Position of Video Games
The Players

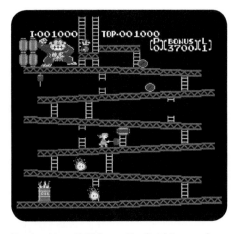

Donkey Kong (1981) was the first hit game for Nintendo and the first to feature Mario, later to become a star himself

This chapter will map the cultural position of video games; that is, we will look at video games as producers of meaning, both for society in general and for the people who play them. Games are a part of a complex cultural system as well as generators of a specific player culture. When you see how *Fortnite* with its dance moves and emotes has made its way into dance classes and mainstream media, you know game culture have become omnipresent— and that separating games from society and culture is harder than ever.

Researchers challenge the idea of the "magic circle" separating games from real life, as described earlier in this book. Celia Pearce has put it beautifully, saying that the "magic circle is more porous than previously believed."[1] Such work has mainly involved observation of MMORPGs, in which, as Geoff King and Tanya Krzywinska say:

Gameplay does not exist in a vacuum, any more than games do as a whole. It is situated instead, within a matrix of potential meaning-creating frameworks. These can operate both at a local level, in the specific associations generated by a particular episode of gameplay and in the context of broader social, cultural and ideological resonances.[2]

This is what we will deal with in this chapter. In the first section, we address the cultural status of video games (as lowbrow, escapist entertainment), and consider how the mass media portrays them. The second section is about the people who play video games and the game communities they create.

THE CULTURAL POSITION OF VIDEO GAMES

No cultural form exists in isolation; rather, it is integrated within a complex system of meanings shaped by society and its institutions. Compared to other cultural forms, such as literature, the medium of the video game is a new member of this fascinating ecology. It is certainly true that the history of cultural media shows an almost instinctive skepticism leveled at new media.[3] It has been true of radio, it has been true of movies, and it has certainly been true of television, which has long fought against the perception that its role was to entertain rather than to enlighten. Many issues factor into the battle for cultural acceptance that most new media must fight. Some are formal, for example, a strong visual basis usually does not help, as this hints that the medium may be one suited for the illiterate; others are social, for instance, the perceived intentions of the producers. Media that are seen as primarily market-driven fare poorly in the quest for acceptance as a culturally valuable activity.

Expressions of taste or distaste about a new medium are not just objective judgments, even though they may appear so; they are probably also strategic or power-related. French sociologist Pierre Bourdieu,[4] opposing the commonly held idea that taste is an individual matter, argued that taste is an altogether social phenomenon. It is a means to establish boundaries by signaling one's membership of a certain social group. Those with power will praise their own tastes in music and books and cultural media in general, and will tend to label other cultural forms as uncivilized or otherwise problematic. In contrast, marginalized groups have historically coalesced around certain activities (or cultural expressions) in order to establish a counterculture that prizes distinct values and tastes. Video games are one of the most potent examples of a novel cultural object; not surprisingly, they too have been immersed in such battles.

Cultures around the world tend to distinguish between forms of expression that are or are not intrinsically worthwhile. In Western societies, for example, painting, literature, and sculpture are traditionally considered more dignified, more worthy of careful attention, than television and games (electronic or otherwise). During the middle part of the twentieth century, however, the traditional hierarchy was challenged by artists who drew upon objects and images from pop culture. This trend was exemplified by the pop art movement. A foundational example of this is Andy

Warhol's series of portraits of Marilyn Monroe. The boundaries between high and low culture were decisively blurred, and to the delight of some and the horror of others, Western culture has been unable fully to separate the two ever since.

Meanwhile, theoretical and scientific developments pushed in the same direction. The rising discipline of media studies, particularly work inspired by semiotics and ethnography, challenged the idea that certain media or genres were inherently better than others. One such movement was the widely influential cultural studies school, which examined contemporary phenomena—often from a neo-Marxist perspective—to understand their meaning and relationship to power structures and the wider culture. Such approaches were typically guided by the beliefs that all cultural phenomena could be "read"—that is, interpreted—and that no particular type should be privileged. The movement also coincided with a growing number of empirical studies that showed how media users appropriated all types of media products for their own purposes and often used (or interpreted) them in ways not necessarily connected with the type or class of products.[5]

All these developments have served to blur, but not erase, the distinction between high culture and pop culture. Games are still categorized within the latter—and still lower—sphere. Many of us, scholars and gamers alike, have argued that games are underrated as an art form, and that games only lose out in comparison to other arts because the criteria are not suited to their particular qualities. Such arguments tend to emphasize the arbitrariness of distinctions between art and nonart, and expose the unfairness of denying the status of art to a form of expression just because it provides entertainment and aspires to a mass market.[6] Whether something is actually art can never definitively be settled through analysis and debate. The question is more significant in terms of the battle for legitimacy. It is at once meaningless—since it merely depends on our definition of art—and of great practical importance, as the answer has consequences for everything from the establishment (and relative importance) of academic departments, to government regulation of the video game industry (by, for example, censorship through ratings), to the cultural obligations of that industry—which conceivably will develop in different ways depending on whether it is a part of the establishment or if it is denied legitimacy. If nothing else, the question is at least an intriguing one, since today's games are the subject of heated argument over what they mean and how we should feel about them. But how do games communicate meaning? What is it about them that is so contemptible?

Games as Cultural Forms

Video games are made to entertain, but this doesn't prevent them from being "means for creative expression," as Mary Flanagan puts it.[7] Like other media, games can have different functions and expressive intentions, side by side with entertainment. It is also possible to design games for "artistic, political, and social critique or intervention,"[8] linking games to larger cultural issues.

However, typically cultural critics see games exclusively as representational objects, and do not take their procedural characteristics into account. Many who have looked at games as producers of meaning in the areas of ethics (especially the issue of representation of violence) or gender studies have ignored the dynamic nature of games.

For example, a study from 1995 looked at representations of women in the most popular 33 games at the time. These portrayals ran the gamut from sex symbols or prizes, to victims of male power, to heroes and action characters. The study also considered the use of violent themes in the games. The verdict was that the most common depiction of women in games was that of "damsel in distress":

> In one example, *The Adventures of Bayou Billy* (1989), the beginning of the video game shows a woman in a low-cut, red dress. This woman has large, well-rounded breasts. A man is holding her and has a knife placed at her throat. Apparently, this man has kidnapped Annabelle and Billy's mission is to save her.[9]

In the games analyzed, aside from victim or sex object, all the female characters had insignificant roles (or very stereotypical ones, in the case of villains). This is not untrue, but instead of looking at how these representations combine with the mechanics of the games, and what actions and choices are afforded to the player, the study hurries to conclude that engaging with this kind of representation is harmful to children of both sexes, "since they will internalize these expectations and accept the idea that women are to be viewed as weak, as victims, and as sex objects,"[10] without reference to any empirical material that would support this claim. There is nothing wrong with taking an exclusively analytical stance, but the formal analysis is also partial, so that the conclusion rests on very thin grounds. It may be that it is correct, but we cannot know for sure if the *playing* of the games is not considered.

An even clearer example of this representational bias—of failing to consider video games in their specificity as a media form—is a study by Urbina Ramirez and colleagues,[11] who through the analysis of covers of games, and without actually playing them, conclude that games promote a subordinate and stereotypical position of women.[12] Video games are seen as representational media *only*. This can be very problematic in a cultural form that is so much more than representation.

We could, for example, make a content analysis of the character of April Ryan in *The Longest Journey*. We would immediately be placed on our guard by and comment critically on her tight clothes, full breasts, large, innocent eyes, and sensuous mouth; it would be easy to conclude that she was a sex object and a passive figure.

Figure 6.1 April Ryan in *The Longest Journey*, on the way to her next destination

However, this would be far from the truth. April Ryan is an independent and resourceful character, who is not only the protagonist of the game but also makes decisions that can alter the fate of the world, and engages in dangerous action without depending on men. The point is that exclusive use of content analysis to evaluate the cultural role of video games will never give us a full and fair picture.

Cultural critics would do well to study those authors who have developed specific theories about how video games communicate ideas, including Ian Bogost,[13] Noah Wardrip-Fruin,[14] and Mary Flanagan,[15] among others. All these authors, inspired more or less explicitly by Janet Murray, insist on procedurality as one of the basic properties of the computer, and by extension of video games. Bogost proposes the term **procedural rhetoric**, defined as "the art of persuasion through rule-based representations and interactions rather than the spoken word, writing, images, or moving pictures."[16] He adds that "videogames are computational artifacts that have cultural meaning *as* computational artifacts."[17] As critics, we need to learn to read these processes, and also to understand how players find meaning in procedural work. In other words, it is not only how games *look* but also what we can *do* in and with them that produces meaning.

In order to illustrate this, Bogost analyzes a myriad of different games, ranging from small, politically motivated games like *September 12th* to commercial products like *Grand Theft Auto: San Andreas* or *America's Army*, produced by the US Army. It is the latter we will use to show how procedural rhetorics work. *America's Army* is a multiplayer first-person shooter created

Procedural rhetoric:
The art of persuasion through rule-based representations and interactions (typically in games) rather than the spoken word, writing, images, or moving pictures.

specifically as a recruiting and communication tool, and released for free on the Internet. It was very successful, especially in the United States, and was hailed as extremely realistic, reflecting both the physical constraints of combat as well as the rule system of the army. Bogost draws attention to two game mechanics that, for him, reveal the underlying ideology of the game: the honor system and the enemy threat. All characters in the game can earn honor points by following orders and respecting the chain of command; if characters behave inappropriately, for example, by pointing a weapon at a superior or swearing, they will be punished. It takes a lot of time and effort to build up honor statistics, so that losing a character would be very frustrating for the player. Thus, the more honor points gained, the more interested players are in following orders. Bogost, who also takes into account the perspective of the game designers,[18] explains:

> Army success entails the selfless execution of tasks that have been handed down from a higher authority, completed without question or reservation. These tasks, like real US Army missions, are decontextualized from geopolitics. Reward comes not from service completed in the conscious interest of a conflict, but from service completed in the absence of political circumstance. The US Army recruit, one learns from *America's Army*, is an apolitical being.[19]

This is reinforced by the procedural rhetoric of enemy threat. In *America's Army*, players fight each other in small groups on opposing sides, but both teams believe they are the good guys. "The perceptual interchangeability of enemy and soldier underscores the contemporary American assumption that matters of military conflict are commutative; that is to say, one global, even transcendental situation guides both sides of the conflict."[20] Opposition is decontextualized, and perceptual equivalence means that the only explanation for the enemy's behavior must be wickedness.

As Wardrip-Fruin observes, examining the expressive qualities of computer processes helps us to understand "the aspects of works that are not apparent on the surface."[21] It is vital to us as citizens of the twenty-first century to be able to understand complex software systems and how they shape our understanding. An appreciation of the procedural expression capabilities of video games will also allow us to extract ethical meaning from games, as the work of Miguel Sicart eloquently demonstrates.

For Sicart, video games are moral objects that make players (who are moral beings) reflect on their actions. Ethical or unethical play design is not a question of the game being more or less sophisticated in its representation of the world; rather, it is a matter of how the game rules shape the moral responsibility of its players. An ethically relevant game forces "the player to face ethical dilemmas."[22] Video games shouldn't take the moral decision-making power away from the player; a game like *XIII*, where shooting a policeman immediately prompts the "game over" screen, doesn't give players a chance to make their own decisions and experience the consequences. In contrast, a reviled game like *Manhunt*, which forces the player to commit murders, can be, paradoxically, more illuminating from an ethical perspective, because it

> is actually designed to make the player enact an unethical experience, showing that there is no fun in committing these acts, but rather mirroring the lack of morals and the desperate situation of the main character in the fictional game world.[23]

Sicart's vision of players as moral beings allows them to follow their own morality and to "decide which values, practices and discourses are morally desirable."[24] From this perspective, players are not dupes who consume violent content; instead they are empowered to choose both the games they play and their playing strategies.

Public Perception of Games

Despite the work presented in the last section, there aren't many cultural critics who deal with games in their own terms, as procedural forms capable of generating new kinds of expression. For most, play and games equal entertainment, one of the most suspect cultural categories. Entertainment plays a crucial—and much-debated—role in contemporary life. It is often considered synonymous with escapism, which carries very strong negative connotations, since it is associated with an unhealthy flight from reality through means such as drugs.

But we could also adopt a wider notion of escapism, one that includes any human activity not immediately geared toward survival. In this definition, video games are certainly escapist but so too is literature and indeed all of the fine arts. The time that is "left over" in our struggle for survival can—and perhaps should—be filled with another reality, one that is more pleasurable and offers relief from the difficulties of living.[25]

The psychologist Andrew Evans differentiates between escapist activities as passive (such as watching bad television) or active (such as gardening). Games would belong to the active category (to return to Sutton-Smith: the rhetoric of "play as the imaginary"[26]). Evans does not consider games a negative activity, since the healthy or unhealthy quality of escapism does not depend on the activity itself but on its context and the way it is performed. (In principle, any kind of escapism can become an addiction.) He considers games a necessity, both for mankind as a species and for children in their psychological development, and looks at the future of advanced console gaming with positive curiosity regarding new possibilities for simulation and what they could offer us.[27]

In the same vein, Mary Flanagan insists that play has always had subversive qualities as well as purely entertaining ones. She draws on examples of Victorian subversive doll play practices, such as "reskinning," "unplaying," and "rewriting," which are strategies for social resistance.[28] In her book

Critical Play, she analyzes many cases of games and artifacts that engage players in activities that make them question different aspects of human life, from the pleasures of familiarity afforded by the video game *The Sims* to artistic interventions like *OUT*, which turns playing *America's Army* into a live urban performance with an antiwar agenda. The main point is that the nature of games as rule-oriented objects makes them specially geared toward activism. Art, games, and an active critical view of society are thus naturally connected:

> Due to the systemic nature of both the product and the process, game makers use particular repeatable processes, or methods. Like activists, game designers also follow an overall scheme of investigation or research, creating processes to address specific concerns and ideas. In addition, the creation of rules of operation makes interesting constraints to provoke innovation in both the designer's process and the player's role.[29]

However, for most other critics, and certainly for the mass media in general, video games are still consistently considered unsophisticated in their form, problematic in their content, the cause of health problems from obesity to addiction, and implicated in amorphous cultural fears—for example, the seemingly ever-present scourge of antisocial, aggressive teenagers. The first video games raised few cultural eyebrows—perhaps because so few people ever played them, or perhaps because their few pixels were so abstract that they had little emotional impact. But it wasn't long before this new form of entertainment raised suspicion. The year 1976 marked the entry of video games into America's culture wars; as seen earlier, *Death Race*—with its goal of running over tiny human-like figures—sounded the first alarm, sparking a media outcry that led to the banning of the game.[30]

From early on reporters and commentators expressed concern over the detrimental effects of gaming, whether physical or moral.[31] Reports in the US popular media in the early 1980s often appeared fascinated with the growing subculture of gaming. For the following three decades, the concerns surrounding games have been remarkably consistent, with few developments.

Concern over violence in games, and the endless argument over whether computerized violence can spill over into violence in the real world, has repeatedly spurred academic and cultural research (see Chapter 9 on "Video Games and Risks"). The results have further fed public discussion, from government think tanks, to outraged parents, to kids themselves.[32]

In their short history, video games have been connected to a wide variety of (often contradictory) effects. As one editorial in the *British Medical Journal* mentioned, game play has been connected with aggression and addiction, while "case studies have reported adverse effects of playing video games, including auditory hallucinations, enuresis, encopresis, wrist pain, neck pain, elbow pain, tenosynovitis, hand-arm vibration syndrome, repetitive strain injuries, peripheral neuropathy, and obesity."[33] Meanwhile, news media regularly report that games have been linked with positive effects like improved hand-eye coordination.

Given that even early arcade games—with their primitive graphics and barely human protagonists—sparked full-fledged controversy, there is no direct link between a game's realism or content and the level of cultural concern. Nevertheless, most of these flare-ups have occurred in the last couple of decades, and are often tied to particularly violent titles. Controversy became especially intense in the United States in the early 1990s. This was just when the console producer Sega sought to distinguish themselves from Nintendo by publishing much more provocative games. While Nintendo's games were family-friendly, Sega tried to appeal to older audiences by betting on adult themes and graphic violence. A number of publishers were more than happy to comply, and launched games that seemed bound to cause alarm.

Mortal Kombat, in particular, was released for the Sega console in 1992[34] (see Chapter 4) and quickly came to symbolize the trend toward ruthless on-screen violence. Acclaim, who released the game for the Sega Genesis/ Megadrive and the Super Nintendo, were told by both Sega and Nintendo to tone the game down; but Sega allowed players, through the use of codes, to unlock the game's full-scale violence. According to Gagne:

> Newspaper articles described *Mortal Kombat* as "offering children exciting new ways to maim, dismember, and murder unsavory opponents in a sadistic martial-arts tournament" in which "it is considered a mark of success . . . to rip the head and spine out of an opponent and wave it in the air while the blood flows to the ground."[35] With such stirring imagery, it was only natural for parents to be concerned about video games as more than a thief of a child's attention.[36]

America was thus primed for upset over *Night Trap* (1992), a horror game released a few months earlier and inspired by the already disreputable slasher film genre. It raised such controversy that it was removed from some US stores in 1993. Moving beyond a reliance on graphics, the game actually used full-motion video to bring to life the player's efforts to save a group of female college students trapped in a lakeside house full of vampires. The game contained both scantily clad screaming young women and lots of blood, so it was a sure recipe for scandal.

The wake left by these and other troubling games led all the way to Washington, DC, and in July 1994 the US Congress debated how to respond. The result was the creation of the Entertainment Software Rating Board (ESRB),[37] established by (what is now called) the Entertainment Software Association[38] at the prompting of Congress. Since 1994, the ESRB has rated every video game published in the United States. The anonymous raters[39] assign a game one of six age ratings, from "Early Childhood" (suitable for age three and older) to "Adults Only" (18 years and older), as well as a series of content descriptors (there are more than 30) such as "Drug Reference,"

"Nudity," or "Strong Language." A similar system, Pan European Games Information (PEGI),[40] exists in Europe with aims and procedures comparable to those of the ESRB. The US rating system, in particular, has been the subject of some controversy, as its methods and rulings have become issues in the continuing debate about how we define violence and immorality. A regular complaint is that any suggestion of sex will cause games to be rated as Adults Only, while games with high doses of violence will receive lower ratings.[41]

As an illustration of this, we can look at the cultural outrage around the *Grand Theft Auto* series. The games from *Grand Theft Auto III* onward have all courted controversy because of the player character's criminal and violent behavior toward police and others. After its 2001 release, *Grand Theft Auto III* was criticized for its focus on crime (carjacking in particular); in 2002 *Vice City* became infamous for a game mechanic allowing the player to have (off-screen) sex with prostitutes. Afterwards, the player could assault the prostitute and steal her money. Though the mechanic was optional, such actions were made possible by the game, and arguably encouraged, since the player received a health bonus by having sex. Unlike players, critics failed to recognize the ironic and satirical humor integral to these games. Their game worlds were inspired by gangster movies and, particularly in the case of *Vice City*, made abundant use of pop culture. To the initiated, the game played like a living pastiche of TV cop shows from the 1980s. Though these sources of inspiration had long been in the cultural mainstream, these video games (and perhaps the industry as a whole) were still too new, and too discomforting, to be accepted.

Two years later, *Grand Theft Auto: San Andreas*—inspired by California gang life in the early 1990s—came under attack in a case curiously similar to the *Mortal Kombat* scandal almost 15 years earlier. The game contained a sex minigame that, even though not accessible in the published version, could be unlocked by installing the PC **mod** *Hot Coffee*.[42] While the developer, Rockstar North, contended that installing the mod that brought the content into the game was a violation of the user's agreement (and that Rockstar therefore couldn't be held responsible), the fact remained that the content was present in both the PC and console versions of the game. This prompted the ESRB in 2005 to re-rate the game as Adults Only, and some stores to remove it from their shelves. Rockstar hurried to produce a version without the *Hot Coffee* content, and recovered the game's "Mature" rating but lost money in the process.[43] Later that year, high-profile politicians including Senators Hillary Clinton and Joe Lieberman used this example in their call for further regulation of computer game content. More recently, *Grand Theft Auto V* attracted its fair share of controversy due, among other things, to an interactive torture sequence.

Though public reactions to video games arise, as we have seen, due to a host of factors, the role of media panic is essential. In using the term "media panic," we are referring to the public's reaction (through traditional media such as newspapers or television) to the form or content of new media;

Mod (modification): A piece of software that modifies the appearance and/or rules of an existing game. Mods are often made and published by enthusiastic players.

typically, the novelty is seen as inherently dangerous for people (readers, viewers, or players, depending on the medium) who are thought incapable of distinguishing fantasy from reality.

In 2004 the British tabloid press caused an outcry over a 17-year-old boy who was allegedly obsessed with the game *Manhunt*, and who killed a friend in a manner similar to that of the sadistic murders of the game. Reports seemed to cement the link between the game and the murder, dabbling in psychiatry, speculating about the troubled boy's motivations, and positing a clear cause-and-effect relationship between the two. It later turned out that it was the victim, not the murderer, who was a player of the game.[44]

In 2011, the Norwegian Anders Breivik killed 77 people in a bombing in Oslo and shooting on the island of Utøya. In the uproar following this horrific episode, several media outlets picked up on the fact that Breivik, in a manifesto supposedly written by him before the mass murder, had admitted to having played video games. He allegedly used *Call of Duty* to train his combat skills, and *World of Warcraft* as "a useful cover story to explain the time one is actually spending plotting attacks."[45] Immediately several stores in Norway removed the offending games, plus a few other "violent games," from their shelves, out of respect for the dead.[46]

There are countless examples in the media of alleged links between video games and extreme violence: the Columbine High School massacre is regularly invoked. Few media outlets resist the urge to make this connection, even though the perpetrators typically have serious psychological and social problems that predate their engagement with whichever cultural medium they favor. Michael Moore plays with the absurdity of media panic in his film *Bowling for Columbine* (2002), in which he wonders whether the fact that the two teenage murderers regularly went bowling should be linked to their crimes as well.

The scientific evidence linking video game (or other media) consumption to real-world violence is highly contested (we'll discuss this link further in Chapter 9). As Henry Jenkins puts it:

> If video game violence was an immediate catalyst, we would have difficulty explaining why none of the shootings involving teens have occurred in movie theaters or video arcades where the direct stimulus of game playing would be most acute. Instead, these murders have tended to occur in schools and we need to look at real-world factors to discover what triggers such violence. Media activists strip aside those careful qualifications, claiming that the computer games are "murder simulators" teaching our children to kill.[47]

Dmitri C. Williams has analyzed the representation of video games in major American news magazines.[48] His results show that media discourse on video games is plagued with misconceptions and frequently vilifies the games themselves. These attacks have little to do with video games per se, Williams argues; rather, they reflect basic conservative fears about new media, and even show the same historical progression of anxiety that other media before them have suffered: "first were fears about negative displacement, then health, and then antisocial behaviors like aggression and violence."[49] He notes that "at the same time as games were drawing the ire of conservative society, they were also used as a means of reinforcing social norms and power relations. This was particularly evident for gender and age."[50] Women players and older players are ignored by the media, so that the media picture of a gamer is still tied to the negative image of the male antisocial teenager.

As this section has shown, video games occupy a contested cultural niche in today's Western societies. We have been suspicious of play and entertainment since Plato. The dominant influence of the Protestant work ethic, among many other things, has made it difficult for adults to justify play and games. Video games have inherited this prejudice, along with all of the other suspicions that are heaped upon new media.

On the other hand, video games have also become more established as a cultural form with a strength of its own, and continue to slide into the mainstream. The number of people who have never played a video game—from first graders to retirees—seems to be dwindling inexorably.[51] Children and adults alike are drawn to video games. And in the midst of these conflicting assumptions—about what we should do with our time and what we want to do, between whether games have a purpose or whether they just expose us to danger—the video game has become a cultural object of importance. Not unlike the many-sided die of the old *Dungeons & Dragons* games, video games yield many answers, depending on how you look at them, and reveal many different things about us as people.

But who are gamers and why do they play? This question is addressed in the next section.

THE PLAYERS

There has been a growing tendency within computer game studies to look beyond an exclusively formal understanding of games (as systems of rules) and adopt a situated play approach instead. The question is not so much "What Is a game?" as "How is this game played?" Studying gamers at play illuminates the ways games operate as interactive objects and how they engender meaning on multiple levels. As Jason Rutter and Jo Bryce put it, this approach moves "away from any basic assumption that digital games have a meaning or form that can be discovered through applying the right analytical cipher to the appropriate game code in a manner removed from social, economic and political contexts." Games are "cultural artefacts which are given value, meaning and position through their production and use."[52]

Why Play?

Most of the people reading this book are, like the authors, intrigued by the world of video games, if not players themselves. But we should not forget the befuddled spouses, not to mention the aggravated fathers and the protective mothers. Because these people ask a very important question: what are you doing spending all that time staring at a screen? And they have a point. Although some people play video games very casually, others seem to live for little else. They play with an all-consuming passion. They spend hours tucked away in their rooms or clustered in Internet cafés, punching buttons and staring at a screen, gripped by the unending possibilities of video games.

So what is it that makes this activity so fascinating? A number of psychologists have tried to answer this question. Juan Alberto Estallo has compiled several explanations based on reinforcement theory, or the boost in self-esteem felt by those who become good at playing. Moreover, players assign symbolic value to the games they play, so that they find their own subjective rewards in the act of playing. Estallo is aware that any self-esteem boosting activity is prone to provoke addiction in certain kinds of people, but he rejects that video games per se are a cause of sociopathologies. He actually stresses the positive qualities of video game players, such as a high level of creativity and extroversion, and a heightened capacity for learning.[53]

Estallo's theories are borne out by the empirical experience of the authors Sue Morris and Talmadge J. Wright, who have written about first-person shooters. In Morris's *Online Gaming Culture*, she argues that some video games provide a degree of "authorship," meaning creativity and autonomy, which is lacking in many other available forms of recreation (as we will see later with regard to the modding community).[54] Wright, Boria, and Breidenbach have studied player communication and conclude that it "can both reproduce and challenge everyday rules of social interaction while also generating interesting and creative innovations in verbal dialogue and non-verbal expressions."[55] Video games would thus allow players to escape alienation in different ways, and to engage in a kind of activity that goes beyond consumerism.

Mihaly Csikszentmihalyi's book *Flow: The Psychology of Optimal Experience* has often been applied to explain the joy people find in video games. His concept of **flow** describes a state of concentration and satisfaction that a person experiences when performing an activity—anything from playing a musical instrument to climbing a mountain—she enjoys very much, and that becomes an "optimal experience." Flow usually refers to activities that fall outside daily routines, and include a certain sense of playfulness. People will achieve it through completely different activities, depending on their preferences. The optimal experience is "an end in itself. Even if initially undertaken for other reasons, the activity that consumes us becomes intrinsically rewarding."[56] The experience of flow is characterized by the following elements of enjoyment:

- A challenging activity that requires skills (not something spontaneous but goal-oriented and with rules)
- The merging of action and awareness (attention is totally absorbed by the activity)

Flow: The flow state is described as the feeling of optimal experience. It is felt when we feel in control of our own fate and have a sense of exhilaration and enjoyment.

- Clear goals and feedback
- Concentration on the task at hand (forgetting about everything else)
- The paradox of control (the sense of exercising control in difficult situations where your abilities are pressed to the limit)
- The loss of self-consciousness
- The transformation of time (either time passes very quickly, or at a key moment a second can be experienced as lasting for a long time).[57]

Csikszentmihalyi suggests that in order to turn an activity into a flow experience, the first step is to make it a game. He suggests that a person establishes her own rules, objectives, and rewards and lets herself be absorbed by a powerful goal. But this goal will only work if it is balanced with the person's abilities: the task should not be too difficult or we will experience anxiety, nor too easy or we will get bored. The reward of flow is the ability to lose oneself and experience ecstasy, understood as a total detachment from the world outside the activity, so that the actor becomes the event.

The theory of flow can help to explain why people enjoy playing video games: games often adapt to the expertise of the player,[58] so there is a match between ability and goal, and anyone who has tried to get the attention of someone immersed in a game knows how the player can lose awareness of everything outside it.

But flow is at the same time such a general concept that it could explain any other activity equally well. The theory ultimately does not offer a specific explanation as to why video games are fun to engage with—why don't players seek flow through other available activities?[59]

In her book *Reality Is Broken*, Jane McGonigal presents an interesting variant of the psychological explanations for why we play. For her, "games are providing what reality cannot."[60] Games make us happy despite being hard work because we prefer rewarding interaction to being entertained passively. With games, flow can be experienced immediately.[61] She identifies a series of intrinsic rewards afforded by games, which is worth quoting at length:

> First and foremost, we crave *satisfying work*. [This] means being immersed in clearly defined, demanding activities that allow us to see the direct impact of our efforts.
>
> Second, we crave *the experience, or at least the hope, of being successful*. We want to feel powerful in our own lives and show off to others what we're good at.
>
> Third, we crave *social connection*. We want to share experiences and build bonds, and we most often accomplish that by doing things that matter together.
>
> Fourth and finally, we crave *meaning*, or the chance to be a part of something larger than ourselves. We want to feel curiosity, awe, and wonder about things that unfold on epic scales.[62]

The chapters of McGonigal's book are organized around these rewards. For her, engaging with games is about happiness hacking; life is hard and difficult, and games make it better. This is an attractive argument: it would be fantastic if games were the cure for all angst and all the difficulties of life. Unfortunately, in contrast to the grandness of this vision, McGonigal's examples seem rather mundane, for instance, a points game to turn household chores (like cleaning the bathroom) into something fun that motivates all housemates to take part. Even without going into the issue of gamification, it seems that both the bleakness of the world and the benefits of game-like activities (like engaging in crowdsourcing or collaborative projects) are overstated. Still, it is an insightful work that sheds optimistic light on how games engage players, and on the possibilities of games as a cultural form.

Sherry Turkle offers another direction of inquiry in her book *Life on the Screen*, an examination of simulated identity and interactions in "inhabited" game worlds.[63] She looks at textual MUDs as spaces where people have a chance to experiment with different identities. Ultimately, the medium allows us to realize—and directly experience—the notion that there is no unified self. Reality is just another window, like the window of a computer screen; what one experiences online has real-life implications and consequences. This is seen as something positive, as Turkle insists on the illuminating and even curative properties of this kind of play, even though she acknowledges that some players experience a dangerous fragmentation of their identity from too much play. Her work on MUDs is certainly relevant to all social game worlds where players adopt a fictive identity, and is a powerful testimony to the profound ways that video games can influence one's sense of self.

Dennis D. Waskul has also dealt with the symbolic boundaries between person, player, and persona that players build in role-playing games, and comes to the conclusion that "boundaries inevitably implode as person, player, and persona blend and blur into an experience that necessarily involves all three."[64] Waskul's essay appears as part of a collection, one of two edited by Williams,[65] which together offer valuable perspectives on how games are linked into the lives of players, and how in-game relationships with other players are an important playing motivation. Torill Mortensen, for example, argues that in games a great deal of pleasure is derived "from a gaming environment that permits personal influence, social interaction and development in relation to other players, not just in relation to the game."[66]

As we can see, people also play games because of the emotions they elicit. Here, the work of Aki Järvinen[67] and Olli Leino[68] springs to mind as some of the most significant contributions to the area.

Inspired by cognitive science, Aki Järvinen links emotions in games to the particular pleasures offered by staged pretense. An interesting implication of his understanding of game emotions is that game systems

not only elicit emotions from players, but also lead them to predict their and fellow players' future emotions during the game. Gaming encounters, thus, presents an "emotional huddle" of sorts, and in its center there lies a game system as an agent, the actions of which are predicted as well—through trial and error of scripts and schemas that are channelled through game mechanics to the game elements and system behaviour.[69]

Leino also makes game emotions dependent on gameplay conditions, in order to find the specificity of games as objects:

> What is common with all players' experiences with single-player computer games, even those with an open-ended "simulation game" like *Sim City 4*, is that they can be described in terms of negotiating the gameplay condition in one way or another. This applies also to "transgressive play," those players' actions which are "symbolic gesture[s] of rebellion against the tyranny of the game" and attempt to break out from the role of "ideal player" implied by the game. . . . Consider for example constructing a city in *Sim City 4* just to raze it by refusing to call in the fire brigade when an accidental blaze breaks out involves negotiating the gameplay condition. Describing the emotions arising from both "constructing" and "razing" the city (including all the smaller-scale projects involved) as meaningful and rational equally necessitate appealing to the gameplay condition as the criteria."[70]

Multiplayer games in particular can create a whole palette of "social feelings" in the gamer; a player might run the emotional gauntlet during a game, feeling anything from rage to joy to betrayal, all because of the trials and tribulations of his on-screen persona. These emotions—even the negative ones—can offer a powerful incentive to keep playing. Jonathan Baron has explored the emotions attached to this kind of game, examining how these simple responses are a powerful element either in motivating or discouraging players, according to their degree of success in the game.[71]

Figure 6.2 Positive in-game emotions: a successful Tauren warrior moving on to the next quest in *World of Warcraft*

There are even players who find joy in destroying the game experience for others. These "grief players" are a part of every gaming community, from the early textual worlds to the game worlds of today, with hundreds of thousands of participants; more to the point, such "players" are a part of every human community. In the world of multiplayer games, these players may wreak havoc, for example, by playing only for the purpose of killing other players or stealing their property. Developers have become more and more aware of the fact that social games not only encourage people to play nicely together but also open the door for a lot of "undesirable behavior." In recent years designers have altered the configuration of games precisely to curb this brand of spiteful activity.[72] Jonas Heide Smith, in his analysis of group behavior in social games, points to the trade-off designers face between allowing a high degree of freedom and restricting action to avoid grief play. He presents indicative data of players' perceptions of different kinds of sabotage in online games, showing that they think sabotage is a significant problem as it can totally spoil their experience of the game.[73] The presence of the grief player reveals the potentially negative reasons why some people, luckily very few, are drawn to video games, and can be linked to the negative effects video game playing can have in some predisposed individuals, as explored in Chapter 9.

Taking a broader approach to the range of parameters affecting players, there is another dimension influencing the ludic experience, which, following Aycock, we call "metaculture." Metaculture includes all the factors beyond the psychological experience of playing, and is defined by a playing community. Aycock uses chess as an example, asking why the satisfaction of winning is greater at some times more than others (when playing an ex-world champion, for instance). The answer lies in the metaculture of chess, which can include everything from international rules, tournaments, and ratings, to journals about the game and the equipment used. All of these elements are significant because they help determine, for example, how important a single game can be, or how players can achieve lasting fame. For instance, the World Cyber Games (WCG) website hosts a "Hall of Fame," where pictures and small bios of the "WCG Legends" are displayed. This title "is given by WGC committee to the players who have won the Grand Final two or more times. WGC and all the world's gamers will remember them forever."[74] Winning, in this case, means much more than just playing a good game.

The metaculture of a game is an array of meanings produced and endorsed by the playing community, something that also occurs for video games, as we will see in a later section. Considering the metaculture of a game completes our understanding of the act of playing, since without it theories of framing such as Csikszentmihalyi's flow (as explained previously) provide an insufficient basis for understanding the experience of playing as a whole.

Who Plays?

You might think that the majority of video game players are maladjusted boys in their teens, but the truth is that the past few years have seen an unprecedented widening of the player base, related to what Jesper Juul has called "a casual revolution." He quotes a report from the Entertainment Software Association that says that 65 percent of US households play video games today, and the average age of a game player is 35 years, as well as a BBC report that says that 59 percent of people between the ages of 6 and 65 play some form of video game.[75] Video games are no longer synonymous with complex and demanding AAA titles; they can also be on-screen solitaire, a round of mahjong, or Wii with the family.

Juul argues that the arcade video games of the 1980s were made for a general audience, but the field became specialized in the 1990s and early 2000s in a way that "alienated many players."[76] The operating difficulty of high-end first-person shooters and the heavy time investment required to play MMORPGs are not for everyone. But even during the years of specialization the biggest successes came from games oriented more toward the mainstream, such as *Myst* or *The Sims*. Juul's point is that lately game designers have begun designing for everyone again, and the casual games of our time "are easy to learn to play, fit well with a large number of players and work in many different situations."[77] He is referring mainly to two new trends: downloadable casual games that can be played in short bursts, like *Cake Mania*, and mimetic interfaces that invite players to use their real-world knowledge and intuition directly, such as *Guitar Hero*. It is rarely the case that games are purely casual or purely hardcore, and most games can be used in different ways (there can be hardcore play of *Bejeweled* and casual play of *Halo*, for example), but the design of a game will tend in one direction or the other.[78]

Hardcore players: People who play games that are difficult to learn and master for extended periods of time. They usually engage with games on a daily basis, and for a larger amount of time.

Perhaps the only sense in which one can meaningfully talk about casual versus **hardcore players** is when considering self-perception. Fewer people will admit to being hardcore players, given the stigma attached to it (uses too much time, is antisocial, etc.), and some people who actually play quite a lot will be hesitant even to admit to playing computer games at all. These people would much rather define themselves as casual gamers. On the other hand, some proud hardcore players are actually afraid that the current focus on casual games will dumb down their hobby.[79]

Regardless, video games are becoming a more "natural" pastime, one that fits into the lives of increasing numbers of people, and this has consequences for the types of games we enjoy and the development of the game industry.

Female Players

In order better to understand the issue of self-perception as a gamer and the position of players in relation to the game industry, we will consider a particular group of players: women. The video game industry is overwhelmingly dominated by men. If we are to fully understand the culture created by those who play video games, we must examine the role of gender in the industry.

Though there are a few well-known female designers—such as Brenda Laurel or Roberta Williams—men control both the production and consumption ends of the industry, with the products themselves mainly targeted at a male audience. However, there is a female game audience: in the United States and Western Europe, female gamers constitute 39 percent and 25 percent, respectively, of the total number of active gamers; in Japan, 36 percent of players are women, and nearly 70 percent of all women have a game machine at home.[80]

In the past, the industry has tried to attract young female players by giving games a more girl-friendly appearance. There is the well-known case of *Ms. Pac-Man*, a game strikingly similar to *Pac-Man*, apart from the pink bow worn by the main character. Nintendo also started marketing a pink version of their Gameboy, aimed at girls even though the games themselves were the same. Now their portable console, the Nintendo DS, is available in a whole rainbow of colors, allowing both boys and girls to choose beyond stereotypes.

For many years video games based on the Barbie doll, such as *Barbie Fashion Designer*, have been typical girl best sellers, even though neutral games such as *Tetris*, *Myst*, or *Frogger* have allegedly enjoyed enduring success among female players. Other games that early on helped open up game culture to girls include music-based games such as *PaRappa the Rapper* or *Fluid*, dancing games such as *Spice World* or *Beatmania*,[81] and games that involve the whole body, such as Wii games. Some of the massively multiplayer online role-playing games have an important fanbase among women; according to Nicholas Yee, 16 percent of *EverQuest* players are female.[82] In recent years the ubiquitous nature of smartphones with almost unlimited supply of games have also paved the way for more gender-balanced availability of games. Games like *Candy Crush Saga* and *Hay Day* have in that sense made an impact similar to *The Sims* or *FarmVille* in drawing in new player types, especially women. Still, the controversy surrounding *Kim Kardashian: Hollywood* suggests that gender is still something that needs to be factored into the equation of game audiences, although the exact implications are still elusive. Allegedly, the Kim Kardashian game became a success because it found a way to reach the female audience not typically attracted to popular builder games like *Clash of Clans* and *Boom Beach*.

From this varied list of games, it is difficult to extract a set of characteristics typical of the games girls prefer.[83] There seem to be some games that attract both boys and girls, although the two genders display different playing strategies, as reported by Kafai in relation to the game *Where in the World Is Carmen Sandiego?* She has studied the differences in children's attitudes to video games by asking boys and girls to design games to teach mathematics and science to younger children, concluding that gender differences might be more context dependent than innate.[84] It is impossible to say if these results can be extrapolated to games in general, but they indicate the importance in empirical research of taking into account the context in which players are observed; for example, changing a parameter like the genre of the game can produce completely different results.

Nevertheless, Schott and Horrell have conducted a series of interviews with girl gamers and have been able to isolate several characteristics:

> Specifically, girl gamers identified a preference for third-person role-play games that contain animal/creature based characters rather than highly gendered human figures. In addition to these factors, games also needed to allow girl gamers the freedom to explore the virtual setting of the game. This was supported by the finding that girl gamers rejected games such as sports games and violent, combat focused games that are not open to creative interpretation.[85]

Girls in this study were also aware of the sexism in games and wished that gender representation was more balanced and realistic. A later study from 2011 stresses that it is important to distinguish between "core" gamers and "noncore" gamers. This distinction resembles the terms "casual gamers" and "hardcore gamers" but has a slightly more precise definition that focuses on classic game genres like shooters, racing, roleplaying ("core"), as opposed to small puzzle games ("noncore"). The core gamers play these at least once per week, whereas the noncore gamers may play once a week but in a different genre.

> Overall, gender remained an element of considerable importance, suggesting that men and women have distinct game playing styles. Those gender differences, however, often depend on a player's previous experience with core genres.[86]

Generally, the study did support that, for example, women had less preference for violent video games but not that women were less interested in competitive games. The study also found that noncore gamers had a preference for simpler games, but this was not a general gender characteristic. Interestingly, the study didn't find any major gender differences in relation to preference for game setting or narrative components.

Female players had a preference for customizing their avatar, which is also in line with previous perceptions. It was found that female players have a stronger preference for playing with an avatar of their own sex, whereas the same was not true for male players.

Concerns of the female players in these studies reflect the two main types of academic research into the area of gender and video games: that which deals with representation of women in video games, often working from a cultural studies or literary perspective; and that which deals with women as players of games, usually from a sociological or ethnographic perspective.

From the former, we have a number of studies that analyze the content of video games to discover how women are represented. These studies are usually very critical of the medium, finding in video games the worst kind of social prejudice and objectification of women. Their arguments are very similar to those of feminist critics dealing with cinema or television, as they concentrate on the symbolic weight of representation; common themes are the stereotypical representation of male and female bodies and behaviors[87] or the male gaze.[88]

The case of Lara Croft, the gun-toting pin-up central character of the *Tomb Raider* series, is paradigmatic of these concerns. The character has drawn the attention of theorists for years, but their analyses have not always paid attention to the game as such.[89] Helen Kennedy's "Lara Croft: Feminist Icon or Cyberbimbo? On the Limits of Textual Analysis" summarizes these arguments, and Lara Croft's ambivalent role as both an action heroine (finally a female character with an active role in a video game!) and an eroticized object of the male gaze with a great deal of voyeuristic appeal. Kennedy argues that watching Lara is not the same as playing as Lara, that is, video games foster a "complex relationship between subject and object."[90] On this same topic, Mary Flanagan has argued that playing (that is, manipulating) Lara's body takes us a step further than watching it:

> More than the indulgence of looking at these stars within filmic worlds, we now embrace the very real pleasures of controlling these desired bodies: Lara is at the apex of a system in which looking manifests into doing, into action.[91]

On the other side of the screen, there is also significant and fruitful research into women and girls as players of video games. A seminal early work in this area is the book co-edited by Justine Cassell and Henry Jenkins, *From Barbie to Mortal Kombat: Gender and Computer Games*, which appeared in 1998 and included a series of contributions from researchers, as well as interviews with women in the game industry and players. The book paints a broad picture of the world of girls and games, going beyond stereotypes and examining what kinds of games girls play and why. It looks at games specifically produced for girls and at how girls play games that are traditionally boy-dominated. More than ten years later, Castell and Jenson suggested in a research paper that the field had not moved forward since then. Often the gender issue was ignored, browsed quickly over, or handled through simplistic and superficial models.

Since its authors are worried about girls being "left out" of the computer revolution, an aim of the book is to offer some answers as to how girls could be integrated into the world of video games without necessarily having to adopt boys' culture and instead modifying the culture itself so that there is space for everybody. The editors believed that female-run and female-oriented game companies could transform the market in what they called "the girl's game movement," something that has not happened yet, even though, as Jenkins argues, the success of games such as *The Sims* might indicate an industry shift.[92] For Jenkins, *The Sims* is an incarnation of the ideal version of a game for girls as described by Brenda Laurel:

- Leading characters are everyday people that girls can easily relate to and are as real to girls as their best friends.

- The goal is to explore and have new experiences, with degrees of success and varying outcomes.
- Play focuses on multisensory immersion, discovery, and strong story lines.
- Games feature everyday "real-life" settings as well as new places to explore.
- Success comes through development of friendships.[93]

If these features become more interesting to both girls and boys, the industry might progress toward gender-neutral gaming, according to Jenkins. We might be getting there through casual games. However, there are still significant differences in the way males and females approach play. Both girls and adult female players dedicate less time to this activity than their male counterparts. In the case of girl gamers, the explanation might lie with the scarcity of attractive game content and the girls' perception that it is a male-dominated culture.[94] This is confirmed by statistics about female players' hours of gaming, which show that younger players spend more time on games than older players.[95]

Beyond game content and player demographics, there is another important aspect to consider in relation to girls and video games: the gendering of gamespaces and gaming practices. According to Jo Bryce and Jason Rutter, public gaming spaces—namely the arcade—are typically male-dominated,[96] and research has found that women prefer playing in domestic spaces. As a result, women are less likely to play certain games, such as first-person shooters. Along with the spaces where games are played, we should also consider the formation of groups of female gamers and the development of their own communities. Bryce and Rutter present a useful introduction to the multifaceted nature of the intersection between gender and computer gaming in "Killing Like a Girl: Gendered Gaming and Girl Gamers' Visibility."[97]

In her report "Girls/Women Just Want to Have Fun: A Study of Adult Female Players of Digital Games," Aphra Kerr, after presenting empirical studies of women gamers and game producers and an analysis of gaming industry advertising strategies, concludes that women gamers are "largely invisible to the wider gaming community and producers."[98]

But why do women play? What pleasure do they derive from engaging with mostly male-oriented games? In her paper "Multiple Pleasures: Women and Online Gaming," T. L. Taylor offers an explanation based on empirical data gathered through extensive ethnographic and interview research centered on MMORPGs, arguably the favorite genre of online female gamers (with the exception of traditional games—from cards to puzzles to trivia-based games—that many people play at their workplaces[99]). Looking at *EverQuest*, Taylor found that women enjoy a very varied range of activities in the game. Some of these won't surprise us, such as socializing or exploring the game world, but other activities are typically associated with male players, including an interest in game standing and progress, identity performance, advancement in the game by way of improved skill, team sports, and combat. From this list, it might be striking to some that girls also seem to enjoy competition and that they do not abhor violence, even stylized as it is in this game. Also revealing is the fact that female *EverQuest* players "often struggle with the conflicting meanings around their avatars," due to their stereotypical appearances, so that, while they enjoy being able to choose an original appearance (instead of a pre-made avatar), they often ignore it during play. What the success of MMORPGs demonstrates is that "games that simply focus on friendship and sociality may overlook the fact that girls are looking for games that also push them to take risks and where there is a chance to be absolutely and unequivocally dominant."[100]

With the so-called Gamergate incident in 2014, the gender discussion took on a life entirely of its own and showed that the issues surrounding gender in games are more complex than ever, and events turned grim like no one could have imagined. Events started out small with an allegedly biased review and eventually escalated into a concentrated campaign of attacks against several women in the game industry and those who defended them, including death and rape threats, hacker attacks, and the threat of a mass shooting.[101]

Gamergate expanded more broadly to involve the entire ecosystem around video games including those who develop games, those who fund them, who write about them, and who play them, just to mention some of the more important stakeholders, all broadly centered around the issue of diversity in gaming. Ultimately, it became a big ugly fight where nobody was quite sure what was up and down in a chaotic web of discussion on pretty much any digital forum invented thus far.

As the dust settled, it was argued that the discussion sparked such strong reactions because games are undergoing a transformation away from subculture and toward the mainstream. Gamergate fundamentally became a battle about what games are and what they should be, as illustrated by Leigh Alexander's Gamasutra article,[102] where she called out the community and brought the issues of sexism in the game community and, more generally, the harassment faced by women online, into the forefront of the discussion. Although it is unfair to label all gamers misogynistic, there is definitely a strong undercurrent. Game culture is today still male dominated on the inside (developers, publishers, journalists, etc.) but less so on the outside where female players are abundant albeit underserved in comparison to the male audience—something that may explain the surprise hit of the app *Kim Kardashian: Hollywood*. Although that game may not be the favorite dish that some feminists are looking for, some actually claim that it is more progressive than most games out there.[103] Changes have happened over the last 20 years with computer science broadly speaking becoming less of a male ghetto and games becoming way more mainstream. Still, we are far away from games becoming a balanced voice for society, and the game community still has strong connotations of what could be described as the smell of deep-fried chicken from the grill bar, where we found the arcade machines hosting some of the first popular video games for teenage boys. As we have seen in Chapter 4, the genres that came to prevail for a long period resembled what would in the 1950s be labeled as good activities for fresh lads— sports, guns, fighting, competition—adrenalin-pumping genres that have now increasingly been challenged by what some gamers decry as "house-wife" games like *Bejeweled, FarmVille,* or *Hay Day.*

The backlash experienced by the female members of the game industry vocal in the debate, most noticeably Zoe Quinn, Brianna Wu, and Anita Sarkeesian, revealed a strong segment of video game culture opposed to the growing diversity in games. Unfortunately, it also meant that the criticism toward the questionable ethics in a lot of game journalism never really received the attention it deserved. Game journalism is in many countries still struggling to come of age and not to be reliant on influence from major game publishers (through for example advertising) to maintain balanced reviews.[104]

Game Communities

As we have seen, video games have now become a way for people to define their identities, to find like-minded individuals, and participate in a world that merges with their "real life" in new and exciting ways. With so many motivations, and so many desires, player culture is a fascinating world, and a crucial element of understanding video games today. One way to look at player culture is to investigate the social clustering of players around their favorite games. Celia Pearce notes that communities of play have existed before video games, and the story of multiplayer games can be studied in terms of communities;[105] but now they are truly flourishing due to the Internet.

In our ever-more networked world, there is a substantial amount of research into virtual communities—which, as opposed to real-life communities, don't meet physically but over the Internet. The research on virtual communities typically focuses on MUDs and social networks of various kinds, from website fora that talk about favorite soaps to dating sites.[106] It is also worth noting that gaming communities (like all other communities) are often exclusive. A player has to prove her worth by living up to community norms and developing a certain amount of social capital. Gaming communities are also prone to some conflict, as we've seen; in addition, socializing has a negative side when people are mobbed or cannot agree about what constitutes appropriate behavior.

Game community:
Players who interact with a high frequency around a game, and may develop a particular set of norms and forms of interaction.

To understand what constitutes a **game community**, let's explore the characteristics of a virtual community, as described by researcher Tom Erickson[107] (as game communities will mostly be virtual[108]). Erickson has summarized the available research on virtual communities and reached the conclusion that most definitions contain the following elements: membership, relationships, commitment, collective values, shared goods, and duration. If we apply them to a persistent online game like *EverQuest,* we will obtain some parameters to understand the kinds of communities that grow up around video games, as well as help us distinguish between them. *EverQuest* has been one of the best-selling fantasy games of all time. It was first published in 1999 and still has a significant online community;[109] because of its size and durability, it offers a good case study in the dynamics of a game community.

- *Membership*: All players must sign up for their own account in order to participate in *EverQuest.* In contrast to the vague standards of some other communities—an online forum, for example, where people can post anonymously and come and go as they please—membership in a game like *EverQuest* is a prerequisite for entering the online world. Membership is tied to the player and not the characters, and one membership account allows a player to maintain several characters at the same time.

- *Relationships*: The fictional world of *EverQuest*, called Norrath, is governed by a set of rules, explained in the game's instructions and on numerous websites. These rules also determine the social relationships between players. A player begins the game by choosing a race and a class (profession) for his characters; this decision determines everything from how other races and classes will view them to what territories they can and cannot venture into. Relationships among races are determined partly by the fictional history of Norrath provided by the game creators, and partly by fantasy literature conventions (for example, dwarves do not like elves). The abilities of the player character also play a role, in that a higher level means a higher social status. Relationships become formalized when players organize in guilds and acquire rights and obligations toward the other members of the guild. For example, a guild might want to carry out a raid on a particular night, and need all its members to participate in order to have a chance of success; this can put pressure on the players to log on, even though they might have other real-life commitments that make it difficult. These social bonds can thus affect the real-world relationships of players.
- *Commitment and generalized reciprocity*: Commitment to *EverQuest* is simple but costly: the game demands hours of your time. Dedicated players spend a large amount of time in the fictional world, and usually expect a similar level of dedication from fellow players, especially if they adventure together in ad hoc groups or organized guilds. Generalized reciprocity means respecting the rules of the game. These rules can be "hard"—the type that game administrators will enforce; for example, the rule that you are not supposed to kill another player unless you're in a PVP (**player versus player**) server—but they can also be "soft"—either informal or unwritten; for example, you shouldn't talk "OOC" (out of character) in a guild meeting as it can annoy fellow players. Different groups of players will share different "soft" conventions.
- *Shared values and practices*: *EverQuest* players are mostly interested in advancing their characters (character advancement is the main goal of the informal genre of role-playing games, and thus the most common practice). Secondary goals can be anything from exploring the virtual environment to engaging in conversation.[110] Players advance their characters with very similar strategies: usually solitary quests and easy killings (rats, snakes) in the first levels, and then more complicated group quests as the levels increase. The shared values of a game community are manifested in game behavior (it is usual, for example, for experienced players to help new ones with their initial quests, and even offer them pieces of equipment as gifts) and on the websites and fora, where players discuss the game and how people should or should not behave.

Player versus player (PVP): Usually refers to a type of online role-playing game in which human players can fight each other.

- *Collective goods*: The main shared collective good is the world of Norrath, duplicated on several servers around the world. Characters also have similar ways of collecting goods; for example, by looting enemy corpses. Sometimes players trade with items from their own inventories. This collective exchange of materials was not intended by the designers of the original game,[111] since every object is supposed to be acquired by a person's "labor" in the game (by killing a monster, for example, or completing a quest). Sharing and other creative exchanges raise the interesting question of who owns the virtual goods in a game world.[112]
- *Duration*: This is one of the main issues when considering typical digital communities: can they be called communities if they do not exist all the time but only in limited time frames (for instance, through email or during sporadic chat meetings)? For some, only the persistent groups are communities, while the majority of researchers are willing to call more sporadic interactions a community. The *EverQuest* world is available 24 hours a day, seven days a week, so a player can join whenever she likes. Even if no other players are online with you, the illusion of a living community still holds, as you can nevertheless explore the world, go on individual quests, and interact with numerous characters (called "bots") controlled by the computer. The community's frontier is also extended by the player's participation in the game's metaculture, as we'll see later—out-of-game fora, in which players use email or instant messaging or Internet chat rooms to discuss various aspects of the game. Some communities go on existing even though the original game world closes, as Celia Pearce has shown.[113]

The dedicated fans of MMORPGs have created thriving game communities, but they are not alone. Other genres, particularly shooting and strategy games, have given rise to communities, growing up around games like *Counter-Strike, Quake, Star Craft*, and *Age of Empires*. The loyal fans of these games belong to clans, maintain dedicated homepages, and participate in intense discussions. Clans and guilds[114] are interesting mini-societies in which power is organized, fought for, and exerted, actions are discussed and planned, and levels of dedication are high.

The strength of game communities is often tied to the persistence of a game, or the amount of time average players dedicate to it. A committed MMORPG player can immerse herself for hundreds of hours in the many quests of the game. However, even if the game world itself is not persistent—as is the case, for example, for most shooters—the community of fans can utilize the game-space to create a sense of continuity. Thus, in a shooter like *Battlefield 1942*, players will create individual derivations of the game with specific rules. A group of people who all play on a particular server might settle on certain rules of behavior, and ways to enforce these. For example, a group of *Battlefield 1942* players might agree that camping[115] is not allowed, even though the game rules cannot prevent it. As more and more groups follow suit, what emerges is a series of subcultures built around the game but each with its own peculiarities, which in turn increase the devotion of its members.

The fan culture has taken a new twist in recent years as more varied publishing formats have arisen. On Steam you can now buy early access to games in development, which is often done by fans to get the latest game, give input and support the game. Through Kickstarter and Indiegogo, fans can support a game even earlier—often all the way from the first visuals. They can support the game by pledging anywhere from $1 to $20,000. Hereby fans earn influence and respect by picking the right game and showing a vested interest. Backers are also usually rewarded on a tiered system, with a number of unique merchandise to demonstrate their devotion beyond just the game itself. Game developers have gone to great lengths to come up with creative rewards for early supporters of their games. This includes, for example, naming a character in the game after a backer or meeting the development team in person, which can easily cost several thousand dollars. The above relationship between players and developers resembles that known from beta testing MMORPGs, but there is a crucial difference: money. The player has actually paid a significant amount betting on the game developer's success, and sometimes has a very particular vision in mind for how the game should turn out. This can lead to conflicts between game developers and players as game development can often drag on, be completely cancelled, or take a turn in a new and unexpected direction.

What does all this accomplish? According to a study by Florence Chee and Richard Smith, game communities provide players with positive values absent from their real lives. They argue that the game helps to fulfill a need, which is not the same as saying that it creates it, and certainly presents no psychological danger for players.[116]

Cooperation and Conflict in Games

Multiplayer games are a balance of cooperation and conflict between players, a crucial point for the formation of player culture. Definitions of computer games usually stress that games imply conflict.[117] Competition can take a number of forms. It can be strictly zero-sum, as in most strategy games where you either win or die trying, or more ambiguous, as when players of a console RPG must cooperate to achieve overall goals but also compete to some extent for resources. These examples all qualify as "intra-mechanic," that is, they concern player relationships that are shaped by the actual game code.

There is also a type of conflict that is "extra-mechanic," which does not stem from the rules of the game itself (though it can be influenced by the game). It is usually this type of conflict which causes serious strife, and not, for instance, that Player A shot down Player B in a competitive game. In other words, conflict in itself is not a problem. An example will serve to illustrate the issue: soon after the 1997 release of the early MMORPG *Ultima Online*, massive tension developed between players who did not agree on the norms of behavior.[118] As one critic commented, the world soon resembled "Afghanistan after the Soviets left: unremitting random violence, feuds, continual victimization of the weak by the strong."[119] Since then, most online game designers have usually gone to great lengths to limit the opportunities for destructive play. Often this has taken the form of severely limiting player options.

Clearly, there are infinite ways in which players may upset other players; and anecdotes from practically every online game abound. Here we shall focus on three main categories of the most common offenses—cheating, the violation of local norms, and grief play.

Although clearly relevant to an understanding of gaming, the world of cheating had received limited academic attention,[120] until Mia Consalvo published her book *Cheating: Gaining Advantage in Videogames*.[121] We can define this transgression as any behavior that gives the cheater an unfair advantage over opponents, and/or anything that runs contrary to the spirit of the game. The terms "unfair" and "spirit of the game" are clearly subjective, and make cheating itself an altogether social construction.

However, some consensus exists and the term is not used in an entirely arbitrary way. Consalvo, who has asked players themselves to define cheating, has isolated three categories: anything other than getting through the game all on your own, breaking the rules of the game (code), or cheating in relation to another human player.[122] In all cases, the advantage obtained must be somehow "unfair." If your brother was an expert *Tekken* player and you had never tried the game before, using those skills to crush you in battle would not be unfair (although it might not live up to higher ideals). Repositioning chess pieces while you were distracted, however, would constitute cheating, since it is unfair, and goes against the spirit of the game (in which strategic skill should decide the winner).

Some techniques may run against the spirit of a game without being technically unfair. These are in fact the most common transgressions. The phenomenon known as "camping" is one example. Camping refers to the less-than-brave tactic of placing one's first-person shooter character in a highly secure spot and then waiting patiently for the enemy to come close enough to be surgically dispatched. Camping is not technically unfair, since the option is equally available to the enemy (in which case the game would grind to a halt). In fact, since camping is such a successful strategy, many players will argue that it actually does not go against the spirit of the game (that is, the intentions of the designers). If so, then camping becomes a question of local norms.

Having the core rules refereed by an impartial machine, video games clearly offer far less opportunity for confusion over winning conditions than do traditional games. But despite the seeming clarity offered by a computer's algorithms, multiplayer games are still often dependent on players reaching a mutual understanding about how the game should be played. Such implicit rules are the subject of intense debate among players. Often such discussions speak directly to the question of the "spirit of the game," while at other times discussion hinges on the interpretation of specific local rules, or player actions as regards these rules.

For instance, if the player community for a real-time strategy game finds that particular civilizations are too powerful, a player who has chosen one of these civilizations might not be accepted for entry into the game. Should the player insist strongly, she may end up being evicted from the game. Interestingly, when an implicit rule reaches a certain broad degree of consensus it is often built into the actual rules of game sequels or later games in the same genre. Consalvo, in her empirical study of cheating practices, has found that a lot of gamers cheat; it is not about subverting the game system; instead it is a way to keep playing through a game that is too difficult, boring, or plain bad.[123]

The broad category of "grief play" includes any player behavior that intentionally causes stress in another player; typically it is unrelated to the winning conditions of the game. A common example is unprovoked harassment through an in-game chat channel. Where stress-inducing behavior is a consequence of a player pursuing a personal goal, Chek Yang Foo and Elina M. I. Koivisto have suggested that the term "greed play" is more appropriate in cases where the player may be unscrupulous but his actions are not motivated by a wish to harm innocent bystanders.[124]

Grief play, in other words, can be understood as the intentional causing of distress in another player. There are gray areas, however, since all players are represented in a gamespace by some type of avatar. Thus, if one player has created an explicitly antisocial character, it can obviously be difficult to distinguish between behavior that is aimed at displeasing another player and behavior that is merely consistent with the character's identity.[125] In general, we should note that grief play is not surprising. It is simply a manifestation of deviance, a gaming parallel of real-world situations that happen every day.

Game Creativity and Metaculture

Some players do not content themselves with just the game. In-game communication with other players (in games where it exists) is not enough. And so, metaculture is born. In order to bring a game beyond the screen, so to speak, players construct elaborate out-of-game meeting places, usually virtual, where they can do anything from discussing a given game to creating ranking systems for evaluating their performances. Modding and official competitions are also group efforts, and range from fully official (for example, a "community" that is based on the game developer's own web page), to semi-official (for example, websites with formal links to developers[126]), to websites wholly independent of the game's creators. The existence of such Internet support can prove essential to the longevity of a game. So even games that have no online component (or only a weak one) may be profoundly affected by the existence of the World Wide Web.

Often dedicated players will keep a game alive long after its release (and long after the developer has turned its attention to marketing other games). An example of this is the website *Age of Kings Heaven*, centered around *Age of Empires II: Age of Kings*.[127] Whereas the original game was released in 1999, players remain active (as of early 2015) posting news stories, strategy guides and other materials, and participating in forum discussions. The modding forum contains over 1.2 million posts, testifying to a level of player interest that goes way beyond a mere desire to play the game itself.

Such dedication among fans means more than sharing information and discussing strategies. As players congregate, they form subcultures centered around a specific game but also placing the players in the wider culture of gaming itself. For instance, avid *Halo* players can feel a sense of belonging when interacting with fellow *Halo* fans. They will develop particular subcultural slang. Such slang will only be fully intelligible to other devoted *Halo* players; it will be partly understandable by fans of other shooters, only vaguely understandable by fans of other genres (like the strategy genre), and close to unintelligible to nongamers.

Undoubtedly, game-specific lingo is a form of metaculture that emerges because it is an efficient way of communicating for the initiated. But it also highlights one's seniority within the social strata that build up around a game. Your language is a way of distinguishing between the experienced and the newcomer, and thus is a way to assert one's position. In other words, even if it was not invented for that purpose, subcultural language becomes a social stratification tool.

Leetspeak: Also referred to as 1337 sp3@k. It is a dialect of online communication (typically between gamers) which is written using certain rules of substitution (e.g. "3" for "E"), and which can be very difficult to understand for anyone who is not active in online communities.

Nowhere is this clearer than in the case of "leetspeak."[128] **Leetspeak** or just "leet" is a code (or more precisely, a cipher) which specifies alternative ways of writing English words.[129] A phenomenon such as leetspeak may well be understood as a reaction to the mainstreaming of gaming—a way to recreate some of the subcultural exclusivity enjoyed by (some) gamers in the past. Certainly one's command of leet, like any other "in-the-know" form of speech, is a signal of one's seniority within gaming.

Beyond language, there are many other creative fan practices, such as modding, as mentioned previously, the creation of walkthroughs, the writing of fan fiction, and so forth. Wirman talks about "game-related fan productivity" and distinguishes between instrumental and expressive forms, interestingly linking it to gamers' different interests and playing styles:

> role-players, players who play the game in-character and attempt to identify with it, are normally seen as interested in the backstory and narrative, while power gamers, players who aim to play as effectively as possible, concentrate on goals, such as completing game quests. In other words, role-players seem expressively productive and power gamers instrumentally productive.[130]

Productive play: Creative activities inspired by games, in which players create scenarios (mods), fiction (fan fiction, movies, machinima, etc.), or game aids (such as walkthroughs) to extend the experience of their favorite games.

A prime example of metaculture is "poaching." This term refers to any activity where fans creatively reuse content from other media. A classic example is a fan writing fiction using the characters from their favorite television series, as Henry Jenkins reports in *Textual Poachers: Television Fans and Participatory Culture*.[131] Celia Pearce has noted that video game–inspired **productive play** goes beyond poaching in other media, as sometimes it can transform the virtual worlds that have spawned the practices, as in the case of the *Uru: Ages Beyond Myst* community.[132] Andrew Burn

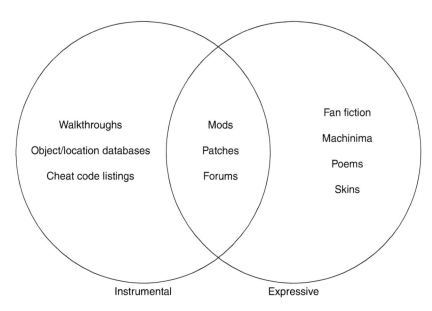

Walkthroughs

Object/location databases

Cheat code listings

Mods

Patches

Forums

Fan fiction

Machinima

Poems

Skins

Instrumental   Expressive

Figure 6.3 Overview of instrumental and expressive productivity

has studied different kinds of fan "poaching" based on video game texts: writing walkthroughs, creative writing that expands game universes, and manga comic strips inspired by characters or events in games.[133] Let's look at these in more detail.

The first involves the production of support texts for games, such as strategy guides, encyclopedias, or walkthroughs (a scene-by-scene reenactment of the experience of navigating your way through a game, with hints about what to do at each turn). Authors present themselves as "experts" in the community, the best-known ones will have their texts downloaded by many, and they will become authorities on a particular game. Creating these documents is an extremely time-consuming activity with uncertain rewards, since nothing guarantees that other players will endorse one's version of the game.

At the other end of the scale, creative fiction writers and manga artists who are inspired by games are not interested in gameplay at all but only in the narrative, or rather the possible narrative inspired by a particular game. They will elaborate on a character's history, retell events that happened in the game, adding explanations and feelings, and even write poetry based on their favorite characters. Stories, poems, and drawings expand the emotional universe in ways that the game cannot.[134]

Another genre of fan fiction that we could call "tribute movies" has also spread quickly across the Internet and has garnered a lot of attention in the gaming community. Some are put together with video editing programs, others with Flash, while still others are recorded using the game engines themselves, so fans can make their own animated films ("**machinima**"[135]). Fan movies reuse characters, settings, and story lines from games, usually with some humorous or ironic purpose, as in the famous "All Your Base Are Belong

Machinima: The practice of manipulating video games to produce animated films.

to Us."[136] Others take their source material to new heights; for example, Alexander Leon's *Mario Brothers* movies.[137] And the machinima genre has grown enormous since the first *Diary of a Camper* movie, based on *Quake*. All these semiotic expansions are the varied efforts of a very active fan community; the result is that favorite games are kept alive as cultural texts far longer than the usual "shelf-life" calculations of industry would predict. Players who make machinima become producers, and some cultural critics argue that this kind of fan production is more active than fan production in traditional media.[138]

"**Mods**" are modifications to or extensions of commercial games; they are created by players and then exchanged with other fans in active online fora. Though players have typically focused most of their modding efforts on shooting games, all types of video games have been modded, from *Civilization* to *Grand Theft Auto*, *SimCity* to *Europa Universalis* to *Amnesia: The Dark Descent*. As with poaching, an important effect of this kind of practice is that it extends the life cycle of successful games. *Half-Life*, a single-player shooter, for example, gave birth in 1999 to the most successful mod of all: a multiplayer version of the same game called *Counter-Strike*. In modifications like this one, fans can correct bugs in the game, construct new levels and maps, create new "skins" (or character avatars), and even modify certain rules so that the result can be a different game entirely.

Modding can probably be traced back to the beginning of video game history, and enthusiasts were already tinkering with Commodore 64 titles in the 1980s. But it was not until the early 1990s that the phenomenon started to spread, when the first modified versions of *Wolfenstein 3D* began flooding the Net. Game developers rapidly realized that this activity could be beneficial, and started facilitating **modders**' work in various ways. Developers began to separate the main program of a game from the media files (such as skins), so that modders would not destroy the original program. The first game to allow for this was *Doom*, in 1993.[139] Some modders have been hired by game companies, and this is increasingly recognized as an acceptable way to get a foot inside the industry.

Modder: A person that makes modifications (mods) of existing games.

But modding is not only interesting from the industry point of view. The study of modding practices can also shed light on the ways video games operate as cultural objects, producers of meaning, and discourses. Hanna Wirman's work on fan practices and their relation to gender discourses is a good example of the kinds of insights this area of study can produce.[140]

A further example of metaculture—which also furthers the connection between devoted fans and the game industry—is beta-tester events. Today, most video game producers use large numbers of "beta testers" while developing a game. The beta testers are usually dedicated players that try new games, helping both to tweak the formal rules and to seed the ground for the more informal culture in the game. From a game developer perspective, this "hotline" to the game community is crucial to ensuring the success of the game, and also to reducing the cost of testing,[141] avoiding the need to hire lots of people and pay them a salary to test the game.

As we can see, some gamers invest themselves deeply in the culture surrounding games and gaming. And as the discussion of modding above

Figure 6.4 Gizmopolitan, a fictitious magazine: productive players of *World of Warcraft*

illustrates, the resources of fan culture are becoming increasingly important in the games business and culture. However, we should be careful of assuming that these practices are more emancipatory than other kinds of media fandom. They are creative and can be seen positively; Celia Pearce talks, for example, of "productive play."[142] However, Hanna Wirman warns that:

> instead of independent DIY culture, game cultures remain very dependent on a mass market, and the most visible fan texts are altered from or based on those popular games. It is also worth noting that in the end, only a small percentage of all the players contribute to the production of new texts. While the highly productive power gamers may appear to

occupy the most extreme position of a cocreator, even they work within the varying economic and legal boundaries and regulations set by global corporations.[143]

E-Sports

e-Sports: The name for video gamers who compete professionally in the most popular games. Also referred to as cyberathletes.

The last area of metaculture we will consider also happens in the shadow of the game industry: the professionalization of play. Just like those who play "physical" sports (for lack of a better way to differentiate), video game "athletes" train by playing a game (or games), find corporate sponsorship, enter gaming tournaments, and win prizes and recognition. As early as 1999, the Descent 3 Championship Tournament had a $50,000 grand prize,[144] and since 2000 the World Cyber Games (WCG) have been held. There are many other championships, but this is the only one where people from six continents play against each other. E-Sports is more evolved in Asia, but the Western world has been catching up during the last years.

Already in 2007, WCG boasted of "a rapidly growing international Olympics in which nearly one million players compete against one another for the title of world champion in separate events."[145]

Many countries now have their own associations and leagues, such as the E-Sports Entertainment Association (ESEA), which organizes tournaments and serves as an information hub for teams and sponsors. In 2007, the ESEA described itself as follows:

> E-Sports EA was created to help promote professional gaming and miti-
> gate the risk and uncertainty that surrounds much of the gaming commu-
> nity. We are creating the infrastructure needed for professional gaming
> teams, players, news sources, and other mediums that are needed to
> develop gaming into an attractive marketing tool. Through strategic
> partnerships and affiliate programs, companies will be able to use differ-
> ent gaming outlets to promote products and services and in turn, allow
> teams to compete in events around the world.[146]

In 2018 just shy of 400 million spectators watched, and the audience is expected to grow with another 15 percent next year. As the audience grows especially driven by better streaming and service like Twitch, so does the revenue. The commercialization of the culture around e-Sports is projected to surpass two billion US dollars within five years.[147]

We also see that sports clubs are joining the area with parallel e-Sports teams, which seems to be driven by the massive audience interest. Apart from helping their members by providing "lessons" on how to play each game or giving them the chance of posting videos of their best game sessions online, the organization has a clear market goal, aimed at making e-Sports as big as traditional sports:

> Spectators fly into different locations just to be amongst the best players, and watch them compete. Media coverage is beginning to catch on, from

traditional news venues like CNN, ABC, and the New York Times to more focused coverage like PC Gamer and Tech TV. With an ever-growing industry in our hands, we must keep feeding the fuel to fire. There is no limit to where competitive gaming will lead to.[148]

From these quotes it is clear that money is still a paramount concern, even when the targeted audience is dedicated gamers. And the cash prizes awarded at the end of a tournament are no doubt a primary motivation for some of these players. But we should not let simple capitalism obscure what is at work here, since gaining fame and glory through playing is an incentive as important as money, if not more so. However, so far, the academic interest has been surprisingly small especially compared to the commercial interest.[149]

The exact definition of e-Sports is still contested, not to mention whether it is even a sport, which continues to be debated.[150] Wagner in 2006 first defined e-Sports as "an area of sport activities in which people develop and train mental or physical abilities in the use of information and communication technologies."[151]

Later researchers have contested this definition as it uses sports without examining the concept in greater detail. Seth, Manning, Keiper, and Olrich (2016) stressed that e-Sports usually is performed online, and under organized formats that is a more fitting starting point. In a closer look they examine whether e-Sports qualifies as a sport. They go through the prerequisites: organized, competitive, skill-based, physical, broad following, and institutionalization.[152] Despite exhibiting a lot of the necessary characteristics and the potential to acquire the missing ones they conclude that e-Sports are not sports. Today e-Sports don't have an institutionalized format that a typical sports discipline will have built over centuries, but the biggest challenge is the lack of gross motor skills (as opposed to fine motor skills). As we will see later indeed e-Sports players stress the physical strain but fundamentally e-Sports involves entirely different muscle groups compared to any other activity typically recognized as sports. In an in-depth study of 26 e-Sports players, the physical strain related to the game exercise is stressed, and they see it akin to sports. They also stressed that the human versus human element and spectator element was a crucial part of the experience—setting it aside from "just" playing video games.[153]

Whether e-Sports may become a "real" sport may change as virtual reality evolves in the future with new interfaces, and e-Sports is consolidated with rules and organizations remains to be seen.

Still, the organized competitions in e-Sports give players the chance to excel at something that might be frowned upon by their families or the general public but that in this way becomes legitimized as a desirable skill and a worthy enterprise.

Is Game Culture Escapism, a Mirror, or Simply Work?

Another group of professional players is the people who "work" in virtual worlds, advancing characters and amassing wealth that they sell to others afterwards for real currency, as explored by Julian Dibbell in his *Play*

Money.[154] The economy of MMORPGs extends into the real world, raising moral and ethical questions related to players' behavior.

We would like to end this chapter by highlighting that player activity and the culture that grows up around video games is not separate from reality, or dismissible as escapism. Gamer activity in its many forms points to the tensions of creative production that characterize the early twenty-first century: the cultural status of the medium, its public perception, and the transitions between play and labor, which Julian Kücklich has aptly named "playbour,"[155] are signs and symptoms of bigger currents in society.

And these meaning-creating frameworks carry implications for the "real world," something that becomes apparent in the struggles around player avatar creation and ownership. What, for example, is an avatar? Is it comparable to a chess piece, or is it in fact an extension of the player, like a virtual limb? The present generation of MMORPGs highlighted the problem, as it became increasingly clear that their status as games (in the magic circle sense) was anything but clear-cut. The status of player activity in these worlds is contested. Does it constitute work (and is it therefore taxable and protected by standard laws) or is it innocent play? The license agreements a user must sign before playing usually take the latter position—not surprisingly, since manufacturers want to make it as easy as possible for players to do nothing more than play. But obviously when they do so players can be spending significant amounts of time and resources living in the game world—building characters, acquiring objects, and anything else they can think of. Many players attach a certain value—even if just gamer's pride—to their activity.

And others agree. Trading websites like eBay serve as markets for game objects and characters (often traded at high real-dollar prices). The monetary value of in-game activities can actually be measured precisely. In *EverQuest* during 2001, the characters in the game combined to produce an annual per capita GNP (gross national product) of $2,266, roughly the same as that of Russia.[156] While this inspired dramatic headlines, we should be clear that this does not mean that *EverQuest* is a rich nation (the number of inhabitants is too small). Giving a rough estimate, Edward Castronova has suggested that the combined economies of all virtual worlds may have an impact on the global economy comparable to that of Namibia or Macedonia.[157]

There are, however, other signs that many virtual worlds cannot be kept separate from real-world influences and legislation. In South Korea more than half of all reported cybercrimes in the first half of 2003 were related to online gaming.[158] In late 2003, a Chinese court ruled that the developers of the online game *Hongyue* were liable for the losses of virtual property suffered by a player. The aggrieved party (one Li Hongchen) argued that the developers had neglected server security, leaving his account vulnerable to hacking.[159]

Meanwhile in 2003, in *The Sims Online*, professor of philosophy Peter Ludlow discovered an in-game brothel with a number of employees played by underage girls. The story made headlines in the *New York Times*, and soon after Ludlow's account was canceled, on the grounds of having advertised his blog within the game (the game developers do not allow the in-game advertisement of real-life goods or services).[160]

Such events highlight the difficulty of separating two spheres of reality, and make it still harder to maintain magic circle notions of the status of games. Players live between the two worlds. In an influential paper on the topic of the application of legal thought to games, Greg Lastowka and Dan Hunter note: "Though virtual worlds may be games now, they are rapidly becoming as significant as real-world places where people interact, shop, sell, and work."[161]

To conclude, we would adhere to T.L. Taylor's words: "My call then is for nondichotomous models. One of the biggest lessons in Internet studies is that the boundary between online and offline life is messy, contested, and constantly under negotiation."[162] Games are of course designed and produced industrially, and have meaning as aesthetic artifacts, but they are transformed by players, who are producers of culture,[163] and how this happens is likely to occupy game scholars for many years.

DISCUSSION QUESTIONS

- Think about your media consumption. What do you expect from different media, such as newspapers, books, music, television, and film? Compare them to video games: what can other media forms do that video games can't, and what can video games do that other media can't?

- Why do you think sections of the public are so worried about the violent content in video games? What is your perception of video game violence?

- Why do people play? Make a list of the different motivations mentioned by students in your class and see which are the most common.

- Think about your identity as a player. Do the people close to you know you play video games? Why, or why not? Is it something you talk about with new people you meet?

- What kind of feelings do you experience when playing games? How do they relate to other players? How is playing games different from other kinds of socializing in this respect?

- Discuss the differences between games that require heavy participation in a community and those played casually. What defines a player as a hardcore rather than a casual gamer?

- Pick a few recent games you all know and discuss how they represent women, and what the female characters can do in the game. Do women like to play them—why, or why not?

- Does your online (video game) life affect your offline life? If yes, how? If not, why not?

- Have you ever created something inspired by a game (e.g. fan fiction, a mod, a walkthrough)? Discuss why players engage in production practices based on their favorite games and what they get out of it.

RECOMMENDED GAMES

America's Army—The game showed how games were becoming more mainstream, and could have an impact on society. Allegedly boosted the number of recruits to the US Army.

Counter-Strike—Began as a mod of *Half-Life* rather than a fully-fledged game. It ended up paving the way for the success of modding—and in the process changed the face of computer games. Now, players can alter computer games quite dramatically. Also, the game is among the top three played e-Sports games.

DOTA 2—The game grows out of *Warcraft III*, and is a multiplayer online arena. Each player controls a hero and cooperate with their team to protect their own base and ultimately destroying the opponents base to claim victory.

FURTHER READINGS

Raessens, J. (2006). Playful identities, or the ludification of culture. *Games and Culture*, *1*(1), 52–57.

(Estimated reading time: 9 minutes)

Shaw, A. (2010). What is video game culture? Cultural studies and game studies. *Games and Culture*, *5*(4), 403–424.

(Estimated reading time: 39 minutes)

Steinkuehler, C. A. (2006). Why game (culture) studies now? *Games and Culture*, *1*(1), 97–102.

(Estimated reading time: 10 minutes)

NOTES

1. Pearce, 2009, p. 177.
2. King and Krzywinska, 2006, p. 38.
3. McLuhan, 1964, p. 199.
4. In his book *Distinction*; Bourdieu, 1987.
5. An example of this might be the popularity of "slash fiction," as examined by Henry Jenkins in *Textual Poachers: Television Fans and Participatory Culture* (1992). This is a particular kind of fan fiction depicting homosexual love between TV or film characters that did not exist in the original; for example, between Captain Kirk and Spock in *Star Trek*.
6. Jenkins, 2005.
7. Flanagan, 2009, p. 1.
8. Flanagan, 2009, p. 2.
9. Dietz, 1998, p. 438.
10. Dietz, 1998.
11. Ramírez, Forteza, Hernando, and Martorell, 2002, replicating Provenzo, 1991.

12. Ramírez et al., 2002.
13. Bogost, 2007, 2008.
14. Wardrip-Fruin, 2009.
15. Flanagan, 2009.
16. Bogost, 2007, p. ix.
17. Bogost, 2007, p. ix.
18. See also a paper written by the game's designers: Zyda et al., 2003.
19. Bogost, 2007, p. 77.
20. Bogost, 2007, p. 78.
21. Wardrip-Fruin, 2009, p. 411.
22. Sicart, 2009, p. 49.
23. Sicart, 2009, p. 89.
24. Sicart, 2009, p. 102.
25. Evans, 2001.
26. Sutton-Smith, 1997.
27. Evans, 2001, pp. 164–180.
28. See Flanagan, 2009, p. 60.
29. Flanagan, 2009, p. 252.
30. On the controversy, see, for example Kent, 2001, pp. 90–92.
31. Consider, for instance, the following quotation from a 1981 *Newsweek* article: "For all their winning ways, video games have been bombarded by controversy. Critics contend that they squander allowances and study time, glorify violence and encourage everything from compulsive gambling to tendinitis (*Space Invaders* wrist). Taking a cue from the pool-troubled elders of the mythical River City, communities from Snellville, Ga., to Boston have recently banned arcades or restricted adolescent access; one legal challenge to the ordinances will be heard by the Supreme Court this week" (Langway, 1981).
32. An example of this is "Video Games and Aggressive Thoughts, Feelings, and Behavior in the Laboratory and in Life," Craig A. Anderson and Karen E. Dill's 2000 study of the effects of violent games. The study begins: "On April 20, 1999, Eric Harris and Dylan Klebold launched an assault on Columbine High School in Littleton, Colorado, murdering 13 and wounding 23 before turning the guns on themselves." The authors thus framed their work as part of the investigation into what caused the tragic school shooting.
33. Griffiths, 2005.
34. The arcade version was released in 1992.
35. Quoting the *Montreal Gazette*, August 7, 1994.
36. Gagne, 2001.
37. www.esrb.org/.
38. A trade group for American game publishers founded in 1994.
39. "Each ESRB rating is based on the consensus of at least three specially trained raters who view content independently of one another. ESRB raters work on a part-time basis and are recruited from one of the most culturally diverse populations— the New York metropolitan area. They must be adults, and typically have experience with children through their profession, education or by being parents or caregivers themselves. They are not required to have advanced skills as computer and video game players since their job is to review content and determine its age-appropriateness, not to assess how challenging or entertaining a particular game is to play. To ensure their objectivity ESRB raters are kept anonymous, and they are not permitted to have any ties to or connections with any individuals or entities in the computer/video game industry" (from the ESRB website, at www.esrb.org/ratings/faq.jsp#14, accessed October 5, 2011).
40. Established in 2003 by the Interactive Software Federation of Europe (ISFE), the trade group for European game publishers. PEGI rates games according to age and by assigning content labels, much as the ESRB does. The difference between the two organizations (apart from the different ratings assigned to individual games) is that the ESRB has agreements with some companies, who pledge not to sell adult-rated games to children. PEGI ratings are entirely voluntary and not enforced by European law, meaning children will be able to buy adult-rated games. Thirty countries use the PEGI rating system. Germany

does not, and has its own, more strict rules for video game content.

41. About this and other controversies, see, for example, GAMEINFORMER, 2006.

42. Developed by Dutch modder Patrick Wildenborg.

43. Around $24.5 million, according to the company's own estimate; GameSpot, 2006.

44. See, for example, BBC News, 2004.

45. See, for example, Good and McWhertor, 2011.

46. Philips, 2011.

47. Jenkins, 2000.

48. Williams, 2003a, 2003b.

49. Williams, 2003a, p. 241.

50. Williams, 2003a, p. 242.

51. See, for example, Schiesel, 2007b.

52. Rutter and Bryce, 2006, pp. 149–150, 162. A good introduction to this approach is "The Use of Games," Chapter 5 in Torill Mortensen's, 2009 book *Perceiving Play: The Art and Study of Computer Games*. The book as a whole is also remarkable for its player focus.

53. Estallo, 1995.

54. Morris, 1999.

55. Wright et al., 2002.

56. Csikszentmihalyi, 1990, p. 67.

57. Csikszentmihalyi, 1990, pp. 46–67.

58. By this we mean that the game's challenges usually start small, giving the player a chance to get used to the interface and the rules, and gradually become more and more difficult as the player masters the game. For example, you can begin as a warrior character in *World of Warcraft* by killing boars with your sword while you learn how the combat system works; as you go up in level, the enemies become more powerful and you need to use more weapons in more complex ways.

59. To this, we could add the fact that video games are different, so that the pleasures of playing *Donkey Kong* are very different from those afforded by a game like *Anarchy Online*. The joy of successful hand-eye coordination in a platform game has nothing (or very little) to do

with that of performance in a role-playing game, even though both activities could prompt players to enter a state of flow.

60. McGonigal, 2011, p. 3.

61. McGonigal, 2011, p. 41.

62. McGonigal, 2011, p. 49.

63. Turkle, 1995. Turkle's book contains extensive empirical information in the form of stories told by participants in multi-user dungeons (MUDs) and role-playing games of various kinds. Other works containing several essays touching on this topic are Williams, Hendricks, and Winkler, 2006; Williams and Smith, 2007.

64. Waskul, 2006, p. 35.

65. Williams et al., 2006; Williams and Smith, 2007.

66. Mortensen, 2007, p. 188.

67. Järvinen, 2008.

68. Particularly his PhD thesis; Leino, 2010.

69. Järvinen, 2008, p. 234.

70. Leino, 2009.

71. Baron, 2004.

72. Talin, 2002.

73. Smith, 2003.

74. WCG, 2010.

75. Juul, 2010, p. 8.

76. Juul, 2010, p. 2.

77. Juul, 2010, p. 5.

78. Juul, 2010, p. 55.

79. Juul, 2010, p. 62.

80. Krotoski, 2004.

81. Schott and Horrell, 2000.

82. Yee, 2001.

83. In Jesper Juul's research on the casual game portal Gamezebo, 93 percent of his survey respondents were female; see Juul, 2010, p. 154. This could be an isolated case or it could reflect the self-selection bias of surveys, but it could also be an indicator that casual gaming is attractive to women.

84. Kafai, 1998.

85. Schott and Horrell, 2000, p. 50. This is consistent with the findings of a report carried out by ELSPA (the Entertainment and Leisure Software Publishers Association), also based on in-depth interviews with women players. Reasons for women's satisfaction with games were "The

presence of a good plot, rich characterisations, choice in how they pursue goals, freedom of self-expression, novelty in challenges, immersion in atmospheric virtual environments, pick-up-and-play capabilities and flexibility" (Krotoski, 2004).

86. Vermeulen, Looy, Courtois, and Grove, 2011.
87. Dietz, 1998; Ramírez et al., 2002.
88. Carr, 2002; Flanagan, 1999.
89. Cassel and Jenkins, 1998; O'Riordan, 2001.
90. Kennedy, 2002.
91. Flanagan, 1999, p. 78.
92. Jenkins, 2000.
93. Jenkins, 2001.
94. Schott and Horrell, 2000.
95. Krotoski, 2004.
96. "Public gaming spaces such as gaming competitions or LAN parties follow similar patterns and can therefore easily be considered to be masculine—i.e. male dominated—spaces. This perception contributes to a constraint on female access and participation in public gaming activities. Such exclusion may be reinforced by the stereotypical and offensive behaviour of males towards females in public gamespaces ranging from belittlement as 'only girls', to patronising female competitors through the well-meaning provision of prize giving, or objectification via the display of pornography at the event" (Bryce and Rutter, 2002, p. 249).
97. Bryce and Rutter, 2002.
98. Kerr, 2003, p. 270.
99. Research indicates that women aged between 35 and 49 "spend more time on online games than any other demographic," referring to the very lucrative online games market of puzzle, card, and trivia-based portals; see Krotoski, 2004, p. 12.
100. Taylor, 2003a, quoting Funk and Buchman.
101. Kain, 2014.
102. Alexander, 2014.
103. http://uk.businessinsider.com/why-kim-kardashian-hollywood-app-is-successful-2015-3?r=US.
104. Nieborg and Sihvonen, 2009.
105. Pearce, 2009, pp. 3–15.
106. See Bell, 2001, pp. 92–110.
107. Erickson, 1997.
108. Even though there is some real-life interaction when people meet physically to play; for example, in championships or conventions.
109. Now both *EverQuest* and *EverQuest II* continue to cater for players, in that they maintain their servers, are open for subscription, and regularly release expansions. However, Sony Online Entertainment doesn't publish data on the current size or composition of its player base.
110. As Richard Bartle describes in relation to the different styles people adopt while playing; Bartle, 1996.
111. Even though trading was later allowed for *EverQuest II* (2005).
112. Taylor, 2002.
113. In *Communities of Play: Emergent Cultures in Multiplayer Games and Virtual Worlds*, Pearce follows the "Uru Diaspora," a community of players of a closed-down world moving across different virtual worlds in search of a new home; Pearce, 2009.
114. These words are usually synonyms, referring to an organized group of players that act together in the game. Some games call them guilds and others clans.
115. For an explanation of "camping," see the next section, on "Cooperation and Conflict in Games."
116. Chee and Smith, 2003.
117. In their account of game design fundamentals, Salen and Zimmerman write, as mentioned earlier, that "a game is a system in which players engage in an artificial conflict, defined by rules, that result in a quantifiable outcome" (2004, p. 80). Similarly, Elliot Avedon and Brian Sutton-Smith define games as "an exercise of voluntary control systems, in which there is a contest between powers, confined by rules in order to produce a disequilibrial outcome" (1971, p. 7). Some

definitions do leave out conflict, e.g. Juul, 2003b.

118. Kim, 1998; King and Borland, 2003.
119. Rollings and Adams, 2003, p. 527.
120. Andy Kuo's student paper, "A (Very) Brief History of Cheating," is often referred to; see also Kücklich, 2004.
121. Consalvo, 2007.
122. Consalvo, 2007, pp. 87–92.
123. Consalvo, 2007, p. 95.
124. For example, "a player persistently camps a high level mob for an item he wants. But because his character isn't advanced enough, this mob kills the player, and proceeds to kill other neighbouring players. The others are unhappy and feel their gaming is being affected, but this player refuses to leave the area and continues to fight the high level mob, as he wants that item" (Foo & Koivisto, 2004, p. 2).
125. See King and Borland, 2003, pp. 161–162.
126. Such as http://heavengames.com.
127. http://aok.heavengames.com.
128. Sherblom-Woodward, 2002.
129. Leetspeak, originating, tellingly, from a version of the word "elite," works mainly through a series of specific alternative spellings (like using "z" instead of "s" in certain circumstances) and the liberal use of non-alphabetic characters to stand for (more or less similarly shaped) letters. Thus "leet" itself is often written "l33t," "ub3r" means über, and "newbie" is often written "n00b."
130. Wirman, 2009, 4.8.
131. Jenkins, 1992.
132. Pearce, 2009, p. 156.
133. Buckingham, Carr, Burn, and Schott, 2005.
134. By UNSC Trooper, posted in July 2007 to: http://halosn.bungie.org/fanfic/?story=UNSC_Trooper0704071531331.html.
135. See Lowood, 2006 or Jones, 2006, among others. Machinima as a form of fan creativity is in itself a big topic in game scholarship.
136. This movie is based on the 2001 Internet craze that saw gamers quoting the often nonsensical sentences from the Japanese video game, *Zero Wing*. The game's terrible English translation turned it into a cult object, and fans started altering photographs from all sorts of situations to include the sentence "All Your Base Are Belong to Us," and the pictures were exchanged and commented upon in many fora. Eventually, a series of these pictures were compiled in a Flash movie that was downloaded thousands of times; www.planettribes.com/allyourbase/AYB2.swf (accessed October 15, 2011).
137. These feature the famous Nintendo brothers Mario and Luigi, in original sprites (two-dimensional figures) from the game, as they engage in an epic journey to save Princess Peach. The five movies create a surprisingly palpable sense of drama, as the cartoonish, almost detail-less brothers are given gravitas by the original dialogue and emotional music. The author, who posted the first movie as a joke in 2003, was very surprised by their success. Available at his website at www.alxlen.com.
138. Jones, 2006.
139. Sotamaa, 2003, pp. 4–6. Sotamaa's works present a thorough examination of modding varieties and the academic interest in modding.
140. For her PhD thesis on female gamers' fan production and female gamer identity, see Wirman, 2010.
141. Postigo, 2003.
142. Pearce, 2009, pp. 155–175.
143. Wirman, 2009, 7.4.
144. Morris, 1999.
145. www.esportsea.com/.
146. www.worldcybergames.com/6th/inside/WCGC/WCGC_structure.asp, retrieved June 3, 2007.
147. Global e-Sports Report, 2019.
148. www.esportsea.com/.
149. Vera and Terrón, 2018.
150. Freeman and Wohn, 2017
151. Wagner, 2006, p. 440.
152. Seth et al., 2016.

153. Freeman and Wohn, 2017.
154. Dibbell, 2006.
155. Hjorth, 2011.
156. Castronova, 2001.
157. Castronova, 2004.
158. Ward, 2003.
159. Lyman, 2003.
160. Harmon, 2004.
161. Lastowka and Hunter, 2004.
162. Taylor, 2006, p. 153.
163. "Consider the range of material productions players are engaged in: the creation of game guides, walk-throughs, answers to frequently asked questions (FAQs), maps, object and monster databases, third-party message boards and mailing lists, play norms, server guidelines, modifications, plug-ins, strategies and strategy guides, auctions/trading, tweaks to user interfaces (UI), macro sharing, fanfic, game movies, counter-narratives, comics, and fan gatherings" (Taylor, 2006, p. 155).

7   Narrative

Storytelling

Reception—The Player's Experience of a Story

A Brief History of Literary Theory and Video Games

BioShock (2007) is widely acclaimed for the richness and depth of its narrative

Let us move away from the cultures created by games and their players, and back to the substance of the games themselves. This chapter explores the importance of narrative in video games. Critics, scholars, and parents alike have found many reasons to dislike and criticize video games. One argument is that the medium cannot tell a story, let alone a good story. Much prominent video game theory centers on what many perceive as an incompatibility between gaming and storytelling. This stands in sharp contrast, however, to the avid nine-year-old fan of *Zelda*, who can offer a step-by-step recitation of the adventures of Link as he travels through the land of Hyrule. So we are left with a basic question: are video games stories?

> The rain has been falling like a dense spittle for weeks now, and as you cruise above the metropolis in your spinner, the neon lights blur below like artist's pastels on a sidewalk. Back on the ground to pursue your mission, the babel of cityspeak washes around you. The last warm smile you can remember came from a geisha grinning off the side of a stark high rise, and that was about as genuine as one of those android snakes they're hawking down in Chinatown.[1]

You are a blade runner. As you search for clues on your first mission, life is not kind in the city. The sound of rain accompanies your character's footsteps; you can nearly smell the food as you step into Howie Lee's bar to ask the owner a few questions. Using your mouse, you click on the screen image of Howie and a menu pops up:

- LUCY PHOTO
- RUNCITER CLUES
- EMPLOYEE
- SMALL TALK
- DONE.

These are your options. What will your next step be? You've just returned from the Runciter shop at the other side of L.A., where an animal murder has taken place, and there you have found a pair of chopsticks with the name of the bar you stand in now. Is this just coincidence or an important lead? As you contemplate this, you notice that the bulky employee behind the bar looks a bit like one of the suspects photographed by the shop's security system. You use your mouse to click on "SMALL TALK," and ask Howie Lee about his employee. He cannot tell you anything, so you click on "EMPLOYEE," and the program guides you around to the back to talk to the guy yourself. He claims maybe to have seen the girl whose picture you are showing him, but then he suddenly throws a boiling pot of water toward you and runs away through the back door. Can you dodge the water? Will you follow him or go back to Howie?

Figure 7.1 Blade Runner: Howie Lee's bar and our character

If this were a movie, the main character would probably run after the suspect in the alley; you as the spectator would not give this interchange a second thought. He might even say something witty as he jumped beyond the arc of the boiling water. You would not need to click over and over again on a simplified list of commands. You would sit back and watch the action unfolding in front of you, pondering connections between the story's elements and wondering what might happen next. However, this is a video game, so nothing will happen unless you act. You need to decide whether to move or wait, choose conversation topics, shoot a suspect or not, arrest people or not, and you need always to look for the clues that might be hiding on the edges of the screen. No matter what happens, the outcome is one that you have helped create. You cannot play *Blade Runner* without paying attention to the story, as at any turn you wouldn't know what to do next. *Blade Runner* is *more* than a story—it is a game—but we can't deny that it is *also* a story. Video game genres (and individual video games) are so different from each other that it would be folly to suggest that a story-centered analysis is always a good idea, but there are many cases in which it is, as we will demonstrate in this chapter.

Blade Runner belongs to the genre of adventure games, a direct descendant of text adventures (see Chapter 4), and arguably the genre in which story is most important. There are other subgenres in which stories are very significant, such as role-playing games or so-called action-adventure games. In the beginning of video game history, only text adventures could be said to integrate stories and games (even though many games used the frame of a plot as advertising); but nowadays there is no popular genre that doesn't use some sort of explicit fictional framework. Early video games were simply too abstract for plot to be a central concern—we can only imagine the triangular ship of *Asteroids* being involved in so many plot-heavy adventures.

But as computing processing power grew, the industry tended toward the production of more representationally sophisticated games. Good graphics have translated into painstakingly detailed and sometimes beautiful worlds, while better AIs allow for more advanced responses to players' actions, including more interesting nonplayer characters, better simulations, and the possibility of handling thousands of players at the same time in huge multiplayer worlds—all of these advances make the game world seem more alive, and each, in turn, changes the possibilities for storytelling.

Narrative is so pervasive that there are video games based on nothing more than a tangential connection to stories in other media; the most popular of these are games directly created from other cultural products, such as films. These games can sometimes have a narrative element, but often the film ends up being a thematic excuse for a platform or action game. Consider, for example, *Star Wars Episode I: Racer*, developed in connection with the movie *The Phantom Menace*. The game draws on the fictional universe of the *Star Wars* series but is based on only one scene from *The Phantom Menace*. As a typical racer game, it contains almost no story, but it nevertheless prompts the player to "take the controls as Jedi-to-be Anakin Skywalker."[2]

There is only a suggestion that the player might frame her actions within the game as part of this specific fictional universe; the act of playing itself will not reproduce the sequence of events as in the movie but allows for many other combinations.

Even in genres where stories are not part of the gameplay at all, such as strategy or simulation, fictional worlds prompt players to imagine that their actions take place within a meaningful narrative frame. For example, Microsoft's successful *Age of Empires* is a strategy game based on the management of resources in the classic setting of "civilization-building," in which your tribe has to develop from nothing to an empire, and compete with others for world domination. The theme of advancing your empire gives a reason for abstract resource management and provides the frame for the game's graphics, settings, and action. Themes and plots—however vague—enable players to figure out game interfaces and the rules of the game: what actions are available to me as a player? And that is why most games use them. *Age of Empires* has a final goal: *advance your culture and dominate all others*, but even video games without any goals, such as the toy-like *The Sims*, coat the simulation with a fictional varnish. In the promotional materials for the game, you are invited to play God in an adult version of a doll's house.[3]

> Create simulated people and build their homes, then help your Sims pursue careers, earn money, make friends, and find romance—or totally mess up their lives. Test your "people skills" as you deal with family, friends, careers, and chaos! There is no right or wrong way to play the game.[4]

Clearly, stories are everywhere. And we will use the general term "narrative video games" to refer to any games in which stories play a significant role. But to avoid the confusion that has haunted many discussions about the role of narrative in games, let us define our concepts.[5] So far, we have been using the words "story," "narrative," "fictional world," and "fiction" in what seems like an interchangeable manner, something that would no doubt horrify many literary scholars.

"Narrative" can be defined as a succession of events. Its basic components are the chronological order of the events themselves (story), their verbal or visual representation (text), and the act of telling or writing (narration).[6] For example, the novel *Dracula* tells us a story of how an ancient vampire comes to England, wreaks havoc in a small community, and is finally destroyed. This story—which is not always clearly or chronologically told—is found in the text, written by Bram Stoker. Bram Stoker (whom we cannot see in the text) creates the narration, both through his own descriptions and through the voices of the characters, who "speak" through their letters and other writings.

Technically "story" and "plot" are "ingredients" of narrative, understood as a succession of events. However, in this chapter, "story" is more of a loose term, referring to fictional worlds projected by the games, unless it is described as "linear story." "Plots" or "narratives" are a scripted succession of events that the player has to perform in a specific order. (In *Blade Runner* you have to find the chopsticks before you can go to Howie Lee's bar, for example.) The events that make up the whole narrative or plot of this kind of game usually allow minimal flexibility in the order of completion.

The other components of narrative—text and narration—are not as essential to our discussion of video games, mainly because these games lack a static text. No matter how many times a book is read, by no matter how many different people, the text is always the same; but in a video game, no two game sessions will be exactly the same. As for narration, the nonfixed text of video games makes it difficult for them to have a single telling; the exception proves the rule here, as there is a very short list of games, such as *Prince of Persia: Sands of Time* or *Max Payne*, that feature a voice-over narration of the type you might have in a movie, which frames the player's actions within a narrative framework that has already been fixed in advance. But this is a trick, of course, because the voice-over only concerns itself with the main plotlines of the story, and it is still possible to have different playing sessions in which minor things are done slightly differently.

As we can see, these terms are concerned with the structural description of a narrative. We should also mention the broader terms "fiction" and "fictional worlds." "Fiction" is not an uncontested term, but we can make a pragmatic distinction between "fiction" as events that have not occurred in "real life" (the basis for novels, films), and "nonfiction" as documentation of events that have occurred (as seen in news items, autobiographies, and film documentaries). Nearly all video game stories are fictional, although there are also games, such as *Battlefield 1942*, based on real World War II battles, which simulate historical events.

A fictional world is an imaginary construct created by the descriptions of a text. Readers—and viewers, and players—infer that there is a make-believe universe in which the events they are reading about (or viewing or performing) make sense. For example, from reading the tale of *Little Red Riding Hood* we can imagine a pre-modern world where people lived close to forests, had tight family relations, and where animals could talk. From our own experience, we know that grandmothers and granddaughters are usually fond of each other, and that little girls shouldn't talk to strangers. This is much less detailed than, say, the fictional world that J.R.R. Tolkien creates in *The Lord of the Rings*, where he invents languages and carefully describes continents, races, animals, plants, and an entire mythology.

However, these two narratives can affect us similarly as readers; the point is that we do not need much descriptive prompting in order to ascertain which kinds of events make sense in a concrete fictional world. As we read, or view, or play, we unconsciously and immediately apply what we know from our own world if it is a realistic setting, and from other fictional worlds if it is not. For example, the player of *Half-Life* assumes the role of a scientist trapped in a secret research facility, where an experiment has gone horribly wrong and brought evil aliens into our world. The player quickly recognizes the science fiction-conspiracy theme (from novels or Hollywood movies) and can almost immediately guess the plot to come: the government will try to eliminate him and all other surviving witnesses. *Half-Life* is full of cues of all kinds: visual, in the dialogues, and in the kinds of actions that we can (and can't) perform with our character. The fictional world is immediately recognizable, and thus believable, because it is similar to many stories we have seen and read before.

Most games have a fictional world, however minimal, and the success of this imaginary creation nearly always influences the player's enjoyment of the game. *Star Wars Episode I: Racer*, as we saw earlier, wouldn't be as engaging if instead of pods and the characters from the *Phantom Menace* movie it featured cars and an unknown set of colored animals as characters. With the visual clues from the movie, the player can imagine her actions as loosely connected to a broader *Star Wars* story outside the game.

Narratives are made of events, and usually contain settings and characters, but both of these ingredients can appear on their own, without being tied to a specific narrative, so that players can imagine how setting or characters fit into the fictional world, relate them to an external story (like *Star Wars*), or simply use them in order narratively to thematize their enjoyment of the game (in *Super Monkey Ball*, for example).

We should point out that it is easy to confuse fictional worlds with narratives. This is because one of the ways we understand a narrative is by filling in the gaps: we postulate connections between events, we interpret the motives of characters, and so on. In other words, we project an imaginary world. In the same confusing way, when video game designers talk about narrative, they usually refer to the introduction of elements that prompt the player into imagining fictional worlds—which could be anything from excellent characters to detailed environments. Many designers abhor the scripting of programmed sequences of events in games, which would actually form a narrative in the literary sense.

Much of the scholarly discussion around narrative and video games deals with the perceived difficulty of combining a playing experience that feels free with the necessary constraints of a narrative structure. In other words, the problem of letting players act freely while ensuring that their actions produce an interesting story.

This chapter will introduce some of the concepts that are important when looking at video games from a narrative perspective—as regards both narrative as a sequence of events and the creation of fictional worlds—in the section called "Storytelling." This section also argues that story and gameplay are integrated in the playing experience, as we will see from the analysis of a particular game. The second part of the chapter, "A Brief History of Literary Theory and Video Games," provides an overview of major theoretical issues in discussion in the video game narrative community. This chapter should give you a fairly extensive idea of the work that has been done in the area, as well as hopefully demonstrating that a consideration of narrative is useful for understanding video games.

STORYTELLING

We will here introduce interesting elements of narrative that are relevant to video games. We have divided the concept of storytelling into three broad categories, which can be thought of as the "who" and the "what," and the "how/why" of a narrative. The categories are "the fictional world," which includes the story's settings and actors; the "mechanics" of the narrative, or how the action of the story is organized; and the **reception**, or the way in which players experience the story and figure out the causality.

The Fictional World: Settings and Actors

Most video games are given a setting that not only helps the player frame her actions but is also engaging enough that it has some value in itself. Players of *Myst* marveled at the beautiful landscapes and eerie atmosphere of the deserted islands. Fans of *The Last Express* no doubt still remember the animated life of the train where the game takes place, full of characters that go on about their business without regard for the protagonist. And those players steeped in *Counter-Strike*, where enemies can appear in any doorway, and where danger lurks around every corner, may even find themselves fantasizing about combat tactics as they walk down corridors in real life. The list of fictional worlds is endless—from the mysterious building where the old *Donkey Kong* takes place (full of jumps and stairs and barrels and dangers for our little Mario) to the terrifying village of *Silent Hill*—and video games have relied upon these imagined spaces from their inception.

But what exactly is the relationship between fictional game worlds and the game experience? Lisbeth Klastrup describes the differences between game worlds and social worlds, and argues that a game world's objects and space are all organized around the act of play.[7] Many of us have tried to open doors and windows that would not move in *Blade Runner*, or tried to climb the trees of *EverQuest*; the fictional world of games is like the stage of a play—it is meant for action, but many of the elements are there to be seen and not used. Only those objects directly related to gameplay will be "usable," although quite a few contemporary games with advanced physics offer the possibility of interacting with objects unrelated to the story. Games indicate which objects are relevant in different ways. In *Blade Runner*, for example, the cursor changes color when the player moves it over a usable object. Others simply try to make as many objects "alive" as possible, in simulations that provide the illusion of a virtual reality. In *Grand Theft Auto V*, we move around in a city where all cars can be stolen, all people beaten up, and a lot of other things done that strictly speaking have nothing to do with the missions we are given. The city, it seems, lives even without us. Although this is, of course, an illusion, as we can only interact with the different kinds of objects in one predetermined way: we can beat people up but not kiss them, for example. Designers have divided opinions as to what kind of world

Reception (studies): In literature, the study of a reader's understanding of the text. In video games, the study of the player's experience of playing a game.

works best, but players' expectations are likely molded by a game's genre: we are more likely to try and explore every nook and cranny of an adventure game as we look for clues, and less likely to care about the surroundings in an action game.

The most important component of a game world is the gamespace,[8] understood as the setting for the gameplay. Gamespaces are not realistic but reductive: they reproduce some features of the real world but create their own rules in order to facilitate gameplay (and to reduce the processing power required by a computer to run the game). For example, in *Myst* (see Chapter 4), the world around us seems open, but in actuality we are forced to follow a very specific route through the landscape, and can't stray off the path or explore.

Espen Aarseth has looked at different kinds of spatial representation in video game history: from two-dimensional to three-dimensional, from open landscapes to landscapes where you can only move in a single direction, and from indoor corridors to space travel and everything in between. He argues that spatial representation is the most innovative aspect of video games. Following on from his main point—that the spaces of video games are fundamentally different from real spaces—he makes an interesting distinction between space in single- and multiplayer games. Single-player games, as in the case of *Myst*, for example, often have landscapes that seem to be open but are actually very restrictive. This is necessary because the game orchestrates the movement of the player in one direction, toward a final goal. Multiplayer landscapes, however, have to be open so that all players can move freely, and so that no player starts with an advantage. The challenge in these games is not the landscape (as it would be in a platform game) but the other players.[9]

Gordon Calleja has examined the importance of gamespace as "a powerful factor in engaging players and giving them the sense that they are inhabiting a place rather than merely perceiving a representation of space."[10]

One of the most contested issues in relation to the fictional world of games has been cut-scenes, cinematic sequences used to relay information to the player. Many games with a sophisticated story use this technique to situate player actions in a fictional world that can thus be described with great authorial control. Play is interrupted and we watch a "film" where the game characters interact or something happens that is out of our control. Cut-scenes are used by designers to create narrative in a variety of ways.

First, they introduce a central narrative tension. Many arcade games used animated cut-scenes to introduce the central conflict of the game. These scenes were brief and served to give the player a chance to get ready for the actual gameplay. As the need to get the player through the game quickly fell away, introductory cut-scenes grew longer, and today's games often have extended movie sequences that introduce characters, and set the scene and the mood.

Figure 7.2 New Zealand Story (1989) cut-scene, where the evil walrus kidnaps the kiwi family but one bird escapes

Second, cut-scenes shape the narrative in a certain direction. They function to ensure that the game protagonist makes certain choices. The player is stripped of his or her influence and the narrative is moved along. In the game *Gabriel Knight III*, for instance, Gabriel walks through a door, triggering a cut-scene in which the player has no control over Gabriel's actions.

Third, cut-scenes compensate for missing game narrative. Many games mark the passing of time within the game using cut-scenes. Sometimes these scenes illustrate a journey; for instance, when the player of *Prince of Persia: Sands of Time* has performed a certain series of tasks the game jumps to a longish cut-scene showing the consequences of the prince having procured the Dagger of Time.

Fourth, they associate the game with contemporary cinema aesthetics as in *Max Payne II*, for example to build a richer game experience through an emotional tie.

Fifth, cut-scenes provide the player with information. Some modern games have integrated cut-scenes much more closely with the gameplay than was previously the norm. Here the cinematics are used to convey useful information, often to serve as a kind of establishing shot describing the layout of a location. As the protagonist enters a new area, the "camera" may swoop through the scene showing the placement of enemies and objects.

Figure 7.3 Max Payne II (2003) cut-scene, where the player is emotionally tied to the main character

The rationale for using cut-scenes in games is disputed. Some hold it to be a case of cinema envy; some argue the technique compensates for game design incompetence, so that the fictional worlds are shown passively instead of letting the player discover them through gameplay.[11]

Others, however, see the attack on cut-scenes as a radical or purist attempt to (over)emphasize what is special about games.[12] In his paper "In Defense of Cutscenes," Rune Klevjer argues that cut-scenes are a manifestation of the author's voice in the creation of the diegetic world, understood as "a fictional world, created by discourse."[13] The importance of cut-scenes is not only retrospective; as we have seen, it also frames the world in which play takes place:

> The cut-scene may indeed be a narrative of re-telling but more importantly: it is a narrative of pre-telling, paving the way for the mimetic event, making it a part of a narrative act, which does not take place after, but before the event. The cut-scene casts its meanings forward, strengthening the diegetic, rhetorical dimensions of the event to come.[14]

Apart from the settings manifested in the gamespaces and conveyed by cut-scenes, the other important ingredient when building fictional worlds is the characters that will populate them. We have talked about "actors" before, because many of these characters are capable of action, and indeed of interacting with the player. If we take a dictionary definition, characters are "the people that the film, book, or play is *about*."[15]

It seems that games (when they have characters) would participate in both modes—the narrative and the dramatic: sometimes we read and imagine worlds (as in adventure games), sometimes we view worlds unfolding (as in cut-scenes in adventure games), but the revolution offered by video games is that we can play some characters ourselves, and that other characters will react to us and do things that we can respond to. Characters in games are not just the people that the game is *about* but also the people who are making action happen and thus producing different stories. Mark J. P. Wolf considers characters to be the driving force of narrative development in video games. He proposes that they be categorized by their function: playing characters, computer-controlled characters and computer-controlled characters with no action in the game (helpers, hinderers, beneficiaries, neutral characters, or narrators).[16]

We propose our own typology of characters in video games, organized according to the extent to which players can interact with them:

- *Stage characters*: Just part of the scenario, moving around but with no personality or function in the game. We cannot interact with them in any way.
- *Functional characters*: Like stage characters but with a general function in the game; for example, in *Grand Theft Auto III* we can attack or be attacked by people walking past, and in *Vampire: The Masquerade—Redemption*, our vampire character once in a while needs to drink blood from anonymous mortals.
- *Cast characters*: Characters with a particular function in the game related to the story. They have personality to different degrees: a minimal amount in the case of the *Blade Runner* bartender we have to interrogate, for example, and a large amount in the case of our friend—later enemy—Sephiroth in *Final Fantasy VII*. Such characters have their own agendas, and can be considered in Proppian terms,[17] as we will explain.
- *Player characters*: The character controlled by the player (except in cut-scenes); we can usually control his actions but his motivations and missions are decided by the story.

Even though all characters can be memorable in their own way, the player character is certainly the crucial one for the player experience. Designer Toby Gard has proposed a typology of player characters, with three categories according to how easy it is for players to identify with them: from avatars to actors, with role-playing game characters occupying a middle position:

> *Avatars* are a non-intrusive representation of ourselves, *actors* are always part of a story (or have a story, albeit minimal sometimes), and *roleplaying* characters have very different abilities that we can raise according to our performance.[18]

Typically, an avatar has no name and cannot be seen, as the game view is first person, so that the player merges with the character, as in *Unreal*, for example. Actors can usually be seen in third-person view and have their own biography integrated with the game story, for instance, Lara Croft of *Tomb Raider*. Role-playing characters are "made" by players, who choose their name, appearance, and abilities, and can often also choose between the first- and third-person views. This last category should in theory offer more room for identification as the player constructs the identity of her own character in play. However, in practice it is hard to really role-play and develop a character within the context of MMORPGs, as MacCallum-Stewart and Parsler have demonstrated.[19]

Tosca has added a fourth category: "iconic" characters. These are characters, such as the *Super Monkey Ball* monkeys, who are empty of personality but allow for the collective channeling of stereotyped expressions in the game performance, such as happiness in victory or dismay when losing.[20]

The importance of being able to identify with a game's characters is something of a recurrent theme in video game design manuals; there is a belief that the stronger the personality of the character, the easier it is for a player to feel alienated from it.[21] The implication—that designers should create characters with only vague attributes—is the opposite of a typical modern literary perspective, where characters are praised for their vivid uniqueness. The fear of alienation is also contradicted by some very popular video game characters, such as Lara Croft, who have very distinctive personalities.

The last point we will consider in relation to characters is that of the creation of better (meaning more active) nonplayer characters, a problem directly related to the development of artificial intelligence[22] and one that has worried many developers for a long time. Brenda Laurel is in fact optimistic, and proposes simplification rather than more complexity:

> the fact is that, thanks to well-internalized dramatic convention, we can enjoy (and believe in) even one-dimensional dramatic characters. In fact, when a minor dramatic character possesses only one or two actionable traits, audience members will impute elaborate histories and motivations as needed to make it believable.[23]

Laurel builds on the work of Meehan,[24] Lebowitz,[25] and others who have established guidelines to create "functional and entertaining characters from a small cluster of well-conceived traits that are realized as goal-formulating and problem-solving styles."[26] Despite constant technological advancements and more and more complex games, good characters do not necessarily have to be lifelike. The techniques mentioned above can allow for the creation of a very interesting array of characters of all categories (stage, functional, cast, and player characters). And of course there is the fascinating possibility of interacting with the characters of fellow gamers in multiplayer titles, an activity that has not been thoroughly explored in the research.

Mechanics: Organizing Narrative Action

We now turn to an examination of what constitutes narrative action in video games, and ways of implementing it. A central preoccupation of game designers is the problem of linearity—how to get a player to move through a game in one particular way, at the same time ensuring that it is interesting. As the narrative possibilities of video games have become more complex, so too has the debate over the mechanics of the narrative. Designers now generally accept that forcing the player through the fictional world does not make a good video game, no matter how compelling the narrative. But if you don't force your player to do things, then how do you create a plot? This is the central question for narrative mechanics.

The basic concept designers use to organize narrative action is "branching." We can define branching as the existence of multiple paths in a narration. Branching leads to the problem of managing the exponential growth of nodes (or individual text spaces) in a narrative. This has been one of the most debated issues among hypertext theorists since the early 1990s. Faced with the same problems, video game designers have generally allowed for moderate branching while implementing plot bottlenecks, through which all players have to pass in order for the story to advance. For example, in *Gabriel Knight: Sins of the Father*, the player has to visit a certain number of locations in order to finish each day; she can do it in different order, but in the end, the day will finish in the same way. Jonas Heide Smith has illustrated the differences between the standard narrative progression of linear fiction (including novels and films) and that of interactive fiction and narrative games.

As illustrated in Figure 7.4, traditional fiction goes only one way—toward a resolution—and does not allow for interruptions or cuts. A traditional narration works because it is a continuous line that plays with a reader's (or viewer's) expectations and orchestrates their emotional trip from beginning to end, controlling important points such as the point of no return and the climax. If we applied the same model to a video game, we could not allow the player to do anything, as any deviation or delay would ruin our carefully planned emotional curve. Imagine the player dying in the middle of the narrative! But a game with such a narrative model would

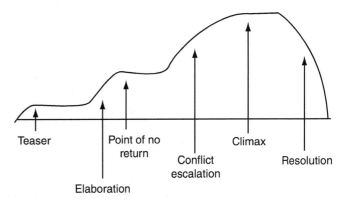

Figure 7.4 A model of classical linear fiction that shows how the story is built up in stages

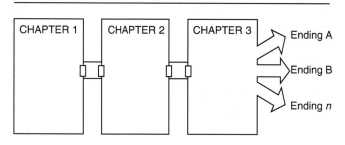

Figure 7.5 A model of interactive fiction that shows the branching of the story

not be much of a game, which is why designers opt for another model (see Figure 7.5).

In this kind of fiction—typical of adventure and action-adventure games—there is no continuous curve. The player has to solve puzzles (or find objects, win battles, or talk to nonplayer characters) within each chapter; usually there is some flexibility as to the order of the tasks, offering a small sense of freedom. In the absence of an emotional curve, designers rely on the emotional satisfaction—the "unambiguous sense of victory"—that solving the puzzles gives the player.[27,28] But ultimately the player is *solving* a story instead of actively *creating* it. The successive chapters work in a cumulative way so that at the end of each a climax or resolution is provided, usually preceded by a difficult "boss fight" to give a greater sense of achievement. As mentioned in Chapter 5 on video game aesthetics, Jesper Juul calls these "progression" games, because the player has to complete a certain sequence of actions in order to get to the end—or endings, as sometimes these games allow for different resolutions according to the player's actions.

Aside from progression games, the other dominant narrative structure—as defined by Juul—is "emergence" games. This type of game follows nothing like the classical linear structure; instead of a prestructured sequence, there is a more active artificial intelligence (AI), in which each object has behaviors. For example, in a progression game, the dragon will always attack the player when she steps into the cave, but in an emergence game this might depend on how the player behaves toward the dragon, which is a more "active" object with a few possible different responses. For both Juul and Smith, an emergent structure is preferable, as it gives players a sense of freedom. Smith calls it "deistic narration," a kind of object-oriented narration in which game designers become architects of space and situations:

> An example: A virtual living room is designed, the avatar is placed on a couch, and a dragon is placed under the couch. What we then *have* is not a story but a story is what we may *get*. What we have is a starting position with narrative potential but without direction.[29]

The key to successful mechanics is to make players feel that they are contributing to creating a plot; the most successful narrative experiences happen in games where our actions have noticeable plot consequences.

Beneath the narrative structure of an entire game, designers must also manage the smaller sequences of events that make up the arc of a game's plot. To explore these building blocks of narrative, some game theorists have investigated **quests**.[30] Quests are small "missions" that players must perform; they structure a game's action and create opportunities for storytelling.

From the designer's point of view, a quest is a set of parameters in the game world (making use of the game's rules and gameplay) that creates a challenge for the player. From the player's point of view, a quest is a set of specific instructions for action; these can be a general goal (overthrow the evil king) or extremely precise (take this bucket to the well, fill it up, and bring it back to me). After the quest has been completed, it can be narrated as a story. Quests are a way of structuring the events that constitute a game, as they manifest causality at two levels. On a semantic level, quests demonstrate how and why a player's actions are connected to each other and to the end of the game's story; on a structural level, quests embody the cause-and-effect relationship between a plan of action and its results, or between the interaction of objects and events. These two levels can be perceived by both the player and the designer, and if the quests are well built, they enhance a player's emotional engagement. Ideally, quests are the glue that holds world, rules, and themes together in a meaningful way.

Most games with a narrative component employ quests—not only adventure games but also role-playing games or multiplayer role-playing games (where the massive presence of player characters does not leave a lot of room for designer-controlled story production). In *World of Warcraft*, for example, at any given time of day or night, thousands of players around the globe are running around their fictional worlds, engrossed in their particular quests: find a book, kill a monster, take a letter to another city. In adventure games, quests are often defined in terms of puzzles or enigmas that have to be solved by collecting objects, using information, and rearranging machinery.

Game designers should ideally avoid quests that are meaningless for the player. The two levels on which quests operate (the semantic and the structural, as discussed) are also the two levels on which quests can fail. Quests generally do not work because they fail to integrate the storytelling elements in a particular game: if quests feel disconnected from the plot, the game world, or our characters, chances are that the bridging of the semantic and structural levels has not succeeded. There seems to be a fairly fixed and small number of typical quests that many games repeat (the exchange, the breach of contract, the discovery of the traitor, and saving the kingdom are among the most popular), and we might ask ourselves if it is desirable to explore new lands and devise new versions of these quests or search for entirely different ones. As Jill Walker suggests in her analysis of *World of Warcraft* quests,[31] some of the classic quests, such as taking a letter from one character to another, can feel more significant if they reveal relationships between the nonplaying characters that populate the world of the game. In other words, designers need not invest a lot of effort in making player characters a part of the quest stories—a narrative can also be richer if the static world is better fleshed out than in most current games. This is also

Jeff Howard's point in his *Quests: Design, Theory and History in Games and Narratives*.[32] More recently, Tanya Krzywinska has looked at the episodic narrative elements of quest games through the repetition of certain patterns ("beats"), using *World of Warcraft* as an example. Here, quests are seen as micronarratives set within an overarching multithreaded narration.[33] These authors have taken the analysis of quests to a level of greater sophistication.

Marie-Laure Ryan[34] has over the years extensively worked with narrative structures, and has mapped out nine fundamental narrative structures that are described below:

1. *The complete graph structure*: In this narrative structure, all the paths are bidirectional and all nodes are linked to each other. The reader has total freedom to navigate. It is almost impossible to guarantee a coherent narrative as the reader has full control of what to do.
2. *The network structure*: In this narrative structure, paths can be either unidirectional or bidirectional. This is the standard structure of literary hypertexts. The reader's navigation is neither entirely free nor limited to one course.
3. *The tree structure*: In this narrative structure, all paths are unidirectional, and progression produces a plot. The reader's progression is carefully controlled, so any choice results in a well-formed story. This structure is sometimes used in adventure games, although the maze structure explained later is more common.
4. *The vector with side branches*: In this narrative structure, there is one main story that progresses chronologically. However, the reader is allowed or even encouraged to make small detours, which in video games are often referred to as "side quests." The structure resembles that of sightseeing with a guide.
5. *The maze structure*: This narrative is the one mostly found in adventure games, where the players have to find the right path to successfully complete the game. There are more ways to reach the end, but you will always get to the same end. The story will be quite coherent as the game's design sets down blockers between each chapter, ensuring that the players go through the key nodes to progress the story appropriately.
6. *The directed network*: This narrative structure is more chaotic, but strong attempts are made constantly to maintain some coherence as the player progresses. The player has some freedom to connect the experiences of the journey in different ways, forming a somewhat unique narrative. The player feels more empowered as the decisions made during the story influence what happens in the later narrative.
7. *The hidden story structure*: This narrative structure is more complex, as it operates with a fixed narrative that the players slowly uncover as they progress through the game. The game is a reconstruction of a fixed narrative that develops into a new narrative. This worked very well in the first *Max Payne* game, where you slowly uncover what happened to the protagonist's family.

8. *The braided plot*: This narrative structure allows the player to experience different perspectives on an unfolding narrative by changing the protagonist and location. This can be by playing characters with different abilities or access to special knowledge.
9. *Action space, epic wandering, and story-world*: In this narrative structure the player can interact on the macro level to choose different incidents (micro-level). Once the player is on the micro-level the narrative is locked down, and a narrative plays out with limited agency for the player.

Not many progression games manage to give players a sense of freedom, but there are some notable attempts, such as *Blade Runner*, mentioned previously. In this game, there are almost no puzzles; instead the player goes through different scenarios in search of clues. The player has a variety of options each time he confronts a replicant (the game's initial villains). Arresting, killing, or letting them go free prompts complex responses; ultimately, the player's actions decide if she turns out to be a replicant herself—one of the most interesting questions raised by the film the game is based on.

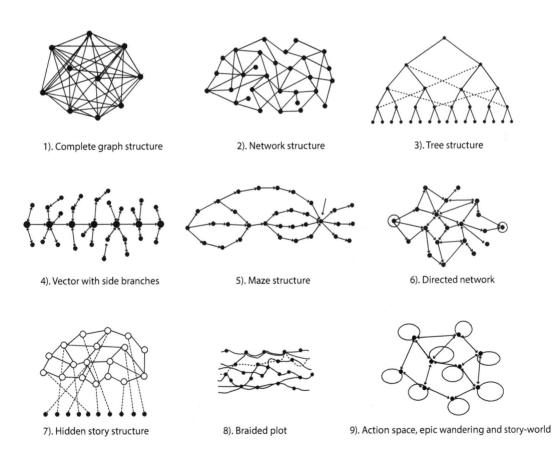

1). Complete graph structure   2). Network structure   3). Tree structure

4). Vector with side branches   5). Maze structure   6). Directed network

7). Hidden story structure   8). Braided plot   9). Action space, epic wandering and story-world

Figure 7.6 A variety of different interactive narratives and how they can fold into each other. (Source: Ryan, 2001b, pp. 247–255, figures 4–11)

Reception—The Player's Experience of a Story

"Reader response criticism" or "reception theory" is a branch of literary theory that focuses on the experience of readers as they interact with texts, and tries to articulate the nature of the reading activity. It is a useful perspective from which to study players' experiences with narrative video games. In what follows, we will argue that a reception theory-based analysis can explain the way that narrative and gameplay together determine the player experience in games that make use of stories. This approach can also answer the question: do we need to pay attention to the story in order to play these kinds of games? A close analysis of the game *Resident Evil Code: Veronica X*[35] will serve to introduce these ideas.

Resident Evil Code: Veronica X is the fourth major title in the very popular *Resident Evil* series. It is somewhere between the adventure genre and the "survival horror" subgenre. Along with other titles like *Silent Hill* and *Alone in the Dark* that fit this hybrid category, the player controls a character who has to get out of some enclosed place, solving puzzles and destroying horrific monsters along the way.

The story in *Resident Evil Code: Veronica X* is about a young woman, Claire Redfield, who travels to Europe to find her brother, Chris. Both siblings are survivors of previous games, and enemies of the evil "Umbrella Corporation," which experiments with biochemical viruses that turn people into zombies and monsters. At the game's outset, Claire is captured by the company and sent to a prison on a monster-infested island, from which she has to escape. Throughout the game, the player alternates between controlling three characters and uncovers yet more of the evil corporation's dark secrets.

Let's begin our analysis with an initial concept, the "literary repertoire," because it will help us understand how readers (in this case, players) can start interpreting a story successfully—that is, how they get into it. The literary repertoire is described by Wolfgang Iser as "the familiar territory within the text,"[36] which can include anything that the reader might already know—references to earlier works, social norms, and historical events. This repertoire brings context into the discussion without opening the door to excessively subjective interpretations or psychological particularities: the reader can only actualize[37] what is already in the text. Understanding the repertoire is a matter of competence, and it can affect both content (for example, recognizing a quote) or form (being able to interpret the conventions of the horror genre). In the case of *Resident Evil Code: Veronica X*, the repertoire includes (among other things):

* *Knowledge of the survival horror genre of video games*: This includes basic premises such as kill all monsters; pick up all objects to solve puzzles; there is a boss, or monster, that is especially difficult to kill at the end of each level or area.

- *Knowledge of the horror B-movies that inspired this kind of game*: These movies place the game in the right cultural context but also offer useful tips; horror devotees all know, for example, that zombies move really slowly, so you can probably dodge them instead of always fighting them (something that will prove particularly useful, since it is easy to run out of ammunition).
- *Knowledge of how to cheat since the player can become stuck, which stops the game*: Savvy players will know to consult a "walkthrough," the detailed turn-by-turn summaries of games discussed earlier. They will also know where to find "cheats," such as pirate programs to optimize their performance in the game. (Note that just as in the case of B-movies, here we are stretching the repertoire to include meta-elements—or elements beyond the game itself—but such "cheats" are now an established part of game communities.)

The repertoire is activated by "clues" in the game (everything from the creepy sounds when you go up the stairs to the dark rain on the fresh tombs) and outside the game (such as the game cover, which shows a zombie reflection in the eyes of the protagonist) which indicate that we are immersed in a survival horror game. Even if we were to start the game knowing nothing about it, we would still be able to summon the right repertoire—the right mental category—soon enough, as we immediately have to face the creaking stairs, and a few minutes later we find ourselves in the first graveyard surrounded by zombies.

If players fail to recall the right repertoire—imagine, perhaps, that we had never played a similar game, or never seen a horror movie—the game cannot be appropriately enjoyed. In the first scene, for example, an injured soldier helps Claire out of her cell. If we wrongly summon the repertoire of "love story" to try to explain this, we will concentrate on the fact that he is wounded, and waste all our time either staying in the cell with him, or trying to find medicine to cure him (which will not happen until we have done many other things in the game).

In reader response criticism, the act of reading is vital, as it transforms the literary text from artifact into aesthetic object. In other words, a text begins as a "dead" object with a lot of potential meanings that only become actualized through reading. Wolfgang Iser attempts to explain how this happens through his theory of "filling in the gaps," in which a reader starts from what the text says and figures out what it does not say. For example, if the text mentions that two new characters who meet in an elevator exchange hateful glances, the reader will wonder what the reason behind it is: maybe they know each other already and have had a fight; maybe they are ex-lovers; maybe they are fans of opposing football teams. As readers, we tend to try and confirm these hypotheses as we read.[38]

While playing a video game, our mind is busy with the story level and the action level at the same time. The first of these, which we experience on

Figure 7.7 The cover of the European version of *Resident Evil Code: Veronica X* for PlayStation

the fly, can be narrated afterwards (it is "tellable"[39]) and makes sense as a story (complete with character motivation and feelings); the second is about solving action problems, and if it was to be narrated it would be as a "walk-through." To illustrate this, let us enter into *Code: Veronica*. The game opens with a cut-scene in which our character, Claire, is captured by the Umbrella Corporation men. The following description of this scene is written by Dan Birlew and Thomas Wilde, who have transposed the *Resident Evil* games into a series of stories.

Story Level

Slowly, someone clutching his stomach shambles into the room and stands outside Claire's cell door. Claire uses her lighter to see who it is, and is surprised to see the face of the man who took her prisoner in Paris.

The man unlocks her cell and opens the door. As Claire hesitantly steps outside her cell, he slumps into a nearby chair and pulls an empty bottle of medicine out of his pocket. He throws it against the floor in frustration. Not looking up, he tells Claire that the place is finished. They've been attacked by what he thinks is a "special forces team." Claire's free to leave the prison grounds, but he warns her that she has no chance of getting off the island.[40]

The gaps here open and close as they do in any narrative: Who is the guy? (open)—Umbrella guard who captured me (close); Why is he opening the door? Maybe he will kill me, maybe he is a spy (open)—he opens it because the base is under attack and wants to give me a chance (close); Do I believe him? (open) Do I have a chance? (open) Who is attacking us? (open) We could continue, but you get the idea: just as when reading a story, the gamer actively works to fill in the gaps.

However, unlike in a novel (or a movie), as the story grows and changes in our minds we also have to act. This walkthrough demonstrates the choices a player must make as they decipher the game's clues.

Action Level

CELLBLOCK ROOM—We are in a cellblock. Start off by going to your item screen. Go to the LIGHTER you see and use "Select" with the action button. This will prompt a cut-scene. After the cut-scene, go back into the cellblock and grab the ever important GREEN HERB. In the small corner of the room, grab the HANDGUN BULLETS. On the desk near the unconscious jailer is a COMBAT KNIFE. Once you have all the items, you may exit the room.[41]

As we can see, the walkthrough is full of things we need to do in order to get out of the cell and to the graveyard, but these things are not worth telling in the previous narration of the plot (in the same way that what the guard says is not worth telling in the walkthrough, which merely states "this will prompt a cut-scene").

When we say that both levels are "active" in our minds at the same time, we do not mean that they are as clearly separated as in our descriptions here. This is an abstraction necessary for analysis, but in fact the act of playing is more than the sum of the two, since actual gameplay is full of doubts, ineffective movement, reloads, and at some point, probably death. This content is also an essential part of playing.

So the act of playing is informed by: our cognitive, often unconscious filling in the gaps, our sense of what we think we have to do within the game, and the hand-eye coordination that gives us our playing ability. Below is Tosca's description of the first time she played the opening scene of *Code: Veronica*, demonstrating the messy reality of actual gameplay:

> I walk around the cell in darkness, it takes some time to find lighter and learn how to operate it. I watch the cut-scene, have no idea what the guy is talking about, if they have been attacked shouldn't the attackers be on my side? Why does he say I have no chance? Maybe it is a trap, am not sure I should trust him but have no option. He doesn't talk anymore even though I try to click on him and approach him. (I don't see the herb they recommend to take in the walkthrough.) I explore a lot of things with no result (try to open cupboard and get closer to the chest of drawers, but it doesn't work). Since I know the game is about zombies and that the guy belongs to the evil corporation, I am not sure he won't turn into a zombie at any minute and kill me, so I stab him repeatedly to finish him off before leaving the cell. This has required equipping the knife instead of the lighter, something that needs several tries before I find out how to do it.

Actual gameplay is full of trial and error—especially at the beginning of the game when we are not familiar with the interface or the story. My description of the endless things I attempted (moving the body, looking in the cupboards), and my rationale for stabbing the man (the implicit association with movies or other games in which the undead come back to haunt you), are all actions appropriate to the unfolding framework of the story. Though they differ from the sequence of actions recommended by the walkthrough above, they are not wrong; the player is simply using the information that she has at that moment as she tries to fill in the gaps. The player will eventually fill the gaps in the right way and find the right sequence of actions to perform (alone or with help of a walkthrough); or, perhaps, she will quit the game in frustration. And here is a remarkable feature of narrative in video games: it is perpetually unfolding, constantly folding back on itself, full of false starts and restarts, as the player contributes to the story's creation with each action.

Our take on the player experience of narrative resonates with Gordon Calleja's more recent concept of "alterbiography," defined as the "active construction of an ongoing story that develops through interaction with the game world's topography, inhabitants, objects, and game rules and simulated environmental properties."[42] Calleja is also influenced by Iser, and talks about how the scripted narrative inspires and becomes a part of the player's alterbiography, creating narrative involvement.

We hope we have demonstrated that a close reading of a video game is not only possible but also that it yields interesting insights about how a game that makes use of stories is experienced by a player. Of course, one should keep in mind that the analysis presented here is very much determined by the genre to which *Resident Evil Code: Veronica X* belongs, just as any similar analysis will be tied to its subject. Different subgenres will require an adaptation of these concepts, but it is our belief that they are flexible enough to be extensively applicable. Using the notion of the "literary repertoire" demonstrates the vital importance of a game's cultural (literary, filmic) context, and its gameplay context (knowledge from other games and genres). Similarly, exploring our innately human tendency to "fill in the gaps" of a story shows us that the interpretive process goes hand in hand with the skill-based operation of the game controls, which we can also call interactivity. Drawing from these and other insights of reader response criticism, we are given an intriguing perspective on narrative video games, one in which story and game are not opposed to each other but merge in a unique combination.

A BRIEF HISTORY OF LITERARY THEORY AND VIDEO GAMES

Having examined some of the applications of ideas about narrative to video games, here we will offer a historical look at the theoretical work that explicitly deals with questions of narrative, storytelling, and fiction in relation to video games.

It is always arbitrary to isolate particular time periods, but there is a basic distinction between the works that appeared in the 1990s (or before) and those that appeared from 2000 onward. The 1990s was an exciting time in the nascent field of digital aesthetics: computers had become widespread, the Internet was becoming a major cultural focus, and various forms of digital art, literature, and games were emerging. A whole group of theorists was attracted to the new digital medium, determined to uncover in what way it was special and different from previous media. These texts tend to consider video games as part of more general theories about digital media, while later works deal with video games as a unique object of study.

The transition is best demonstrated by Espen Aarseth's groundbreaking book *Cybertext*, from 1997, still a landmark in the theoretical study of new media and narrativity. He makes a sharp analysis of the changes in textuality (the nature of the text) brought about by the digital era. Aarseth proposes a new model of textuality that can accommodate (among other things) print books, hypertexts, and video games, which he classifies according to an innovative typology. According to Aarseth, video games are "cybertexts," that is, "texts that involve calculation in their production of scriptons,"[43] which means that the participation of the reader/user is not trivial, and the degree of involvement goes beyond the activity of reading. Aarseth's foundation is **narratology** and reader response theories, which he develops to fit the digital medium. His main point is that reading a normal book requires an interpretive effort on the part of the reader, but engaging with a cybertext requires something more, as it is a configurative activity. Cybertexts have existed for a long time (the *I-Ching*, for example, a book that uses printed symbols to decode the tosses of a group of coins, has been around for nearly three millennia[44]), but only with the computer do their properties become widespread and easy to implement.

Narratology: The study of narratives. Within computer game research narratology is often seen as opposed to ludology.

Cybertext examines the main genres of cybertextuality available at the time: hypertext, video games (in the form of adventure games), machine-generated literature, and MUDs. It was an important work in that it opened the textual paradigm to the texts of the digital era, offering an attractive alternative to the dominant hypertext theory of the time (which emphasized the similarities of the new kinds of text with postmodern theories of dispersion).

Other pioneering work in the area was done by Janet Murray, in her *Hamlet on the Holodeck*, also from 1997, which we will consider later in this chapter; also by Marie-Laure Ryan[45] and Mark J.P. Wolf,[46] who attempts to describe video games as an independent medium within a framework of cultural and media history, leaning heavily on film studies, although he also considers the "formal aspects" of the video game (space, time, and narrative).

Both of these first theorists and those who came after have been concerned with a number of issues very much framed by the typical theoretical problems of the digital era. These have kept hypertext theorists and digital aesthetic critics busy since the early 1990s:

Ludology: The study of games, particularly computer games. Ludology is often defined as the study of game structure (or gameplay) as opposed to the study of games as narratives or games as a visual medium.

- **Ludology** versus narratology
- Interaction versus narrative
- The interactive storytelling paradigm: in search of quality
- The fictional status of video games.

We can use these headlines as a way to thematize the theoretical discussions in the field.

Ludology Versus Narratology

From our earlier discussion of literary theory, it seems like looking for stories in video games would be quite straightforward, utilizing the accumulated knowledge of literary theory in order to approach our new aesthetic object. But this approach has not been uncontested. Quite the opposite—the use of literary theory has caused the biggest clash of paradigms in video game studies so far: the "war" between ludology and narratology.

Literature is one the oldest subjects of study in the humanities, and as such its methods have been exported to the study of newer media, such as cinema; first steps in new disciplines are usually inspired by older ones. We could say that the same has happened in the case of video games, as some early approaches to the study of games centered on their representational quality, and thus authors have been able to apply literary and dramatic models to the description and cultural understanding of video games.[47]

However, some of these attempts have been rejected by a group of researchers, identified (by themselves and others) as "ludologists."[48] Their aim is to consider video games as games and not as narratives or anything else. The term "ludology" was introduced into video game studies by game theorist Gonzalo Frasca. He suggested that ludology be thought of simply as the "discipline that studies game and play activities."[49] In that broad sense there is no inherent opposition to literary approaches, and indeed "ludology" *is* sometimes used to merely refer to "the study of games" (using any approach). Expanding on this stance, however, Frasca has since specified that a ludological stance implies that "games cannot be understood through theories derived from narrative."[50]

Jesper Juul's article "Computer Games Telling Stories?" offers a balanced introduction to the debate. He argues that part of the problem arises from the indiscriminate use of the word "narrative." If everything is a narrative, it is of course not very useful to say that video games can also be described as such. Juul also gives three reasons for why it is easy to confuse narratives with video games:

1. The player can tell stories of a game session.
2. Many video games contain narrative elements, and in many cases the player may play to see a cut-scene or realize a narrative sequence.
3. Video games and narratives share some structural traits.[51]

Juul argues that we should resist the temptation to confuse the two forms, because it is impossible to translate video games into stories and vice versa.[52] He also discusses how understanding narrative simply as a retelling of events can be misleading and how the experience of playing a game is very different from that of reading a story.

Ludologists have found a wide variety of reasons why subsuming video games under the headline of narrative is a bad idea; the most damning is that the approach can lead us to overlook the "intrinsic properties" of video games. The Finnish theorist Markku Eskelinen has overtaken Frasca's less confrontational stance and is in the vanguard of ludology's most radical anti-narrative critics. As he forcefully puts it:

> The old and new game components, their dynamic combination and distribution, the registers, the necessary manipulation of temporal, causal, spatial and functional relations and properties not to mention the rules and the goals and the lack of audience should suffice to set games and the gaming situation apart from narrative and drama, and to annihilate for good the discussion of computer games as stories, narratives or cinema.[53]

But the extremity of such a stance has further stoked the debate. The idea that games are first and foremost games—an argument bordering on the tautological—can be taken to mean that the formal properties of video games are more important, more *intrinsic*, than the stories in the games (or the graphics, or the social activity that games promote). The debate has raged on for the last several years, with ludologists attacking the colonization of the new field of game studies by alien disciplines such as literature. Controversy is sometimes good, and from a pragmatic perspective we can say that this discussion has helped bring the study of video games into the spotlight.[54]

The debate has continued among game scholars, although lately the ludologists have been identified as "essentialists," and narrative is no longer the enemy. The new struggle is between those who prefer to concentrate on the formalistic properties of games (the ludologists) and those who want to consider them as situated practices.[55]

To return to the focus of this chapter, literary theorists have criticized radical ludology for viewing stories as "just uninteresting ornaments or gift wrappings to games, and laying any emphasis on studying these kinds of marketing tools is just a waste of time and energy."[56] Scholars like Marie-Laure Ryan, and later Julian Kücklich,[57] see ludology as a threat to the fruitful application of narrative concepts to the study of video games.

Computer games function as what Kendall Walton would call a "prop in a game of make-believe." It may not be the raison d'être of computer games, but it plays such an important role as a stimulant for the imagination that many recent computer games use lengthy film clips, which interrupt the game, to immerse the player in the game world.[58]

From this it follows that the two sides seem to be talking about different things when they say "narrative," as ludologists see it as a fixed sequence of events forced on the player, while literary theorists see it as a loose fictional frame.

Paradoxically, certain ludologists have come to agree with the importance of stories. Jesper Juul's *Half-Real: Video Games between Real Rules and Fictional Worlds* represents a move away from his earlier radical position, as he argues that the essence of video games as a cultural product is the unique way in which they combine "the rules that the player interacts with in real time with a fictional, imagined world."[59]

Beyond the squabbles, we should recognize the ludology-narratology wars as a symptom of the struggle to define the new discipline of game studies, beyond the dominant paradigms—the hypertextual[60] and the cinematic[61]—of the beginnings of the study of digital textuality.

Interaction Versus Narrative

A game has to be interactive. This is the greatest strength of video games, but it is also a challenge. If the point of video games is that players do things (gameplay), the fact that in some video games they are forced to "sit and watch" (for example, cut-scenes) is seen by some designers and others as an unwelcome invasion. And if designers are able truly to integrate stories into the game, how can narratives ever be fully engaging if they always have to offer the player the possibility of winning? And how can artificial intelligences ever become interesting fictional characters? All these questions are derived from the ongoing debate of interaction versus narrative, a problem inherited from earlier discussions about the status of digital literature, mostly from the field of hypertext theory.[62]

One solution to this problem is to separate interaction from narration and situate them in different planes, as Janet Murray does when she conceives of video games as symbolic dramas:

> In games, therefore, we have *a chance to* enact our most basic relationship to the world—our desire to prevail over adversity, to survive our inevitable defeats, to shape our environment, to master complexity, and to make our lives fit together like the pieces of a jigsaw puzzle. Each move in a game is *like* a plot event in one of these simple but compelling stories. *Like* the religious ceremonies of passage by which we mark birth, coming of age, marriage and death, games are ritual actions allowing us to *symbolically* enact the patterns that give meaning to our lives.[63]

The trouble with this answer is of course the *like*, which puts video games and stories at different abstract levels. This might explain how narratively we make sense of the conflicts posed by video games but doesn't tell us much about how stories actually work *within* them. We could also say that it seems much easier to create symbolic dramas than real interactive stories (at plot level), since anything can be read as a symbolic drama. Even *Tetris*, after all, has "clear dramatic content."[64]

An alternative is Atkins's analysis of video games that effectively integrate narrative and gameplay. *More than a Game* is dedicated to four video games that he sees "as having a central narrative impetus, that develop story over time, rather than simply repeat with minimal difference in a move from level to level of increasing excess."[65] The chosen games are *Tomb Raider, Half-Life, Close Combat*, and *SimCity*—which seem like strange choices since there are no adventure or role-playing video games among them, the two subgenres with a stronger narrative component.[66] Each of the four games represents a good example of an effective strategy for integrating narrative and gameplay: *Tomb Raider* is a model of open-endedness and the use of quests; *Half-Life* employs innovative themes and perspective; *Close Combat* takes the concept of realism to new heights; and *SimCity*'s simulation rules can be read narratively, which means that game rules can have ideological implications. The book concludes with a discussion on the status of video games as a fictional form. It is a very compelling approach, but no links to previous theory are made, which undermines the author's credibility when he tackles highly contested issues in the field of digital culture—such as interactivity or immersion—as if for the first time.

The narrative versus interactivity debate also crops up in most video game design textbooks, although the authors might not identify it as such.[67] For instance, game designer Richard Rouse argues that all out-of-game storytelling should be avoided, as it goes against the interactive experience of gaming. Rouse uses examples from bad cut-scenes (for example, from the game *Tekken*) to argue that very often they are not integrated into the game.[68] In-game storytelling is the preferable option, which Rouse describes as "showing," compared to the "telling" which occurs with out-of-game narrative. In-game storytelling is achieved by, for example, creating a believable world that gives a context to the plot, and by nonplayer characters with personalities. *Deus Ex*, with its successful in-game storytelling, is a good example of how to achieve both narrative and interaction; the gameplay offers the choice of acting in a violent or more pacifist way, so that players can create different stories as they go. "For in-game storytelling, players get to experience the story themselves instead of being told it secondhand"; it also maintains the player's immersion in the game world.[69]

Rouse is not alone in proposing a way to use "storytelling" to thematize the rules in games. Designers and theorists alike argue that fiction might actually have a very important function in video games.[70] This connection is explored by Jesper Juul by looking at examples of "clashes" between rules and fiction:

> In the game of *Grand Theft Auto 3*, a blue arrow is placed over whatever object or target the player has to reach in a mission. Even though the game has been lauded for its elaborate world and detailed environments, the blue arrow clearly points to the *rules* of the game. This is at odds with a certain mode of thought that claims that a good game should never remind the player that he/she is playing a game. I claim that the player is always aware that the game is a game, and that this is part of the reason why we can accept incoherence in game worlds.[71]

Juul argues that the fictional world is also needed in video games to enable players to infer the rules (to let them know which repertoire applies)—which in "good" games are anyway hidden from immediate perception.[72] This compromise is a step forward from early ludological positions, and certainly demonstrates a more effective way of reconciling literary theory and video games.

Perhaps further reconciliation is possible through a reexamination of our terminology. As we have already suggested, the idea that narrative and interactivity oppose each other springs from a definition of narrative as a linear unfolding of events; while this is true in many instances, it is not very interesting, as Jonas Heide Smith remarks.[73] There are other forms of narrative than the traditional sequence, and especially interesting possibilities have recently bloomed, with the growth of multiplayer online games. We might even speculate that this argument will soon be a thing of the past, as we move past the dominant influence of single-player games. As we move forward, we might want to look at how narratives are produced in multiplayer environments, for example, in which the parameters of the story are not all fixed by a designer and where new kinds of experiences arise due to the unpredictability of the players' behavior.[74]

In the same spirit, Henry Jenkins argues that games tell stories in their own unique way, and that their narratives are not equivalent to a simplistic, linear idea of a story of the type found in films or novels.[75] Jenkins proposes, instead, that game stories are "spatial" and "environmental." Spatial stories are related to those works of literature that tell a hero's odyssey, or travel narratives; in the case of computer games the traveling would be done not only by the characters but also by the player. Environmental stories are related to the genres of literature that focus on the depiction of worlds, such as fantasy or science fiction; in computer games, it is the player that does the exploring. In order to construct a world that tells a story, game designers act like creators of amusement park rides; they are not storytellers but architects of narrative. Accordingly, Jenkins describes four ways in which narrative can appear in games:

- *Evoked narratives*: When video games reproduce a world that is known to players through other works of fiction, so that the games are part of an encompassing system of meanings. For example, the game *Blade Runner* reproduces the world of the film and the novel, so that players will be able to "live out" the stories that exist in their imagination by visiting that world.
- *Enacted narratives*: Where, as Jenkins puts it, "the story itself may be structured around the character's movement through space and the features of the environment may retard or accelerate that plot trajectory."[76] This category encompasses the spatial and environmental stories mentioned above. These are typically not appreciated by literary scholars, as they privilege spatial exploration over plot development. This form is very well suited to video games, as a designer can create the world that the player will have to traverse and conquer.
- *Embedded narratives*: When "the gamespace becomes a memory palace whose contents must be deciphered as the player tries to reconstruct the plot."[77] The classical embedded narrative would be a detective story, such as those found in adventure games, where players encounter a world of clues that have to be deciphered in order to find out about the story that has already happened. A good example of this is *Myst*.
- *Emergent narratives*: When "gamespaces are designed to be rich with narrative potential, enabling the story-constructing activity of players." We have seen Juul's description of these narratives earlier, in the section on "Mechanics"; both Juul and Heide Smith have called this "object-oriented narration," in which the gamespace is filled with objects with their own behaviors, so that the player interaction creates unique events that feel significant. Henry Jenkins gives the example of *The Sims*, which allows players to create their own stories.[78]

These four kinds of narratives fail to address many of the elements discussed in the first part of this chapter, such as the sequential storytelling we find in quests, or other literary ingredients such as characterization. However, they may help move us beyond the frozen narrative versus interactivity discussion. Because these categories highlight other qualities of video game stories, such as their spatial component, and provide a way to introduce contextual elements (using the evoked narratives category, for example).

Figure 7.8 Myst (1994), with its special embedded narrative, attracted a new audience to video games

They offer a different and fruitful use of literary theory in relation to video games.

The Interactive Storytelling Paradigm: In Search of Quality

During the 1990s, the idea of the "interactive narrative" gained a certain prominence. It refers not to video games, nor hypertext (or other forms of digital literature) but rather to a sort of role-playing in which the computer can anticipate the player's reactions and give an illusion of total interactivity. It is considered an ideal form of digital storytelling, deeply engaging and immersive. This paradigm approaches narrative from an Aristotelian and structuralist perspective, and its proponents are typically interested in the problems inherent in automatic generation of stories, or how to improve artificial intelligence. The field of interactive narrative has attracted scholars that work with design and programming of games, such as Craig A. Lindley or Michael Mateas,[79] as well as theorists such as Marie-Laure Ryan.[80]

The most influential work in this area is *Hamlet on the Holodeck*, by Janet Murray, an enthusiastic defense of the computer as the new storytelling medium, because of the way its four defining properties facilitate digital narration:

> Digital environments are *procedural, participatory, spatial* and *encyclo-pedic.* The first two properties make up most of what we mean by the vaguely used word interactive; the remaining two properties help to make digital creations seem as explorable and extensive as the actual world, making up much of what we mean when we say that cyberspace is *immersive.*[81]

The "procedural" property refers to the computer's ability to execute rules in succession and thus generate behaviors. For Murray, the computer character Eliza, created by Joseph Weizenbaum in 1966, is a good example of how the procedural property can produce the illusion of a "living person." Eliza was able to converse with humans as if she was a psychologist that always turned your statements back at you. For example, if you typed: "I am worried," the program would respond: "What are you worried about?" Inspired by this, authors like Ian Bogost and Noah Wardrip-Fruin have developed theories about the specific expressive power of video games (and other digital cultural forms) that are specifically tied to the procedural property (see Chapter 6).

The second, "participatory" property refers to the fact that we can influence the production of behavior when interacting with a computer; an example is the textual adventure game *Zork*, in which the program responds to the textual input of the player and produces lines of text that describe her progress in the game, thus creating a story. Computers are also "spatial," that is, able to represent navigable space.

Finally, the "encyclopedic" property points to the storage capacity of computers, whose memories can hold enormous amounts of information and allow us to interact with information-rich environments, from fan websites to MUDs to enormous games like *SimCity* and *Civilization*.

Without going into a detailed discussion of the four properties, it is not hard to see that video games turn out perfectly to embody each of them, and are thus, it could be argued, the perfect vehicle for digital storytelling.

Murray is inspired by the "holodeck," the entertainment system of the *Star Trek* universe. The holodeck is an immersive entertainment environment, a virtual reality machine that makes stories come to life and lets "readers"—in this case the ship's crew—participate as actors in completely realistic virtual environments that make use of all five senses. An example Murray gives is that of the female starship captain in the series *Star Trek: Voyager* who is entertained with a story inspired by *Jane Eyre*, in which she plays a nineteenth-century governess and nearly falls in love—in "real" life—with the virtual hero.[82]

Following the promise of the holodeck, Murray's dream is that of a "cyberbard"—a Homer or Shakespeare of the future, able to bend the computer to more artistic uses than those we know today. Murray's book is inspiring, filled with rich personal anecdotes about new media experiences, even though it also suffers from excessive utopianism. The book overstates the interest that interactive narrative might hold for average audiences, and projects the idea of the romantic author into the future. As for computer games, even though Murray identifies them as the greatest commercial success and creative effort in digital storytelling, she thinks they are not yet mature as a medium: "The narrative content of these games is thin, and is often imported from other media or supplied by sketchy and stereotypical characters."[83]

Janet Murray was influenced by an earlier book by Brenda Laurel, *Computers as Theatre*, from 1991, about interface design and drama, although it also deals with video games and offers a dramatic model for computer-human interaction. Laurel's opinion of video games, however, regardless of their technological advancements, is also not very positive: "I find most video games to be boring, frustrating and 'obstructionist' in the sense that they require players to solve puzzles primarily for the purpose of extending the duration of game play."[84]

The dubious opinions these scholars hold of video games are in part due to their judging them by the quality standards of other media, such as movies or print novels. They suggest that the simplicity of game narratives can be overcome in different ways, involving everything from complex artificial intelligence or more detailed fictional worlds. Mark J. P. Wolf, another author worried about the quality of video games, seems to equate the emotional complexity of a player's experience with the level of detail in the games' visual imagery. He writes, for example, that *Myst* is a turning point in the development of the video game's diegetic world, because of the light effects that create a rich world and that inspire contemplative moods in the player.[85]

Murray offers some guidelines for creating engaging, interactive storytelling. To begin with, formulaic storytelling could make use of the same plots all stories are made of, combined in an interesting way that possibly involves powerful artificial intelligence.[86] Murray suggests that procedural storytelling could be similar to ancient oral storytelling (the bardic system), although how this inspiration can be used to combine plots is not entirely clear. She also stresses the importance of using well-known genres (like mystery or science fiction) in order to exploit knowledge that the user already has—in a way similar to the "repertoire" concept of reader response theory.

Vladimir Propp's "morphology of the folktale" might be another tool to help create digital stories. His system, created in 1928, describes how Russian folktales can be analyzed by isolating small narrative units that are combined in different ways but essentially repeat themselves in many tales (for example, the hero leaves home, or the hero gets a present). Murray argues that interactive narrative would benefit from reproducing his formulaic system of story elements, symbols, and character functions. According to Murray, Propp's algorithm is much more complex than "most electronic computer games currently on the market," which are limited to two or three themes such as "fight bad guy," "solve puzzle," and "die." Without considering the economic reasons behind this simplicity, she sees it as a problem that video games "do not allow substitution of thematic plot elements" that would require much more ambitious programming.[87]

A productive take on these problems is exemplified by the work of scholar and designer Michael Mateas, who together with Andrew Stern has created the most successful interactive drama to date, *Façade*. This piece combines both a credible and engaging plot with believable characters, while allowing real interaction on the part of the player, who communicates with the program using natural language.

Mateas and Stern explicitly wanted to create an Aristotelian plot arc.[88] Their AI system tries to respond to the input of players and change dramatic

Figure 7.9 Façade (2005) attempts to use natural language interaction to create a deeper interactive narrative experience

values so that the interaction actually has an effect on the development of the story. What lies behind the relatively simple interface is a carefully planned programming of story units, which they call "beats." "Roughly, a beat consists of an action/reaction pair between characters. Beats are sequenced to make scenes, scenes to make acts, acts to make stories. The AI plot system contains a library of beats appropriate for our story."[89] *Façade* is both a simulation and a plotted narrative. At any moment, the player experiences the freedom to interact in natural language and to send the action one way or the other, but a "drama manager"

> continuously monitors the simulation and proactively adds and retracts procedures (behaviors) and discourse contexts by which Grace and Trip operate. That is, the rules of the simulation are regularly being updated in an attempt to give the player a well-formed overall experience with unity, efficiency and pacing.[90]

And it works. Even though there are occasions on which the system fails to recognize player input, most interactions elicit an appropriate answer, and the story can be played a few times with different outcomes.

The paradigm of the interactive narrative does have a lot to offer our study of video games. In the relentless search for quality advocated by Murray, Laurel, and others—in their insistence on the ways that narrative can be adapted to new technologies—we have to admire their enthusiasm about the possibilities of the new medium and their attempt to describe what it is about interactivity that people desire so much.

The Fictional Status of Video Games

From the foregoing discussion, it seems clear that fiction in video games does not work according to the same parameters as in representational media; it should also be clear that we cannot apply literary theories wholesale to the study or design of video games without considering their specific properties. A variety of authors have begun to move beyond the quagmire of narrative, to focus instead on what kinds of fictions video games are, and how we could delimit their fictional properties.

A foundational theoretical premise for these scholars is to decide what the game world is. Is the game world a prop for the player's imagination (in Walton's sense), or is the world a virtual object or stage for the game to take place on? In Marie-Laure Ryan's words:

> In an abstract sense, of course, most if not all games create a "game-world," or self-enclosed playing space, and the passion that the player brings to the game may be regarded as immersion in this game-world. But I would like to draw a distinction between "world" as a set of rules and tokens, and "world" as imaginary space, furnished with individuated objects. The pieces of a chess game may be labeled king, queen, bishop, or knight, but chess players do not relate to them as fictional persons, nor do they imagine a royal court, a castle, an army, and a war between rival kingdoms.[91]

One of the consequences of such a distinction is that the world we imagine in our heads is not equivalent to the visual appearance of the virtual world of the game. Thus, we should consider the whole world experience and not just what has been called, by authors such as Wolf, the "diegetic representation" of a world, which is just the "world on screen."[92] For Wolf, this is different from "extradiegetic narration," that is, how video games point to other diegetic worlds (television shows, movies, novels, and the like). Wolf's examples of extradiegetic narration are of intro movies, cut-scenes, intro screens, and game manuals. However, the meta level of genre references not only points to stories in other media, it also calls up the player's game repertoire[93]—as discussed in relation to reader response theory—so that the player can also infer how the game world will work. In other words, the world allows us to make inferences about the rules.

Salen and Zimmerman's concept of the "narrative descriptor" is a good example of elements beyond the game. Narrative descriptors are "representations, which means that they are depictions of one or more aspects of the game world";[94] these can be graphics on the side of the arcade cabinet, manuals, soundtracks, cut-scenes, and so on. Let us, for example, look at their description of the action in *Asteroids*, from which players will be able to infer much about interaction and gameplay:

> Shoot the asteroids while avoiding collisions with them. Occasionally a flying saucer will appear and attempt to shoot you down with guided missiles. Destroy it or the missiles for more points.[95]

These few sentences remind us not only of a genre that is related to other media—science fiction—but also of typical video game conventions—in this case the reward system. Video game conventions, for example, having several "lives," are very important for the gaming experience, even if they wouldn't make sense in a traditional narration. Imagine an account of *Romeo and Juliet* where Romeo was allowed to start all over again after discovering his lover dead, as many times as it took for them to be together and live happily ever after. We would perceive this not only as incoherent but also as totally destructive of the play's dramatic effect. Jesper Juul argues that the incoherence and instability of video game fictions does not mean that these fictions are of lesser quality than those found in other media; rather, they just need to be considered from their own perspective:

> The worlds that video games project are often ontologically unstable, but the rules of video games are very ontologically stable. While we may not be able to explain *why* Mario reappears in *Donkey Kong*, we always know for certain how many lives we have left. That the majority of fictional game worlds are incoherent does not mean that video games are dysfunctional providers of fiction, but rather that they project fictional worlds in their own flickering, provisional, and optional way.[96]

Espen Aarseth has also dealt with the question of fiction in video games, and comes to the conclusion that computer games are not fictions in the same way as, say, books or films are, even though they do contain fictional elements. Some of the fictional elements in computer games are just representations (for example, a door that cannot be opened), but others can be operated in the same way as objects in the real world (some doors can be opened, closed, and locked). These would have a middle status, a combination of representation and simulation. Aarseth talks about "virtuality," and concludes that "instead of the common notion that game worlds are fictional, we should start to see them as composites where the fictional element is but one of the many types of world-building ingredients."[97]

In a remarkable conjunction of ideas, other authors from Henry Jenkins to Julian Kücklich have also proposed literary approaches to the study of video games based on their capacity to evoke fictions, and not on their narrative qualities,[98] which takes us out of the cul-de-sac of the narratology-ludology debate. The fictional worlds approach has also opened the door to studying video games as a part of wider ecologies of fiction, such as transmedia worlds, where the specific strengths of video games for storytelling purposes are considered in relation to other media products such as books, films, or television series.[99]

TRANSMEDIA GAMES

Transmedia studies have become a field in its own right[100] and grown very much in scope since Marsha Kinder identified video games as a crucial part of what she called "commercial transmedia supersystem,"[101] which we today might rather call transmedia franchises. Kinder proposed that intertextuality could emerge from products such as toys and of course games. Also Henry Jenkins, who coined the expression "transmedia storytelling," considered games as one more brick in complex entertainment systems, where

> In the ideal form of transmedia storytelling, each medium does what it does best-so that a story might be introduced in a film, expanded through television, novels, and comics, and its world might be explored and experienced through game play.[102]

This somehow subordinate position of video games (at least in story-related terms) has been the rule whenever video games have been part of complex transmedia systems, also today, they are "characterized by an adaptation aesthetic, a process through which the images and characters from the film become playable and/or navigable."[103] Transmedial studies as a field spans over several disciplines, ranging from media studies to communication to the humanities, so video games are interesting objects of study from different angles (as part of franchises, as carrying specific affordances, as fulfilling narrative roles). The narrative-centric transmedia research is best represented by the work of Marie-Laure Ryan[104] and Jan-Noel Thon,[105] who both have argued in favor of separating the concept of transmediality from an attachment to a particular medium and instead work toward an overarching theory of transmedia narratives that would also include video games:

> I am thinking here of principles such as extending the timeline, creating prequels and sequels, telling the story of secondary characters, extending the geography of the storyworld, telling the story from a different point of view and leaving some unresolved issues that can be answered in another narrative. These principles are timeless and independent of medium.[106]

FINAL REMARKS

Perhaps these developments mean that the field is moving toward more stimulating discussions that also take into account more contemporary literary theory. However, postmodern literary theory has not been a part of the debate so far, and perhaps it never will be. Stories in computer games are still in their infancy, and the heavily loaded postmodernist theories about deconstruction or other dispersions of the text wouldn't be of much help at this stage.

So let us return to the question we posed at the beginning of the chapter: are video games stories? Yes, we would answer. Many video games are stories, as well as games. Some games contain more narrative than others, but even the most abstract usually include the sketched elements of a fictional world. And we need to take into account the narrative elements of a video game if we are to fully understand the medium and how player interaction is shaped.

DISCUSSION QUESTIONS

- Think about a game you have played where you liked the story. How is it different from other kinds of stories, such as those in books or movies? What do you like and dislike in video game stories?

- Think about a memorable video game character (including player characters) and discuss why you remember him or her. How are characters in games different from characters in other media?

- What makes a good quest in a game? Why? Use examples to illustrate your answer.

- Summarize a good story-based game you have played. What do you leave out when you summarize it? Why?

- Are interactivity and narrative totally opposed? In other words, can a game designer give options to her players while at the same time making sure they experience a good story? Discuss, using theory from the chapter as well as examples from your own experience.

RECOMMENDED GAMES

Resident Evil Code: Veronica X—A great example of the narrative strength that can come to play in computer games.

BioShock series—A great example of how narrative can work in games, and where the moral nature of your choices adds an extra dimension to the game experience. *BioShock* shows how the story and the game can really work together, where too often the narrative almost gets in the way of the game.

Baldur's Gate 2—A classic example of how narrative is used in games to enrich the classic game mechanics. Very well executed with a few interesting twists where the narrative sometimes breaks the artificial boundary between the game and the story—allowing the story to overtake the game experience at key points in the story.

Façade—An early example of interactive fiction heavily relying on artificial intelligence to construct a unique experience every time you play the game. Often seen as one of the first successful examples of a truly interactive narrative able to respond to player actions.

Silent Hill 2—An intriguing example of how well narrative can work to infuse the game experience, where your actions in the game influence how the story develops. The twist of the narrative undermining your protagonist is as disturbing as it is effective in creating a unique experience.

FURTHER READINGS

Aarseth, E. (2012, May). A narrative theory of games. In *Proceedings of the International Conference on the Foundations of Digital Games* (pp. 129–133). ACM.

(Estimated reading time: 22 minutes)

Fernández-Vara, C. (2011). Game spaces speak volumes: Indexical storytelling. *Proceedings of DiGRA 2011 Conference: Think Design Play*.

(Estimated reading time: 28 minutes)

Kücklich, J. (2001, September). Literary theory and computer games. In *Proceedings of the First Conference on Computational Semiotics for Games and New Media (COSIGN)*.

(Estimated reading time: 35 minutes)

NOTES

1. From the game package of Westwood's *Blade Runner*. Just like the film, the game is set in Los Angeles in 2019, and the player has the role of a rookie blade runner named Ray McCoy, who has to deal with several dangerous replicants.

2. www.lucasarts.com/products/starwarsracer/default.htm.

3. On the similarity of *The Sims* and doll's house play, see Flanagan, 2003; Krotoski, 2004, p. 12.

4. From promotional material for the game, as quoted at, for example, www.metacritic.com/game/gamecube/the-sims.

5. The discussion here builds on Rimmon Kenan, 2002.

6. As Rimmon Kenan herself notes, these distinctions have been given different names by different literary theorists; for example, Genette's *histoire*, *récit*, and *narration*. This is not the place to discuss them and compare them, as we are only interested in definitions that will help us understand computer games.

7. In her PhD thesis, *Towards a Poetics of Virtual Worlds: Multiuser Textuality and the Emergence of Story* (Klastrup, 2003, p. 19).

8. Aarseth, 2000.

9. Aarseth, 2000.

10. Calleja, 2011, p. 92.

11. Rouse, 2001, p. 223.

12. Klevjer, 2002; Wolf, 2001.

13. Klevjer, 2002, p. 198. This definition follows Gérard Genette, for whom "diegesis" would mean the narrative of a work of fiction, that is, the story, so that everything that did not belong to the main story would be "extradiegetic." Later, in film theory, diegesis has been understood to include the elements that belong to the main story (for example, the background of the characters that has led to their situation).

14. Klevjer, 2002, p. 200.

15. *Collins English Dictionary*. Italics added.

16. Wolf, 2001, p. 98. Unlike characters in other media, who are deeper and capable of development, characters in video games follow a goal, which can be "score oriented, conflict oriented, task oriented or some combination of these." However, Wolf's argument suffers from a confusion between the personality of the fictitious characters (in many cases absent) and the actions players

have to take when controlling them. There is no reason why a playing character cannot be a narrator, for example.

17. Vladimir Propp published his *Morphology of the Folk Tale* in 1928, offering among other things a typology of characters according to their function in these narratives, such as: the hero, the villain, the donor, the dispatcher, the false hero, the helper, the princess, and the father (of the princess); Propp, 1969.
18. Gard, 2000.
19. MacCallum-Stewart and Parsler, 2008.
20. Tosca, 2003a.
21. Rouse, 2001, p. 235. However, some theorists disagree. Ken Perlin, for example, maintains that we cannot identify with game characters unless they have a strong personality, since if they are empty and only "filled" through our agency, identification is impossible; Perlin, 2004.
22. See, for instance, Bringsjord, 2001.
23. Laurel, 1993, p. 145.
24. Meehan, 1976.
25. Lebowitz, 1984.
26. Lebowitz, 1984, p. 146.
27. Smith, 2000a.
28. Juul, 2001.
29. Smith, 2000b.
30. Tronstad, 2001; Tosca, 2003b; Aarseth, 2003; Howard, 2008. The analysis here is based on Tosca, 2003b.
31. Walker, 2007.
32. Howard, 2008.
33. Krzywinska, 2009.
34. Ryan, ML (2001b).
35. Released in 2001 for the PlayStation as an updated version of the original 2000 Dreamcast game.
36. Iser, 1979, p. 69.
37. "Actualize" here means to understand the cues provided by the text and call up the relevant repertoire—in other words, make the appropriate projections.
38. Iser, 1979, p. 169.
39. In Marie Laure Ryan's sense; Ryan, 1991.
40. From a 135-page document entitled "A Detailed Plot Analysis of the *Resident Evil* Videogame Series," by Dan Birlew and Thomas Wilde. Downloaded from http://db.gamefaqs.com/console/psx/file/resident_evil_plot.txt (June 30, 2005).
41. This walkthrough by CVXFREAK was downloaded from http://db.gamefaqs.com/console/dreamcast/file/resident_evil_code_veronica_complete.txt (June 30, 2005).
42. Calleja, 2011, p. 127.
43. Aarseth, 1997, p. 75. "Scriptons" are the text units the reader sees on-screen after having manipulated the text. They are different from "textons," which are all the units that make up the text but which are not necessarily visible to the reader, for example, the programming language.
44. The *I-Ching* is a multi-authored text whose current written version probably dates from around 800 years before Christ. It consists of 64 symbols, each of which contains a main text and six smaller texts. Readers have to toss three coins in order to combine these fragments, and the random result (1 of 4,096 possibilities) is used in predictions and future-telling; Aarseth, 1997, p. 75.
45. Ryan, 1991, 2001b.
46. Wolf, 2001.
47. Laurel, 1993; Murray, 1997; Ryan, 1991, 2001b; Aarseth, 1997.
48. See Frasca, 2003b, for a history of the concept. *Ludus* means "game" in Latin, therefore "ludology" would be the study of games. The (mostly Scandinavian) researchers associated with this term are Markku Eskelinen, Gonzalo Frasca, Aki Jaarvinen, Jesper Juul, and Espen Aarseth.
49. Frasca, 1999.
50. Frasca, 2001b.
51. Juul, 2001.
52. Although he doesn't mention adaptation of fictional universes, which is certainly possible, as in the case of the *Blade Runner* game, even though the same sequence of events is not maintained.

53. Eskelinen, 2001.
54. A good summary of the history of the controversy can be found in Frasca, 2003b.
55. See, for example, Taylor, 2006; Malaby, 2007; Consalvo, 2009.
56. Eskelinen, 2001.
57. Kücklich, 2002, 2003a.
58. Ryan, 2001a.
59. Juul, 2005, p. 145.
60. Landow, 1992.
61. Manovich, 2001.
62. Authors like Landow, 1992 or Douglas, 1992 discuss the break with traditional narrative brought about by hypertext narrative.
63. Murray, 1997, p. 143. Italics added.
64. Murray, 1997, p. 144.
65. Atkins, 2003, p. 20.
66. There might be a historical explanation, though, since the classic genre of adventure computer games is no longer so popular, but its characteristics have been incorporated into other subgenres, such as action-adventure or survival horror.
67. Salen and Zimmerman call this opposition "crafted story" versus "emergent experience"; see Salen and Zimmerman, 2004, pp. 383–384.
68. Rouse, 2001, p. 223.
69. Rouse, 2001, p. 227.
70. For example, Ryan, 2001a; Wolf, 2001, pp. 109–110; or Laurel, 1993, p. 106, who talks about goals as framework for action.
71. Juul, 2003a, p. 146.
72. Juul, 2003a, p. 163.
73. Smith, 2000b.
74. Smith, 2000b. This is a rather underexplored area in computer game studies, with the exception of the work of Anders Drachen (later published under the name Anders Tychsen); Tychsen, Hitchens, Brolund, McIlwain, and Kavakli, 2008, Tychsen, Hitchens, and Brolund, 2008; Drachen and Smith, 2008.
75. Jenkins, 2003a.
76. Jenkins, 2003a, p. 129.
77. Jenkins, 2003a, p. 129.
78. Jenkins, 2003a.
79. Examples of their work include Lindley, 2002; Mateas, 2001.
80. In her books Possible Worlds, Artificial Intelligence, and Narrative Theory and Narrative as Virtual Reality; Ryan, 1991, 2001b. Ryan's work connects literary theories of possible worlds to the realm of the digital, and engages with literary definitions of virtual reality, simulation, and immersion in relationship to narrative.
81. Murray, 1997, p. 71. Italics added.
82. In the episode "Persistence of Vision"; see Murray, 1997, ch. 1.
83. Murray, 1997, p. 51.
84. Laurel, 1993, p. 167.
85. Wolf, 2001.
86. Murray, 1997, p. 186.
87. Murray, 1997, p. 197.
88. Mateas, 2001, p. 151.
89. Mateas, 2001, pp. 151–152.
90. Mateas and Stern, 2003, pp. 5–6.
91. Ryan, 2001b, p. 307. Jesper Juul also makes a distinction between "the worlds we find in computer games and how computer games cue the players into imagining worlds"; Juul, 2003a, p. 109.
92. Wolf, 2001, p. 94.
93. Tosca, 2003c.
94. Salen and Zimmerman, 2004, p. 399.
95. Salen and Zimmerman, 2004, p. 400.
96. Juul, 2003a, p. 169.
97. Aarseth, 2005, p. 4.
98. Jenkins, 2003; Kücklich, 2003b.
99. Jenkins, 2003; Klastrup and Tosca, 2004, 2011.
100. Freeman and Rampazzo Gambaratto, 2018.
101. Kinder, 1991, p. 38.
102. Jenkins, 2003.
103. Kennedy, 2018, p. 72.
104. Ryan, 2014, 2016.
105. Thon, 2016.
106. Ryan, 2016, p. 7.

Serious Games and Gamification—When Entertainment Is Not Enough

The Oregon Trail (1971) was among the first learning games and has remained immensely popular

Games continues to grow. During the last 25 years the game industry grew in value from €15 billion to €120 billion, and each week the people of this planet are spending something like three billion hours playing.[1] We're playing in a number of different ways. We see people doing it on their phones, on Facebook, on TV screens, on websites, and in virtual reality. The range of platforms, channels, and genres offered for different player types is immense, and the game industry seems to have "cracked the code" for making games a mainstream offer.

Looking back 20 years, the general perception of games was quite different from that of today. Which would have been the first games to come to mind back then? It could well have been the pervasive *Counter-Strike*. Today the mainstream game landscape is far more varied and a casual title like *Minecraft* is hugely popular, and not violent in the classic, gory sense. Although we still have hugely popular more classic games favored by teenagers like *Clash Royal* and *Counter-Strike*, things have indeed changed.

It used to be mostly about entertainment, and now it's about pretty much everything else as well. The area of "serious games" and "gamification" has benefited from the omnipresence of games but has also helped influence the perception of games by showing how games can be so much more than run-of-the-mill shooters for teenage boys. Serious games and gamification have played a large role in this transition and will probably go on to have a still larger impact on the face of gaming. Especially since the barriers for larger penetration in schools, corporations, government (such as limited hardware, legacy IT system, and teacher's IT competence) are slowly evaporating. As these barriers disappear, the market may grow even more rapidly. Market research companies like Gartner, IDATE, and Allied Market Research predict an even larger serious games market just around the corner. Allied Market Research, for example, predicts growth from $2,731 million in 2016 to $9,167 million in 2023.[2] Mordor Intelligence estimates the gamification market at $5.5 billion in 2018, and growing 30.31 percent over the next five years.[3]

Few other entertainment media have managed to encroach on other lives like this—maybe with the exception of social media. As the dust is settling, we can get a clearer picture of exactly what we know—where the marketing hype stops and the research evidence solidifies.

This chapter will examine the area in more detail. The question is: what do players take away from video games? Not on a cultural level but on an individual level. Do players learn from video games, and if so, what do they learn? Can we change players' behavior by using a simple game loop like points, badges, and leaderboards, as gamification evangelists claim—or does it require a bit more, as a growing body of game researchers insists? Before diving deeper into the research area, it is also worth noting that as any emerging space there often exist different themes and terminology that can easily result in confusion when entering this field.

OVERVIEW AND THEMATIC AREAS

Many researchers and practitioners in the serious games and gamification area will refer to subareas like school, military, health, or corporate. These are areas where there is historically a strong tradition for both use of and research on the use of serious games and gamification. In general, these labels can safely be ignored as they do not have any real research significance as they mainly denote a context-of-use, and no significant difference in the subject of study. You will also find some other terms for the area like games-for-change, games-for-health, advertainment, political games, and news games. These are often somewhat random terms but are often centered around specific initiatives, agendas, conferences, or communities. When looking for research it is important to have these different research and professional communities in mind, as you may otherwise miss a lot of research that are not available in the classic serious games and gamification journals, conferences and other publications. We cover each of these key areas briefly without going into detail, as that would require several chapters.

GAMES-FOR-CHANGE

The games-for-change area is almost a movement. It focuses on using games to change the world for the better. The Games for Change Festival, founded in 2004, spearheads the efforts, and over the years there has been at least one yearly festival—spreading from the United States to other continents. This includes games like *PeaceMaker*, about creating peace between Israeli and Palestinian; *Stop Disasters*, on how to stop flooding; *Escape from Woomera*, about detention camps in Australia; *Third World Farmer*, about the daily hardships of farmers in Africa; *Darfur Is Dying*, based on the unfolding humanitarian catastrophe in Darfur; and *Ways2Sort*, a fast-paced puzzle game to learn and internalize waste sorting. In recent years a game like *Papers, Please* garnered a lot of attention by putting the player in control of an immigrations officer.

In general, there exists limited direct research evidence that games can change the world despite the very influential work by Jane McGonigal. McGonigal, with her book *Reality Is Broken*, has been very influential in arguing that one of our favorite pastimes can serve as backdrop for serious collaboration, thinking, and reflection. Her focus is on games based around epic challenges, collaboration to solve problems, and giving a role to everyone. Games can bring us leverage to solve real problems like in the alternate reality game (ARG) *World Without Oil*, where players enter a community that most try to engineer, develop, and build solutions in a world with an oil shortage. She promotes so-called ARGs, which weave together fiction and reality to engage people in solving real-life problems in an epic setting. Her vision is that the impact of games can reach a level such that it warrants a Nobel Prize—quite an ambition.[4] In general, the games-for-change area draws on more general research on serious games and gamification in relation to learning and changing behaviors rather than its own dedicated research.

In 2012 Constance Steinkuehler along with research colleagues launched a serious games project with the White House in Washington to help solve public challenges, like saving fuel in the US Navy or similar. The White House cooled off with the Trump presidency, and although the direct impact is still to be seen, it very well illustrates the monumental leap games have taken over the last 40 years—from the local diner's arcade machine across the teenage bedroom to the Oval Office.

Games-for-change:
A subgenre within serious games that focuses on creating games that can lead to the world becoming a better place, from the foundation that games should actively try to change the world.

GAMES-FOR-HEALTH

This area has a lot of similarities with the evolvement of games-for-change. Its birth was closely tied to the conference Games-for-Health out of Boston. It launched in 2004 but closed down in 2010. However, not before exporting it to Europe where the conference continues with its own organization. It also resulted in the establishment of the *Games for Health Journal* that still attracts numerous research publications within the field.

The area is vast and encompasses multiple subdomains and extensive research. It may be the most researched area within serious games, but being focused on a very specific area around health makes it hard for game researchers to enter and transfer directly to other domains. In a review study from 2018, 1,738 health games were identified.[5] The games and research span the full health area both for staff and patients. It cuts across treatment, rehabilitation, compliance, and training, to name a few. Especially, the area of *exer-gaming* has received a lot of positive research attention, to combat obesity by using new interfaces that force players to move while playing.[6]

NEWS GAMES

The term refers to the idea of using video games as commentary on a news story, where a game can involve the users. The genre experienced some popularity back in 2010–2011 with games like *Playing the News* and *Cutthroat Capitalism*.

Ian Bogost spearheaded the field from an academic point of view, alongside more hands-on work by Gonzalo Frasca.[7] Increasingly, it is suggested that for news games to thrive they need to be integrated with the news organizations rather than an externally inserted "plugin" that journalists do not have a close relationship to. One can say that journalists almost need to become game designers and game developers in their own right.[8] Despite many attempts and projects across the globe (e.g. United States, France, and Denmark), this has never really gained a strong foothold that can challenge the popularity of, say, fantasy leagues.

POLITICAL GAMES

In political games you aim directly at pushing a political message to the player by putting them in a specific position. The historical traditions date back to the 1980s for example with games like *Nuclear War, Balance of Power, Hidden Agenda*, and the neo-Nazi game *Purging Germany*. All of these games tried to set a political agenda and could in some sense be called educational; however, their goals were quite specific. Some served more as comic strips or propaganda leaflets than real games. They wanted to present a particular message, and this message had strong political undertones. In *Nuclear War*, for example, the inevitable destructive consequences of nuclear war were caricatured in "Spitting Image" style, a cartoonist's caricature of current world leaders. The subversive use of video games has always been present within game culture but became less of a factor as the industry matured commercially during the 1990s.

Political games made a comeback in gaming subculture with the terrorist attacks of September 11, 2001 with especially the game *September 12th*. *September 12th* serves as a good example of this crop. In this simple, single-screen game, the player overlooks a village filled with both terrorists and civilians. The player's only option is to fire missiles to kill the terrorists or do nothing; the firing of the missile will inevitably result in civilian casualties. The deaths of innocent victims will draw mourners, who will also be drawn toward terrorism; the player watches as almost the entire village population become terrorists. The player cannot win the game and does not get any points. All he can do is observe and become more frustrated in his powerlessness. Circulated on the web in 2003 by Gonzalo Frasca, developer of the game and game researcher, *September 12th* is barely a game, but its criticism of the war on terror is clear.

The subgenre never quite did get a foothold, and research is quite limited. Although news articles hailed political games as "the next big thing," this has not come to pass.[9]

The following examples fit the definition of political games presented by Karlsson, who writes that a political game:

> wants to communicate a specific message or perception of the world. Play becomes secondary. This does not mean that the gameplay necessarily lacks in any way. *America's Army* is hugely popular because of excellent gameplay, but play is still instrumental as regards to the US Army's overriding goal.[10]

Figure 8.1 September 12th (2004) provides the player with the military means to attack terrorists but also shows the unexpected repercussions

The game Karlsson refers to is one of the most successful projects within political gaming, although some will deny its political connotations. Available free on its own homepage, it is explicitly offered as a promotional tool to "inspire" young men and women to join the US Army. However, its popularity was a huge surprise for many, and some speculate, partly in jest, that without the game the United States would not have been able to continue the war in Iraq due to the lack of recruits. *America's Army* in this way spills into another subdomain, namely advertainment, which is meant to promote a specific product, whether it be the US Army, Nike apparel, or Dole bananas.

Advertainment/ advergame: The use of games for advertising rather than just entertainment.

ADVERTAINMENT

Advertainment is a fusion of advertising and entertainment, and refers to video games used for marketing purposes. Advertainment grew considerably since its origins in the mid-1990s up until the late 2000s, led by increasing interest from major companies around the world—assuming that building a game would make customers flock around their products.

A small sampling of games includes *The Beast*, developed for the Steven Spielberg movie *AI*, which set new standards for alternate reality games; the *Three King Games* made by fast-food franchise Burger King in 2006 set a benchmark by getting to the Xbox store as a paid product. LEGO has also used free online and mobile games for years as a way to build their brand and engage children.

Companies especially appreciate the active participation required to play these games; while playing, we are relentlessly exposed to the companies' products, which are incorporated into the gameplay in more or less creative ways. While playing an advertainment title, in other words, we are literally helping to build the company's brand in our own and others' consciousness.[11] Gardner stresses the difference between "integral" games and "giveaway" games,[12] referring to a classic problem in using video games for serious purposes. Some serious games will not really integrate the message they want to get across with the gameplay. These are called giveaways, whereas integral games integrate the message into the gameplay. Integral games are usually more difficult and expensive to develop but also arguably result in a stronger impression and user experience (see later discussion on exogenous versus endogenous design). The rationale behind advertainment (build it and they will come) increasingly came out-of-sync with reality as games became abundant online and on smartphones.

Today, advertainment still exist but most marketeers have realized that it's hard to attract people with an original game, so instead they rely on sweepstakes wrapped in a very simple quiz-like or other basic game mechanic. In addition, e-Sports now allows an easier way to reach the same audience.

TWO RESEARCH DOMAINS

Now that we have an overview of the complexity and diversity of the field, it's time to look at the central area of the field. We approach the area through two lenses: serious games and gamification. Taken at face value they look quite similar as they deal with the use of games in nonentertainment settings. However, they differ in their theoretical focus, foundation, approach, and strategies.

1. Serious games (product): The concept that *video games* can be developed for and used in a variety of nonentertainment settings to *learn things*.
2. Gamification (process): The concept that *game mechanics* can be used in a variety of nonentertainment settings to *change behaviors*.

To set the stage here are two brief examples. In *Dragon Box* (serious game), you learn about algebra by playing a game, where you have to solve a number of puzzles. The game introduces key concepts related to algebra that you need to apply successfully to progress in the game. In *Sales Force Motivation* (gamification), the sales staff is challenged to get points on the score board by selling. Through the leaderboard salespeople are constantly engaged and motivated to sell the most to beat their colleagues.

Despite huge debate about the exact definitions, and indeed whether gamification even warrants its own label, there exists a clear and important demarcation line between serious games and gamification.[13] Serious games are a virtual container, where you typically simulate or represent something that you want players to learn about. Gamification, on the other hand, is rather a layer you put on top of real life to change the way players learn, behave, or think. As such gamification draws on disciplines like behavioral design, social psychology, and design thinking, whereas serious games draw on instructional design, educational theories, and education psychology. Because gamification usually happens in the wild, you have a stronger focus on how it is used by people in a social context, and how players interact during the experience, as part of a real-world setting. Serious games can definitely also have a focus on the larger context-of-use, but this will often not take precedence, and not be an integrated part of the core experience that exists by itself. You still see the experience very much from the perspective of an individual player that is doing something in a virtual world that the player may or may not be learning from.

Table 8.1 summarizes the two different approaches that we will explore in more detail throughout the chapter, and as such is a simplification. However, it works well to guide us, and make sense of the landscape. As the above suggests, the concepts of serious games and gamification has spread wide. We will look more closely at their definitions, key findings, and effectiveness.

One key thing to keep in mind when venturing into this area is that it is potentially quite confusing. Researchers can have very different starting points both in what theories and ontologies they draw and what type of phenomena they are examining. These phenomena can cut across target group, context-of-use, theoretical foundations, and knowledge type to start with the most obvious. Often contradictions in the research fields stem from the fact that researchers are examining different phenomena or have radically different starting points on humans and learning.

Table 8.1 The key differences between serious games and gamification

	Serious Games	Gamification
Alternative names	Edutainment, learning games, game-based learning, educational games, simulation games	Gameful design, playful design, motivational design, ludification
Scientific and theoretical starting point	Educational theories, instructional design, education psychology, simulation theory	Behavioral design, behavioral economics, game theory, social psychology, nudging
Focus	Product	Process
Player actions	Virtual	Real
Center	Individual	Group
Game role	Simulation/representation	Layer/tracker/tool
Purpose	Create learning	Change behavior

Two examples will prove the point starting with serious games. One study may look at how surgeons can improve specific motor skills during their professional work through a simulation game, where you do surgery. Another may examine how primary students can learn about Vikings in history class with a role-playing game. On a high level, you can of course compare whether the students learned what they needed to, but that is also pretty much the only similarity. There are marked difference in target group, knowledge type, context-of-use, game genre, duration, game mechanics, proficiency starting level, and group dynamics.

Similar challenges can be found within gamification, where you may have a study of how to use a gamification layer to create a better classroom learning environment for college students, whereas another study examines improvement of sales effort in a corporation context. Here we also find that the variety is so marked that it becomes hard to really compare the two experiences. This should caution us when comparing studies but still we will try to distill the essence.

Serious games: Games intentionally created with a primary agenda other than entertainment.

SERIOUS GAMES

It is clear that "serious games" is a diverse topic. The area presents quite a complex array of factions, all talking about the same issues in different terms. No matter the language used, they all argue that games can be used for more than entertainment, and often research is aimed at documenting positive outcomes. To further complicate matters, the topic is crowded with competing terminologies and related domains. To simplify matters in this book, we focus on research on serious games that are used for the education of children, young people, and adults for learning knowledge and skills.

For the origins of the expression "serious games," we must look to the 1960s. The term was coined by Clark Abt in 1970 and formed the title of his influential book.[14] Other, early examples of early research interest into serious video games are the work of psychologist Patricia Greenfield, including her 1984 book *Mind and Media*, which deals among other things with how computer games influence individual development; Thomas Malone with his work on motivation, education, and video games;[15] and psychologists Geoffrey and Elizabeth Loftus with their 1983 book *Mind at Play*, about the cognitive learning gains from video games.

Pre-serious Games: Nondigital Games Show the Way

Although the term was coined later, the serious games "movement" was born in the late 1950s, with nonelectronic, pen-and-paper, and board games. By the 1970s, educational games had exploded in popularity, and were becoming an important pedagogical tool, especially for teaching in American businesses and the military. Back then, the games used in such settings were primarily simulations, aimed at replicating precisely a real-world event, from landing a plane to implementing city taxes, rather than the broader category of fictional games including action, adventure, and strategy, in which the replication of the real world can be less exact. One of the first educational nonelectronic games, for example, was *Inter-Nation Simulation* from 1958, used in high school social studies classes to teach international relations. Here, players control one of up to seven hypothetical nations, and need to negotiate with the other nations in order to solve problems ranging from minor international crises to nuclear war.

Since these initial efforts, the creation and use of such nonelectronic—or "traditional"—games have been relatively constant, and continue to see a stable level of use and following. They were popular with some teachers but have never become a core feature of the educational system despite widespread use. Alongside this popularity, research into the educational use of traditional games is now well established, with peer-reviewed journals, well-known researchers, and substantial research topics. Over the last 50 years, researchers have addressed varied topics, from the learning outcomes of traditional games to the practical barriers to using such games. The majority of these findings are relevant to the educational use of video games. Here we present the most important implications, with brief discussions of the key topics for video games: effectiveness, motivation, debriefing, and the influence of teachers and setting.[16]

The number of studies on the effectiveness of traditional games in education is quite high, spanning more than 40 years of research, and offering some clear findings. The studies so far suggest that games are a viable alternative to traditional teaching, and provide approximately the same learning outcome—that is, a student has the same chance of positive learning outcome from using a game as he/she does through another media for learning. Games cannot necessarily be said to be more effective than other teaching forms, although most studies have offered evidence of higher motivation, better retention over time and potentially better transfer.[17] Students also tend to subjectively rate their learning outcome higher when they use games, and to prefer gaming to other teaching methods. Thus, for good or bad, even though we cannot objectively measure an increased learning outcome, students often feel they have learned more. Indeed, the preference of students for games fits well with the increased motivation consistently found when examining the educational use of nondigital games.[18]

The effectiveness of nondigital games relies heavily on exactly how they are used in a teaching environment. Debriefing—the process of reflection after the game has finished—is especially important. Researchers have found that students can make incorrect assumptions based on their game experiences.[19] Therefore debriefing is key, as the teacher needs to take time to correct any mistakes, clarify misconceptions, and expand on the game experiences.[20]

The role of teachers and the setting for serious games have caused a number of problems in these studies. The school setting—with its physical limits in terms of classroom size and logistical limits in terms of available time for teaching—is not very appropriate for games. In addition, most teachers have little experience of using games, and this jeopardizes the learning experience. The teacher's theories of learning—not to mention their opinions about the value of alternative teaching strategies—may also hinder the effectiveness of games.[21]

As we can see, research into nondigital games has addressed some of the tough questions about the proper role of games in education, and the area still enjoys great popularity—a popularity that has not become less as board games have made a comeback in popular culture.[22] This research effort shows no sign of abating, as the use of games in education has continued to grow. And today more and more of these educational games are electronic. As we turn to video games, the more than 40 years of research into nondigital games offers interesting insights. In particular, as we will see later in this chapter, many of the ideas from pre-digital games research are relevant to serious games in the digital domain.

Categorizing Serious Games: Edutainment, Commercial Off-the-Shelf Games, and Educational Serious Games

Research into serious games struggles with complexity as we have seen, and one of the most important risks is if we ignore just how different serious games can be. It covers a wide variety of fields and has been growing fast. From 2007–2017 it grew from 42 yearly research publications to 237.[23]

The first important step is therefore to get a clear understanding of the three categories within serious games. When we later look at the effectiveness across meta-studies, for example, there is often no differentiation between different types of serious games even if they have wildly different approaches to the player, learning, and praxis around it.

The most important point in table 8.2 is that the different types of serious games focus on teaching people different things, and often with quite different underling instructional theories to achieve this.

The next two elements to consider is motivation and game mechanics. Motivation can be either extrinsic (external) or intrinsic (internal). When motivation is extrinsic the game draws on game elements that are external and ad hoc to the gameplay (e.g. points, leader board, or level completion). In other words, you can easily add or remove these components across

Table 8.2 An overview of the three different subcategories within serious games

	Edutainment	Commercial off-the-shelf games (COTS)	Educational serious games
Game learning focus	Skills and knowledge	None or Knowledge	Skills, knowledge and affective
Instructional theory	Behavioristic	Common sense	Behavioristic, cognitive, constructivism
Motivation	Extrinsic	Intrinsic	Intrinsic
Game mechanics	Exogenous	Mixed	Endogenous
Player agency	Passive	Active	Active
Teacher role	None	Ad hoc	Active
Debriefing	None	Ad hoc	Integrated
Game examples	*Math Blaster, Monkey Math School*	*Minecraft, Civilization, SimCity*	*Oregon Trail, Dragon Box*

different gameplays. In intrinsic motivation you rely on the game play by itself to motivate and engage, and don't have to add external motivation elements although you will often add it for extra effect.

Closely related, to the motivation structure is whether the game mechanics are *exogenous* (external) or *endogenous* (internal)[24], which describes how closely linked the game activity and the learning activities are. In an endogenous game mechanic, the learning element is directly embedded in the gameplay as part of in the actions you take to play and win the game. Contrary to this is an exogenous game mechanic, where there is not such a direct relationship. In other words, you can play *Space Invaders*, and then get interrupted by an algebra question you need to solve to progress in the game. An easy way to spot an exogenous game mechanic is whether it can easily be changed, removed, or re-used without changing the game experience, as for example with a leader board or achievement system.

The next factors in table 8.2 look at the position of the player, which is crucial as this may be one of the most defining characteristics of serious games compared to other instructional methods. When a player is passive, this implies that the player is merely consuming the educational content, for example through video, text, or audio. In other words, they don't engage with the content actively, and don't do anything with it to influence the virtual world.

The final two factors relate to the teacher's role, and how debriefing is structured. We previously saw that research on pre-digital serious games found these to be key factors to achieve a good learning outcome. When the teachers take an active role, they are key to ensure the optimal game and learning experience but especially in the debriefing you ensure that the learning is discussed and reflected to bring it beyond the game experience.

Edutainment—Keep It Simple Stupid

Historically, edutainment started out in the United States in the 1970s as a very fragmented field, with different developers picking their own favorite theory from the major learning approaches (behaviorism, cognitivism, or constructivism). Early on, edutainment drew heavily on existing traditions within educational media, but this tendency became even more marked in the early 1980s. By then, edutainment basically relied on the learning principles of behaviorism, articulated first by John Watson in 1919.

Edutainment focuses on teaching the player certain specific skills: algebra, spelling, problem-solving, or other basic skills.[25]

According to legend, in 1984 Trip Hawkins, founder of Electronic Arts, coined the term "edutainment" to refer to electronic games that use entertainment in the service of education.[26] The label was used with great success for the top-seller *Seven Cities of Gold*, a game about the Spanish colonization of Latin America in the sixteenth century.

While edutainment in general conversation often refers broadly to any electronic use of entertainment for educational purposes we here use it quite specifically for a certain game genre.

Edutainment titles typically target younger children and include for example *Pajama Sam, Castle of Dr. Brain*, and *Math Blaster*. In the *Math Blaster series*, the player must shoot down the right answer to an arithmetical problem to progress; with any luck, the player learns basic math along the way. Many edutainment games are consciously devised to mimic "normal" video games in order to make them more appealing. However, the implemented gameplay and graphics are usually quite dated and simplistic—definitely quite far from modern gameplay. Edutainment titles have a strong educational component, albeit often quite mechanistic, and often do not achieve the high levels of engagement associated with commercial titles because they lack intrinsic motivation.[27]

Today, we still have edutainment titles similar to those from the 1970s and 1980s that rely on a behaviorist approach. These are less concerned with the actual connection between the game and the learning experience; the game often simply serves as a reward for learning. So, although edutainment does not have to be behavioristic, and definitely wasn't when edutainment first entered the market place (e.g. *Oregon Trail* or *Where in the World Is Carmen Sandiego?*), it often is so today. So, while edutainment started out as a serious attempt to create video games that could teach children various subjects, it was quickly marred. The reliance on behaviorism resulted in games that relied heavily on simple game mechanics and quite traditional learning principles, to the disappointment of researchers and many parents.[28] Today edutainment has become synonym for video games with simple game structures, which provide a limited learning experience because they feed the player information, rather than encouraging curiosity and exploration.

The formula settled on by most edutainment titles in the 1980s that are still with us today can be defined by the following characteristics:

- *Drill-and-practice learning*: The learning principles in edutainment are inspired by drill-and-practice thinking rather than understanding. Games encourage the player to memorize the answers—for example, that two plus two equals four—but don't necessarily teach the underlying rules that make this true.

- *Little intrinsic motivation*: Edutainment relies on extrinsic motivation— the promise of rewards—rather than intrinsic motivation, arising from the game activity per se. Extrinsic motivation is not related to the game but consists of arbitrary rewards, such as getting points for completing a level; intrinsic motivation, on the other hand, might be a feeling of mastery from mastering a specific part of the game.
- *Exogenous game mechanics*: There is no integration between the learning activities and the game mechanics. Most edutainment is unable to integrate the experience of playing with the experience of learning, so the latter is subordinated to the more palpable experience of play. The player will often concentrate on playing the game rather than learning from the game.
- *Player agency is limited*: The player will often not be able to do anything actively with the game content they are learning. The content is often presented in text, images, or videos that cannot be influenced, and is quite static in the game world. The player doesn't have any real agency in the game world, and if they have this is removed from the learning mechanics.
- *No teacher presence*: Edutainment hardly demands anything of teachers or parents; it assumes that students can simply be put in front of a given game title, and through gameplay alone they will learn the given content or skills. Often the consequences are not that big for edutainment games' learning outcome because they focus on training basic skills, but for more complex games or subjects it becomes a challenge.

We must also acknowledge that edutainment, from early on, primarily became driven by business interests. This pedagogically mostly unambitious perspective has arguably undermined the market by producing a long string of low-quality games that simply aren't very engaging to play.[29] The edutainment category also includes a number of titles with questionable educational content, developed by opportunists seeing a chance to capitalize on parents' hopes for such games. These are often found attached to a license such as Disney, Garfield, or another favorite dish of the day, and have fielded some of the more spurious examples—games that focus on the same basic content and offer little that is new in the way of teaching math and spelling (which remain among the most popular topics).[30] A commercially successful edutainment title, *Chefren's Pyramid*, can serve as an example. Here the player might read something about the pyramids, then play a bit of backgammon, and solve some calculations. This hardly facilitates a meaningful learning experience. A way to overcome this would be for games to implicitly use educational material as part of the basic conflict (or goal) of the game, as suggested by Malone.[31] Or, in technical terms, the game's victory conditions would require the desired learning outcome. The players have to utilize the desired knowledge, attitude or skill in order to win. For instance, gaining geographical knowledge in *Civilization* is crucial to taking full advantage of the map, and knowledge of the historical development of a certain region is very beneficial in *Europa Universalis II*. Whether you get this information before, during, or after playing the game is not important. It is important that you will actually need educationally relevant knowledge, skills, or attitudes to succeed in the game, because you will then find it relevant and meaningful while playing the game, and worth "holding" on to. However, a fruitful connection between educational content and the basic game structure often remains difficult to construct. The simple structure of video games limits the amount of material one can include and this material must be integrated with the core game activities. Otherwise the player risks learning only one thing, namely, how to play the game.

Consequently, the attitude among educators, researchers, and game developers toward edutainment titles is often one of deep skepticism. The game design, the learning principles, and the graphics are all criticized heavily by both children and parents.[32] Almost none of the current edutainment titles is built on research that verifies their educational benefits. The ghettoized position of edutainment games has inspired developers, educators, and researchers to look at the commercial game industry for new ideas. The diminishing success of edutainment titles over the last ten years implies that children are unlikely to be attracted to discount games.[33] The clearest place to see this multifaceted development is on the App Store, which serves as one big laboratory (for better and worse) for trying to find more or less creative ways of combining learning and gaming content. But even here

Figure 8.2 Dragon Box—Algebra 5+ (2012) elegantly teaches students equation through game puzzles of increasing complexity that shows an alternative to classic edutainment titles

the picture is quite mixed as edutainment continues to shoot up, whereas educational serious games that we will turn to later remains rare. Many researchers instead looked at using **COTS** (Commercial-off-the-shelves-games) that takes a very different approach than edutainment.

Commercial Off-the-Shelf Games—Just Copy-Paste

As a reaction to the limited success of edutainment researchers and educators turned their attention directly to "real" entertainment computer games to see whether they could be repurposed for an educational setting. The rationale went something like this: if we cannot make learning games that are as engaging as commercial entertainment video games, then maybe we can turn commercial entertainment video games into learning. The tradition dates back to the 1990s but gained momentum from the early 2000s. Some key academic contributions came from James Paul Gee on basic learning principles of mainstream entertainment games and socio-cultural theory,[34] and by Kurt Squire on the implications of actually using mainstream entertainment games in real classrooms.[35] In general it has been the discipline of education that has tried most rigorously to understand the educational potential of COTS, for example, in the work of Angela McFarlane and colleagues,[36] Marc Prensky,[37] John Kirriemuir,[38] and Simon Egenfeldt-Nielsen.[39] In recent years especially, *Minecraft* has been almost a perfect poster face, which we will look a bit more closely at later in the chapter.

COTS rarely focus exclusively on teaching a specific topic or skill that can be clearly mapped to a curriculum. Games in this category include *SimCity, Civilization, The Sims*, and *Minecraft* that have been used by numerous schools but also less obvious ones like *Call of Duty* or *World of Warcraft*. In the game *SimCity*, a prime example of a commercial game with educational potential, players have to plan and run a small city, developing it from a hole in the ground to a bustling metropolis. In order to do so, they must understand many of the basic principles of urban planning, such as zoning, sewage, land prices, pollution, crime, and unemployment. The educational goals of commercial video games are mostly indirect rather than direct, and this can lead to a skewed focus in the learning process. However, their strength is that their motivational effect is well documented by their success on the commercial entertainment market. When commercial games like *SimCity*[40] get it right and are used correctly, they are a powerful educational experience. Below we outline the characteristics of COTS based on our earlier matrix.

- *Explorative learning*: The learning principles in COTS are often indirect or tangential, and rely on the companion material and the teachers' ability to put the games into the right context.
- *Highly intrinsic motivation*: As COTS are first and foremost games, they enjoy a strong intrinsic motivation, where the core gameplay is the key motivation.

- *Mixed game mechanics*: In some cases, a COTS may fit very well with the learning objectives resulting in an endogenous game, but it requires careful usage. Often what educators believe are endogenous mechanics are really exogenous mechanics. Thereby, COTS can fall into the same trap as edutainment.
- *Player agency is strong*: With the complex universe and gameplay found in most COTS, players are actively involved in the game experience. The questions is often whether the agency focus is on the right areas, as it is centered first and foremost on the game, which may be more or less separated from the learning.[41]
- *Strong teacher presence*: Most COTS rely heavily on the involvement of teachers to support and facilitate the learning objectives that are often tacit in the game experience or quite tangential. However, the game rarely supports this with a teacher manual or an integrated debriefing, which has led to dedicated educational manuals for popular games like *SimCity*[42] or *Civilization*.[43]

Most of the research into COTS have been along two strands: (1) the challenges in bringing entertainment into a school environment; (2) the innate tension between fun and learning. Despite great interest among both teachers and students, computer games are not well designed for classroom use.[44] Challenges include teachers' lacking understanding games, installation, licensing, steep learning curves, and high preparation time.[45] COTS are still not mainstream, and many speculate that it stems from the introduction of smartphones, tablets, and Chromebooks in schools that made it even more difficult to use entertainment games. Indeed, schools are often left with quite simple edutainment titles on these platforms despite some exceptions to the rule like *Dragonbox* and *Minecraft*.

The more innate challenge that COTS face is closely tied to their core advantage: intrinsically motivating gameplay that engages students, but often not in the right things. In *Civilization*, Squire[46] has detailed just how a COTS can serve as a powerful serious game inside a school. However, you need to carefully observe the details of how that game is designed and used as it is not easily transferable to most other games. In the game you build up a civilization by developing your city and technology while trading and battling with opponents. On the face of it, this sounds like any other war game. However, *Civilization* is inspired by the theory behind the famous history book called *Guns, Germs and Steel*,[47] and these rules are built into the game. So, to master the game you need to master this theory and go about implementing it. The actual active player actions and feedback on these will relate to this theory, and this also makes it quite easy for the teacher to construct just-in-time lectures around the game fostering discussion and reflection. However, if we look at another famous historical strategy game, *Age of Empires*, which is similar on a high level, the dynamics pan out very differently. In *Age of Empires* you indeed also develop your city through technology, getting resources and warfare. However, here the theory is more akin to an advanced model of rock-paper-scissors, and any learning is rather tacit or tangential. You may get interested in the historical period you play but the game in essence has very little to offer except maybe the historical scenario introductions that take two minutes, and that players can easily skip.

Due to the importance of the teacher to offset the limitations of the COTS, this has been a key focus area for research, and one such strong model is suggested by Eck. In his iNtegrating Technology through inquiry (NTEQ) model,[48] he defines five key qualities for a successful use of COTS in the classroom that also is supported by other researchers:[49]

1. The teacher is technologically competent and assumes the roles of designer, manager, and facilitator.
2. The student actively engages in the learning process, assumes the role of researcher, and becomes technologically competent.
3. The computer is used as a tool, as it is in the workplace, to enhance learning through the use of real-world data to solve problems.
4. The lesson is student centered, problem based, and authentic, and technology is an integral component.
5. The environment incorporates multiple resource-rich activities.

Educational Serious Games—Hard Fun

The last category is educational serious games, which historically started as a challenger to the formula used by edutainment.[50] Within educational serious games there are different approaches, but they are united by a desire for intrinsic motivation and endogenous design coupled with a strong player agency, where you actively use the learning as part of the game experience. Examples include *Oregon Trail*, *Logical Journey of the Zoombinis*, *Quest of Atlantis*, and *Global Conflicts: Palestine*. In *Global Conflicts: Palestine* (produced by one of the authors of this book), you play a journalist arriving in Jerusalem. You have to write stories and, in the process, find sources and information, and recognize different perspectives and agendas to get the right story.

The educational serious games often present new approaches and provide strong evidence for learning outcomes. However, they often lack the budget and technical quality to compete directly with COTS. Successful educational serious games are still few and far between but show that there is a way to combine the strengths of commercial entertainment games with education without necessarily limiting oneself to the edutainment formula or being dependent on COTS that may more or less randomly stumble over topics relevant for education. The chances of developing better educational serious games have also increased, as the tools for making computer games have been commodified, most clearly shown by the success of Unity3D game engine.

Historically, educational computer games were often put under the same label as edutainment. However, looking back there are distinct differences, which are important to stress both in regard to examining learning outcomes, and if one is to design good serious games in the future. A key driver for educational serious games was during the 1980s, the cognitive theorist Thomas Malone who elaborated on the approach needed to make educational serious games. He stressed that to be effective, gameplay and educational content must be integrated. Malone identifies a number of factors relevant to designing educational video games, and especially stresses the need for intrinsic motivation. In 1987, Malone and Mark Lepper[51] wrote arguably the most influential papers in the research on educational video games. The authors list the elements needed to achieve intrinsic motivation in a game, which is one of the key shortcomings of edutainment but crucial to achieve strong educational computer games that are comparable to entertainment computer games:

- *Fantasy*: The game activity can increase intrinsic motivation by using fantasies as a part of the game universe. All entertainment games rely heavily on building fantasies for players to explore, and educational serious games should be similar rather than abstract and distant. A fantasy can be internal or external to the game. In a missing letter game, you can easily provide an external fantasy; for example, that you need to find the letter to free the princess. An internal fantasy is more motivating, but it also requires that the fantasy is tied more closely to the actual gameplay, and is not merely ad hoc.
- *Control*: The player gains the overall feeling of being the controlling party while playing. The sense of feeling in control is present in most entertainment games, and many fans of the best-selling *Grand Theft Auto* series describe the control and freedom as the defining element of the series. All games have a sense of control, given their interactive nature, but the degree of control can vary widely. Basically, as Raph Koster[52] would say, games are about verbs not nouns, things you can do, and many educational computer games are just way more limiting than their entertainment counterparts.[53]
- *Challenge*: The activity should be at the appropriate level of difficulty for the player to be pushed to the limit of his or her capacity. Here again we see that most entertainment games do this extraordinarily well, whereas many educational computer games have to rely on the lowest common denominator among players. They make it too easy (or sometimes too hard). Indeed, balancing a game is always a very difficult assignment.
- *Curiosity*: The information in the game should be complex and unknown to encourage exploration and reorganization of the information. So games must always have more to show, whether literally in the exploration of a visual universe, in the form of conversations or events in role-playing games, or in the relationships between variables and the dynamics of the underlying system in strategy games. Here entertainment games are also ahead of educational computer games as they provide more areas to explore and reconcile, whereas many educational computer games

(especially edutainment) make the mistake of serving information well chewed and ordered for the player.

Over the years, the above principles served as guidelines to many researchers and some game designers. It seems, however, that although Malone and Lepper's contribution is important, the focus is too narrowly on the game structure itself. The principles leave little room for the social dynamics around the game and learning experience. Although later revisions of Malone and Lepper's work tried to integrate the collaboration around video games, the context of the game is arguably downplayed in this framework.

Another influential theory to shape educational serious games emerged from constructivism. Constructivism is particularly critical of the reliance on behaviorism and cognitive learning theory found in edutainment. They argue that a too mechanic approach confines the player's agency in the virtual world, and how the player learns. Constructivist theorists stress different elements, such as the player's freedom to explore the game universe and the process of constructing knowledge in a meaningful and personal way. For some constructionist thinkers, video games hold fantastic promise; they make it possible for the learners to approach a subject in an active way and construct their own representations. In an ideal game, constructivists argue, the learning experience of the students draws on different perspectives, gives rise to a variety of actions, and offers a fuller understanding of the given topic.

For these thinkers, the main focus is the actual construction process of knowledge facilitated by interaction with the game; as a consequence, constructivist-based research has focused on open-ended games, on students making their own simple games, and on so-called microworlds. A microworld is a simulation of a system—anything from a small universe with laws of physics to a city with basic urban planning actions—which is simplified and constructed so that a player can work with the system's concrete objects. When players interact with objects in a video game, they are learning about the properties of these objects, their connections and applications. From a constructionist perspective, this is an optimal way to learn.[54]

From the behaviorist perspective, the challenge of educational video games is transmitting information from the video game to the player. The context of this information is irrelevant, and the transmission of content relies on conditioning and reinforcement (much like "drill-and-practice"). From a constructivist position, the transmission of information is not sufficient for a successful educational experience. Players must actively engage in a video game and construct their own knowledge using the artifacts of the game world.

Among the most noticeable early constructivist contributions within this field, the work by Yasmin Kafai remains central. In the mid-1990s, Kafai researched how to use the actual game design process as a new way for students to engage with a subject. Seymour Papert, often seen as the father of constructivism, inspired Kafai's work. Kafai envisioned children not just as players of games but as the actual designers of these games, thereby turning children into producers of knowledge and in a very concrete way letting them play with knowledge.[55] This approach gained new momentum with *Minecraft* that was a perfect combination of COTS and constructionist approach. This materialized with the dedicated platform for education *Minecraft Edu*. In research studies the unique potential of *Minecraft* have been reported to support scientific, inquiry, peer collaboration problem-solving, and as a strong arena to explore any **STEM** subject[56] with promising learning outcome.[57] According to Kafai (2017), *Minecraft* may even be pointing to a new type of serious games that bridge the gap between edutainment reliance on instructional approach, and educational serious games constructivist. She calls for a new are to be developed called "Connected gaming, where both playing and making games are part of the learning process."

STEM: A popular abbreviation for science, technology, engineering, and mathematics, used to group this educational area and curriculum as one entity.

Another important research approach focuses on the players themselves and the context around the game—something that is lacking in Malone's early work. This position is championed by James Paul Gee, David Williamson Schaffer, Sasha Barab, and Kurt Squire. From their socio-cultural perspective, video games are tools for the players in constructing viable learning experiences. Games mediate discussion, reflection, and analysis. The video game experience is facilitated by the surrounding classroom culture and the student's identity. This approach is argued to be very useful for understanding video games that are surrounded by strong social networks, which facilitate the learning experience.[58] Here, the content of a video game itself is less significant than its way of initiating new explorations and journeys into knowledge.

Gee has given the strongest account of the approach and presents five main areas of interest concerning video games for educational purposes.[59] He does not see these as limited to school settings but as intrinsic qualities for learning through video games:

- *Semiotic domains*: Like other activities in life, video games are a semiotic domain—a realm of signs and symbols—that one slowly learns to interpret. The player learns to make sense of and navigate through a video game, and in doing so is pointed to other interesting domains, like science and history.
- *Learning and identity*: When the student is involved with the material, video games give new opportunities for learning experiences. Namely, video games are quite good at creating agency and identification: they develop the player's sense of control and encourage the player to identify with other people. Both of these spark critical thinking and deepen the learning experience.
- *Situated meaning and learning*: Video games are well suited for new forms of learning in which the player is situated in the domain and understands it from the inside. Players can interact with the game world

through probing, can choose different ways to learn, and can see a topic in its larger context.

- *Telling and doing*: Games can amplify the important elements in an area to facilitate easier understanding, and represent subsets of domains enabling the player to practice in a safe environment with constant feedback. Games also lend themselves well to transfer between domains, so that you can apply facts you learned about astronomy in a video game to real-life stargazing. This is due to the fact that games are virtual worlds with meaningful, concrete, and rich audiovisual learning experiences rather than abstract bits of concepts put together in a textbook.
- *Cultural models*: The content in games represents ways of perceiving the world, and uses a lot of information implicit in the game universes. This content also has a bearing on other domains of life, and can be both good and bad, depending on your values and norms.

The preceding elements are also clearly found in Sasha Barab's research on transformational play, where the player's role and agency are key. The player must use a conceptual understanding of the topic directly in the game world to transform a problem, and in the process themselves. Learners can take on roles like scientist or journalist, and slowly apply increasingly complex skills to solve still more complicated problems. An important point is that in transformational play you take a holistic perspective, where you both know and use science.

This approach has produced promising results, evidenced, for example, in a study of *Quest Atlantis*. In the scenario Taiga Fishkill, students were found to learn more and also retain the knowledge better. Interestingly, children also changed their primary motivation for participating in the course: 97 percent of the nongame participants said their primary motivation to complete the course was to get a good grade or because a teacher told them—only 36 percent of the game participants chose the same. Instead, 46 percent of the game participants said that they completed the course because they wanted to.[60]

Key Research Challenges in Serious Games

In the following we walk through some of the topics that have been on the research agenda for many years.

Learning Versus Playing

Some researchers question the viability of packaging education as fun. They fear that using video games for learning sends the implicit message that learning is not necessarily hard work, and must always be fun.[61] However, this problem seems to spring more from these researchers' beliefs about education, as they are not supported by any direct studies.

But a related and more crucial issue is the potentially inherent contradiction between learning and playing. Researchers increasingly suggest that a student should clearly see that a particular game is about learning a specific topic and appreciate the expected result. Without explicitly framing the experience as educational, the differing goals and rules within a play context take over. The clash of play and learning is evident when the game goals work against the learning goals. This is all too often the case, as much educational use of video games relies on commercial titles, and many edutainment titles split the game and learning parts.[62]

Another problem between playing and learning relates to students' interest and engagement, which will vary considerably between lessons. Students see the educational experiences with games as a playful, voluntary activity, an activity that they control. Likewise, within a game the player remains in control; this is very different from the more explicit demands that traditional classroom learning makes on a student. The player feels that the control should not be tainted by outside interference but may also criticize the lack of direct educational intervention. On the one hand, that player control is a critical characteristic in video games is stressed by all researchers, but it is also a fact that many studies show the benefit of carefully guiding, supporting, scaffolding, introducing, and debriefing the player after the video game experience. This guiding is actually part of most game cultures but becomes problematic in school settings. The lack of a firm setting confuses students who are uncertain of the expectations when playing and learning. Ultimately, students are unsure whether to approach the video game as play or learning.[63]

Indeed, sometimes the playful approach may ruin the educational experience. On a very basic level, relying on games mean that some students will not trust the educational experience, while others may trust it too much. Research indicates that when students experience a contrast between their own knowledge and information presented in the game, they stick with their own knowledge.[64] Other studies indicate that students sometimes have a blind belief in the game.[65] Neither approach is very beneficial: blind belief is a poor starting point for critical reflection and complete denial is similarly problematic.

Drill-and-Practice Versus Microworlds

Today, most researchers seem to shy away from a narrow focus on the drill-and-practice games of behaviorist edutainment; but many designers still indirectly assume that parts of the game have drill-and-practice elements that can transfer facts and support development of different skills. In fact, research indicates that drill-and-practice can be useful but works best in combination with other teaching forms.[66] Maria Klawe[67] stresses that video games should be used for math activities that are otherwise hard to introduce in a classroom, while specifically pointing to the limitations of drill-and-practice.

Most of the early mathematical video games focused on drill-and-practice of simple number operations and concepts. Such games are easy to develop.

Moreover, playing such games is an effective and motivating method of increasing fluency for many students. However, drill-and-practice is only one of many components of mathematics learning and can be achieved via a variety of noncomputer-based methods.[68]

The preference for drill-and-practice is understandable not just in the most obvious domain of math: it replicates the rote repetition that is the basic method of many traditional classrooms, and thus may feel more familiar to many designers; furthermore, drill-and-practice games are easy to develop compared to the design challenges facing other types of titles. Microworlds, for example, have proven significantly harder to design than classic drill-and-practice games.[69]

In microworlds, the player is confronted with a virtual world that contains a condensed version of the most important variables and characteristics of a given domain. This could be a physics environment, where you explore the different mechanics and interrelationships between atoms by constructing strings of molecules. It could also be a simulation of Williamsburg in colonial times, in which you get a look at the important elements of everyday life, interactions, and routines. When you look at most educational serious games, they will evolve around a microworld to allow for active player agency in an endogenous game that is intrinsically motivating.

Immersion Versus Transfer

In discussing the challenges of the game design process, Klawe[70] raises some of the central problems with educational video games. Most of her conclusions are backed up by an earlier study by Kamran Sedighian and Andishe Sedighian,[71] the researchers responsible for the *Super Tangram* component of the E-Gems series of educational titles. Klawe points out that the immersive effect of video games leads to a lack of awareness of the mathematical structures and concepts integrated in the video game. This results in a weak transfer of game experience to other contexts. Students may learn some content or skills in the game universe and apply them in the game context, but most games are not constructed in a way that makes the knowledge accessible in other contexts. In an earlier study, Klawe and Eileen Phillips found that when students wrote down math problems on paper while playing a math video game, they were more successful in transferring the video game skills to other classroom practice.[72] The engagement with paper and pencil, these researchers found, forces students to construct the knowledge actively.

The transfer of knowledge seems to represent a double bind. On one hand, many researchers assume that the learning experience must be undetectable by children—that an educational video game should resemble a traditional video game. It should not give itself away as children will then shy away from the educational title.[73] On the other hand, it seems that if the players are not aware of the learning elements, the learning experience—and especially the student's ability to transfer the information elsewhere—will be undermined.

The transfer of game skills to other contexts has to be made explicit (and here, as we'll see in the next section, the teacher can play a crucial role).

Teacher Role and Intervention

Contemporary research consistently shows that teachers play an important role in facilitating learning with video games: teachers steer the use of a game in the right direction and provide an effective debriefing that can catch misperceptions and important differences in students' experiences while playing. Many edutainment titles adhering to behaviorism neglect the teacher's role, and assume that no outside intervention is necessary for learning. In more recent titles designed with a constructivist approach (although few and far between), the teacher is made essential.

Many researchers argue that video games should not be thought of as explicitly educational but as tools that provide opportunities for interested teachers. Thus, the teacher's role is imperative for creating the learning experience. This is especially true of commercial entertainment titles that find their way into educational settings—such as *The Sims* and *Civilization*—and that have not been developed with the curriculum explicitly in mind.[74]

In recent years the teacher's role has received more attention. Thorkild Hanghøj and Christian Engel Brund[75] outline four different teacher roles that approach games very differently in the classroom: instructor, playmaker, guide, and evaluator. The instructor relates to teachers' attempts to plan and communicate the overall goals of the game in relation to specific learning objectives. The playmaker is described as the teacher's ability to communicate the tasks, goals, and dynamics of a particular game from the students' perspective. The guide focuses on the teacher's facilitation or scaffolding of students in meeting specific learning objectives through playing the game. The teacher is also crucial as an evaluator who explores, understands, and responds to the students' gameplay. The teacher roles are not discrete, absolute, or normative but rather in flux. Teachers can move between them to best advantage during their teaching with games.

Assessment

Assessment plays a key role in serious games for assessing learning outcomes but also have special challenges and qualities due to the interactive and dynamic nature of the game medium. Initially, serious games should enable players to learn, and optimally better than other formats. To assess this we can use two different approaches: (1) formative: this assessment is done during the game is played; (2) summative: this assessment is done after the game is finished.

There are numerous ways to do either formative or summative assessment but that is beyond the scope here. However, two characteristics of serious games should be stressed: (1) serious games are harder to assess due to their dynamic progression, and (2) serious games have a special potential for assessment during the game experience (formative), as it intrinsically measures players (e.g. with actions, decisions, points, and levels).

A key problem in our assessment of games is that defining "educational effectiveness" is incredibly difficult. Measuring the learning outcome of a given activity is never easy, but the interactive nature of video games makes such quantification even harder. Computer games are dynamic systems and each player will have a different experience. For instance, in the ambitious educational strategy game *Making History: The Calm and the Storm* by Muzzy Lane, one student may not acquire information about the Japanese occupation of Manchuria in 1931, whereas another player will. This makes it very hard to compare learning outcomes between students and classes, and also causes teachers concern. What is one to measure, what should teachers discuss in plenary, and what will students learn the right things? We also must acknowledge that different kinds of computer games focus on different forms of knowledge, which are not easy to measure.[76] Some of these knowledge forms will go largely unnoticed if we rely on, for example, simple multiple-choice tests (e.g. the ability to solve problems).

While the summative assessment provides challenges, the special format of serious games with intrinsic measurement have led some to speculate on games can even be exclusively used for a different kind of assessment. This has sometimes been referred to as stealth assessment. Here you directly gather data during gameplay or integrate elements that through the game assess key area. This approach has the advantage of measuring more directly the learning outcomes, and can also encompass a broader range of competences compared to summative approaches.[77] In the research area game analysis the formative assessment is also used outside serious games to explore a multitude of topics.[78]

The Educational Effectiveness of Serious Games

The question that continues to haunt the educational use of games is whether it is really worth the trouble. The research findings regarding the effectiveness of video games for educational use have consistently build up over the years, and there is a growing body of evidence that serious games lead to stronger learning outcomes across both genders and all ages.[79] Despite claiming to consolidate the area, it still seems that there are different definitions of what is included in the field, which is also reflected in the meta-studies below.

In 2006 Vogel[80] conducted a meta-study across all age groups, where they found higher cognitive gains from serious games compared to traditional teaching methods. They look more closely at possible variables that positively or negatively influence outcome. They find that age and gender do not influence outcomes. They also find that students are more motivated to learn from serious games. This is especially the case when the player controls the game rather than being steered through it. More interestingly, they

Table 8.3 An overview of the key meta-studies on learning outcomes from serious games, simulation games, and educational games. Only true recent meta-studies are included not overview articles. Table inspired by Clark, Tanner-Smith, and Killingsworth (2013) but revised and expanded.

Reference	Genre	Studies	Participants	Results (+ indicates positive impact)
Vogel et al. (2006)	Computer games and interactive simulations	32	All age groups	+ learning outcome in cognitive + students' motivation + player control game
Sitzmann and Ely (2010)	Simulation games	65	+18 years	+ declarative and procedural learning + higher self-efficacy + player active + higher retention and better transfer
Connolly, Boyle, MacArthur, Hainey, and Boyle (2012)	Computer games and serious game	120	+14 years	+ Learning outcomes in all area except soft skills
Wouters and Oostendorp (2013)	Serious games	39	All age groups	+ Improvement in knowledge + Improvements in skills + Instructional support + Collaborative games
Clark et al. (2013)	Digital games	69	K-16 students	+ Learning outcomes + Noncompetitive games + Learning theory informed games
Lamb, Annetta, Firestone, and Etopio (2018)	Serious educational games, educational simulations and serious games	46	Secondary to university	+ Learning outcome in cognitive, affective and skills

also found that learners controlling the path through the video games positively impact the learning outcome. They didn't find any better learning outcomes when playing in groups rather than alone.

Traci Sitzmann and Katherine Ely's 2010 meta-study focused on adults use computer-based simulation games, and they found positive learning outcomes. They also add a lot more details around the factors that influence the outcomes. For example, they are the only meta-study to put a percentage on the additional learning outcome. They find that self-efficacy increases by 20 percent—so when learning from games the learner acts with greater confidence in their own knowledge. This meta-study also shows that both declarative knowledge (up with 11 percent) and procedural knowledge (up with 14 percent) increase when using simulation games, compared to an array of other teaching methods. Finally, the study found that retention increased by 9 percent and transfer by 5 percent. Overall, it showed that you learn more from game-based learning. You will remember it better, and be better able to transfer it to a real-life situation, which is in line with nondigital findings as discussed earlier.[81]

Sitzmann and Ely also find a number of key accelerators for getting the most out of game-based learning. First of all, the games do not necessarily need to be entertaining, and have a stronger impact when learners have free access to them. They also find that game-based learning is most effective when combined with other forms of instruction. Finally, they find that game-based learning that requires an active approach, as opposed to passive, is more effective compared to traditional teaching methods. So, when games require the learner to make decisions and infer rules from the game system, the learning effect from simulation games increases, compared to other instructional methods. However, an important caveat is that when they compare simulation games to instructional methods that require the learner to be active, the simulation games are not superior.

Wouters and Oostendorp[82] focus specifically on serious games for all age groups, and especially have an emphasis on the importance of instructional support. They also go through some effort to examine whether specific characteristics of a game or domain have better impact. They find that schematic games provide better learning outcomes compared to realistic games or cartoon-like games. They find that instructional support is very important to get the best learning outcomes both for learning knowledge and acquiring skills. Across ten factors they find support for six factors that are all in line with theoretical assumptions. Interestingly, they find no evidence that interactivity increases learning outcome nor narrative framing, which contradicts some early theory (e.g. Malone but also the results found by Sitzmann and Ely, and Vogel). The instructional support factors that result in better learning outcomes are reflection, modeling, collaboration, modality, feedback and personalization. This is in line with results from multimedia research.[83]

Another important meta study of video games by Clark, Tanner-Smith, and Killingsworth is from 2013, and focused on K-12 Education. They conclude that:

> beneficial effects on cognitive competencies are primarily based on knowledge outcome measures rather than cognitive processes/strategies outcome measures, of which there are fewer, or creativity outcome measures, of which there are none.[84]

As we see, meta-studies consistently document better learning outcomes, so Clark et al. move the focus to see what conditions influence outcomes positively. This is the first meta-study to examine whether serious games augmented by a learning theory lead to better learning outcomes, and they find good evidence for this. Interestingly, they also find that the complexity of the game mechanics doesn't make a difference. As they conclude "simple gami-fication as well as more sophisticated game mechanics can prove effective."[85] Finally, they did not find an effect of whether you play in a group or as individuals. However, they find an interesting related relationship, where competitive single-player games underperform compared to other combinations.

In the last study by Lamb et al. from 2017, learning outcome is also found to be positive across all areas but not necessarily for older age groups, which contradicts earlier findings by Sitzmann and Ely. They also find mixed results in relation to the game's type and modality influence on learning outcome but conclude that overall these factors do influence learning outcomes, and warrants further studies. Overall, they conclude that 3D games for skills-based cognitive retraining have the strongest effect across all age groups.

Overall, the meta-studies support that the type of serious game does influence learning outcomes. They show that the theoretical foundation built up over the years holds up under the scrutiny of empirical studies, although clear evidence is still emerging. There is clear evidence that serious games informed by learning theory perform better even if this doesn't necessarily need to imply complicated game mechanics. We also see clear indications that instructional support in numerous areas is important to gain the highest learning outcome. Neither the teacher role nor debriefing is explicitly addressed in any of the meta-studies, which is surprising as research from nondigital games suggest debriefing by a facilitator as a crucial factor.

The meta-studies have certainly moved forward since the early ones by Randel et al. (1992) and Lee (1999) by including moderator variables to show under what conditions learning outcomes are best achieved. However, even if the meta-studies do include important theoretical concepts like motivation, narrative, player agency, and type of game mechanics, this is often not quite precise enough. For example, narrative is not found to be a contributor toward higher learning outcomes, but this is also too imprecise a variable, if we look to previous theory. The theoretical foundation would advise a differentiation between extrinsic and intrinsic narratives as a key element to include. Another example is game mechanics, which is examined in terms of whether a simple or complex mechanic benefits learning outcome. However, according to theory discussed earlier, the important variable is not the complexity but rather whether the mechanics are endogenous or exogenous. Another, key challenge is that theory would predict that different types of games are appropriate for different types of learners to learn different things. None of the meta-studies examines this, which is a real problem. One could definitely speculate that a 3D simulation game would be appropriate for procedural learning, for example in firefighting for professionals, but not necessarily novices that need a more schematic approach. A 3D simulation game would allow for an intrinsically motivating endogenous game experience, whereas a 3D quiz game to master declarative knowledge around the periodic table in chemistry would be a questionable candidate for a 3D environment. In such a game, chances are you would draw on extrinsic motivation and exogenous game mechanics. Such complexity may explain why a meta-study like Wouters[86] found that schematic games work best, whereas Lamb[87] found that 3D simulation games support best learning outcomes.

Where Should Serious Games Go

If we look back on the different categories of serious games it is hard to make a final verdict toward whether edutainment deserves the criticism aimed at it. However, from the perspective of learning outcomes, there is some evidence that supports the critique of edutainment. First, the meta-studies show that player agency needs to be active to achieve best learning outcomes, which is directly at odds with edutainment. Second, studies show that games informed by learning theory fare better, which is often not the case for edutainment. Third, one meta-study finds that competitive single-player games do worse, which is typically a core element in the edutainment drill-and-practice approach. Summing up, there is clear direction for future studies, and definitely also take-aways for future educational game designers. As Wouters and Oostendorp conclude:

> Also for designers of GBL the results of the meta-analysis yield some guidelines. They should focus on the learning content and less on the visual design. When a narrative is important, consider to integrate it with the learning content. Apply instructional support to foster cognitive skills and the acquisition of knowledge rather than to stimulate in-game performance.[88]

Unfortunately, chances are that developers of edutainment titles will continue to ignore research evidence as it, from a commercial perspective, is cheaper and easier—and nobody is yet calling them out. This is clearly the case from the real-life laboratory called the Apple App Store. Here traditional edutainment still dominates with its clear, compelling, and simple messages that are easy to pick up by parents and teachers. Next we will turn to gamification, which has certainly been an interesting laboratory since the late 2000s.

GAMIFICATION—CONQUERING THE WORLD, ONE POINT AT A TIME

The idea of using games for more than entertainment was historically focused on bringing content, attitudes, or skills into a gaming context to improve the related learning experience. However, in recent years the idea of gamification has taken off, turning things upside down. In *gamification*, you bring the game into the activity you are trying to enrich, rather than the other way around. Gamification has gained a huge following, with more or less powerful anecdotal evidence testifying to its effect often followed by significant controversy.

Initially, the area was driven by marketing hype claims, but over the years research has grown exponentially in the area. We definitely saw precursors to the concept of gamification early on in classic game theorists like Huizinga, Caillois, Sutton-Smith, and Csikszentmihalyi. Some have even traced the roots of gamification at least back to the seventeenth century with religious card games, gamified prayer books, and music-composing gamified systems.[89] In more recent times, loyalty programs are offered as an example of early gamification systems. The birth of "modern" gamification is somewhat contested, but the term is today ascribed to Nick Pelling's failed business venture Conundra, which ran from 2002 to 2006 with no significant traction.[90] It was not until the US-based company Bunchball launched their platform in 2007 that things started to pick up.

Definitions of Gamification

The battle for gamification is still raging, and there is also a discussion about what a game really is; as we saw in Chapter 3, there is not a straightforward answer to this. Raczkowski[91] provides three different game ontologies that influence the perception and approach to gamification:

- *Games as experimental grounds*: Games are simulation systems where you can mimic and train a number of procedures safely.
- *Games as sources of flow*: Games can transform any mundane activity into a meaningful experience through optimal flow.
- *Games as governed by points and high score*: Games are first and foremost an activity that is about collecting points to get the best score.

Especially, the third approach to game has been criticized strongly as too simplistic by Bogost,[92] Deterding,[93] and Juul,[94] or as not even a real phenomenon by Klabbers[95] worthy of any research attention. The criticism is especially leveled at commercial entities that take a commercial approach to the area and build companies and applications on top of gamification hype. The more successful the commercial side, the harsher the critique from research circles. However, others have argued that such a critique of the gamification industry approach seems to be driven more by personal opinion rather than research evidence.[96]

On closer examination, the majority of the classic gamification "gurus"[97] books, no matter how commercial, do not argue for a gamification that is restricted to a very mechanical approach driven by a behavioristic worldview as evident in the definitions we will go through a bit later. If we look at some quick interviews[98] with 16 "gurus," many of them stress going beyond a simple approach focused on PBL (points, badges, and leaderboards) but then go on to mention (and build) gamification solutions that are mostly quite mechanical. So despite better intentions, commercial products often rely on a mechanical approach sometimes paraphrased as the PBL formula.[99] However, the reason for this is probably very simple—it is much cheaper, easier, faster, and more scalable to develop an experience and slap on some points, badges, and a high score to make it stand out—especially when most customers don't really understand games and the drivers that ultimately make them work. In this sense, gamification is haunted by similar challenges that serious games experience with the limitations of the edutainment formula.

The definition of gamification was already fairly well agreed on from 2011:

Deterding, Dixon, Khaled, & Nacke, 2011: "Gamification is the use of game design elements in non-game contexts."[100]

Zichermann & Cunningham, 2011: "the process of game-thinking and game mechanics to engage users and solve problems."[101]

Kapp, 2012: "gamification is using game-based mechanics, aesthetics, and game-thinking to engage people, motivate action, promote learning, and solve problems."[102]

Werbach & Hunter, 2012: "The use of game elements and game-design techniques in non-game contexts."[103]

Zichermann & Linder, 2013: "implementing design concepts from games, loyalty programs, and behavioral economics to drive user engagement."[104]

Merriam-Webster's Dictionary, 2018: "the process of adding games or gamelike elements to something (such as a task) so as to encourage participation."

Table 8.4 outlines gamification in more detail by listing five levels of game design elements in gamification, which would probably also be agreed to by most of the theorists—in theory but not necessarily praxis.

Table 8.4 The different elements in design gamification experiences

Level	Description	Example
Game interface design patterns	Common, successful interaction design components and design solutions for a known problem in a context, including prototypical implementations	Badge, leaderboard, level
Game design patterns and mechanics	Commonly reoccurring parts of the design of a game that concern gameplay	Time constraint, limited resources, turns
Game design principles and heuristics	Evaluative guidelines to approach a design problem or analyze a given design solution	Enduring play, clear goals, variety of game styles
Game models	Conceptual models of the components of games or game experience	MDA; challenge, fantasy, curiosity; game design atoms; CEGE
Game design methods	Game design-specific practices and processes	Playtesting, playcentric design, value conscious game design

Source: Deterding et al. (2011, p. 6).

There is a pretty consistent understanding of the concept of gamification centering around using two key components in nontraditional game contexts: the application of game thinking and the use of game elements. In contrast, the end goal of gamification is a bit more elusive although it tends to include motivation, engagement, learning, and change. In the introduction to this chapter, we settled on a high-level definition that excludes learning and focuses on behavior change to clearly set it aside from serious games: the concept that *game mechanics* can be used in a variety of nonentertainment settings to *change behaviors*. Although learning can be a component of change, this is not always necessary and rarely the primary focus when using gamification. The primary purpose is to change behavior—sometimes to increase learning but definitely not always.

Also, this definition allows us to unfold two different types of gamification that is inspired by some of the thinking in Deterding's work on eudaimonic design, deep/shallow gamification by Lieberoth, and Nicholson's meaningful gamification:[105] the instrumentalist and idealist approach.

This distinction is useful for seeing through the disagreement in the field and to focus on the elements that researchers believe are crucial for successful gamification. It is only recently that the research area of gamification has realized a clear enough sense of what gamification is to examine what impact and significance different gamification elements and approaches can have. In this sense the gamification field is research-wise much less mature than the serious games area.

Categorizing Gamification: Instrumentalist or Idealist

The instrumentalist approach has been by far the most influential in society, since it delivers what people want. It delivers the "how" of behavioral change through gaming, without worrying too much about the simple "why." The idealist approach, on the other hand, stresses that the gamified activity should not only get people to do things but also provide a deeper, more meaningful activity that wants people to do it. We shouldn't just log into Foursquare to get points, level up, and achieve status; we should do it for a deeper purpose, such as socializing with friends and creating new relationships. The instrumentalist argument is, yes, we can create a deeper experience, but really, it's not so important as long as we achieve the goals we set out to accomplish. Both sides agree that it's usually harder to get both the why and the how right. The idealist will argue that the instrumentalist approach is shortsighted, and people will realize that they are trying to do something that lacks meaning. The truth is probably somewhere in between. You may get a stronger and more sustainable gamification experience if you combine the why with the how, but you can to a large extent settle for using only the instrumental approach for quick gains. In Table 8.5 we outline some of the key areas where the two approaches differ.[106]

Cleary, we see different areas where the two schools are more or less widespread because they have different backgrounds, needs, and focus.

Table 8.5 The two schools within gamification and their characteristics

	Instrumentalist	*Idealist*
Area	Marketing, corporation, health	Research, schools
Player agency	Outer locus of control (*force* people to do things)	Inner locus of control (*help* people do things)
Game ontology	Ludus	Paidia
Motivation	Extrinsic	Intrinsic
Mechanics	Exogenous	Endogenous
Object	Game	Experience

These include the view on players, motivation, mechanics, and what games are.

When we look at player agency, the instrumentalist in general tries to tightly control the actions of the players, whereas the idealist wants the player to maintain as much freedom as possible. As such, the idealist starts from the free and explorative mode of play that Caillois describes as paidia rather than the more rule-based and restricted ludus. The instrumentalist will use extrinsic motivation to achieve this result, whereas the idealist will rely on players to engage in intrinsically motivated actions because of their meaningfulness and self-interest. To ensure that the player perceives the activity as meaningful and pursues the right areas, the mechanics need to be endogenous. You cannot rely on external rewards as they will move the player toward a superficial focus on the subject. Finally, the idealist will not be restricted to just looking at the game as a deterministic set of rules but will have a more holistic view of the full experience that involves social interactions and interpretations by the players.

The preceding shows us that even if the two schools on the surface can agree what gamification is on a high-level—game elements and game thinking—they hardly agree on what constitutes a "real" game. If we think back on Chapter 3, indeed we see that a concept like make-believe and magic circle is challenged when we move "outside" of the game's safe rules and directly into real life. This may very well be what has sparked colorful language from researchers like "exploitationware"[107] or "bullshit."[108] Nevertheless, it is clear that both the instrumentalist and the idealist draw strongly on game elements and game thinking in their work—one may speculate that maybe marketing people are just pretty horrible game designers who prefer the instrumentalist approach because they are good marketing people.

Instrumentalist Approach

Overall, the instrumentalist approach is much more commercial in its approach compared to idealism, and attempts to offer clear-cut recipes for how to succeed with gamification. Gamification is about using game mechanics to enhance existing structures, sites, services, products, or experiences, and it very much ends up sounding more like marketing than anything else, although it doesn't have to be like that.[109] The instrumentalist cookie-cutter approach has really given gamification traction with major corporations. Gamification companies like Bunchball and Badgeville offer a turnkey solution for getting started quickly and embedding game mechanics in your organization, product, or service.

The classic example usually mentioned first is Nike+, which a lot of people know about, and therefore easily can demonstrate how gamification works for example with run challenges, badges, status, network, and comments.[110] Another example is when accounting firm Deloitte employed Badgeville to use gamification structures for their new leadership training. In the new setup, leaders would be encouraged to complete the training through badges, leader boards, and status symbols. This resulted in much quicker certification completion (whether it was better is not known).[111]

The key argument behind instrumentalist gamification is that by quantifying, tracking, and rewarding behaviors toward a specific goal, we are able to induce people to act in ways they normally would not. This underlying approach obviously stirs great controversy, since it incorporates quite a mechanistic view of human nature. As with any discussion ultimately based on ontological assumptions, there really isn't a right or wrong answer—although of course you may through research in specific cases find more or less backing for a given approach in a given context.

Tom Chatfield[112] has given one of the clearer accounts on how games from a neuroscience perspective can be harnessed to engage people. This has been adapted by the instrumentalist approach. He describes seven core components: experience systems, short/long term goals, reward for effort, rapid/frequent/clear feedback, uncertainty, and other people.

- Experience systems give us a sense of achievement for reaching milestones and keep us working toward them. For example, the LinkedIn progress bar shows how much profile information is needed and outlines what is needed to achieve that goal.
- Short- and long-term goals allow us to achieve success on a micro scale while simultaneously making progression toward the macro goal seem more achievable.
- Rewards for effort trigger releases of feel-good chemicals in our brain, which train us toward a desired behavior.
- Rapid, frequent, and clear feedback to a user's actions will also set off the reward centers in our brains. For example, Facebook is addictive partly because it allows us to receive real-time feedback on our actions.
- Uncertainty is crucially important for a strong reward scheme. Gamblers become addicted to slot machines due to the unpredictable nature of the payoffs.[113] It is the element of uncertainty that has people constantly checking their email or buying loot boxes.
- Enhanced attention is used to make the experience more intense through, for example, updates, contest, or similar.

- Other people probably provide humans with the greatest rewards, as we are social creatures by nature. Adding other people into your experience is a no-brainer, as evidenced by the rise of social media.

Zichermann is a strong proponent of the instrumentalist approach, and an intensive speaker. He describes the gamification loop as the pointification loop that is defined by challenges, points, win condition, leader boards, badges, social networking, and status.[114] The elements are fairly similar to Chatfield's. The argument goes that through experience and points, you can create a status that gives you power, access, and stuff; this formula involves a number of key principles inherited from the game world. The idea is that any (real) activity you engage with gives you points. Effectively, points serve as an indicator for your experience level and progression. No matter what you do, you will feel a sense of progression (however superficial this may be, it often works).[115] As you gain experience, this will give you privileges that can take different forms. They can be about the basic need for feeling included (access), the feeling of empowerment by influencing surroundings (power), or the need to acquire desirable goods (stuff). The basic idea is that these principles can be applied across the board. The content is of less importance, as you always quantify something and hence turn it into a game. For example, a child's reluctance to get dressed in the morning can be overcome in an instant if it's turned into a competition—who gets their clothes on first?[116]

Idealist Approach

The idealist argues that we need something more than just points, badges, and leader boards. According to Deterding, we need to focus on creating meaning, mastery, and autonomy in the game experience. You can create meaning in a number of ways—through, for example, being part of a community or setting up meaningful goals. However, the activity has to be relevant on some level. The second requirement is that you actually have to do something real and feel the fulfillment of achieving mastery in a new domain. Without mastery, scoring points or pinning on badges will seem empty. You need to make the game about interesting choices, balancing options, and challenge—it should not be trivial. Rules are crucial here because they set the constraints that make things more difficult, and goals communicate clearly when you are successful at a new level of mastery. Finally, it is stressed that autonomy is key to creating the engagement characteristic of games, and that framing is crucial. You will engage in quite "numbing" activities for a greater purpose, if you find it meaningful and you choose to do it. However, if you feel something is forced upon you—no matter how good the game—it will lose a lot of its attraction.[117] Nicholson pursues a similar line of reasoning, where he stresses the importance of relevance in a given context. He stresses that relevance is created by allowing the player to choose what goals are important for them in a given activity, and a freedom in demonstrating mastery toward these goals. One example of this is *Chore Wars* from 2007, where players can set up their own household activities, points, and short/long-term goals. The key point is that you maintain freedom, autonomy, and mastery driven by the player. Another example is the Toyota Prius, where a green plant in the dashboard shows how green you are driving. It is up to the players to create their own challenges and goals around the system.

The Impact of Gamification

Even if the area has matured considerably and overview articles have emerged, it is still early. It is clear that the instrumentalist gamification approach was most represented in research studies. When looking at game elements, PBL elements were by far the most common, followed by social networking equally between cooperative and competitive. When looking at the outcomes, enjoyment featured prominently followed by behavioral change and social aspects. Only 27.7 percent of the 65 experimental quantitative studies report clear positive results; 47.7 percent reported mixed but positive results; 21.5 percent reported mixed but negative results; and only 3.1 percent of the studies reported negative results.[118]

In the following we have brought forward two interesting studies that show the way forward for gamification, and provide interesting insights into what impact gamification has. The two different experimental studies both look at gamification within a classroom setting for university students. Corporations have used gamification more, but unfortunately they often don't allow research to be conducted, and only report very selective metrics that typically are meant to advance their own agenda, and have to be treated with some care. The two studies look at how gamification can increase learning in the classroom and come to quite different results.

Negative Results

Holistically, the results suggest that some common mechanics used in classroom gamification (i.e. competitive context, badges, and leaderboards) may harm some educational outcomes. We found that though students from each course started at the same levels of intrinsic motivation, satisfaction, effort, social comparison, and empowerment, over time students in the gamified course tended to decrease in motivation, satisfaction, and empowerment relative to the non-gamified course.[119]

Positive Results

We have found that gamification can help in many ways our students, from increasing passing rates and participation, to high student satisfaction and heart-warming testimonials.[120]

On the surface, they both deploy a similar gamification design, namely PBL. It is a fairly straight-up intervention where they add a gamification layer with badges that are rewards. However, there are also some important differences, and it seems that the interventions are also somewhat different, although it is hard to judge due to limited information on the exact gamification design. The study that finds negative results seems to deploy a very instrumentalist version of gamification, where some badges are flicked together and can be achieved by performing a task. The badges are designed so they primarily rely on quantitative measures, and only very indirectly relate to the behavior that the course aims at. The study with the positive results reports that they spend one week in preparing the gamification design and several days of overhead throughout the course to score it properly. They have also made their own toolbox and focus on social interactions as a key element. It certainly suggests that they have a much more fine-grained and precise system.

In the study by Hanus and Fox with the negative results, the examples are badges. For example, get the bookworm by exceeding the minimum number of required sources in a paper, playing a video, or writing a critical review. On the face of it, this looks like badges that have problematic win conditions and feedback loops that fall squarely in the instrumentalist camp. While on the face of it, they look relevant, they will highly likely encourage wrong behavior, reward behavior that doesn't demonstrate mastery, and defocus the course. For example, let's say that one student wants to write a good paper, and chooses three hard but relevant sources (no points), whereas another student writes a good paper but with five irrelevant easy sources (extra points). All kinds of ramifications can easily be imagined. For instance, some students write good papers but just go for the achievements, which is a well-established risk of weak gamification design. Indeed, Hanus and Fox report that the intrinsic motivation decreases for the students in the gamification group, and that this negatively impacts their course outcome. Maybe the badges were better designed in the "negative study" but it doesn't look like it, and it shows that plug and play gamification platform is a difficult path as we need to consider relevance and context.

We cannot necessarily conclude that we will always see negative results from a more instrumental approach, which a study from 2014 by Andreas Lieberoth convincingly demonstrates. Through a very shallow gamified framing, he finds that gamification in the short term can achieve a large impact on people's engagement in a given activity.

The mixed results reported throughout gamification studies are reviewed by Toda, Valle, and Isotani (2018) to understand what and when gamification works and for whom. They find that indeed gamification can result in worse learning performance in some situations, in some instances due to lack of understanding rules or not appreciating getting scored. In one study it was showed that the players who engaged the most with the gamification performed worse afterwards. Second, they report that in many situations the gamification intervention produced unexpected undesired behaviors due to the context-of-use or due to planning issues. Sometimes the points and badges were simply not perceived as motivating or sometimes too motivating, resulting in over-the-top competition. Finally, it was often reported that the effect of gamification declined over time.

Both the reviews by Toda, Valle, and Isotani and by Koivisto and Hamari warn of severe method flaws, and a large variety in the quality of the gamification interventions. Indeed, it can sometimes be hard to see whether it's the concept of gamification that is not working, a specific poor gamification design, or just a weak experimental research design. Nevertheless, it seems clear that the cookie-cutter approach, where you just implement gamification, is far away from the realities in the classroom. Indeed, gamification may do more harm than good if implemented poorly, both in the short and long term.

Also, it is worth noting that the above is akin to what we would expect from studies in the serious games area, and the critique researchers level at the instrumentalist approach to gamification.

Criticism of Gamification

We have already seen several examples of critique of gamification and an ongoing struggle for what the field should be. Several discussions have piggybacked on this fundamental debate, relating to the relation between extrinsic and intrinsic motivation, as well as inner and outer control. Several studies suggest the external/extrinsic can undermine the internal/intrinsic. After significant controversy over the years at conferences and in blogs, more than one commentator has lost perspective. However, Jesper Juul has tried to sum it up, describing three main threads in gamification criticism:[121]

1. Extrinsic rewards demotivate in the long term.[122] If you play football to win matches and forget about love of the game, you will become de-motivated. This argument ignores the fact that, for a lot of activities (especially those gamified), there may not really be any love to lose. However, there is indeed a valid concern when we use gamification principles, for example, for motivating learning (such as the grading system). Students may forget that they are not learning to get good grades but because it's interesting, important, and opens new doors. There is also bigger question with regard to whether reliance on extrinsic motivation in one knowledge domain will spill over into other areas.

2. Some suggest that gamification comes close to repression,[123] and that it encourages shallow understanding of an activity, potentially leading to a "seduction of the masses." This is really an empty line of reasoning— it may very well be true but no more so than for most other strategies for influencing people, and for media consumption in general. This line of reasoning seems to be more a question of passion and outrage than informed reasoning. Especially since the success of *FarmVille*, *EpicWin*, *Weight Watchers*, and *Foursquare*, to name a few, gamification hits can be hugely successful—labeling these as seduction of the masses may not be completely inaccurate, but on the other hand it may also be somewhat of a stretch to see them as much more than the next phase of entertainment, following the reality wave.

3. Finally, Juul suggests that player optimization and performance measurement, which have worked inside games, may not work outside games.

Implementation needs to be careful, but this criticism seems rather general and is made without giving concrete examples.

These three criticisms attack gamification somewhat differently, but the first two are more ethical than anything, while Juul's final point is rather vague. The ethical criticisms seem better founded, although still difficult to generalize from. It is still too early to define the exact merits of gamification but we clearly see a more murky picture than for serious games. This may very well be a consequence of an emerging field with huge variations in gamification designs but also that a lot of gamification is simply implemented with an instrumental approach, which can be problematic. It should be stressed though that there are probably situations where both approaches will work but that we still need to tread carefully.

FINAL REMARKS

Serious games and gamification have certainly developed, and maybe this is the area that is in most dire need of game researchers. Clearly, there are enough pitfalls to navigate and plenty of areas that need clarification to make sure we truly can harness the full potential of games for pursuits beyond pure entertainment. The industry within the area is still trying to figure out exactly how they should approach the field.

Some researchers early on argued that we should be careful about investing large sums of money in expensive educational video games before we have evidence that they are worth the investment.[124] On the other hand, it is very hard to gain the necessary experience to develop effective titles without experimental use and research. Though to date it is still difficult to prove conclusively that serious games and gamification are worth the investment, it definitely looks like they can bring both engagement and learning to the table.

DISCUSSION QUESTIONS

- How do "serious games" compare to "regular" video games? Why are they different?
- What challenges do you see in using games for purposes other than entertainment?
- What potential is there for using games for purposes other than entertainment? Include considerations of the changes in platforms, distribution, target groups, and controllers.
- Revisit Chapter 3 and discuss how gamification is at odds with the different definitions of a game. You can for example consider concepts like make-believe, magic circle, conflict, and safety. When does a game stop being a game?
- Do advertising, games-for-change, gamification, and political games present game developers with ethical and moral dilemmas?

RECOMMENDED GAMES

Oregon Trail—Among the first and surely most played educational games of all time.

Math Blaster—Perhaps the game that defines best the classic edutainment genre with its classic, shoot-down-the-right-answer formula.

Global Conflicts: Palestine—Shows that games can tackle some of the most difficult issues through engaging narratives.

This War of Mine—A role-playing game taking a very different approach to game mechanics, and showing the potential of endogenous serious games.

Dragonbox—Set a new standard for integration of gameplay and mathematics learning through a simple puzzle game mechanic.

FURTHER READINGS

Baranowski, T., Blumberg, F., Buday, R., DeSmet, A., Fiellin, L. E., Green, C. S., & Young, K. (2016). Games for health for children-current status and needed research. *Games for Health Journal*, 5(1), 1–12.

(Estimated reading time: 28 minutes)

Egenfeldt-Nielsen, S. (2011, February). What makes a good learning game? Going beyond edutainment. *eLearn Magazine*. ACM.

(Estimated reading time: 10 minutes)

NOTES

1. IDATE, 2018; McGonigal, 2011.
2. Allied Market Research, 2018.
3. Mordor Intelligence, 2018.
4. McGonigal, 2011.
5. Lu and Kharrazi (2018).
6. Lu, Kharrazi, Gharghabi, and Thompson (2013).
7. Bogost, Ferrari, and Schweizer, 2010; Delwiche, 2007; Frasca, 2007.
8. www.ludology.org/ or www.impactgames.com/playthenews.php.
9. Erard, 2004.
10. Karlsson, 2004, p. 4.
11. Gardner, 2001; Lindstrøm, 2003; Rodgers, 2004; Tønner, 2000.
12. Gardner, 2001.
13. Deterding et al., 2011; Bouça, 2012.
14. Abt, 1970.
15. Malone, 1980; Malone and Lepper, 1987a, 1987b.
16. Greenblat and Duke, 1981.
17. Egenfeldt-Nielsen, 2007.
18. Clegg, 1991; Randel, Morris, Wetzel, and Whitehill, 1992; Van Sickle, 1986; Wentworth and Lewis, 1973.
19. Egenfeldt-Nielsen, 2007.
20. Lederman and Fumitoshi, 1995.
21. Saegesser, 1981.
22. Silverman, 2018.
23. Çiftci, 2018; de Freitas, 2018.
24. Rieber, 1996; Squire, 2006.

25. Egenfeldt-Nielsen, 2007.
26. Cheung, Li, and Zapart (2006).
27. Facer, Furlong, Furlong, and Sutherland, 2003; Leyland, 1996.
28. Buckingham and Scanlon, 2002; Leyland, 1996.
29. Buckingham and Scanlon, 2002; Egenfeldt-Nielsen, 2005.
30. Buckingham and Scanlon, 2002; Egenfeldt-Nielsen, 2005.
31. Malone, 1980.
32. Buckingham and Scanlon, 2002.
33. Buckingham and Scanlon, 2002.
34. Gee, 2003.
35. Squire, 2004a.
36. McFarlane, Sparrowhawk, and Heald, 2002.
37. Prensky, 2001.
38. Kirriemuir, 2002.
39. Egenfeldt-Nielsen, 2005.
40. Adams, 1998.
41. Egenfeldt-Nielsen, 2011.
42. Kuntz, 1999.
43. Shippee, 2017.
44. Wastiau, Kearney, and Van den Berghe (2009).
45. Egenfeldt-Nielsen, 2007.
46. Squire, 2004a.
47. Diamond, 1997.
48. Van Eck, 2009, p. 6.
49. E.g. Egenfeldt-Nielsen, 2007.
50. See e.g. Hancock and Osterweil, 1996; Malone and Lepper, 1987a.
51. 1987a, 1987b.
52. Koster, 2004.
53. Buckingham and Scanlon, 2002.
54. Rieber, 1996.
55. Kafai, 1996.
56. Cipollone, Schifter, and Moffat, 2014; Ekaputra, Lim, and Kho, 2014; Karsenti, Bugmann, and Gros, 2017.
57. Callaghan, 2016.
58. Gee, 2003; Jessen, 2001; Linderoth, 2002; Shaffer, 2006; Squire, 2004b.
59. Gee, 2003.
60. Barab, Gresalfi, and Ingram-Goble, 2010.
61. Healy, 1999; Kafai, 2001; Okan, 2003.
62. Egenfeldt-Nielsen, 2005; Grundy, 1991; Healy, 1999; Magnussen and Misfeldt, 2004.
63. Egenfeldt-Nielsen, 2005; Jillian, Upitis, Koch, and Young, 1999; Leutner, 1993; Squire, 2004a.
64. Egenfeldt-Nielsen, 2005.
65. Grundy, 1991.
66. Cotton, 1991; Loftus and Loftus, 1983.
67. Klawe, 1998.
68. Klawe, 1998, p. 9.
69. Kafai, 1995, 2001; Papert, 1998.
70. Klawe, 1998.
71. Sedighian and Sedighian, 1996.
72. Klawe and Phillips, 1995.
73. Brody, 1993.
74. Cavallari et al., 1992; Egenfeldt-Nielsen, 2005; Grundy, 1991; Klawe, 1998; Squire, 2004a.
75. Hanghøj and Brund, 2011.
76. Bellotti, Kapralos, Lee, Moreno-Ger, and Berta, 2013.
77. Shute and Ke, 2015.
78. Fernández-Vara, 2019.
79. Vogel et al., 2006; Sitzmann and Ely, 2010; Connolly et al., 2012; Wouters and Oostendorp, 2013; Clark et al., 2013; Lamb et al., 2018.
80. Vogel et al., 2006.
81. Sitzmann and Ely, 2010.
82. Wouters and Oostendorp, 2013.
83. Mayer, 2001.
84. Clark et al., 2013, p. 3.
85. Clark et al., 2013, p. 11.
86. Wouters, 2013.
87. Lamb, 2018.
88. Wouters and Oostendorp, 2013, p. 423.
89. Fuchs, 2014.
90. Pelling, 2011.
91. Raczkowski, 2014.
92. Bogost, 2011a, 2011b.
93. Deterding, 2013.
94. Juul, 2011.
95. Klabbers, 2018.
96. Landers et al., 2018.
97. Werbach and Hunter, 2012; Zichermann and Cunningham, 2011; Kapp, 2012; Zichermann and Linder, 2013.
98. Garcia, 2018.
99. Werbach and Hunter, 2012.
100. p. 10.
101. p. xiv.
102. p. 10.
103. p. 26.
104. p. xii.
105. Deterding, 2013; Nicholson, 2012; Lieberoth, 2014.

106. Nacke and Deterding, 2017.
107. Bogost, 2011a.
108. Bogost, 2011b.
109. Raymer, 2011.
110. Zichermann, 2010.
111. Bradt, 2013.
112. Chatfield, 2010.
113. Montague and Berns, 2002.
114. Zichermann, 2010.
115. Lieberoth, 2014.
116. Zichermann and Cunningham, 2011; Zichermann, 2010.
117. Deterding, 2011.
118. Koivisto and Hamari, 2016.
119. Hanus and Fox, 2015.
120. Iosup and Epema, 2014.
121. Juul, 2011.
122. Nicholson, 2012.
123. Chaplin, 2011.
124. Grundy, 1991; Jillian et al., 1999.

9 Video Games and Risks

The Walking Dead (2012), a zombie game

Two Research Perspectives
The Active Media Perspective
The Active User Perspective
Other Questions
Final Remarks

This chapter explores the risks involved with playing video games—or, in popular parlance, the potential harmful effects of video game play. This is an issue that everyone in the industry—and just as many people who have nothing to do with video games—seems to have an opinion about. For angry parents and determined teenagers, for dismissive developers and anxious educators, and seemingly for everyone in between, video games seem to contain an element of danger. Over the years, the question of harm has received massive attention in both public debate and research circles. Although the interest may not be as great as in the last millennium, the area has still regularly received attention, especially from the general media that often looks for causal links between shootings and playing video games.

Was the Columbine High School shooting of 1999 aided by the killers' fondness for violent video games? In 2011, did the Norwegian killer Anders Breivik plan and carry out his crimes with the help of computer games? Can violent video games make you more aggressive? Questions like these never seem far from the public agenda, and researchers of various stripes have for the last few decades tried to answer them.

We discuss this Pandora's box by contrasting two competing research perspectives: the "Active User" perspective and the "Active Media" perspective. The discussion will make clear that the link between violent games and player aggression has received most attention but that beneath this issue lie even more basic disagreements about how we experience and perceive video games.

As we have seen throughout this book, academic research has been conducted on many elements of video games; however, the study of dangers in connection with games remains a key research avenue, as it continues to receive massive media attention and is still an arena for great controversy. As mentioned, research within this area has primarily been centered on the question of whether video games lead to increased aggression in players. This concern has been driven by regular bursts of public concern in relation to violent video games, most noticeable on the release of *Death Race* in 1976, *Mortal Kombat* in 1994, *Grand Theft Auto III* in 2001, *Medal of Honor* in 2010, *South Park: The Stick of Truth* in 2014, *Hatred* in 2015, and *Rape Day* in 2019.

Until the late 1990s, the majority of funded game research involved a risk perspective. This century, it has become somewhat of an orphan in games research, as more than a few researchers have flatly refused to take part in studies of risk. These researchers, as we'll discuss further, typically feel that video games as a medium are treated unfairly—that the discussion of games and aggression is essentially an attempt to turn games into a scapegoat for more complex societal problems; they also fear that the link to aggression is a precursor to censorship not leveled at other media, which is a valid concern given the continual attempts, especially in the United States, to pass laws to curb video games.[1,2] Also, Steam has over the years been under heavy fire to censor games on their distribution platform. Scholars who refuse to engage in this debate may well be interested in the aggression question itself but simply resent what they see as unfair criticism of video games, and suspect that opponents of games may have ulterior motives.

TWO RESEARCH PERSPECTIVES

Active Media perspective: A school of thought that believes that media actively influence a mostly passive recipient, the player.

Active User perspective: A school of thought that stresses the active interpretation and filtering players exhibit when playing video games.

The **Active Media** perspective refers to a school of thought that believes that media actively influence a mostly passive recipient, the player. Its proponents typically use "classical" methods of research, often based in a laboratory, and are influenced mainly by social psychology and behaviorism. This perspective mostly exists outside mainstream games research; "risk" researchers do not consider themselves games researchers, do not attend games conferences, and often do not play games. This split has at times led to problematic research, lacking a basic knowledge of (or interest in) video games, although recent years have seen more rigorous studies.

In contrast, the **Active User** perspective refers to a school of thought that stresses the active interpretation and filtering players exhibit when playing video games. The Active User perspective will gather empirical data from natural settings and will tend to look to anthropology, cultural studies, and media theory for theoretical ammunition.

We should note that the distinction between the Active Media and Active User perspectives is an artificial one, set up by us to recognize some basic differences between researchers examining the risks of computer games. In the following pages the Active Media perspective and the Active User perspective are discussed in a way that provides the necessary knowledge for understanding the debate on risks, both in research circles and in the general press. The chapter should also give the reader a starting point for conducting studies in both areas with an eye to potential problems and limitations.

Over the last 35 years, more than 200 studies have been conducted to try to understand the relationship between video games and risk. Taken as a whole, this body of knowledge has been influenced more by the Active Media than the Active User perspective. The former has imbued this research with a social psychological perspective, and a reliance on what Active Media researchers refer to as "the effect tradition," that is, an almost automatic relationship between playing violent video games and becoming more violent. In the Active Media perspective, video games are conceived as having a direct, objective, and measurable effect on players.

An Active User perspective, which takes the opposite starting point, has over the years tried to challenge this tradition. According to researchers from this latter perspective, video games do not have the same effect on everybody but are mediated by a variety of factors such as playing context, genre expectations, and the individual player's interpretation. The player is not seen as a passive recipient of the content in video games but rather as an active, selective, and critical user.

In the sections that follow we present typical research designs for each perspective. It should be stressed that in principle the two perspectives (or "theories") are not directly linked to specific academic fields, although researchers within each are typically allied with certain methodologies, as we'll see below. These research designs summarize the specific ways that each group prefers to conduct a scientific study. By examining a standard example of these two research approaches, we hope to show that the way the question of harmful video games is formulated and examined will to a large extent decide the answers arrived at.

A Typical Research Design for the Active Media Perspective

A typical study in this tradition will start out with two groups of subjects; they can number anywhere from 8 to 100. One group plays a violent video game (for instance, the action game *Quake*) while the other group plays a nonviolent video game (for instance, the racing game *Need for Speed*). Before subjects start playing, their level of aggression is measured—different methods may be used, from a standard multiple-choice psychological questionnaire to a physiological test that involves taking swabs of saliva to find the amount of cortisol in the player's body. This measurement is repeated for both groups after they have played their games. The assumption is that any difference in the change in aggression levels between the two groups can be attributed to the difference between the two games. The effect of one violent game can then be generalized to other violent video games that these groups might play.

A Typical Research Design for the Active User Perspective

In a classic study following an Active User perspective, the researchers observe and interview a group of children playing different video games in a natural setting (such as an after-school club) over a relatively long period (say, three months). Through their observations the researchers note behavioral characteristics such as verbal and physical violence. Questions could range from the children's perception of dying in a game to whether they have bad dreams. The researchers aim to describe the full experience of gameplay and the context in which these children play games; the ultimate goal is to understand how the players integrate video games into their daily life—how players use the games.

The effect of playing certain games (or types of games) is just one potential focus of an Active User study and is rarely looked for specifically. When incidences of aggression are found, they are analyzed in the specific context in which they arose; researchers hesitate to generalize actions or behaviors to other situations because they believe that each player perceives each game differently and the context of play is important for the player's perception. Furthermore, because everything that the children do is seen as dependent on the context (in this case the after-school program, the particular group of subjects, and the specific games they play), the researchers are not able to isolate "violence" as a variable.

The focus of these two research designs makes all the difference. The Active Media perspective looks at what a video game does to a player, whereas the Active User perspective is interested in what the players do with the video game. This crucial difference stems from a very basic theoretical disagreement on how we should understand people's psychological functioning. This split also runs through a number of other disciplines and may be exemplified by the disagreement evident in the statements made by the two groups.

An Active Media proponent concludes, based on laboratory studies, that

> exposure to violent video games is significantly linked to increases in aggressive behaviour, aggressive cognition, aggressive affect, and cardiovascular arousal, and to decreases in helping behaviour.[3]

Compare the following statement from a group of Active User proponents:

> Many scholars believe that trying to understand the media's impact on human development through laboratory measurements and other numerical methods is inherently flawed.[4]

Table 9.1 The differences between the Active Media perspective and the Active User perspective

	Active Media perspective	Active User perspective
Scientific and theoretical starting point	Behaviorism, social psychology, experimental psychology	Anthropology, ethnography, literary studies/ semiotics, cultural studies, media theory
Research methods	Predominantly quantitative (controlled studies)	Predominantly qualitative (interview and observation)
Main interest	The effects of media on attitude, perception and behavior	Meaning, role, and function of media
Research object	The video game (what effect the game has on the player)	The player (what the player does with the game)

Though Table 9.1 simplifies each perspective slightly, laying out their basic characteristics side by side gives us a graphic appreciation of the differences. Whereas the Active Media perspective involves generalizing, researchers within the Active User perspective usually avoid making general claims. The Active Media perspective examines the specific influence of violent video games, while the Active User perspective examines video games in a broader way. Researchers within the two perspectives do share some notions of what qualifies as science—both groups agree, for example, that logic, argument, and reasoning are pillars of science. However, it is unlikely that studies taking an Active Media perspective will ever fully convince Active User researchers and vice versa. As we look at the basic assumptions of the two groups, it seems less likely that they are directly disagreeing with another and more likely that they are having different conversations. Their theoretical assumptions are dramatically different from each other.

Attempts have recently been made to combine the approaches to achieve a stronger research design and to facilitate better dialogue between the two perspectives.[5] Traditionally, the two research positions have seldom engaged in direct discussion of each other's research; the occasional public debates are centered on the Active User perspective's skepticism toward the basic premises of the Active Media perspective. Within the last five years, however, the Active Media perspective has begun to engage with the criticism, trying to refute some of the critiques.[6] Media researcher David Buckingham criticizes both positions for building barriers but also states that "despite the more complex views of meaning which have been developed, much of the work on violence has remained stubbornly tied to behaviorist assumptions."[7]

Let us deepen our understanding of the risk issue by exploring the thinking behind each of these perspectives, as well as the relevant criticisms of each. We will begin with the Active Media perspective, since it remains the most dominant perspective.

THE ACTIVE MEDIA PERSPECTIVE

The Active Media perspective has set the agenda for research into the risks of video games since the early 1980s; though it is less dominant today, its influence continues to be felt, with more than 130 published studies in the last two decades. The Active Media perspective has its theoretical roots in North American psychology, and the "behaviorist tradition" constitutes an important part of its foundation. Another basic building block is communication theory (often defined as "who says what to whom in what channel with what effect"), particularly the branches inspired more by classical social sciences than by hermeneutic approaches to media use.

With its origins in the 1910s, behaviorism conceptualizes human beings as fairly simple systems that respond to the stimuli around them; classical behaviorists avoided discussing inner mental processes. The Active Media perspective relies on behaviorism, especially its use of theory for understanding empirical results but is offering still more sophisticated theoretical frameworks to guide predictions and interpretations.

Active Media research can technically employ most types of methodologies, from experimental studies to cross-section correlation. Nevertheless, these studies share a basic assumption that a particular medium (such as video games or violent video games) has one particular effect on people (who are basically similar); this assumption often leads to experiments with a fairly standard research design, similar to the example presented earlier.

The most used research design is usually referred to as an experimental study. Ideally these take place in a laboratory setting, and by filtering out confounding variables the researcher aims to measure the exact effect of a given variable. The two other typical research designs are cross-section correlation studies and longitudinal correlation studies.

Cross-section correlation studies look at a group's use of video games and level of aggression at a given point in time. A correlation is said to exist if the players of violent video games are more aggressive than the nonplayers. So, if a group of gamers plays more violent video games and is more aggressive than others, this denotes a correlation.

Longitudinal correlation studies typically follow a given group of people over a number of years. If, over time, a correlation is ascertained between the fact that those who play violent video games also exhibit more aggressive behavior (and that behavior was not present at the start) then there is a causal correlation: violent video games in those cases lead to aggressive behavior. There are still few studies of this type that have been undertaken and none really before 2005, even though they potentially offer the strongest evidence for establishing a clear cause-and-effect relationship between violent video games and aggressive behavior.

Following a lot of criticism, research designs have been improved and attempts have been made to review earlier research in the related field of meta-studies (which we'll discuss later). There is still disagreement among researchers within the field that the results from these three typical effect studies are not strong enough by themselves to give a final verdict on whether video games promote aggression. However, overall, Active Media researchers are increasingly convinced that video games pose a threat that needs to be dealt with.

We will return to some concrete research results after we have looked at common theories in the Active Media perspective.

Theories and Methods

Researchers within the Active Media perspective have a variety of theoretical starting points. Albert Bandura's social learning theory from the 1970s has often been preferred, but over the years other approaches have been applied. Here, we will introduce the ones that have historically played a role: catharsis theory, cultivation theory, social learning theory, general arousal theory, the cognitive neo-association model of aggression, and the general aggression model. See Dill and Dill,[8] Calvert,[9] and Barlett and Anderson[10] for other introductions.

- *Catharsis theory*:[11] The idea of catharsis has a long history in psychology, dating back to Sigmund Freud in the late 1890s, but in video games research a newer version of the theory is often used. Seymour Feshbach and Robert Singer proposed this theory in the early 1970s, pointing out that experiencing depictions of violence in media (whether video games, movies, or television) can actually reduce aggressive feelings. The idea is that one's own aggressive feelings will be mirrored in the media, and experiencing them will reduce internal tension. In video games, the active role of the player further enhances this effect as the aggressive feelings are not only seen on the screen but also actively performed by moving an avatar on the screen.

  The application of catharsis theory within the Active Media tradition is limited to a few studies, but the theory is often used in less scientific discussions. The limited interest in catharsis as an explanatory theory could also be attributed to the inclination among effect researchers to focus on the dangers of video games; they are less likely to seek out arguments that games reduce aggression. In the last decade, the catharsis theory has also become less acceptable in psychology in general.[12]
- *Cultivation theory*:[13] Cultivation theory is built on television research, and attempts to explain to what degree media lead to a distorted perception of social reality, for example, through stereotyped perceptions. The theory has been less used in relation to video games; though there are certainly characters in video games that are based on ethnic or gender stereotypes, it is still uncertain what stereotyping, if any, video games can produce in the player.
- *Social learning theory*:[14] According to social learning theory, behavior is learned through imitation of attractive models with attached rewards. Supporters stress that video games exemplify this model of learning: they

demand the player's full attention and entail active identification with characters on the computer screen. Furthermore, rewards are attached directly to the performance of symbolic violence (getting points, for example, by killing opponents). Therefore it is more likely that these aggressive actions are transferred to the outside world.

- *The general arousal theory:*[15] This theory claims that video games will increase the player's arousal level and thus increase his energy and the intensity of his actions. The increased arousal will not necessarily lead to different player actions but more likely a heightened intensity in these actions. Supporters of this theory point out that especially violent video games provide the arousal necessary to facilitate more aggressive behavior. Getting into an argument with a friend while playing a violent video game may accelerate into a fierce discussion, or you may be more likely to get irritated when someone pokes you after playing a game than after talking on the phone or washing dishes.

- *Cognitive neo-association model of aggression:*[16] This theory holds that violent media lead to hostility and aggression due to reinforcement of related association nodes in the brain. These nodes can be created and strengthened by video games; through them, aggressive thoughts will be transformed into physical action.

- *General aggression model:*[17] The general aggression model (GAM) is one of the newest theories in the field and combines earlier theories on aggression with cognitive schemata theory. Today this is the de facto standard in the field, and there has been made extension of it over the years. Cognitive schemata theory suggests that we order our experiences in different schemata which we use when we perceive new experiences. According to the model, violent media content causes aggressive behavior by influencing the person's internal state, which researchers measure by looking at a variety of cognitive, affective, and arousal variables. Violent media content increases aggressive behavior in several concrete ways: by teaching the player how to perform aggressive actions, by influencing underlying aggressive and cognitive schematas, by increasing arousal, and by creating an emotional and aggressive mental state.

From these descriptions it should be clear that most theories refer to media in general; the one exception is the general aggression model, which was developed with video games in mind. The theories, mostly developed in the 1970s and 1980s, reflect the strong influence of behaviorism and cognitivism at that time. This is also true of most of the research questions posed, research designs constructed, and methods used. They are also heavily inspired by research on television and violence.

Important Studies

In the last 15 years, Active Media research has to a large extent been pushed forward by meta-analyses of earlier studies and the emergence of longitudinal studies—in other words, looking at previous studies and combining their results to make a stronger case for the risks associated with video games, while looking at the longer term effects. However, there are some notable exceptions that we will cover here. As noted earlier, the total number of studies is at least 130 but is hard to estimate, and depends on what one chooses to include as a research study.

In their 2000 study, Anderson and Dill examine video games in relation to aggressive thoughts, feelings, and behavior, both in the artificial setting of a laboratory and from data on real-life behavior. This study consists of two parts; the first part is the most interesting, as it represents a classic research design and findings typical of the effect perspective.

More than 220 psychology students participated in the first part of the study: a majority were women, the average age was 19, and the students were awarded course points for participating. The subjects filled out a questionnaire describing their five favorite games, and their experience with the content, violence, and playing style of these games. The students were also asked about the amount of time they spent playing. From these questionnaires the researchers extracted information about the subjects' aggressive behavior, criminal record, game habits, and general worldview.

The results showed that male players felt more secure, played more violent video games, and spent more time playing than women. The more a participant played violent games, the more likely it was that he or she had engaged in criminal activities. Academic achievements were also hampered by a high playing time. Those who played violent video games did even worse academically, and were more involved in aggressive crimes like theft.

The second part of the research consisted of an experimental study. It confirmed that violent video games reinforce aggressive thoughts, with men being more aggressive than women. The overall conclusion was that there is a causal relationship between realistic violent video games, aggressive behavior, and crime.

In their 2002 study, Active Media researchers Steve Durkin and Bonnie Barber examined a number of links between video games and adolescents. There were 1,304 participants, all adolescents, covering a broad socio-demographic profile and with an average age of 16. The study captured both positive and negative effects of video games. The researchers divided the participants into three groups based on their video game usage and rated them according to the following variables: family closeness, activity involvement, positive school engagement, positive mental health, substance use, self-concept, friendship network, and disobedience. The overall conclusion was that "computer games can be a positive feature of a healthy adolescence."[18] Though noting the potential negative impact of video games, Durkin and Barber also found that games can offer a variety of positive effects in the lives of adolescents; the optimism of their work is in surprising contrast to traditional studies within the Active Media perspective.

The study measured the game use of youngsters on a scale from 1 to 7 (1 = never, 7 = daily). Looking more closely at the results, it is clear that the group with low usage of video games (defined as answering 2, 3, or 4) rates better than both the group that does not play video games and the group that plays video games regularly (defined as answering 5, 6, or 7). The results indicate that the group with low usage has less depressed mood, better self-esteem, and better academic achievement. The group that does not play video games at all is more deviant and is more prone to criminal behavior. The study did not find differences between the groups in relation to self-reported aggression.

A 2001 study by Thomas N. Robinson, Marta L. Wilde, Lisa C. Navracruz, K. Farish Haydel, and Ann Varady stands out for its nontraditional research design: it looks at what happens when we change children's media habits. The study involved children from two different schools with an average age of 9. The goal was to reduce media consumption (television, video, and video games) and examine the consequences. The participants were split into two groups: the first group maintained its normal level of media usage, without outside interference. The second group was allowed to maintain its normal media habits but was educated about media use during a six-month course. The course used social learning theory to help the children explain what happened to their behavior and emotions when they used media. It also introduced turn-off television days, a parents' information campaign, and discussions in general. After the course, the children were encouraged to reduce their media consumption to around seven hours a week.

The results showed that the trained group was perceived as less aggressive by their friends and showed less verbal aggression. Researchers also witnessed a tendency toward less physical aggression, but the decrease was not statistically significant. This study is particularly interesting because it points to realistic ways to limit the influence of aggression by educating players of video games to become critical and self-aware. This is quite different from the traditional Active Media perspective, where players are seen as helpless victims in the hands of video games. It also turns the research design upside down, in comparison with traditional Active Media research. Instead of measuring what happens when one plays video games, it measures what happens when one does not. Of course the problem with the above study is that it doesn't focus exclusively on video games but media use in general.

Another recent trend in examining the effect of violent video games is to apply more advanced statistical analysis than previous studies. This has revealed interesting problems with earlier research. Earlier studies had looked primarily at whether there was any relation between playing violent video games and measures of aggression—not at how big the effect of playing violent video games was. These early studies found that, yes, you become more violent when playing video games. However, they did not say anything about the size of the effect of video games compared to other factors such as parental involvement. Attempts to remedy this problem are seen in more recent studies from 2004, for example, by Gentile and colleagues[19] and by Funk and colleagues.[20]

Studies carried out in the last ten years have increasingly attempted to introduce more subtlety into their analyses. In 2004, Douglas Gentile and colleagues found that adolescents who played video games with more violent content were more hostile, got into more arguments with teachers, and were more involved in physical fights compared to their contemporaries who didn't play violent video games to the same extent. These adolescents also seemed to perform worse in school. The superficial evidence pointed to a damning correlation between video game violence and a broad spectrum of problematic behavior.

However, when the researchers included additional variables—especially the gender of the subjects and involvement of their parents—the results were radically different. When these factors were considered the effect of violent video game exposures on physical fights practically disappeared. When you look only at the relationship between violent video games and violence, underlying variables may actually account for the apparent link. For example, let's say that less parental involvement leads to more playing of violent video games. Let's also say that less parental involvement leads to more violence. From a simple statistical analysis you might conclude that violent video games lead to more violence. However, this would not be a valid conclusion, as in this example the true explanatory factor is parental involvement.

These findings stress the importance of looking for additional variables, rather than limiting studies to focus exclusively on the relation between playing violent video games and aggression. Ultimately, the study indicated that parental involvement and gender differences were a more powerful underlying explanation for aggression than video games. This lends some support to Active User criticism of the Active Media perspective for using overly simple models of humans and their behaviors.

Attention deficit/hyperactivity disorder (ADHD) is a relatively newly defined and controversial condition, which some have associated with video games. A 2010 study links exposure to video games with ADHD. In the study, 1,533 participants with ages ranging from middle childhood to early adulthood were assessed during the course of a year.[21] For younger participants, parents, teachers, and the children themselves reported on media exposure and attention problems, while older participants used self-reporting. The study found that, for all ages, exposure to video games (and television) was correlated with ADHD. It was suggested that video games may be a predictor. It also seems that longer exposure to video games increases the risk, likewise that the risk is higher the younger you are, and higher among males. The authors warn that the nature of the experimental setup does not make it possible to account for any unknown factors that might explain some of the correlation. Finally, it is stressed that the catch-all of "video games" is problematic, as there is a huge difference among different types of video games.

Longitudinal Studies

Active Media perspective research is often criticized heavily for looking only at short-term effects. One 2005 study, however, examined the effect of violent games one month after play. The study was conducted with 213 participants aged 14 to 68 (with an average age of 28), who played *Asheron's Call 2* for one month. The study found no increased aggression on any measure after the trial period.[22]

More rigorous studies have followed, however: in 2008 a joint US-Japanese study included 1,595 subjects with an age range of 9 to 18 years, who were measured on video game use and physical aggression at the start and end of a school year. The study found that those who played a lot of violent video games became relatively more physically aggressive across genders. It also found the effect of video games to be greater among younger students. Finally, it demonstrated that the effect of violent video games on physical aggression was not mediated by living in a collective culture (Japanese) or in a more individualistic culture (United States).[23]

Krahe and Möller's 2010 study followed 1,237 German high school students over 12 months through self-reporting on media use including video games. It found that media violence is correlated with physical aggression and lower empathy, albeit with a quite small effect size of 2 percent—meaning that only 2 percent of the variation in aggression can be explained by the differences in media usage. This study did not focus exclusively on video games but does offer some valuable longitudinal evidence.

In a study from 2011 by Ferguson, Miguel, Garza, and Jerabeck, 165 youngsters were followed to examine whether youth aggression could be a consequence of playing violent video games. The study had an initial interview, a one-year follow-up, and a three-year follow-up. The study found no relation or negative outcomes based on exposure to violent video games. Rather, family violence and peer influence was found to be the biggest influence.

A later study from 2012 by Willoughby, Adachi, and Good surveyed 1,492 youngsters in grades 9 through 12 about their video game habits and aggressive behaviors. Interestingly, the study looked at the classic issue, which is the selection versus socialization hypothesis. The selection hypothesis implies that a person selects aggressive video games because they already have a preference for aggression, whereas the socialization hypothesis predicts the subject becomes aggressive from playing aggressive video games. The study supported the socialization hypothesis: It was found that violent video games predicted higher aggression, whereas nonviolent video games did not.

In a German study from 2014 by Mößle, Kliem, and Rehbein the effect of violent video games on aggression was similarly examined. Special focus was given to the role of empathy as a moderator of the effect of violent video games. The 1,207 school children in the study were on average 10.4 years old at the start of the study and 12.4 years old at the end. The results showed that there was a relation between violent video games and aggression. However, it was also found that empathy was a key variable to mediate the effect of violent video games, although only in boys. This may suggest that violent video games only have a negative effect when empathy is not developed through other appropriate interpersonal activities. Thus, it may not be so much the exact effect of violent video games that is crucial to examine but rather whether players have developed important empathy skills outside the game world.

In 2018 a new longitudinal study supported a cautious approach to blaming video games for aggression. In the game the researchers made three different interventions over a two-month period (*GTA V, The Sims 3*, and no game) with 90 participants aged 28 years with even distribution of gender. The participants needed to play the game at least 30 minutes a day during the study. To measure aggression, several standard questionnaires were used but none of them found any effect after the two months.[24]

The efforts to improve the rigor with which violent video games is examined reached a new high in 2019 with a study focused on providing a better research design, and especially changing the method to measure aggression. The study examined 1,000 British adolescents aged 14–15 years. The study asked participants for the top three games they played, and then coded them based on official game ratings to see if they were associated with higher report aggressive behavior or less prosocial behavior. The aggression was measured by asking parents to report real aggressive behavior. The study found no link.[25]

This is in line with past criticism of researchers that even if you can measure indirect effects of aggressions in children after playing violent video games this does not translate into real-life behavior, a point that was again stressed by Fergusson along with colleagues in Society for Media Psychology and Technology under APA.[26] Indeed, nobody has so far been able to find relationship between video games and real-life violence on a societal level.[27]

Meta-Studies

A large number of meta-studies (studies combining the results of previous Active Media research) have been conducted in the past 15 years. Though they all seek a larger sample, and thereby a stronger dataset for making statistical analyses, these studies vary in their intentions. Some simply review earlier studies and look for overall tendencies. The more ambitious collate original data from earlier research and carry out new statistical analyses. Here we present examples of both types, as they have different strengths. The conclusions from the newest of these studies, conducted within the last 15 years, have become increasingly mixed. The main differences among conclusions of the meta-studies is how seriously they take the problems of method presented in most earlier studies. Does one dismiss these studies entirely because they are flawed, or does one insist that the relationship between violent video games and aggression (that many studies find, although not all) should lead to a cautious approach until stronger method designs are available?[28]

In their 2001 meta-study, psychology professors Craig Anderson and Brad Bushman offer a straightforward and potent conclusion: "Violent video games increase aggressive behavior in children and young adults."[29] This conclusion is strengthened by the study's critique of the flawed methodology of many previous studies. The authors focus on the difference in effect size between flawed experiments and stronger experiments, and find that the effect size (the actual harmful impact of video games, not just the strength of the relationship) increases with the strength of a study's methodology. The conclusion is that the current combination of correlation studies and experimental studies provides strong evidence that violent video games lead to aggressive behavior in real life.

Communication researcher John Sherry does not disagree, although he is less convinced. He stresses that the effect of video games is smaller than that of violent television.[30] British psychology professor Mark Griffiths is even less convinced, stating that the only consistent finding from the many studies he has analyzed is that young children are affected by violence more than teenagers and older children.[31]

Psychologist Jonathan Freedman stresses that the research is limited and finds it very problematic that strong claims are made. He states:

> I cannot think of another important issue for which scientists have been willing to reach conclusions on such a small body of research. Even if the research had been designed and conducted perfectly, there is far too little evidence to reach any firm conclusions.[32]

As the meta-analysis has gained in strength, it has attracted its own criticism, including publication bias and unreliable statistical measures.[33] Some see the meta-analysis as the ultimate answer to the question of video games' malign effect. However, one should remember that all the criticism of methodology and theoretical assumptions still holds true, no matter how many such studies are carried out. Simply put, 300×0 is still 0. This is not to say that the Active Media approach is not making headway, but the meta-analysis should be approached with open eyes, particularly in view of the complexity of these studies, which has led to controversy. This is very clearly stated in the following quote:

> Meta-analyses of video games similarly produce weak and inconsistent results. Two early meta-analyses claimed to find small but significant effects for video game violence on aggression, although a subsequent review of these meta-analyses during a court case revealed that the authors may have simply ignored research that didn't fit with their hypotheses (ESA, VSDA and IRMA v. Blagojevich, Madigan, & Devine, 2005).[34]

In their meta-analysis from 2010, Craig and colleagues include 136 studies on aggressive behavior, including most studies within the Active Media perspective. The study does respond to a number of the criticisms leveled at previous meta-studies. However, as many of the studies are duplicates from previous meta-studies, some problematic elements have been carried over. The authors conclude:

> we believe that debates can and should finally move beyond the simple question of whether violent video game play is a causal risk factor for aggressive behavior; the scientific literature has effectively and clearly shown the answer to be "yes." Instead, we believe the public policy debate should move to questions concerning how best to deal with this risk factor. Public education about this risk factor—and about how parents, schools, and society at large can deal with it—could be very useful.[35]

Despite the strong stance of Anderson and Bushman, a large number of Active Media researchers favor Freedman's more cautious approach.[36] The exceptions are usually in research studies either co-authored by Craig Anderson or by his colleagues.[37]

In recent years, Christopher Ferguson has become one of the most vocal critics of the casual link between games and violence. In early 2015, he released a study that changed the battlefield by looking at the actual societal impact of more media violence. Previously, this has often been anecdotal evidence that would go something like this: If violent video games were so bad wouldn't our society have collapsed with the rapid rise of violent television and video games during the last 20 years? In this approach, Ferguson looks at how much violent video games were played during specific years (1996–2011) and how this correlates with violent crimes in the same period. Indeed, he finds no effect—actually he finds an inverse effect, which would suggest that the opposite was true. Although he makes no such claims, it suggests that the findings are quite strong.

However, the methodical weaknesses of such a study are legion. There are many potential confounding variables when you look on a societal level, all of which need to be controlled for—for example, the general development in equality and income level in society at large. Also, how do you measure what people actually play? Ferguson uses the most sold games from the Internet Movie Database (IMDb), but sales data has become quite weak since the mid-2000s with the emergence of online and mobile games, where data is fragmented.

The most recent meta-analysis of the relationship between violent video game play and physical aggression over time came out in 2018. Here Prescott, Sargent, and Hull look at 24 studies with a total of 17,000 participants. The study does find a link strongest with white participants, less strong among Asian participants, and not reliably for Hispanic participants. Despite a small effect size that explains only around 1 percent of the variance, they stress that this is still practically significant. As APA attests to whether an effect size is large or small in a given domain depends on the eye looking—in other words, this is a subjective question.[38]

It is also noteworthy that a number of healthcare associations have made strong statements about the risks of video games—for example, the

American Psychiatric Association has spoken out against them—although here there is also disagreement.[39] In 2007 the American Psychiatric Association refused to include video game addiction in their diagnostic system, known as the DSM-IV, due to limited and inconclusive research: "the APA does not consider 'video game addiction' to be a mental disorder at this time."[40] However, with the DSM-5 in 2013, "Internet Gaming Disorder" was included on the watch list warranting more research, and it is likely that APA will update its stance on the issue in the coming years. In 2015 the APA Task Force on Violent Media published a new report to bring APA's position from 2005 up to date with most recent research results, and revise their resolution on violent video games.[41] Here, they concluded:

> "The research demonstrates a consistent relation between violent video game use and increases in aggressive behavior, aggressive cognitions and aggressive affect, and decreases in prosocial behavior, empathy and sensitivity to aggression. . . . No single risk factor consistently leads a person to act aggressively or violently," the report states. "Rather, it is the accumulation of risk factors that tends to lead to aggressive or violent behavior. The research reviewed here demonstrates that violent video game use is one such risk factor."[42]

Based on the technical report the APA put into place a resolution with a number of warnings in relation to video games.[43]

Overall, meta-studies do find a relation between violent video games and aggression albeit the discussion remains what the small effect size shows—and that no real link has yet been established on a societal level. Ultimately, the results are too mixed to warrant any strong conclusions, although the group of researchers around Craig Anderson are very firm in concluding that video games lead to aggression. Even if there is a correlation, and some effect size, it seems that the link to actually observable aggression from playing video games is weak.

Indeed, numerous researchers are far from convinced, and in line with common research practice it would be premature to conclude that there is a link between violent video games and real-life aggression. However, there are enough indications to warrant further studies, and a cautious approach. And those who prefer can conclude from these studies that a cautious stand is the safest: they can avoid violent video games, and in doing so avoid any potential (though not yet proven) long-term real-life harmful effects.

Criticism

Criticism of the effect perspective has grown with surprising intensity over the last 15 years, and has been more explicit than that leveled at the Active User perspective. The criticism has been focused at different levels, spanning basic differences over ontological approach, disagreement about what constitutes scientific evidence, and specific faults in methodology. Criticism directed at the competing Active User perspective has also grown stronger over the last ten years, however. Psychology in general has broadened its approaches and challenged basic assumptions about how to do research and what methods to use. Some are inclined to disqualify all published Active Media studies due to severe problems of method. The influential comparative media scholar, Henry Jenkins, is very skeptical of the simplistic conclusions often put forward. He cautions against looking for links in studies that do not reflect real-life media use.[44]

The primary criticisms leveled against the Active Media perspective are described in the sections that follow.

Laboratory Versus Everyday Situations

The Active Media perspective relies heavily on laboratory studies to establish a relationship between video games and aggression. However, the laboratory is not similar to everyday situations, and although the differences may seem obvious, Active Media researchers continue to apply results gained in an experimental setting to real-life behavior. The majority of laboratory studies do a very bad job at replicating the phenomena they want to study. Important variables—such as the social experience around the video game, the player's control of the situation, and the desire to play video games—are absent. Usually, players are not in charge of how long they play, what they play, or how they play. This is hardly representative of an activity that is mostly driven by pleasure.

Another distortion created by the laboratory is that the length of the play session in these studies can vary from 4 to 75 minutes. This range could very well have an important bearing on how the video game is experienced. The players with brief play periods are abruptly interrupted, and although this may also happen when you play normally, the short time span is not representative of most play. In any case, the interruption is arbitrary, and not linked to the actual experience of playing violent games. Participants given a long play duration may also experience something different from real life, where they may be used to taking turns or playing for shorter periods. The longer play time may also, especially for inexperienced players, lead to tiredness. This tiredness then becomes a confounding variable, which can distort the results. Sherry's 2001 meta-analysis finds that less aggressive behavior is exhibited the longer one plays. This seems counterintuitive, and could unintentionally demonstrate that the artificial setting of the laboratory may lead to an increase in aggressive behavior. In long play sessions, on the other hand, players may be less aggressive because they get used to the artificial situation and hence do not feel uncomfortable.

Within the structures of the laboratory, participants are inevitably led in specific directions by a study; there is always the danger that they might anticipate what the researchers are looking for and adjust their answers accordingly. Though we can't prove a connection, look at the different results from the studies we examined earlier by Durkin and Barber[45] and Anderson and Dill.[46] Each research team began with different expectations: how can we be sure that these expectations didn't influence the different results they obtained? Due to their starting point the majority of Active Media researchers expect to find a negative effect; not surprisingly, the majority of them do.

Problems of Causality

A second source of criticism is the problem of causality, which Ferguson[47] also refers to as the "third variable" effect. Even within the carefully controlled laboratory environment, we cannot be certain how to explain a given effect. If players of violent games exhibit aggressive behavior, how do we know this isn't because they weren't able to choose the game themselves, and were "forced" to play a title they didn't like? Such problems are even more pronounced in cross-section correlation studies. Here, a study may find that people who show a preference for violent games exhibit more aggressive behavior than those who play more peaceful games, or who do not play at all. But from this result alone causality cannot be established: aggression could be caused by the violent games or the preference for violent games could be caused by the person's aggressive tendencies. In the case of longitudinal correlation, this problem is less acute. However, such studies cannot completely assure validity. The gaming variable may theoretically be tied to other variables—anything from parental involvement to gender, as we saw earlier—which may in fact be the actual cause of the increased aggression. Theoretically, we can even go so far as to say that the aggression could be caused by the social stigma assigned to players of violent games, rather than by the games themselves.

Defining Aggression

Another basic problem in studies within the Active Media perspective is the inconsistent use of the term "aggression": both what constitutes aggression and how it is measured. This problem is not limited to media studies but applies to studies of aggression in general.[48] Researchers have used all of the following as measures of aggression: aggressive thoughts, hitting a doll, playing patterns, verbal aggression, aggressive behavior, physical fights, or the more obscure willingness to donate money to charity. These different variables in turn draw on different theoretical traditions that can be contradictory in their assumptions and unclear in their measurement criteria.

It is interesting to note that Geen[49] offers a very simple working definition of aggression: actions that do harm or the intention to do harm. This disqualifies a number of studies into the effects of video games, which instead look for violent thoughts or preferences for certain aggressive words. However, Geen acknowledges that underlying variables, such as those presented by Anderson and Bushman in their general aggression model, can mediate aggression. Aggression continues to be an ambiguous concept, and the exact relation between aggressive schemata, aggressive play, verbal aggression, and physical aggression is unresolved.

Video Games Are a Rich and Varied Phenomenon

The Active Media perspective does not approach video games as a varied phenomenon but implies that they are homogeneous, with only slight differences in their content. For most researchers within the Active Media perspective, the only relevant difference seems to be whether this content is violent or nonviolent. This approach would be problematic even with other media. To compare the effect of a nonviolent soap opera with a violent action movie, for example, would hardly make sense. They use very different artistic effects, and aspire to different goals, and one runs the risk of not measuring violent content but simply the general impact of different formats.

The enormous differences between video games are obvious to video game researchers but seem less clear to psychologists and other Active Media researchers from other traditions. Despite the evolution of game research over the last 20 years, a certain degree of ignorance remains about even the most basic differences between video games. A somewhat dated study by Anderson and Dill[50] loses its persuasiveness when the researchers choose to compare *Wolfenstein 3D* (a violent action game) with *Myst* (a peaceful adventure game). When we recall the large differences between the adventure genre and the action genre, we cannot help but doubt the study's implication that the only important difference between the games is the level of violence.

Statistical Problems

Ferguson, in particular, has in his research been critical of the statistical implications of the Active Media approach. In his 2007 study he shows that "studies employing less standardized and reliable measures of aggression tended to produce larger effect sizes."[51] He has also documented a tendency for studies showing greater effects of videos games on aggression to get published more frequently. In two other articles, Ferguson points out that the standards accepted for evidence are quite low, compared to other research areas, and that the so-called clinical cutoff point is not really applied. The clinical cutoff is the point at which an observed behavior becomes pathological. Hence, it may be that someone consistently becomes more aggressive from playing video games, but that doesn't mean that they become aggressive enough for this to actually lead to malign or pathological behavior. This is supported by the lack of any increase in violence on a societal level at a time when the popularity of games has increased massively.

Criticism of Basic Assumptions

Throughout this chapter, we have argued that the starting point for the Active Media perspective in examining the effect of video games is problematic. When investigating the relation between video games and aggression, opponents of Active Media have argued that a researcher ought to look in the places where aggression is actually found. They might, as a starting point, interview hardened young criminals, look at whether video games trigger fights in clubs or bars, or visit the local arcade. Beginning with actual events (rather than in a laboratory) results in a hypothesis informed by empirical data. The researcher can then analyze this data and devise further tests to see if the results can be generalized to other real-life situations.

Strangely, Active Media researchers do not examine the actual places where a direct link between video games and violent behavior might be found. It is interesting, as Jenkins points out, that in the few studies of arcades, we find very little violence in the places where games are actually played.[52] We still need to establish a real-world link between playing video games and violence, beyond the often overhyped media descriptions of single, tragic events like the Columbine shootings, for which, on closer examination, the link to video games is at best sketchy.

Professor David Gauntlett has also suggested that the Active Media perspective offers a conservative perception of children and young people, one that runs contrary to modern developmental psychology. In modern psychology, as mentioned earlier, context is essential for framing an experience; individuals, far from being passive, construct their understanding of a situation. Recognition of humans' basic ability to interpret experiences is lacking in Active Media research. For Active Media researchers it seems irrelevant whether a player is killing someone to save the world or killing someone for the fun of it.[53]

Ultimately, one may have to accept the fundamental assumptions of positivism and behaviorism if the Active Media perspective is to be meaningful. But in the United States and much of Europe, as well as many other places around the world, these theoretical assumptions are no longer the dominant psychological approach. The Active Media perspective remains haunted by its inherent problems of method, mentioned above, and by a sustained and withering critique of its basic theoretical assumptions. Though its legacy remains strong, these problems have limited the impact that Active Media research has had on the broader video game research community.

THE ACTIVE USER PERSPECTIVE

If we can generalize, the video game research community typically approaches its work from an angle closer to this perspective. Active User researchers are mostly from the humanities, particularly from the fields of cultural studies, anthropology, and pedagogy; these researchers share many of the same theoretical assumptions about people, methods, and what research entails. When dealing with video games and risks, the Active User perspective has drawn on methods from the humanities and certain parts of the social sciences, with a preference for qualitative methods such as interviews and field observations. This highlights the attitude that players are competent and selective, not just passive recipients of information. In other words, agency belongs to the player; the player, and not the medium, is in charge.

No two people experience a book, a film, a game, or any other medium in exactly the same way. The experience largely depends on their personal background and the context in which they "absorb" the medium. An individual's experience with media can be completely unpredictable for researchers, no matter how thoroughly the media product itself has been analyzed and dissected. Thus, Active User researchers hesitate to draw a direct line linking a media product's content with a change in the behavior or attitude of the user.

Specifically, when someone plays a video game, the activity cannot be understood without considering the context he is playing in. The player may have friends hanging around, be alone in a big house, or be just stopping by the local game café. It seems problematic, these researchers argue, to insist that certain games are dangerous, as the meaning of playing a game is not a static entity to be discovered by looking at the game. As Carsten Jessen states:

> Computer games primarily acquire their meaning and content through their concrete use in concrete situations. In this sense they are more a kind of tool for social relations than a means of communicating the messages one normally looks for in the media. This should not be seen as a claim that there is no content in computer games, or that this does not matter; it should be taken as an indication that we cannot interpret a content outside the concrete practice which also provides the framework of understanding.[54]

When an outsider views a video game, assumptions are the easiest thing to make. A well-meaning researcher—not to mention an anxious parent—sees a child playing a video game, gleefully shooting other children, and eventually being shot himself. The adults may be horrified. For the child, this is play. The player is not really killing other children but competing against the like-minded, exploring worlds of intrigue and adventure, and socializing with others through a fascinating medium. If this defense of video games seems hard to stomach, remember that violent, unspeakable acts are abundant in fairy-tales, which hardly raise an eyebrow.

Theories and Methods

The Active User perspective cannot be understood as a close-knit research community; rather it is a varied group of researchers with a shared mindset. The perspective has been strongest in the Nordic countries and the UK. Researchers tend to draw on a variety of theories and methods, and do not see them as mutually exclusive.

Literary Theories of Reader Response and Reception

"Reader response" theories originate in literary studies, and assign more interpretive agency to the reader (or user) than to the text itself. This approach began with work on theories of aesthetic response by Hans Robert Jauss and Wolfgang Iser in the 1970s. These authors proposed that readers create meaning by engaging with texts in a variety of ways. For example, as we have seen, readers unconsciously "fill in the gaps" while reading; they are able to follow the plot even though some information is usually missing. Readers do a lot of mental work when reading, using their encyclopedic knowledge of the world and their ability to relate cause and effect to interpret texts.

Another interesting branch of reader response theory is represented by Stanley Fish, who makes the radical proposal that texts have no meaning other than the meaning they are assigned by interpretive communities. For example, if a reader believes that Shakespeare is the peak of all literature, his ardor will unavoidably affect his reading.

All these perspectives insist, although in different ways, on the active participation of readers. Reader response theories have been exported to other media such as television, partly to contest the common view of audiences as passive consumers. It is also easy to export this point of view to video games. Theories of the Active User perspective all take for granted that engaging with video games is a worthwhile activity, and that a game's meaning is built only with a player's active participation.

Play as Meta-Communication[55]

Gregory Bateson points out that humans are capable of communicating that actions should be interpreted based on their context, and that play is crucial for developing this ability. The concept of "frame" refers to the context we use for interpreting a given activity; as a result, the meaning of a given activity depends on the persons involved. When a group of children is play-fighting in a backyard, a bystander may see it as aggressive and dangerous behavior. But for the children it can just as well be play; should someone be hurt by accident, it would not be interpreted as aggression but as an unfortunate side effect of playing. It is not possible to interpret another person's behavior without taking into account his own interpretation and perspective.

The Children's Perspective[56]

Flemming Mouritsen[57] and Carsten Jessen[58] attempt to get closer to children's use of video games. They see children as capable of constructing a frame around their play and culture that is almost impenetrable by adults. According to some researchers of children's culture, it is almost impossible for adults to see beyond their own frame of reference and approach video games with an open mind. Still, many studies from the Active User perspective attempt to understand the meaning of video games by seeing these games through children's eyes. The difficulty of this approach is obvious, but Active User researchers believe that the only way to really understand children's use of video games is to be a part of children's game culture—by observing, participating, and thus opening up themselves as researchers to other interpretations.

Catalyst Model[59]

Ferguson has become one of the strongest critics of the Active Media Perspective, and through the Catalyst model shifts focus toward the individual's disposition for being influenced by violent video games. The Catalyst Model stresses that individuals have different predispositions that are more important predictors (whether they be biological or environmental) of adverse effects from violent games than the violent video games themselves. As such, you can say that he accepts that media can have malign effects but that it has to be seen in complex interplay of different variables—and not as one size fits all.

Though the above theories vary widely in their origins and uses, all prioritize the individual, internal perspective of each human being, and stress that the creation of meaning is central to any media experience, including video games. As opposed to the Active Media perspective's positivist approach, the scientific standpoint of Active User researchers is hermeneutic: the aim of research is to constantly revisit a problem and construct an increasingly valid interpretation. The goal is not so much to generalize the results to all people but rather to offer reflections, insights, and understanding of a specific phenomenon that will be increasingly convincing, although never conclusive.

Most researchers in the broad Active User group will draw on some of these theoretical perspectives, although their influence may be implicit. Fish's theory, for example, is often seen as too extreme, but Iser's foundational reader response work still has an impact though researchers may not explicitly mention him.

Important Studies

It should be noted that the number of Active User studies that directly examine video games and risks is quite limited. Compared to the hundreds of studies coming from the Active Media camp over the last generation, Active User researchers have only made limited forays into the topic. As mentioned at the beginning of this chapter, many game researchers shy away from this subject as they find it hard to generalize from a single media object. Video games are so diverse, and mean so many different things to different people, that from an Active User perspective it hardly makes sense to ask the broad question: "Are video games dangerous?" or even a more humble question such as: "Do violent video games lead to aggression?" For one 5-year-old, a video game may be conceived as dangerous, violent, and scary, while another child can perceive the same game completely differently at the same age. Instead, the goal is to create a multifaceted picture of video games, rather than limiting research by replicating existing stereotypes and assumptions. We can see the Active User perspective at work in a few key examples.

In 2000, Birgitte Holm Sørensen and Carsten Jessen[60] studied 31 children in Denmark, aged from 5 to 17 years. The children were interviewed in small groups, and then the researchers observed about 20 of them playing video games. The goal was simple: to arrive at a picture of children's perception of playing video games, their ability to distinguish between fiction and reality, and their appreciation of interactivity. The study found that the potential negative influence from violent content in video games is smaller than that of violence in other media. The researchers also see video games as close to ordinary play activities, and concluded that the children used video games as yet another toy.

Several other studies have turned their focus on adults, and found that adults often have a stereotyped and limited knowledge of video games. They therefore cannot predict how a person will understand a specific media product. They have little experience with video games and often approach the medium with a wish to censor, regulate, and change the experience into something they know and understand. From this perspective, computer games will seldom fulfill an adult's conception of an acceptable activity for children. As we saw in Chapter 3, adults have a tendency to idealize children's play; adults understand video games in relation to how they think children should play and behave.

An adult's interpretation may thus be very far from how children themselves understand the activity of playing video games.[61] Active User researchers insist that violent video game content cannot be taken at face value. Video games may on the surface look like simple, bloody fighting games, when in fact their basic story lines help us handle the difficult realities of life. In a hostile and scary world, video games may be just what a lot of children need to address their fears and insecurities.[62]

In the large European research project "Children, Young People and the Changing Media Environment," organized by Sonia Livingstone,[63] video games play a central part. The study looks at 12 European countries, and combines qualitative and quantitative methods. In total, close to 15,000 children aged between 6 and 16 participated. The researchers found that media increasingly plays a central role in private homes, and that video games are prominent in this.

Another important contribution to the field is the American psychologist Sherry Turkle's work, presented in her books *The Second Self*[64] and *Life on the Screen*.[65] Turkle has examined different perceptions of technology and tried to assess what computers and virtual worlds mean for us as human beings. She carried out a range of studies inspired by ethnography, and although the results are perhaps stretched too far, they are interesting. Turkle points out that computers inspire the user to think nonlinearly, and how the computer's interactive capacity forces the user to reconsider the relation between nothing less than man and machine, and life and death. According to Turkle,[66] people think that technology is merely a useful tool. Certainly technology is often useful; however, we fail to appreciate the more subtle ways it influences our lives every single day. Technology, including games, offers children new ways of thinking and relating to each other. Turkle finds that technology can have an effect but that this is probably neither predominantly positive nor negative. This effect does not exist in a vacuum but is a part of everyday interactions and formed by each child and their surroundings.

The ambiguity of media is also attested to in another study, by Laura Ermi and Frans Mäyrä.[67] They maintain that video games can captivate children through features such as challenges, vast virtual worlds, and freedom. It may be this very freedom and the chance to get away from the restrictions of the real world that lead children to prefer video games to other play activities. This preference is a conscious one, as the researchers found that even their 10- to 12-year-old subjects could engage in a debate concerning the adverse effects of video games:

> In conclusion, the image of a child in contemporary game culture that emerges from our research is not one of helpless victim. On the contrary, many children seem to be very articulate about their preferences and capable of sharply criticizing games.[68]

Based on a recent study by Cheryl Olson, it seems that the Active User approach may be gaining ground in the United States, which has traditionally been more inclined toward the Active Media approach. Her focus is on describing the playing of video games through both qualitative and quantitative studies, and in relation to developmental stage, environment, and personality. She concludes: "Compared with other media such as books, films, and radio, electronic games appear to have an unusually expansive appeal and serve a surprising number of emotional, social, and intellectual needs."[69]

Games allow social interaction, joyful competition, peer learning, making friends, expressing creativity, and experimenting with different identities, and they serve as a means of relaxation or an outlet for difficult emotions. Based on the data collected, she argues that violent video games reflect a long tradition within toys more generally, and as such lie within the range of normal development. Violent video games are often favored not because of violent content but rather because they fit well with, in particular, boys' preferences for competition and mastery.

The above examples make clear that risk is far from central to the Active User perspective. However, the field's research does have some bearing on the relationship between video games and risks. Video games are used very differently and it is too simple to talk of general media effects.

Criticism

It seems that there is a double standard at work. When Active User researchers criticize the effect perspective, they challenge the reliability and validity of the research results. This is leveled at all areas of Active Media research, from its basic theoretical assumptions about how humans work, to the concrete ways of measuring effect. These rigorous demands are, however, rarely applied to Active User researchers' own studies. This leads the Active Media perspective to adopt a dismissive attitude toward Active User studies. The former considers the experimental designs of the latter as fuzzy and lacking in scientific rigor; some Active Media proponents consider Active User work a lesser form of research (or, worse yet, not research at all).

More concretely, criticism of the Active User perspective is aimed at the limited scope of results and a weakness in documentation. This criticism, however, is usually not explicitly brought forward by the competing perspective. The Active Media perspective seems to have a limited interest in Active User studies, and finds that attacking the findings is not really worth much time and effort. As described earlier, Active User researchers, on the other hand, are quite ready to deliver criticism in the other direction.

It is clear that the theoretical framework outlined above makes it very hard (or even undesirable) for Active User researchers to generalize from their results. These researchers believe that observations of a group of children's reactions toward violence do not necessarily apply to other children. Still, data is sometimes stretched to provide general conclusions. This is problematic when you use qualitative research methods that are not capable of being—nor intended to be—used to support broader conclusions. A researcher may have performed observations in an after-school program over a couple of weeks, and formed an opinion on the children's interactions. These results cannot, however, be easily generalized as we have no way of knowing if these students are representative. The samples in Active User studies are not random, and are almost always too small to generalize to the whole population. Further, it is seldom possible for others to gain access to the exact data that form the researcher's opinions, and this makes it hard to test the conclusions of a given study.

OTHER QUESTIONS

The Active Media perspective has primarily examined the effect of violent video games on aggression in children and adolescents. However, other topics have been examined in relation to risks associated with video games and these are presented in the sections that follow.

The Content of Video Games

More and more people—academics and pundits alike—have questioned the unbalanced content of video games. The most pressing question is whether games present a stereotyped, perhaps even discriminatory, picture of the world.

The models for solving problems, stereotyped game universes, and frequent depictions of violence are just a few examples of problematic content. The Active Media studies examining this question offer various conclusions: they find that aggression is often a part of games, although the degree of violence depicted varies significantly both between video games and according to the individual researchers analyzing content. Karen Dill and colleagues[70] have found that 79 to 85 percent of all video games contain violence, but Schierbeck and Carstens[71] stress that only 5 percent contain extreme violence. It makes a difference whether we are talking about the "war game," chess, or the almost vicious beat-'em-up *Mortal Kombat*.

Social Relations, Gender, and Exposed Groups

Another currently popular question is whether some groups are more exposed to the effects of video games than others. From the start, video games have appealed more to males than to females, and there are clear gender differences in video game preferences. As we saw in Chapter 4, the lack of strong female game characters has been lamented until (and also since) Lara Croft entered the scene. The difference gender makes has been closely investigated, especially in Justine Cassel and Henry Jenkins's *From Barbie to Mortal Kombat*, published in 1998. Recently, some researchers have bemoaned the lack of development in gender studies related to video games (see Chapter 6).

Studies on gender differences from the Active Media perspective have conflicting results. Some studies[72] find that females become more aggressive playing violent video games than males, while others do not find this effect.[73] The greater response of some women might be a result of female test subjects being less used to video games in general. They may therefore find it more intense, alien, and overwhelming to play a violent video game, which could trigger a more aggressive reaction.

Researchers from both the Active Media and Active User perspectives have stressed that age may play an important role in how someone is influenced by video games. Developmental psychology argues that young children (below 8 years) can have trouble distinguishing between reality and fiction. The lack of this ability is especially problematic if we look at children from the social learning theoretical perspective: children may imitate in real life what they see in video games. At least one Active User study, however, stresses that children may be capable early on of telling fiction from reality.[74] Dill and Dill[75] have challenged this claim, stating that the case for the existence of young, media-competent children may be exaggerated.

Extending this argument, Active Media researchers have claimed that video games affect our perception of the surrounding world. The results are remarkably in agreement, and show that violent video games result in a more negative perception of the real world.[76] A consequence of this may be that players perceive the world as a more hostile and dangerous place. They may also transfer behaviors from the game to the real world, leading to what can be labeled as crime.

It has been suggested that increases in crime may be a consequence of video games, although most studies supporting a link between crime and video games are based on arcade games (and violent crime in the United States has been decreasing for some time). Arcade games cost money to play, and could therefore give players an incentive for finding what we might call alternative funding sources. This is, however, entirely different from most current video game playing, where one can play without incurring great cost. Some studies have also found that academic achievement can be affected by video games, but others have failed to find the same relationship.[77]

On the positive side, some have pointed out that players with low self-esteem may improve their sense of self by mastering video games. The relevant studies are now relatively old and have contradictory results. The conclusion—not surprisingly—is often that the relationship between self-esteem and video games varies depending on the player.[78] These correlations, however, have only been explored to a limited extent to date.

Addiction

Addiction to video games as a research topic has grown over the years since British psychologist Mark Griffiths and his co-researchers pioneered the field almost 20 years ago. Still, the definition of addiction causes a number of problems for these Active Media studies, and a satisfactory description has yet to be found. In the DSM-5, video game addiction was included under the classification Internet Gaming Disorder (but on the watch list warranting more research before official inclusion), and the methods for measuring this condition remain elusive. Indeed, a meta-study from 2013 on available protocols by King et al. found large inconsistences across 63 different studies. Video game addiction was measured with 18 different methods, and although the meta-study found that these methods could in the future form the foundation for a sound method, this is not the case yet. Rather, in these studies we see, for example, variations in coverage of key indicators for addiction, varying cutoff points for the appropriate clinical status, and lack of inter-rater reliability. In common words, the methods do not cover all areas of addiction and are not consistent between assessments by different testers, and therefore may result in different clinical conclusions.

Addiction to video games does not have the same repercussions as other forms of addiction. The secondary consequences that are normally associated with addiction, such as crime and debt, are not part of the pathology of video game addiction. Thus, labeling a person as a video game addict often seems to be based more on subjective values than scientific rationale. A reasonable conclusion on addiction is reached by Mark Griffiths:

> It is this author's belief that videogame addiction does indeed exist but that it affects only a very small minority of players. There appear to be many people who use video games excessively, but are not addicted as measured by these (or any other) criteria.[79]

Different definitions of addiction result in quite different estimates of the number of addicted players. In one study, 19.9 percent of players are found to display addictive behavior in relation to video games,[80] while in another—by the same researcher, in fact—arrives at the significantly higher figure of 37.5 percent.[81] However, both of these numbers are adjusted downwards by the researchers, as most addicted players do not seem troubled by their playing pattern—nor does gameplay seem to harm their lives or their relationships. In a later article from 2005, Griffiths and Davies settle on the estimate that 7 percent of the total number of video game players are addicted, based on a definition of addiction as playing more than 30 hours a week, following the guidelines set out in the DSM-III-R protocol; as previously mentioned, however, these protocols have changed in the versions since the DSM-III-R.

The validity of Griffiths' early work was challenged in a study by Gentile in 2011.[82] In a survey, 1,178 American youths aged 8 to 18 were asked questions about game preferences. It was concluded that about 8.5 percent of video game players in this sample exhibited pathological patterns of play, as defined by a score based on the DSM-IV pathological gambling criteria. The study also found a correlation between young people exhibiting pathological gaming and attention deficit disorder. Indeed, pathological gamers were twice as likely to suffer from attention disorder, although one can only speculate about any causal relationship.

A later study, conducted in Singapore in 2011 with 3,034 schoolchildren, found a similar prevalence, of around 9 percent.[83] This was a two-year longitudinal study, which offered a unique opportunity to address the question of causality. The study found that greater amounts of gaming, lower social competence, and greater impulsivity seem to act as risk factors for becoming pathological gamers. It also found that the outcomes of pathological gaming were depression, anxiety, social phobias, and lower school performance. The study suggested that the relationship between pathological gaming and psychological disorders may be reciprocal, that is, they reinforce each other. Other studies have found similar findings, for example in the recent study by Brunborg, Mentzoni, and Frøyland (2014).

With the increasing number of studies on game addiction, Dara Kush and Mark Griffiths in 2012[84] decided to carry out a meta-study based on 30 studies of adolescents. The meta-study indicated that gaming addiction does exist despite what diagnosis method you use, and it can be categorized as a behavioral addiction rather than a disorder related to impulse control, which has implications for developing proper treatment. A meta-study from 2011 puts the most likely prevalence of gaming addiction to around 3.1 percent, which is considerably lower than most previous meta-studies. However, it was lent credence in another recent study with 8,807 European students, in which the prevalence of gaming addiction was noted at 3.62 percent (Strittmatter et al., 2015).

FINAL REMARKS

The potential adverse effects of video games have long been the subject of debate. This debate intensified in the 1990s as certain games became still more realistic and detailed in their depictions of violence. In recent years, a number of violent incidents have been linked—especially in public debate—to the perpetrators' fascination with violent games. At the same time, more realistic audio and graphics, as well as more complex games, have reactivated worries about whether video games could damage those who play them.

We have summarized the volumes of research into the risks associated with video games, focusing specifically on the keystone of this research over the past two decades: the relationship between violent video games and increased aggression in gamers. The results have, however, often pointed in different directions. Whereas some researchers have found clear signs of aggressive behavior caused by video games, others have not been able to replicate their results, and still others have been strongly critical of the methods and underlying theories used in these studies.

This tangle of conflicting conclusions can be maddening, especially for parents desperate to protect their children, and governments eager to defend against any threats to a country's youth. But as we have seen, by dividing the research into two ideological camps we can gain a much better understanding of the nuts and bolts of this disagreement.

The *Active Media* perspective is based on medical and psychological traditions. The researchers usually try to study the question with the help of specially staged experiments, in which people are exposed to different types of games under controlled (but not very realistic) conditions. The perspective has the strong support of certain academic groups in the US.

The *Active User* perspective derives inspiration from ethnography and culturally oriented media studies. Researchers in this paradigm stress the fact that the user constructs meaning from each piece of media, and the process is always dependent on the context. According to this perspective, it is not possible to study the potentially adverse effect of violent video games in artificial settings, or without attempting to understand the player's own perspective. The Active User perspective is strongly represented in Scandinavia and Great Britain.

These two academic traditions are in fundamental disagreement over how (and even whether) to answer the question: "Do video games cause players any harm?" The majority of Active User researchers answer either that video games do not seem to cause harm in any direct sense, or, more likely, that the question is quite simply too general to answer. Some Active Media researchers, by contrast, answer in the affirmative, while others say that there might be a connection between video games and harm but are uncertain as to the extent.

We may never be able to provide a definitive answer, to this and to many other knotty problems. But after more than four decades of video games, decades of academic research, and untold hours of gameplay, we do know a few things. Video games are here to stay. Video games have been successful because they are beguiling. They inspire the full gamut of emotional reactions, from fear and hatred to utter devotion. As they become more and more a part of our lives, and as they grow in directions we can today only barely imagine, the field of video game studies will need new talent, both to develop these creations and to seek to understand them. We hope that this book has given you a feel for the key avenues to understanding video games. And if you are intrigued, we invite you to explore further this astounding medium.

DISCUSSION QUESTIONS

- Which research perspective is best supported? Why is it difficult for researchers to engage in a fruitful debate?
- How would you criticize the Active User perspective?
- How would you criticize the Active Media perspective?
- What, if anything, makes the study of video games more complex than studying other media?
- Why is it important to research the malign effects of video games? What is your position on the issue? How would you research the potential malign effects?

RECOMMENDED GAMES

Mortal Kombat—one of the games to spark most controversy with its fatality moves, leading to studies on the risks associated with playing video games.

Doom—A very successful game to spark controversy at the time due its detailed graphics and violent content.

Grand Theft Auto V—The latest versions of the hugely successful game, where you play in an open-ended world, and can be just the bad boy you dream of.

FURTHER READINGS

Burgess, M., Dill-Shackleford, K., Stermer, P., Brown, B., & Brown, P. (2011, September). Playing with prejudice: The prevalence and consequences of racial stereotypes in video games. *Media Psychology*, *14*(3), 289–311.

(Estimated reading time: 40 minutes)

NOTES

1. Jenkins, 2007.
2. For an overview, see GamePolitics. com at http://gamepolitics.com/ legislation.htm (accessed February 17, 2012).
3. Anderson, 2004, p. 113.
4. Heins et al., 2001.
5. Williams, 2003b.
6. Anderson, 2003.
7. Buckingham, 2001, p. 67.
8. Dill and Dill, 1998.
9. Calvert, 1999.
10. Barlett and Anderson, 2012.
11. Feshbach and Singer, 1971.
12. Bushman, Baumeister, and Stack, 1999; Olson, 2010.
13. Chandler, 1995; Gerbner, 1973.
14. Bandura, 1977.
15. Zillmann, 1979.
16. Berkowitz, 1984.
17. Anderson and Bushman, 2001.
18. Durkin and Barber, 2002, p. 373.
19. Gentile and colleagues, 2004.
20. Funk and colleagues, 2004.
21. Swing, Gentile, Anderson, and Walsh, 2010.
22. Williams and Skoric, 2005.
23. Anderson et al., 2008.
24. Kühn et al., 2018.
25. Przybylski and Weinstein, 2019.
26. Ferguson et al., 2017.
27. Cunningham, Engelstätter, and Ward, 2016.
28. Bensley and Van Eenwyk, 2001; Emes, 1997; Freedman, 2001; Robinson, Wilde, Navracruz, Haydel, and Varady, 2001.
29. Anderson and Bushman, 2001, p. 353.
30. Sherry, 2001.
31. Griffiths, 1999.
32. Freedman, 2001, p. 2.
33. Ferguson, 2009.
34. Ferguson, 2010a, p. 73.
35. Craig et al., 2010, p. 171.
36. Bensley and Van Eenwyk, 2001; Dill and Dill, 1998; Freedman, 2001; Goldstein, 2001; Ivory, 2001; Sherry, 2001; Ferguson, 2009.
37. Anderson et al., 2004; Anderson and Bushman, 2001.
38. Prescott, Sargent, and Hull, 2018.
39. For a summary, see Grossman and DeGaetano, 1999.
40. American Psychiatric Association, 2007.
41. American Psychiatric Association, 2015a.
42. American Psychiatric Association, 2015b.
43. American Psychiatric Association, 2015c.
44. http://henryjenkins.org/2007/04/a_few_thoughts_on_media_violen.html#sthash.WV5g1L4p.dpuf.
45. Durkin and Barber, 2002.
46. Anderson and Dill, 2000.
47. Ferguson, 2010a.
48. Geen, 2001.
49. 2001, p. 3.
50. Anderson and Dill, 2000.
51. Ferguson, 2007, p. 470.
52. Jenkins, 2000.
53. Gauntlett, 2001.
54. Jessen, 1998.
55. Bateson, 1972.
56. Jessen, 1998.
57. Mouritsen, 2003.
58. Jessen, 2001.
59. Elson and Ferguson, 2014.
60. Jessen, 2001; Sørensen and Jessen, 2000.
61. Jessen, 1998.
62. Jones, 2002.
63. Livingstone, 2002.
64. Turkle, 1984.
65. Turkle, 1995.
66. Turkle, 1995.
67. Ermi and Mäyrä, 2003.
68. Ermi and Mäyrä, 2003, p. 244.
69. Olson, 2010, p. 185.
70. Dill and colleagues, 2005.
71. Schierbeck and Carstens, 1999.
72. For example, Cooper and Mackie, 1986.
73. For example, Durkin and Barber, 2002.
74. Buckingham, 2000.
75. Dill and Dill, 1998.
76. Anderson and Dill, 2000; Kirsh, 2003; Lynch, Gentile, Olson, and Brederode, 2001.

77. Durkin and Barber, 2002; Harris, 2001.
78. Harris, 2001.
79. Griffiths and Davies, 2005.
80. Griffiths and Hunt, 1998.
81. Griffiths, 1997.
82. Gentile, 2009.
83. Gentile et al., 2011.
84. Kuss and Griffiths, 2012.

Video Game Timeline

3500 BC   Egyptians are playing the board game *Senet*.

400 BC   Vikings are playing the board game *Tafl*.

AD 822   The Moors in Spain are playing chess.

1400   The nobility in Europe play card suit games.

1600   *Go*, originally of Chinese origins, is played throughout Japan.

1812   The first war game, *Kriegsspiel*, sees the light in Prussia as a chess variant.

1841   First international chess competition is held in London.

1896   *Ludo* is patented in England.

1904   *The Landlord's Game* is patented as one of the first overtly serious games.

1952   PhD student A.S. Douglas develops a version of *Noughts and Crosses* for the EDSAC computer at the University of Cambridge.

1958   Physicist William Higinbotham runs the electronic (but noncomputerized) game *Tennis For Two* as a demonstration tool at Brookhaven National Laboratory in Upton, New York.

1961   Steven Russell and friends develop the two-player space shooter *Spacewar!* at MIT.

1970   *Simulation & Gaming* journal is founded.

1971   The first arcade game, *Computer Space*, is released. The game, inspired by *Spacewar!*, is not a great success, most likely because it is too difficult to learn to play quickly.

1972   Influential early game developer Atari is founded in California.

        Atari releases the *Pong* arcade game, which is hugely successful.

        Magnavox launches the Odyssey console.

        Hunt the Wumpus

1974   The *Dungeons & Dragons* tabletop role-playing game is commercially launched.

1976   *Night Driver*

      Death Race

      Adventure (aka Colossal Cave Adventure)

1977   Atari launches the Video Computer System, one of the first game consoles to use cartridges (and therefore able to play games not built into the system). The machine later becomes known as the Atari 2600.

1978   *Space Invaders*

      Empire

1979   *Adventure* (Atari)

      Asteroids

      Galaxian

1980   *Mystery House*

      Battlezone

      Pac-Man

      Defender

      Zork

      Space Panic

      Ultima

      MUD (first persistent online multiplayer game, initially developed in 1978)

1981   *Donkey Kong*

1982   *Microsoft Flight Simulator*

1983   *Dragon's Lair*

      Mario Bros.

      Nintendo's Famicom console (to be known in the West as the Nintendo Entertainment System) is launched in Japan.

1984   A severe crash in sales, beginning the previous year, leads many to doubt the future of the game industry.

      Tetris

      King's Quest

      Elite

1985   Mary Ann Buckles writes a PhD dissertation entitled *Interactive Fiction: The Computer Storygame "Adventure."*

The Nintendo Entertainment System is launched in the United States.

Gauntlet

Super Mario Bros.

Balance of Power

1986   The Sega Master System console is launched in the United States.

The Legend of Zelda

Habitat

1987   *Leisure Suit Larry in the Land of the Lounge Lizards*

Maniac Mansion

1989   Nintendo launches the Game Boy handheld console worldwide.

The Sega Genesis console is launched in the United States.

Herzog Zwei

SimCity

1990   *The Secret of Monkey Island*

1991   The Super Nintendo Entertainment System console is launched in the United States.

Sid Meier's Civilization

1992   *Wolfenstein 3D*

Mortal Kombat

Dune II

1993   *Doom*

Myst

1994   The Entertainment Software Rating Board is created.

Sony's PlayStation console is launched in Japan (to be launched in the United States the year after).

1996   The Nintendo 64 console is launched in Japan (to be launched in the United States the following year).

Tomb Raider

Madden NFL 97

Meridian 59

1997	*Ultima Online*
1998	Sega's Dreamcast console is launched in Japan.
	Dance Dance Revolution released in arcades.
	StarCraft
1999	The Columbine High School shootings lead to increased worry over violent video games.
	EverQuest
2000	Sony's PlayStation 2 console is launched in the United States.
	The Sims
2001	*Grand Theft Auto III*
	Bejeweled
	Halo
	Microsoft launches the Xbox console.
	The peer-reviewed *Game Studies: The International Journal of Computer Game Research* is launched.
2003	First large-scale international conference of DiGRA, the Digital Games Research Association.
	Call of Duty
2004	Nintendo launches the Nintendo DS handheld console.
	World of Warcraft
2005	Sony launches the PlayStation Portable handheld console in the United States.
	Microsoft launches the Xbox 360 console in the United States.
	Guitar Hero
2006	Sony launches the PlayStation 3 console.
	Nintendo launches the Wii console.
	The peer-reviewed *Games and Culture* journal is launched.
2007	*Halo 3* is launched and becomes the fastest-selling game in history.
	Assassin's Creed
	The iPhone is released. With the subsequent launch of the App Store, mobile gaming gets a powerful boost.
2009	*Angry Birds* is launched and soon becomes a global phenomenon, helping to shine the spotlight on casual games.

FarmVille is launched on Facebook, generating intense interest in social gaming.

2010   The Kinect system is launched for Xbox 360.

Sony launches Move for PlayStation 3.

"Gamification" becomes a widely used term (at least among marketers), in response to the ideas of game designer Jesse Schell and others.

Games using 3D projection begin to appear.

2011   Nintendo launches the 3DS handheld console.

Minecraft

Twitch game services makes its debut.

2012   Nintendo launches the Wii U.

Sony releases the PlayStation Vita handheld game console.

Journey

Walking Dead

Candy Crush

2013   Microsoft releases the Xbox One.

Sony releases the PlayStation 4.

Grand Theft Auto V

The Last of Us

DOTA 2

Papers, Please

2014   Oculus VR is bought by Facebook.

The Gamergate controversy brings new attention to sexism and harassment in video games.

Hearthstone

Shovel Knight

Dark Souls 2

2015

Fallout 4

Witcher 3

Her Story

Rocket League

2016	Hololens is released.
	Steam hits more than 50 million new users per year.
	Pokemon Go
	Overwatch
	Clash Royal
2017	Nintendo Switch is released.
	PlayerUnknown's Battlegrounds
	Fortnite
	Unchartered 4
2018	e-Sports named potential next Olympic discipline.
	Red Dead Redemption 2
	Spider-Man
	Loot boxes removed from several games due to similarities with gambling.
2019	Magic Leap is released.

Glossary

AAA: The term used for video games with the highest development budgets, e.g. the *Grand Theft Auto* and *Assassin's Creed* series.

Action games: Games focusing on speed and physical drama that make high demands on the player's reflexes and coordination skills.

Active Media perspective: A school of thought that believes that media actively influence a mostly passive recipient, the player.

Active User perspective: A school of thought that stresses the active interpretation and filtering players exhibit when playing video games.

Adventure games: Games focusing on puzzle-solving within a narrative framework. These games typically demand strict, logical thought.

Advertainment/advergame: The use of games for advertising rather than just entertainment.

Aesthetics (of a video game): All aspects of a video game that are experienced by the player, whether directly (such as audio and graphics) or indirectly (such as rules). (Note that **aesthetics** is an ambiguous term used in many ways across disciplines.)

Agency: The player's ability to influence the game world through their decisions and actions.

AI (artificial intelligence): Often used to describe the behavior patterns of computer opponents.

Alternate reality games: A game genre that mixes the game world with reality, so the boundaries become blurred—for example, using real websites as part of the game.

Arcade: Public gaming facility offering computer games (arcade games). Arcades were highly popular in the early 1980s. A game would typically begin when the player inserted the equivalent of a US quarter. Action games were especially well suited to arcades.

Arcade game: Game played on dedicated "arcade" machines. The player inserts coins to play and a game is typically quite brief.

Augmented reality: A game that works by putting a virtual layer over the physical world, often with the aid of a built-in camera for mobile games.

Autofire: Feature of certain joysticks, sending "fire" impulses to the game in short, rapid bursts.

Avatar: Graphical representation of the user in an online forum, especially a role-playing game.

Boot: To "boot" or to "kick" a player is to exclude him or her from an online game.

Bot: Computer-controlled ally or opponent (typically in action and strategy games).

Camper: (1) In multiplayer team games, a player who only values his or her own survival without caring for the condition of other team members. (2) Player who hides in a safe place, taking down the enemy as he approaches without placing himself in any real danger.

Casual games: Games with a modest learning curve and that require little time investment in order to be enjoyed, such as a brief online card game.

Casual players: People who play games but only rarely, or who engage mostly with casual games.

CGI (computer-generated imagery): Special effects (in movies, for instance) created by computer graphics.

Clipping: The act of removing graphics that move outside the player's logical line of vision.

Console: A computer designed for the sole purpose of playing games. Often sold without a keyboard.

Controller: The hardware through which the player sends his or her input to the game, typically a "pad" with a number of buttons that can be mapped to perform various functions depending on the game.

COTS: Commercial-off-the-shelves-games.

Cut-scene: Dramatically important sequence, often displayed without the interaction of the player. The scene is typically shown to motivate a shift in the "plot" of the game and displayed outside of the game engine.

DOT (damage over time): Refers to damage dealt to players or computer-controlled characters in combat games. Damage over time is a type of damage that occurs at set intervals over a limited period of time, such as poisonous effects.

Dynamics: The processes and events in a game that are generated by the relationships between rules, game world physics, player input, etc.

Edutainment: A combination of the terms "education" and "entertainment." Label for games with a pronounced educational ambition.

Emergence: (1) The phenomenon whereby a complex, interesting, high-level function is produced as a result of combining simple, low-level mechanisms in simple ways. (2) The phenomenon whereby a system is designed according to certain principles, but interesting properties arise that are not included in the goals of the designer.

Endogenous games: A game that closely integrates the key game elements and the learning activity.

Engine: The basic code that defines the relation between game objects and determines the limits of graphics and sound.

e-Sports: The concept describes the discipline of video gamers competing professionally in the most popular games for example Counter Strike or StarCraft.

Exogenous games: A game where the game's key elements are so weakly related to the learning activity that it can easily be replaced with another game's mechanics.

Flow: The flow state is described as the feeling of optimal experience. It is felt when we feel in control of our own fate and have a sense of exhilaration and enjoyment.

Frag: A kill in an action game, typically a 3D shooter.

Freemium: Games (often apps) that players can download for free but for which they then have to pay a fee in order to proceed past a certain point, to eliminate advertising, or to unlock more of the game (for example, new levels or better items).

FPS: (1) "Frames per second," or the number of images displayed on a screen every second to create the illusion of motion (often referred to as "frame rate"). (2) "First-person shooter," a shoot-'em-up game that plays from a first-person perspective (or from the view of the character).

Game community: Players who interact with a high frequency around a game, and may develop a particular set of norms and forms of interaction.

Game object: A distinct entity in a game world, such as a character, a sword, or a car. Does not refer to things like background graphics, sounds, interface details, etc.

Gameplay: Ambiguous term for the total effect of all active game elements. Refers to the holistic game experience and the ability of the game to command the attention of the player.

Games-for-change: A subgenre within serious games that focuses on creating games that can lead to the world becoming a better place, from the foundation that games should actively try to change the world.

Gamespace: The entire space (or world, or universe) presented by a game.

Gamification: The act of inserting game mechanics into a product, site, or service to make it more engaging.

Genre: A category (of video games, in this instance) based on certain shared characteristics.

Hardcore players: People who play games that are difficult to learn and master for extended periods of time. They usually engage with games on a daily basis, and for a larger amount of time.

Hardware: Tangible elements of a computer or console, such as the processor, graphics card, or hard drive (as opposed to software).

Health games: A subgenre within serious games that denotes the use of games designed to inform and improve health—rehabilitation games and exercise games have been especially popular.

HUD: "Heads-up display." Usually shows the player's remaining health, ammo count, and armor level.

Indie games: Independent games, developed outside of the large studios (and often published without traditional publishers).

Interactive fiction: Contested label for types of fiction based on high user participation. Normally the term refers to computer-based types of fiction, but role-playing games such as *Dungeons & Dragons* and special forms of paper-based literature may also deserve the label "interactive." (Sometimes used to refer solely to text adventure games.)

Interactivity: A term used in many fields but typically as a measure of user influence. The higher the degree of interactivity, the more influence the user has on the form and course of a media product.

Interface: The graphical or textual form of interaction between user and software. Through the interface the user may give commands to the software that are then translated into instructions that the computer can interpret.

Isometric perspective: Also referred to as 2.5D because it tries to mimic the 3D effect. However, although it may look like 3D, the objects are drawn (and are viewable) from only one perspective.

Joystick: A type of **controller**. The player chooses "direction" by manipulating a stick (as in a fighter airplane).

KS (kill steal): The act of killing an enemy who was already the target of another human player, thereby gaining the credit for the kill. This is considered rude.

Lag: Decreased game speed typically due to low bandwidth.

Latency: In online multiplayer games, the time it takes to transmit data from the player's machine to the server and back.

Leet speak: Also referred to as 1337 sp3@k. It is a dialect of online communication (typically between gamers) which is written using certain rules of substitution (e.g. "3" for "E"), and which can be very difficult to understand for anyone who is not active in online communities.

Ludology: The study of games, particularly computer games. Ludology is often defined as the study of game structure (or gameplay) as opposed to the study of games as narratives or games as a visual medium.

Machinima: The practice of manipulating video games to produce animated films.

Mechanics: Ambiguous term often referring to events or actions that the game design allows for; for instance, driving, regaining health, or shooting. May be thought of as the "verbs" of a game, i.e. what the player can do.

Microtransaction: A payment exchanged for virtual/in-game services, often used in otherwise free-to-play games (and a staple in freemium titles).

MMO (Massively Multiplayer Online): See **Online role-playing games**.

Mod (modification): A piece of software that modifies the appearance and/ or rules of an existing game. Mods are often made and published by enthusiastic players.

Modder: A person that makes modifications (mods) of existing games.

MS-DOS: A nongraphical operating system developed by Microsoft that was dominant before Windows.

MUD (multiuser dungeon): A system for virtual role-playing. Can be conceived of as a thematically charged chat room with a focus on role-playing. Certain types—so-called MOOs (MUD, object-oriented)—operate with objects that the players/users can interact with (and sometimes alter or create). Many online role-playing games are direct descendants of MUDs.

Narrative: A string of connected events making up a story.

Narratology: The study of narratives. Within computer game research narratology is often seen as opposed to ludology.

NPC (nonplayer character): Any character in a game not controlled by the player.

Online role-playing games: Game type in which players (typically several thousand of them) act simultaneously in the same server-based world. Users normally pay a monthly fee and connect through their Internet account. An online role-playing game is a graphically illustrated MUD. This type of game is often termed a MMORPG (massively multiplayer online role-playing game).

Parser: The function that interprets the (adventure game) player's textual input.

Play: Ambiguous term (when contrasted to "games"), often referring to the relatively unstructured, relatively goalless activity of children's (or adults') playful behavior.

Player character (PC): In-game character controlled by a human player.

Player killing: One player killing another within the game world (typically in MMORPGs). Sometimes considered a serious problem.

Player versus environment (PVE): Usually refers to a type of online role-playing game in which human players only fight computer-controlled opponents.

Player versus player (PVP): Usually refers to a type of online role-playing game in which human players can fight each other.

Polygon: Geometric figure; a closed-plane figure bounded by straight lines. 3D graphics usually consist of polygons and are therefore not dependent upon a fixed perspective.

Procedural rhetoric: The art of persuasion through rule-based representations and interactions (typically in games) rather than the spoken word, writing, images, or moving pictures.

Productive play: Creative activities inspired by games, in which players create scenarios (mods), fiction (fan fiction, movies, machinima, etc.), or game aids (such as walkthroughs) to extend the experience of their favorite games.

Quest: A mission in a game, structuring action for the player.

Real-time strategy game: Strategy game in which the action is played out continuously, without breaks (as opposed to **turn-based strategy games**).

Reception (studies): In literature, the study of a reader's understanding of the text. In video games, the study of the player's experience of playing a game.

Serious games: Games intentionally created with a primary agenda other than entertainment.

Shoot-'em-up: Action game with an extreme focus on shooting down enemies. Seldom used to describe 3D shooters; often refers to more abstract games using a third-person perspective.

Simulation games: Games focusing on realism. Typically they make heavy demands on the player's ability to understand and remember complex principles and relations.

Source code: Basic instructions describing how a game works. The source code reveals the secrets of a piece of software and is therefore often carefully guarded.

Spawning: The event of someone or something appearing in a game environment.

STEM: A popular abbreviation for science, technology, engineering, and mathematics, used to group this educational area and curriculum as one entity.

Strategy games: Games focusing on the ability to deal with dynamic priorities, typically in a context of resource shortage. Strategy games may be divided into **real-time strategy games** and **turn-based strategy games**.

Text game: Game that only uses textual input and output. These are often adventure games (for which the textual form was popular in the 1980s).

3D games: Refers to gamespaces modeled in three dimensions, or to three-dimensional projection, in which the player's eyes are "tricked" into perceiving depth in the image.

3D shooter: Action games in which the action is seen through the eyes of the protagonist and where the graphics are three-dimensional (and often constructed of polygons). Synonym: first-person shooter (**FPS**).

Turn-based strategy games: Strategy games divided into "turns," as in board games (and as opposed to real-time strategy games). Typically a player moves all his or her units, then the next player moves all their units, and so on.

User-generated content: The idea that you can empower players to seamlessly generate new content to a game continuously to keep the game fresh.

Vector graphics: Graphics defined and generated on the basis of mathematical statements, meaning the perspective becomes flexible.

Virtual world: Multiplayer (or multiuser) system presented as having a large-scale geography. May be divided into game worlds and social worlds, the latter having no objectives or goals.

Games Cited

Format: *Title*, Developer, Year, Publisher

Advanced Dungeons & Dragons, Gary Gygax, 1977, TSR

Adventure (aka Colossal Cave Adventure), Will Crowther and Don Woods, 1976

Adventure, Atari, 1979, Atari

The Adventures of Bayou Billy, Konami, 1988, Konami

Adventures of Bayou Billy, Konami, 1989, Konami

Age of Empires, Ensemble Studios, 1997, Microsoft

Age of Empires II: The Age of Kings, Ensemble Studios, 1999, Microsoft

Age of Empires II: The Conquerors Expansion, Ensemble Studios, 2000, Microsoft

Age of Empires III, Ensemble Studios, 2005, Microsoft Game Studios

Age of Mythology, Ensemble Studios, 2002, Microsoft Game Studios

Aion: Steel Cavalry, Aion Team Development, 2008 (Korea), NCsoft

Airport Security, Persuasive Games, 2006, Shockwave.com

Akalabeth, Richard Garriot, 1980, California Pacific Computer

Aliens, Activision, 1986, Activision

Alone in the Dark, Infogrames, 1992, Infogrames

America's Army, US Army, 2002, US Army

Amnesia: The Dark Descent, Frictional Games, 2010, Frictional Games

Anarchy Online, Funcom, 2001, Funcom

Angry Birds, Rovio Mobile, 2009, Rovio

Arkham Horror, Richard Launius, 2008, Chaosium

Asheron's Call, Turbine Entertainment Software, 1999, Microsoft/Turbine

Asheron's Call 2: Fallen Kings, Turbine Entertainment Software, 2002, Microsoft Game Studios

Assassin's Creed, Ubisoft Montreal, 2007, Ubisoft

Assassin's Creed: Unity, Ubisoft, 2014, Ubisoft

Asteroids, Atari, 1979, Atari

A Story About My Uncle, Coffee Stain Studios, 2014, Coffee Stain Studios

Backpacker, TATI Mixedia, 1995, BMG Interactive

Balance of Power, Chris Crawford, 1985, Mindscape

Baldur's Gate, BioWare, 1998, Interplay

Baldur's Gate II: Shadows of Amn, BioWare, 2000, Interplay

Barbie Fashion Designer, Digital Domain, 1996, Mattel

Batman: Arkham City, Rocksteady Studios, 2011, Warner Bros. Interactive Entertainment

Battlefield 1942, Digital Illusions, 2002, Electronic Arts

Battlezone, Atari, 1980, Atari

The Beast Within: A Gabriel Knight Mystery, Sierra On-Line, 1995, Sierra On-Line

The Beast, Microsoft, 2001, Microsoft

Beatmania, Konami, 1997, Konami

Bejeweled, PopCap Games, 2001, PopCap Games

Beyond Good and Evil, Ubisoft Montpellier Studios, 2003, UbiSoft

Big Fish Casino, Self Aware Games, 2012, Big Fish Games

BioShock, 2K Boston, 2007, 2K Games

Black & White, Lionhead Studios, 2001, Electronic Arts

Blade Runner, Westwood Studios, 1997, Virgin Interactive Entertainment

Blood Money, DMA Design, 1989, Psygnosis

Blue Block, Martin Demers, 2010, Martin Demers

Blue Max, Synapse Software, 1983, Synapse Software

Bomb Jack, Tehkan, 1984, Tehkan

Boom Beach, Supercell, 2013, Supercell

Broken Sword: The Sleeping Dragon, Revolution Software, 2003, THQ

Bruce Lee, Datasoft, 1984, Datasoft

Bump'n'Jump, Data East, 1982, Bally/Midway

Burnout 3: Takedown, Criterion Games, 2004, Electronic Arts

Burnout Crash! Criterion Games, 2011, Electronic Arts

B.U.T.T.O.N, Copenhagen Game Collective, 2010, Copenhagen Game Collective

Cake Mania, Sandlot Games, 2006, Sandlot Games

California Games, Epyx, 1987, Epyx

Call of Duty, Infinity Ward, 2003, Activision

Call of Duty: Modern Warfare 2, Infinity Ward, 2009, Activision

Canabalt, Semi-Secret Software, 2009, Semi-Secret Software

Candy Crush Saga, King, 2012, King

Carmageddon, Stainless Games, 1997, Interplay/SCI

Castle of Dr. Brain, Sierra On-Line, 1991, Sierra On-Line

Castle Wolfenstein, Muse Software, 1981, Muse Software

Championship Manager 4, Sports Interactive, 2003, Eidos Interactive

Championship Manager 11, Dynamo Games, 2011, Square Enix

Champions of Krynn, SSI, 1990, SSI

Chore Wars, Kevan Davis, 2001

The Chronicles of Riddick: Escape from Butcher Bay, Starbreeze Studios, 2004, Vivendi Games

Clash of Clans, Supercell, 2012, Supercell

Clash Royal, Supercell, 2016, Supercell

Close Combat, Atomic Games, 1996, Microsoft

Command & Conquer, Westwood Studios, 1995, Virgin Interactive

Command & Conquer: Generals, Electronic Arts Pacific, 2003, Electronic Arts

Commando, Capcom, 1985, Capcom

Computer Space, Nutting Associates, 1971, Nutting Associates

Counter-Strike, Valve, 1999, Sierra Entertainment

Counter-Strike Online, Valve, 2008, Valve

Crash Bandicoot, Naughty Dog, 1996, Sony

CrossFire, SmileGate, 2007 (South Korea), Neowiz Games

Cutthroat Capitalism, Smallbore Webworks, 2009, Smallbore Webworks

Dance Dance Revolution, Konami, 1998, Konami

Darfur Is Dying, Susana Ruiz, 2006, shareware, MtvU

Dark Age of Camelot, Mythic Entertainment, 2001, Vivendi/Electronic Arts

Darklands, MicroProse, 1992, MicroProse

Darwinia, Introversion Software, 2005, Introversion Software

Day of the Tentacle, LucasArts, 1993, LucasArts

Deadline, Infocom, 1982, Infocom

Death Race, Exidy, 1976, Exidy

Decathlon, Activision, 1983, Activision

Defender, Williams, 1981, Williams

Defender of the Crown, Cinemaware, 1986, Cinemaware

Delta Force, Nova Logic, 1998, Nova Logic

Depression Quest, Zoe Quinn, 2013, Zoe Quinn

Desktop Tower Defense, Paul Preece, 2007, Kongregate

Deus Ex, Ion Storm, 2000, Eidos Interactive

Diablo, Blizzard North, 1996, Blizzard Entertainment

Digital: A Love Story, Christine Love, 2010, Christine Love

Dishonored, Arkane Studios, 2012, Bethesda Softworks

Donkey Kong, Nintendo, 1981, Nintendo

Donkey Konga, Namco, 2003, Nintendo

Don't Starve, Klei Entertainment, 2013, Klei Entertainment

Doodle Jump, Lima Sky, 2009, Lima Sky

Doom, id Software, 1993, GT Interactive

Doom II: Hell on Earth, id Software, 1994, GT Interactive

Doom III, id Software, 2004, Activision

DOTA 2, Valve, 2013, Valve

Double Dragon, Technōs Japan, 1987, Taito

Dragon Age: Origins, Electronic Arts, 2009, Electronic Arts/Valve

Dragonbox, We Want to Know, 2012, We Want to Know

Dragon's Lair, Advanced Microcomputer Systems, 1983, Cinematronics

Dreamfall: The Longest Journey, Funcom Oslo, 2006, Aspyr

Drop7, Area/Code Entertainment, 2009, Zynga

Dune II: The Building of a Dynasty, Westwood Studios, 1992, Virgin Interactive

Dungeon Fighter Online, Neople, 2005 (South Korea), Neople

The Elder Scrolls III: Morrowind, Bethesda Game Studios, 2002, Bethesda Softworks

The Elder Scrolls IV: Oblivion, Bethesda Game Studios, 2006, 2K Games

Elevator Action, Taito, 1983, Taito

Elite, David Braben and Ian Bell, 1984, Acornsoft

Empire, Walter Bright, 1978

Empires: Dawn of the Modern World, Stainless Steel Studios, 2003, Activision

Enter the Matrix, Shiny Entertainment, 2003, Atari

EpicWin, Supermono Ltd, 2010, Supermono Ltd

Escape from Woomera, 2004 (incomplete), unreleased

E.T. the Extra-Terrestrial, Atari, 1982, Atari

Europa Universalis, Paradox Development Studio, 2000, Strategy First

Europa Universalis II, Paradox Development Studio, 2001, Strategy First

Euro Truck Simulator, SCS Software, 2008, SCS Software

EverQuest, 989 Studios/Verant Interactive, 1999, Sony Online Entertainment

Eye of the Beholder, Westwood Studios, 1990, SSI

Façade, Michael Mateas and Andrew Stern, 2005

Fallout, Interplay, 1997, Interplay

Fallout 4, Bethesda Game Studios, 2015, Bethesda Softworks

Far Cry, Crytek, 2004, Ubisoft

FarmVille, Zynga, 2009, Zynga

FarmVille 2: Country Escape, Zynga, 2014, Zynga

Fez, Polytron, 2012, Trapdoor

Fieldrunners, Subatomic Studios, 2008, Subatomic Studios

FIFA 12, Electronic Arts Canada, 2011, Electronic Arts

FIFA 2004, Electronic Arts Canada, 2003, Electronic Arts

FIFA 2005, Electronic Arts Canada, 2004, Electronic Arts

Final Fantasy, Square, 1987, Square

Final Fantasy VII, Square, 1997, Square

Final Fantasy XI, Square Enix, 2003, Sony Online Entertainment

Flight Simulator 2002, Microsoft Game Studios, 2001, Microsoft Game Studios

Fluid, Opus, 1996, Sony

Food Import Folly, Persuasive Games, 2007, Persuasive Games

Fortnite, Epic Games, 2017, Epic Games

Forza Motorsport, Turn 10 Studios, 2005, Microsoft Game Studios

FreeSpace 2, Volition, Inc., 1999, Interplay

Frogger, Konami, 1981, Sega-Gremlin

Gabriel Knight: Sins of the Fathers, Sierra On-Line, 1993, Sierra On-Line

Gabriel Knight 3: Blood of the Sacred, Blood of the Damned, Sierra On-Line, 1999, Sierra On-Line

Galaxian, Namco, 1979, Namco

Gauntlet, Atari, 1985, Atari

Gettysburg: The Turning Point, SSI, 1986, SSI

Ghostbusters, Activision, 1984, Activision

Ghosts 'n Goblins, Capcom, 1985, Capcom

Glitch, Tiny Speck, 2011, Tiny Speck

Global Conflicts: Palestine, Serious Games Interactive, 2007, Serious Games Interactive

Glow Puzzle, Nexx Studio, 2010, Nexx Crunch Sdn

Goat Simulator, Coffee Stain Studios, 2014, Coffee Stain Studios

Golden Axe, Sega, 1989, Sega

Gorf, Midway, 1981, Midway

Grand Theft Auto, DMA Design, 1997, BMG Interactive

Grand Theft Auto III, DMA Design, 2001, Rockstar Games

Grand Theft Auto V, Rockstar North, 2013, Rockstar Games

Grand Theft Auto: Vice City, Rockstar North, 2002, Rockstar Games

Gran Turismo, Polyphony Digital, 1997, Sony

Gran Turismo 5, Polyphony Digital, 2010, Sony

Gremlins, Atari, 1984, Atari

Grim Fandango, LucasArts, 1998, LucasArts

Guitar Hero, Harmonix, 2005, RedOctane

Gun Fight, Midway, 1975, Midway

Habitat, Lucasfilm, 1986, Quantum Link

Half the Sky Movement: The Game, Half the Sky Movement, 2012, Half the Sky Movement

Half-Life, Valve Corporation, 1998, Sierra Entertainment

Half-Life 2, Valve Corporation, 2004, Valve Corporation

Halo 2, Bungie, 2004, Microsoft Game Studios

Halo 3, Bungie, 2007, Microsoft Game Studios

Halo: Combat Evolved, Bungie, 2001, Microsoft Game Studios

Halo: Reach, Bungie, 2010, Microsoft

Hamurabi, David Ahl, 1978

Hang-On, Sega, 1985, Sega

Hatred, Destructive Creations, 2015, Destructive Creations

Hay Day, Supercell, 2012, Supercell

HearthStone, Blizzard, 2014, Blizzard Entertainment

Hearts of Iron, Paradox Development Studio, 2002, Strategy First

Heavy Rain, Quantic Dream, 2010, Sony

Heretic, Raven Software, 1994, id Software

Her Story, Sam Barlow, 2015, Sam Barlow

Herzog Zwei, Technosoft, 1989, Technosoft

Hexen, Raven Software, 1996, id Software

Hidden Agenda, Trans Fiction System, 1988, Springboard

Hitman: Codename 47, IO Interactive, 2000, Eidos Interactive

Hunt the Wumpus, Gregory Yob, 1972

The I of It, Armor Games, 2011, Kongregate

iCopter, Lawlmart, 2009, Lawlmart

Impasse, Wanderlands, 2011, Kongregate

Impossible Mission, Epyx, 1984, Epyx

Indiana Jones and the Last Crusade, LucasArts, 1989, LucasArts

Indiana Jones and the Temple of Doom, Atari Games, 1985, Atari Games

International Karate+, System 3 Software, 1987, Epyx

iShoot, Ethan Nicholas, 2008, Ethan Nicholas

Jelly Car, Walaber, 2008, Walaber

Jet Set Radio, Smilebit, 2000, Sega

Johann Sebastian Joust, Die Gute Fabrik, 2011, Die Gute Fabrik

Journey, Thatgamecompany, 2012, Sony

Joust, Williams Electronics, 1982, Williams Electronics

Kampfgruppe, SSI, 1985, SSI

Karate Champ, Technōs Japan, 1984, Data East Corporation

Kim Kardashian: Hollywood, Glu Games, 2014, Glu Games

King of Chicago, Cinemaware, 1987, Cinemaware

King's Quest, Sierra On-Line, 1983, Sierra On-Line

Knight Lore, Tim and Chris Stamper, 1984, Ultimate Play the Game

Kung-Fu Master, Irem, 1984, Irem

The Last Express, Smoking Car Productions, 1997, Brøderbund Software

The Last of Us, Naughty Dog, 2013, Sony

League of Legends, Riot Games, 2009, Riot Games

The Legend of Zelda, Nintendo, 1986, Nintendo

The Legend of Zelda: The Wind Waker, Nintendo EAD, 2002, Nintendo

Leisure Suit Larry 3: Passionate Patti in Pursuit of the Pulsating Pectorals, Sierra Entertainment, 1989, Sierra Entertainment

Leisure Suit Larry in the Land of the Lounge Lizards, Sierra On-Line, 1987, Sierra On-Line

Lemmings, DMA Design, 1991, Psygnosis

Limbo, Playdead, 2010, Microsoft

Lineage II: The Chaotic Chronicle, NCsoft, 2004, NCsoft

Lineage: The Bloodpledge, NCsoft, 1998, NCsoft

Line Rider, Boštjan Čadež, 2006, Boštjan Čadež

Little Computer People, Activision, 1985, Activision

Logical Journey of the Zoombinis, Brøderbund, 1996, Brøderbund

The Longest Journey, Funcom, 1999, Empire Interactive

Loom, Lucasfilm Games, 1990, Lucasfilm Games

Lords of the Rising Sun, Cinemaware, 1989, Cinemaware

Lotus Esprit Turbo Challenge, Magnetic Fields, 1990, Gremlins Graphics Software

Lunar Lander, Atari, 1979, Atari

Madden NFL 97, EA Tiburon, 1996, EA Sports

Madden NFL 07, EA Tiburon, 2006, EA Sports

Mafia Wars, Zynga, 2008, Zynga

Majestic, Anim-X, 2001, Electronic Arts

Making History: The Calm and The Storm, Muzzy Lane, 2007, Muzzy Lane

Manhunt, Rockstar North, 2003, Rockstar Games

Maniac Mansion, Lucasfilm Games, 1987, Lucasfilm Games

Maplestory, Wizet, 2003 (South Korea), Nexon

Marble Madness, Atari Games, 1984, Atari Games

Mario Bros., Nintendo Corporation, 1983, Nintendo Corporation

Mass Effect 3, BioWare, 2012, Electronic Arts

Master of Orion, Simtex, 1993, MicroProse

Math Blaster, Davidson & Associates, 1983, Davidson & Associates

Max and the Magic Marker, Press Play, 2010, The Games Company

Max Payne II: The Fall of Max Payne, Remedy Entertainment, 2003, Rockstar Games

Medal of Honor, DreamWorks Interactive, 1999, Electronic Arts

Medal of Honor, Danger Close Games/EA Digital Illusions CE, 2010, Electronic Arts

Medal of Honor: Allied Assault, 2015, Inc., 2002, Electronic Arts Games

Meridian 59, Archetype Interactive, 1996, The 3DO Company

Metal Gear Solid Touch, Kojima Productions, 2009, Konami

Metroid Prime, Retro Studios, 2002, Nintendo

Microsoft Flight Simulator, SubLOGIC, 1982, Microsoft Game Studios

Microsoft Solitaire, Wes Cherry, 1990 (Windows 3.0), Microsoft

Microsoft Train Simulator, Kuju Entertainment, 2001, Microsoft

Minecraft, Mojang, 2011, Mojang

Minecraft Edu, TeacherGaming, 2016, Mojang

Monkey Math School, THUP Games, 2011, THUP Games

Moon Patrol, Irem, 1982, Irem

Mortal Kombat, Midway Games, 1992, Acclaim Entertainment

MotorStorm, Evolution Studios, 2006, Sony

MotorStorm: Apocalypse, Evolution Studios, 2011, Sony

MotorStorm: Pacific Rift, Evolution Studios, 2008, Sony

Ms. Pac-Man, Bally/Midway, 1982, Bally/Midway

MUD, Richard Bartle and Roy Trubshaw, 1978

Myst, Cyan Worlds, 1993, Brøderbund Software

Mystery House, On-Line Systems, 1980, On-Line Systems

Need for Speed, Electronic Arts Canada, 1994, Electronic Arts

Never Alone, Upper One Games, 2014, E-Line Media

Neverwinter Nights, BioWare Corporation, 2002, Infogrames

New Super Mario Bros., Nintendo, 2006, Nintendo

The New Zealand Story, Taito, 1988, Ocean

Night Driver, Micronetics, 1976, Atari

Night Trap, Digital Pictures, 1992, Sega

Nike Goooal, Framfab Denmark, 2004, Nike

1942, Capcom, 1984, Capcom

Nintendogs, Nintendo, 2005, Nintendo

No Pain No Game, Volker Morawe and Tilman Reiff, 2001, Volker Morawe and Tilman Reiff

Nokia Game, Nokia, 1999–2003, Nokia

North & South, Infogrames, 1989, Infogrames

Nuclear War, New World Computing, 1989, US Gold

Operation Wolf, Taito, 1987, Taito

The Oregon Trail, MECC, 1971, Brøderbund Software

Oregon Trail, MECC, 1985, Brøderbund

Out Run, Sega, 1986, Sega

Overwatch, Blizzard Entertainment, 2016, Blizzard Entertainment

Pac-Land, Namco, 1984, Namco

Pac-Man, Namco, 1980, Midway

Pajama Sam, Humongous Entertainment, 1996, Humongous Entertainment

Papa Sangre, Somethin' Else, 2010, Somethin' Else

Paperboy, Atari, 1985, Atari

Papers, Please, Lucas Pope, 2013, Lucas Pope

PaRappa the Rapper, NanaOn-Sha, 1996, Sony

PeaceMaker, ImpactGames, 2007, ImpactGames

Phantasmagoria, Sierra On-Line, 1995, Sierra On-Line

Pikmin, Nintendo, 2001, Nintendo

Pitstop, Epyx, 1983, Epyx

Pitstop II, Epyx, 1984, Epyx

Planescape: Torment, Black Isle Studios, 1999, Interplay

Planetfall, Infocom, 1983, Infocom

Plants vs. Zombies, PopCap Games, 2010 (mobile version), PopCap Games

PlayerUnknown's Battlegrounds, PUBG Corporation, 2017, PUBG Corporation

Playing the News, Impact Games, 2009, Impact Games

Pokemon Go, The Pokémon Company, 2016, Niantic

Pole Position, Namco, 1982, Atari

Pong, Atari, 1972, Atari

Populous, Bullfrog Productions, 1989, Electronic Arts

Prince of Persia, Brøderbund, 1989, Brøderbund

Prince of Persia: The Sands of Time, Ubisoft Montreal, 2003, Ubisoft

Project Gotham Racing, Bizarre Creations, 2001, Microsoft Game Studios

Quest Atlantis, 2003, Indiana University

Qix, Taito, 1981, Taito

Quake, id software, 1996, GT Interactive

Quake III: Arena, id Software, 1999, Activision

Quest for Oil, Serious Games Interactive, 2013, Maersk Group

Ragnarok Online, Gravity Corporation, 2002, Gravity Corporation

Railroad Tycoon, MicroProse, 1990, MicroProse

Rainbow Islands, Taito, 1987, Taito

Rape day, Unknown developer, 2019, Unpublished

Red Dead Redemption, Rockstar San Diego, 2010, Rockstar Games

Red Dead Redemption 2, Rockstar San Diego, 2018, Rockstar Games

Resident Evil, Capcom, 1996, Capcom

Resident Evil 2, Capcom, 1998, Capcom

Resident Evil 4, Capcom Production Studio 4, 2005, Capcom

Resident Evil Code: Veronica X, Capcom, 2000, Capcom

Return to Castle Wolfenstein, Gray Matter Interactive, 2001, Activision

Rez, United Game Artists, 2001, Sega

Rhythm Racer, AvatarLabs, 2009, AvatarLabs

Riddim Ribbon, Tapulous, 2010, Tapulous

Ripper, Take-Two Interactive, 1996, Take-Two Interactive

Rise of Nations, Big Huge Games, 2003, Microsoft Game Studios

Riven, Cyan Worlds, 1997, Brøderbund

Robot Unicorn Attack, Spiritonin Media Games, 2010, Adult Swim

Rock Band, Harmonix Music Systems, 2007, MTV Games/Electronic Arts

Rocket League, Psyonix, 2015, Psyonix

RuneScape, Jagex Games Studio, 2001, Jagex Games Studio

Sales Force Motivation, Bunchball, 2011

Scorched Earth, Wendell Hicken, 1991, shareware

Scramble, Konami, 1981, Stern

Second Life, Linden Lab, 2003, Linden Lab

The Secret of Monkey Island, Lucasfilm Games, 1990, LucasArts

The Secret of Monkey Island: Special Edition, Lucasfilm Games, 2009, LucasArts

September 12th, Gonzalo Frasca, 2003, Newsgaming

Seven Cities of Gold, Ozark Softscape, 1984, Electronic Arts

The 7th Guest, Trilobyte, 1993, Virgin Interactive

Shadow of the Beast, Reflections, 1989, Psygnosis

Shark Jaws, Atari, 1975, Atari

Shovel Knight, Yacht Club Games, 2014, Yacht Club Games

Sid Meier's Civilization, MicroProse, 1991, MicroProse

Sid Meier's Civilization III, Firaxis Games, 2001, Infogrames

Sid Meier's Civilization III: Play the World, Firaxis Games, 2002, Infogrames

Sid Meier's Civilization IV, Firaxis Games, 2005, 2K Games

Sid Meier's Civilization V, Firaxis Games, 2010, 2K Games

Sid Meier's Civilization: Beyond Earth, Firaxis Games, 2014, 2K Games

Sid Meier's Pirates! MicroProse, 1987, MicroProse

Silent Hill, Konami, 1999, Konami

Silent Hill: The Escape, Konami, 2009, Konami

SimCity, Maxis Software, 1989, Brøderbund Software

SimCity 2000, Maxis Software, 1994, Maxis Software

SimCity 4, Maxis Software, 2003, Electronic Arts

SimEarth, Maxis Software, 1990, Maxis

The Sims Online, Maxis Software, 2002, Electronic Arts

The Sims, Maxis Software, 2000, Electronic Arts

SingStar, London Studio, 2004, Sony

688 Attack Sub, Electronic Arts, 1989, Electronic Arts

Slotomania, Playtika, 2011, Playtika

SoftPorn Adventure, On-Line Systems, 1981, On-Line Systems

Sonic the Hedgehog, Sonic Team, 1991, Sega

SoulCalibur, Project Soul, 1998, Namco

South Park: The Stick of Truth, Obsidian Entertainment/South Park Digital Studios, 2014, Ubisoft

Space Invaders, Taito, 1978, Midway

Space Panic, Universal, 1980, Universal

Space Quest: Chapter 1—The Sarien Encounter, Sierra, 1986, Sierra On-Line

Space Race, Atari, 1973, Atari

Space Wars, Cinematronics, 1977, Cinematronics

Spacewar!, Stewart Russell (and others), 1962

Spice World, SCEE, 1998, SCEE

Spore, Maxis Software, 2008, Electronic Arts

Sprint 2, Kee Games, 1976, Kee Games

Spy Hunter, Bally Midway, 1983, Bally Midway

SSX 3, Electronic Arts Canada, 2003, EA Sports Big

StarCraft, Blizzard Entertainment, 1998, Blizzard Entertainment

StarCraft II: Wings of Liberty, Blizzard Entertainment, 2010, Blizzard Entertainment

Star Wars Episode I: Racer, LucasArts, 1999, LucasArts

Star Wars Galaxies: An Empire Divided, Sony Online Entertainment, 2003, LucasArts

Star Wars: Knights of the Old Republic, BioWare Corporation, 2003, LucasArts

Stationfall, Infocom, 1987, Infocom

Stop Disasters, Playerthree, 2007, International Strategy for Disaster Reduction

Storm Across Europe, SSI, 1989, SSI

Street Fighter, Capcom, 1987, Capcom

Stunt Car Racer, Geoff Crammond, 1988, MicroStyle

Sub Battle Simulator, Digital Illusions, 1987, Epyx

Summer Games, Epyx, 1984, US Gold

Summer Games II, Epyx, 1985, Commodore Gaming

Super Cars II, Magnetic Fields, 1991, Gremlins Graphics

Super Mario Bros., Nintendo, 1985, Nintendo

Super Mario Kart, Nintendo, 1992, Nintendo

Super Monkey Ball, Amusement Vision, 2001, Sega

Suspect, Infocom, 1984, Infocom

Sword of Aragon, SSI, 1989, SSI

Syberia, Microïds, 2002, Mycroïds

Tales of the Unknown, Volume I: The Bard's Tale, Interplay, 1985, Electronic
Arts

Tank, Kee Games, 1974, Kee Games

TapDefense, Tapjoy, 2008, Tapjoy

Tap Tap Revenge, Tapulous, 2008, Tapulous

Tekken, Namco, 1994, Namco

Tempest, Atari, 1981, Atari

Test Drive, Distinctive Software Inc., 1987, Accolade

Tetris, Alexey Pajitnov, 1984, Tetris

There.com, There Inc., 2003, There Inc.

Thief: Deadly Shadows, Ion Storm, 2004, Eidos Interactive

Third World Farmer, 3rdWorldFarmer Team, 2014 (latest release), shareware

This War of Mine, 11 Bit Studios, 2014, 11 Bit Studios

The Three Kings Games, Blitz Games, 2006, Burger King

3-D Helicopter Simulator, Sierra Online, 1987, Sierra On-Line

Time Pilot, Konami, 1982, Centuri

Titanic: Adventure Out of Time, Cyberflix, 1996, GTE Entertainment

Tom Clancy's Splinter Cell, Ubisoft, 2002, Ubisoft

Tomb Raider, Core Design, 1996, Eidos Interactive

Tomb Raider II, Core Design, 1997, Eidos Interactive

Top Spin 4, 2K Czech, 2011, 2K Sports

Track & Field, Konami, 1983, Konami

Trials HD, RedLynx, 2009, Microsoft Game Studios

UFO: Enemy Unknown (X-COM: UFO Defense in North America), Mythos Games/MicroProse, 1994, MicroProse

Ultima, Richard Garriott, 1981, California Pacific Computer

Ultima Online, Origin Systems, 1997, Electronic Arts

Ultima Underworld: The Stygian Abyss, Blue Sky Productions, 1992, Origin Systems

Ulysses and the Golden Fleece, Sierra On-Line, 1981, Sierra On-Line

Uncharted: Drake's Fortune, Naughty Dog, 2007, Sony

Uncharted 2: Among Thieves, Naughty Dog, 2009, Sony

Uncharted 3: Drake's Deception, Naughty Dog, 2011, Sony

Uncharted 4: A Thief's End, Naughty Dog, 2016, Sony

Under a Killing Moon, Access Software, 1994, Access Software

Unreal, Epic Games/Digital Extremes, 1998, GT Interactive

Unreal II: The Awakening, Legend Entertainment, 2003, Atari

Unreal Tournament, Epic Games/Digital Extremes, 1999, GT Interactive

Uru: Ages Beyond Myst, Cyan Worlds, 2003, Ubisoft

Vampire: The Masquerade—Redemption, Nihilistic Software, 2000, Activision

VibRibbon, NanaOn-Sha, 1999, Sony

Walking Dead, Telltale Games, 2012, Telltale Games

WarCraft II: Tides of Darkness, Blizzard Entertainment, 1995, Blizzard Entertainment

WarCraft III: Reign of Chaos, Blizzard Entertainment, 2002, Blizzard Entertainment

WarCraft: Orcs and Humans, Blizzard Entertainment, 1994, Blizzard Entertainment

Warhammer 40,000: Dawn of War, Relic Entertainment, 2004, THQ

Warlords, SSG Strategic Studies Group, 1990, SSG Strategic Studies Group

Ways2Sort, Serious Games Interactive, 2019, Serious Games Interactive

Where in the World is Carmen Sandiego? Brøderbund Software, 1985, Brøderbund Software

Wii Sports, Nintendo, 2006, Nintendo

Winter Games, Epyx, 1986, Epyx

The Witcher 3: Wild Hunt, CD Projekt Red, 2015, CD Projekt Red

The Witness, Infocom, 1983, Infocom

Wizardry: Proving Grounds of the Mad Overlord, Sir-Tech Software, 1981, Sir-Tech Software

Wolfenstein 3D, id Software, 1992, Apogee Software

Wonder Boy, Sega, 1986, Sega

World Games, Epyx, 1986, Epyx

World of Tanks, Wargaming, 2010 (Russia), Wargaming

World of Warcraft, Blizzard Entertainment, 2004, Blizzard Entertainment

World Without Oil, Ken Eklund, 2007

Worms, Team17, 1995, Ocean Software

Xevious, Atari, 1982, Atari

XIII, Ubisoft Paris, 2003, Ubisoft

Yie Ar Kung-Fu, Konami, 1984, Konami

Zak McKracken and the Alien Mindbenders, Lucasfilm Games, 1988, Lucasfilm Games

Zaxxon, Sega, 1982, Sega

Zero Wing, Toaplan, 1989, Taito

Zoo Tycoon, Blue Fang Games, 2001, Microsoft Game Studios

Zork: The Great Underground Empire, Infocom, 1980, Infocom

Bibliography

Aarseth, E. (1997). *Cybertext: Perspectives on ergodic literature.* London: Johns Hopkins University Press.

Aarseth, E. (2000). Allegories of space: The question of spatiality in computer games. In M. Eskelinen & R. Koskimaa (Eds.), *Cybertext yearbook 2000.* Jyväskylä: University of Jyväskylä.

Aarseth, E. (2001). Computer game studies, year one. *Game Studies, 1*(1).

Aarseth, E. (2003). Beyond the frontier: Quest computer games as post-narrative discourse. In M.L. Ryan (Ed.), *Narrative across media.* Lincoln: University of Nebraska Press.

Aarseth, E. (2004). Genre trouble: Narrativism and the art of simulation. In N. Wardrip-Fruin & P. Harrigan (Eds.), *First person: New media as story, performance, and game* (p. 48). Cambridge, MA: The MIT Press.

Aarseth, E. (2005). *Doors and perception: Fiction vs. simulation in games.* Paper presented at the Digital Arts and Culture conference, Copenhagen. https://www.researchgate.net/publication/228953402_Doors_and_Perception_Fiction_vs_Simulation_in_Games

Aarseth, E. (2012, May). *A narrative theory of games.* FDG '12 Proceedings of the International Conference on the Foundations of Digital Games. ACM, pp. 129–133.

Aarseth, E., Sunnanå, L., & Smedstad, S.M. (2003, November 4–6). *A multi-dimensional typology of games.* Paper presented at the Level Up—Digital Games Research Conference, Utrecht.

Abt, C. (1968). Games for learning. In E.O. Schild (Ed.), *Simulation games in learning.* London: Sage Publications.

Abt, C. (1970). *Serious games.* New York: The Viking Press.

Ackerman, D. (1998). *Deep play.* New York: Vintage Press.

Adams, E. (2004, July 9). *Postmodernism and the three types of immersion.* Retrieved February 21, 2012, from www.gamasutra.com/features/20040709/adams_01.shtml#

Adams, P. C. (1998). Teaching and learning with SimCity 2000. *Journal of Geography*, *97*(2), 47–55.

Alexander, L. (2014). *"Gamers" don't have to be your audience: "Gamers" are over.* Retrieved February 20, 2015, from www.gamasutra.com/view/news/224400/Gamers_dont_have_to_be_your_audience_Gamers_are_over.php

Allied Market Research. (2018). *Serious games market expected to reach $9,167 million, globally, by 2023.* Retrieved April 16, 2019, from www.alliedmarketresearch.com/press-release/serious-games-market.html

American Psychiatric Association. (2007). *Statement of the American Psychiatric Association on "Video Game Addiction."* Retrieved August 3, 2007, from www.psych.org/news_room/press_releases/07-47videogameaddiction_2_.pdf

American Psychiatric Association. (2015a). *Technical report on the review of the violent video games literature.* Retrieved April 15, 2019, from www.apa.org/pi/families/review-video-games.pdf

American Psychiatric Association. (2015b). *APA review confirms link between playing violent video games and aggression.* Retrieved April 15, 2019, from www.apa.org/news/press/releases/2015/08/violent-video-games

American Psychiatric Association. (2015c). *Resolution on violent video games.* Retrieved April 15, 2019, from www.apa.org/about/policy/violent-video-games

Anderson, C. (2003). *Violent video games: Myths, facts, and unanswered questions.* Retrieved August 9, 2004, from www.apa.org/science/sb-anderson.pdf

Anderson, C. (2004). An update on the effects of playing violent video games. *Journal of Adolescence, 27,* 113–122.

Anderson, C. A., & Bushman, B. J. (2001). Effects of violent video games on aggressive behavior, aggressive cognition, aggressive affect, physiological arousal, and prosocial behavior: A meta-analytic review of the scientific literature. *Psychological Science, 12*(5), 353–359.

Anderson, C. A., & Dill, K. E. (2000). Video games and aggressive thoughts, feelings, and behavior in the laboratory and in life. *Journal of Personality and Social Psychology, 78*(4), 772–791.

Anderson, C., Funk, J., & Griffith, M. (2004). Contemporary issues in adolescent video game playing: Brief overview and introduction to the special issue. *Journal of Adolescence, 27,* 1–3.

Anderson, C., Sakamoto, A., Gentile, D. A., Ihori, N., Shibuya, A., Yukawa, S., . . . Kumiko, K. (2008). Longitudinal effects of violent video games on aggression in Japan and the United States. *Pediatrics, 122*(5).

Anderson, J. (1996). *The reality of illusion: An ecological approach to cognitive film theory.* Carbondale: Southern Illinois University Press.

Apperley, T. (2006). Genre and game studies: Toward a critical approach to video game genres. *Simulation & Gaming, 37*(1), 6–23.

Ars Technica. (2014). *Updated numbers show PS4 with at least 65 percent of two-console market.* Retrieved January 3, 2015, from http://arstechnica.com/gaming/2014/10/updated-numbers-show-ps4-with-at-least-65-percent-of-two-console-market

Ashcraft, B. (2016, December 27). The 31 most important Japanese games ever made. *Kotaku.* Retrieved May 12, 2019, from https://kotaku.com/the-31-most-important-japanese-games-ever-made-1782936854

Atkins, B. (2003). *More than a game: The computer game as a fictional form.* Manchester: Manchester University Press.

Avedon, E. M., & Sutton-Smith, B. (1971). *The study of games.* New York: John Wiley & Sons Inc.

Badham, J. (Director). (1983). *WarGames* (film). USA.

Bandura, A. (1977). *Social learning theory.* Englewood Cliffs, NJ: Prentice-Hall.

Barab, S., Gresalfi, M., & Ingram-Goble, A. (2010). Transformational play: Using games to position person, content, and context. *Educational Researcher, 39*(7), 525–536.

Barab, S., Gresalfi, M., Dodge, T., & Ingram-Goble, A. (2010, January–March). Narratizing disciplines and disciplinizing narratives: Games as 21st century curriculum. *International Journal of Gaming and Computer-Mediated Simulations, 2*(1), 17–30.

Baranowski, T., Blumberg, F., Buday, R., DeSmet, A., Fiellin, L. E., Green, C. S., & Young, K. (2016). Games for health for children-current status and needed research. *Games for Health Journal, 5*(1), 1–12.

Barlett, C. P., & Anderson, C. A. (2012). Examining media effects. *The International Encyclopedia of Media Studies, 5*(1), 4.

Baron, J. (2004). Glory and shame: Powerful psychology in multiplayer online games. In J. Mulligan & B. Patrovsky (Eds.), *Developing online games: An insider's guide.* Boston, MA: New Riders Media.

Bartle, R. (1990). *Interactive multi-user computer games.* London: British Telecom.

Bartle, R. (1996). *Hearts, clubs, diamonds, spades: Players who suit MUDs.* Retrieved November 27, 2003, from www.mud.co.uk/richard/hcds.htm

Bartle, R. (2003). *Designing virtual worlds.* Indianapolis: New Riders.

Bateson, G. (1972). *Steps to an ecology of mind.* Chicago, IL: University of Chicago Press.

Battle.net. (2003, September 30). *StarCraft, Diablo II,* and *Warcraft III accounts closed.* Retrieved November 14, 2003, from www.battle.net/news/0309.shtml

BBC News. (2002). *"Shocking" Xbox advert banned.* Retrieved August 3, 2007, from http://news.bbc.co.uk/2/hi/entertainment/2028725.stm

BBC News. (2003, July 8). Thailand restricts online gamers. *BBC News*. Retrieved February 21, 2012, from http://news.bbc.co.uk/2/hi/technology/3054590.stm

BBC News. (2004). *Police reject game link to murder*. Retrieved August 3, 2007, from http://news.bbc.co.uk/1/hi/england/leicestershire/3538066.stm

BBC News. (2005, July 26). Uproar grows over GTA sex scenes. *BBC News*. Retrieved February 21, 2012, from http://news.bbc.co.uk/2/hi/technology/4717139.stm

Bell, D. (2001). *An introduction to cybercultures*. London: Routledge.

Bellotti, F., Kapralos, B., Lee, K., Moreno-Ger, P., & Berta, R. (2013). Assessment in and of serious games: An overview. *Advances in Human-Computer Interaction, 201*.

Bensley, L., & Van Eenwyk, J. (2001). Video games and real-life aggression: Review of the literature. *Journal of Adolescent Health, 29*(4).

Berkowitz, L. (1984). Some effects of thoughts on the anti- and prosocial influences of media events: A cognitive neoassociationistic analysis. *Psychological Bulletin, 95*, 410–427.

Bloom, B.S., Engelhart, M.D., Furst, E.J., Hill, W.H., & Krathwohl, D.R. (1956). *Taxonomy of educational objectives: The classification of educational goals: Handbook I: Cognitive domain*. New York: David McKay Company.

Bogost, I. (2007). *Persuasive games: The expressive power of videogames*. Boston, MA: The MIT Press.

Bogost, I. (2008). *Unit operations: An approach to videogame criticism*. Boston, MA: The MIT Press.

Bogost, I. (2011a, May 3). Persuasive games: Exploitationware. *Gamasutra*. Retrieved May 13, 2019, from www.gamasutra.com/view/feature/6366/persuasive_games_exploitationware.php

Bogost, I. (2011b). *Gamification is bullshit*. Wharton Gamification Symposium. Retrieved April 28, 2019, from http://bogost.com/writing/blog/gamification_is_bullshit/

Bogost, I., Ferrari, S., & Schweizer, B. (2010). *Newsgames: Journalism at play*. Cambridge, MA: MIT Press.

Book, B. (2003). "These bodies are free, so get one now!" Advertising and branding in social virtual worlds. *Interactive media forum: Identity and cultures in cyberspace*. Miami University in Oxford, Ohio, SSRN.

Bouça, M. (2012, October 3–5). Mobile communication, gamification and ludification. *MindTrek 2012*, Tampere, Finland.

Bourdieu, P. (1987). *Distinction: A social critique of the judgement of taste*. Boston, MA: Harvard University Press.

Boyer, B. (2009). *The running man: Behind the sketchbooks of Adam Saltsman's Canabalt*. Retrieved November 15, 2009, from http://boingboing.net/2009/11/11/the-running-man-behi.html

Bradt, G. (2013). How salesforce and Deloitte tackle employee engagement with gamification. *Forbes*. Retrieved May 5, 2019, from www.forbes.com/sites/georgebradt/2013/07/03/how-salesforce-and-deloitte-tackle-employee-engagement-with-gamification

Bransford, W. (1998). The past was no illusion. In C. Dodsworth (Ed.), *Digital illusion: Entertaining the future with high technology*. Boston, MA: ACM Press, Addison Wesley.

Briceno, H., Chao, W., Glenn, A., Hu, S., Krishnamurthy, A., & Tsuchida, B. (2000). *Down from the top of its game: The story of Infocom, Inc.* Cambridge, MA: The MIT Press.

Bringsjord, S. (2001). Is it possible to build dramatically compelling interactive digital entertainment (in the form, e.g., of computer games)? *Game Studies*, *1*(1).

Brody, H. (1993). Video games that teach? *Technology Review*, *96*(8), 51–57.

Brunborg, G. S., Mentzoni, R. A., & Frøyland, L. R. (2014). Is video gaming, or video game addiction, associated with depression, academic achievement, heavy episodic drinking, or conduct problems? *Journal of Behavioral Addictions*, *3*(1), 27–32.

Bryce, J., & Rutter, J. (2002). Killing like a girl: Gendered gaming and girl gamers' visibility. In F. Mayrä (Ed.), *CGDC conference proceedings* (pp. 243–255). Tampere, Finland: Tampere University Press.

Buckingham, D. (2000). *After the death of childhood: Growing up in the age of electronic media*. London: Polity Press.

Buckingham, D. (2001). Electronic child abuse? Rethinking the media's effects on children. In M. Barker & J. Petley (Eds.), *Ill effects: The media/violence debate*. London: Routledge.

Buckingham, D., & Scanlon, M. (2002). *Education, edutainment, and learning in the home*. Cambridge: Open University Press.

Buckingham, D., Carr, D., Burn, A., & Schott, G. (2005). *Videogames: Text, narrative, play*. Cambridge: Polity Press.

Burgess, M., Dill-Shackleford, K., Stermer, P., Brown, B., & Brown, P. (2011, September). Playing with prejudice: The prevalence and consequences of racial stereotypes in video games. *Media Psychology*, *14*(3), 289–311.

Burnham, V. (2001). *Supercade: A visual history of the videogame age 1971–1984*. Cambridge, MA: MIT Press.

Burnham, V. (2003). Television gaming apparatus. In *Supercade: A visual history of the videogame age 1971–1984* (pp. 52–55). Cambridge, MA: The MIT Press.

Bushman, B. J. (2002). Does venting anger feed or extinguish the flame? Catharsis, rumination, distraction, anger, and aggressive responding. *Personality and Social Psychology Bulletin*, *28*.

Bushman, B. J., Baumeister, R. F., & Stack, A. D. (1999). Catharsis, aggression, and persuasive influence: Self-fulfilling or self-defeating prophecies? *Journal of Personality and Social Psychology*, *76*(3), 367–376.

Caillois, R. (2001, first published 1958). *Man, play and games*. Urbana: University of Illinois Press.

Callaghan, N. (2016). Investigating the role of Minecraft in educational learning environments. *Educational Media International, 53*(4), 244–260.

Calleja, G. (2011). *In-game: From immersion to incorporation*. Boston, MA: The MIT Press.

Calvert, S. L. (1999). *Children's journeys through the information age*. Boston, MA: McGraw-Hill.

Carr, D. (2002). Playing with Lara. In T. Krzywinska (Ed.), *ScreenPlay: Cinema/videogames/interfaces*. London: Wallflower Press.

Cashmore, P. (2010). *FarmVille surpasses 80 million users*. Retrieved February 20, 2010, from http://mashable.com/2010/02/20/farmville-80-million-users/

Cassell, J., & Jenkins, H. (1998). *From Barbie to Mortal Kombat: Gender and computer games*. Cambridge, MA: The MIT Press.

Castronova, E. (2001). Virtual worlds: A first-hand account of market and society on the cyberian frontier. *The Gruter Institute Working Papers on Law, Economics and Evolutionary Biology, 2*(1), 1–68.

Castronova, E. (2004, August 3). *Virtual world economy: It's Namibia, basically*. Retrieved February 21, 2012, from http://terranova.blogs.com/terra_nova/2004/08/virtual_world_e.html

Cavallari, J., Hedberg, J., & Harper, B. (1992). Adventure games in education: A review. *Australian Journal of Educational Technology, 8*(2), 172–184.

CBS. (2002, October 18). Addicted: Suicide over Everquest? *CBS News*. Retrieved February 21, 2012, from www.cbsnews.com/stories/2002/10/17/48hours/main525965.shtml

Chandler, D. (1995). *Cultivation theory*. Retrieved January 20, 2004, from www.aber.ac.uk/media/Documents/short/cultiv.html

Chaplin, H. (2011, March 29). I don't want to be a superhero: Ditching reality for a game isn't as fun as it sounds. *Slate*. Retrieved June 2019, from https://slate.com/technology/2011/03/gamification-ditching-reality-for-a-game-isn-t-as-fun-as-it-sounds.htm

Chatfield, T. (2010, July). 7 ways games reward the brain. *TED Talk Global*. Retrieved May 5, 2019, from www.ted.com/talks/tom_chatfield_7_ways_games_reward_the_brain

Chee, F., & Smith, R. (2003). *Is electronic community an addictive substance?* Paper presented at the Level Up—Digital Games Research Conference, Utrecht.

Chen, B. X. (2009). *Coder's half-million-dollar baby proves iPhone gold rush is still on*. Retrieved February 12, 2009, from www.wired.com/gadgetlab/2009/02/shoot-is-iphone/all/1

Cheung, M., Li, R., & Zapart, T. (2006). Computer-based edutainment for children aged 3 to 5 years old. In M. Khosrow-Po (Eds.), *Emerging Trends and Challenges in Information Technology Management, 1*(2).

Çiftci, S. (2018). Trends of serious games research from 2007 to 2017: Trends of serious games research from 2007 to 2017. *Journal of Education and Training Studies, 6*(2).

Cipollone, M., Schifter, C., & Moffat, R. A. (2014). Minecraft as a creative tool: A case study. *International Journal of Game-Based Learning, 4*(2), 1–14.

Clark, D. B., Tanner-Smith, E. E., & Killingsworth, S. (2013, May). *Digital games for learning: A systematic review and meta-analysis.* Menlo Park: SRI International.

Clegg, A. A. (1991). Games and simulations in social studies education. In J. P. Shaver (Ed.), *Handbook of research on social studies teaching and learning.* New York: Macmillan.

Computer Industry Almanac. (2003). *Worldwide cumulative PC sales exceed 1 billion: PCs-in-use tops 200M in USA. Cumulative PC sales surpass 400M.* Retrieved February 21, 2012, from www.c-i-a.com/pr0203.htm

Connolly, T., Boyle, E., MacArthur, E., Hainey, T., & Boyle, J. (2012). A systematic literature review of empirical evidence on computer games and serious games. *Computers & Education, 59,* 661–686.

Consalvo, M. (2003). It's no videogame: News commentary and the second Gulf war. In M. Copier (Ed.), *Proceedings of Level Up conference.* Utrecht: University of Utrecht Press.

Consalvo, M. (2007). *Cheating: Gaining advantage in videogames.* Boston, MA: The MIT Press.

Consalvo, M. (2009). There is no magic circle. *Games and Culture, 4*(4), 408–417.

Consolazio, D. (2018, October 18). The history of esports. *Hotspawn.* Retrieved May 12, 2019, from www.hotspawn.com/the-history-of-esports/

Cooper, J., & Mackie, D. (1986). Video games and aggression in children. *Journal of Applied Social Psychology, 16*(8), 726–744.

Cotton, K. (1991). *Computer-assisted instruction (No. 10). The school improvement research series.* Portland: School Improvement Program of the Northwest Regional Educational Laboratory.

Craig, A., Nobuko, I., Bushman, B. J., Rothstein, H. R., Shibuya, A., Swing, E. L., . . . Saleem, M. (2010). Violent video game effects on aggression, empathy, and prosocial behavior in Eastern and Western countries: A meta-analytic review. *Psychological Bulletin, 136*(2), 151–173.

Crawford, C. (1982). *The art of computer game design.* Berkeley, CA: McGraw-Hill.

Crawford, C. (2003). *Chris Crawford on game design.* Boston, MA: New Riders.

Crossley, R. (2010). *Study: Average dev costs as high as $28m.* Retrieved January 11, 2010, from www.develop-online.net/news/33625/Study-Average-dev-cost-as-high-as-28m

Csikszentmihalyi, M. (1990). *Flow: The psychology of optimal experience.* New York: Harper Perennial.

Cunningham, S., Engelstätter, B., & Ward, M. (2016). Violent video games and violent crime. *Southern Economic Association, 8*(4).

de Freitas, S. (2018). Are games effective learning tools? A review of educational games. *Educational Technology & Society, 21*(2), 74–84.

Delwiche, A. (2007). From the Green Berets to America's army: Video-games as a vehicle for political propaganda. In P. Williams & J.H. Smith (Eds.), *The players' realm: Studies on the culture of video games and gaming.* Jefferson, NC: McFarland.

DeMaria, R., & Wilson, J.L. (2002). *High score! The illustrated history of electronic games.* New York: McGraw-Hill, Osborne.

Deterding, S. (2011, January). Meaningful play: Getting gamification right. *Google Tech Talk* [Video]. Retrieved February 21, 2012, from www.youtube.com/watch?v=7ZGCPap7GkY

Deterding, S. (2013). Eudaimonic design, or: Six invitations to rethink gamification. (2013). In M. Fuchs, S. Fizek, P. Ruffino, & N. Schrape (Eds.), *Rethinking gamification* (pp. 305–321). Lüneburg: Meson Press. Retrieved from http://meson.press/books/rethinking-gamification

Deterding, S., Dixon, D., Khaled, R., & Nacke, L. (2011). *From game design elements to gamefulness: Defining "gamification."* MindTrek 2011. Proceedings of the 15th International Academic MindTrek Conference: Envisioning Future Media Environments. New York: ACM.

Deterding, S., Sicart, M., Nacke, L., O'Hara, K., & Dixon, D. (2011, May 7–12). *Gamification: Using game design elements in non-gaming contexts.* CHI 2011, Workshop, Vancouver, Canada.

Diamond, J. (1997). *Guns, germs, and steel: The fates of human societies.* New York: Norton & Company.

Dibbell, J. (2003, December). The unreal estate boom. *Wired.* Retrieved February 21, 2012, from www.wired.com/wired/archive/11.01/gaming.html

Dibbell, J. (2006). *Play money: Or, how I quit my day job and made millions trading virtual loot.* New York: Basic Books.

Dietz, T. (1998). An examination of violence and gender role portrayals in video games: Implications for gender socialization and aggressive behavior. *Sex Roles: A Journal of Research, 38*, 425–442.

Dignan, A. (2011). *Game frame: Unlocking the power of game dynamics in business and in life.* New York: The Free Press.

Dill, K.E., & Dill, J.C. (1998). Video games violence: A review of the empirical literature. *Aggression and Violent Behavior: A Review Journal, 3*(4), 407–428.

Dill, K.E., Gentile, D.A., Richter, W.A., & Dill, J.C. (2005). Violence, sex, race and age in popular video games: A content analysis. In D.J. Henderson (Ed.), *Featuring females: Feminist analyses of the media.* Washington, DC: American Psychological Association.

Donovan, T. (2010). *Replay: The history of video games.* East Sussex: Yellow Ant.

Dorval, M., & Pepin, M. (1986). Effect of playing a video game on a measure of spatial visualization. *Perceptual Motor Skills, 62*(1), 159–162.

Douglas, J.Y. (1992). *Print pathways and interactive Labyrinths: How hypertext narratives affect the act of reading* (PhD thesis), New York University, New York.

Drachen, A., & Canossa, A. (2009). Towards gameplay analysis via gameplay metrics. In *Proceedings of the 13th MindTrek 2009* (pp. 202–209). Tampere, Finland: ACM-SIGCHI Publishers.

Drachen, A., & Smith, J.H. (2008). Player talk—the functions of communication in multi-player role playing games. *ACM Computers in Entertainment, 6*(4).

Dredge, S. (2014). Facebook closes its $2bn Oculus Rift acquisition. What next? Retrieved 21st July 2018, https://www.theguardian.com/technology/2014/jul/22/facebook-oculus-rift-acquisition-virtual-reality

Ducheneaut, N., & Moore, R.J. (2004, November 6–10). *The social side of gaming: A study of interaction patterns in a massively multiplayer online game.* Paper presented at the CSCW2004, Chicago, IL.

Ducheneaut, N., Moore, R.J., & Nickell, E. (2004). *Designing for sociability in massively multiplayer games: An examination of the "Third Places" of SWG.* Paper presented at the Other Players Conference, IT University of Copenhagen, Copenhagen.

Durkin, K., & Barber, B. (2002). Not so doomed: Computer game play and positive adolescent development. *Applied Development Psychology, 23*(4), 373–392.

Dyer, R. (2002). *Only entertainment* (2nd ed.). New York: Routledge.

Egenfeldt-Nielsen, S. (2003). *Keep the monkey rolling: Eye—hand coordination in super monkey ball.* Paper presented at the Level Up—Digital Games Research Conference, Utrecht.

Egenfeldt-Nielsen, S. (2005). *Beyond edutainment: Exploring the educational potential of computer games* (PhD thesis), IT University of Copenhagen, Copenhagen.

Egenfeldt-Nielsen, S. (2006, May 3). *Case study of global conflicts.* Paper presented at the Games@IULM Conference, Milan.

Egenfeldt-Nielsen, S. (2007). *Educational potential of computer games.* New York: Continuum International Publishing Group.

Egenfeldt-Nielsen, S. (2011, February). What makes a good learning game? Going beyond edutainment. *eLearn Magazine.* ACM. Retrieved May 11, 2019, from https://elearnmag.acm.org/archive.cfm?aid=1943210

Ekaputra, G., Lim, C., & Kho, I. (2014). *Minecraft: A game as an education and scientific learning tool*. Conference, The Information Systems International Conference (ISICO) 2013, Bali, Indonesia.

Eladhari, M. (2003, May 2). *Trends in MMOG development*. Retrieved January 14, 2004, from www.game-research.com/art_trends_in_mmog.asp

Elson, M., & Ferguson, C.J. (2014). Twenty-five years of research on violence in digital games and aggression: Empirical evidence, perspectives, and a debate gone astray. *European Psychologist, 19*(1), 33–46.

ELSPA. (2002). *Screen digest: Interactive leisure software report 4th edition*. Retrieved March 21, 2004, from www.elspa.com/serv/screendigestintro.asp

ELSPA. (2003). *The cultural life of computer and video games: A cross industry study*. Retrieved May 2004, from www.elspa.com

Emery, G. (2002). What's in a name: Product placement in games. *USA Today*. Retrieved February 21, 2012, from www.usatoday.com/tech/techreviews/games/2002/1/30/spotlight.htm

Emes, C. (1997). Is Mr. Pac man eating our children? A review of the effect of video games on children. *The Canadian Journal of Psychiatry, 42*(4), 409–414.

Erard, M. (2004). In these games, the points are all political. *New York Times*. Retrieved June 29, 2019, from https://www.nytimes.com/2004/07/01/technology/in-these-games-the-points-are-all-political.html

Erickson, T. (1997). Social interaction on the net: Virtual community as participatory genre. In J.F.J. Nunamaker & R.H.J. Sprague (Eds.), *IEEE 13th proceedings* (Vol. 6). Los Alamitos, CA: IEEE Computer Society Press.

Ermi, L., & Mäyrä, F. (2003). Power and control of games: Children as the actors of game cultures. In J. Raessens (Ed.), *Digital games research conference*. Utrecht: Utrecht University.

Ermi, L., & Mäyrä, F. (2005). Fundamental components of the gameplay experience: Analysing immersion. In S. Castell & J. Jenson (Eds.), *Selected papers of the digital games research association's second international conference*. Vancouver: Simon Fraser University.

ESA. (2004). *Essential facts about the computer and video game industry 2004*. Washington, DC: The Interactive Digital Software Association.

Eskelinen, M. (2001). The gaming situation. *Game Studies, 1*(1).

ESRB. (undated). *Who decides which rating a game should get?* Retrieved October 5, 2011, from www.esrb.org/ratings/faq.jsp#14

Estallo, J.A. (1995). *Los Videojuegos. Juicios y Prejuicios*. Barcelona: Planeta.

Evans, A. (2001). *This virtual life: Escapism and simulation in our media world*. London: Vision.

Faber, L. (1998). *Re:play*. London: Lawrence King Publishing.

Facer, K., Furlong, J., Furlong, R., & Sutherland, R. (2003). "Edutainment" software: A site for cultures in conflict. In R. Sutherland, G. Claxton, & A. Pollard (Eds.), *Learning and teaching where worldviews meet*. London: Trentham Books.

Fagen, R. (1995). Animal play, games of angels, biology and Brian. In A.D. Pellegrini (Ed.), *The future of play theory: A multidisciplinary inquiry into the contributions of Brian Sutton-Smith*. Albany: State University of New York Press.

Farokhmanesh, M. (2014, July). The most progressive game of the summer is the one you're probably not playing. *Polygon*. Retrieved April 29, 2014, from www.polygon.com/2014/7/24/5930655/kim-kardashian-game-progressive?utm_source=Gaming+Insiders+Weekly&utm_campaign=d7f6c1d2a2-Weekly_July_23rd_2014&utm_medium=email&utm_term=0_27af250667-d7f6c1d2a2-114968729

Ferguson, C.J. (2007). Evidence for publication bias in video game violence effects literature: A meta-analytic review. *Aggression and Violent Behavior, 12*, 470–482.

Ferguson, C.J. (2009). Media violence effects: Confirmed truth or just another x-file? *Journal of Forensic Psychology Practice, 9*(2), 103–126.

Ferguson, C.J. (2010a). Blazing angels or resident evil? Can violent video games be a force for good? *Review of General Psychology, 14*(2), 68–81.

Ferguson, C.J. (2010b). Children's motivations for video game play in the context of normal development. *Review of General Psychology, 14*(2), 180–187.

Ferguson, C.J. (2015). Does movie or video game violence predict societal violence? It depends on what you look at and when. *Journal of Communication, 65*(1), 193–212.

Ferguson, C.J., Miguel, C. S., Garza, A., & Jerabeck, J.M. (2012, February). A longitudinal test of video game violence influences on dating and aggression: A 3-year longitudinal study of adolescents. *Journal of Psychiatric Research, 46*(2), 141–146.

Ferguson, C., Klisinan, D., Hogg, J., Wilson, J., Markey, P., Przybylski, A., Elson, M., Ivory, J., Linebarger, D., Gregerson, M. M Farley, F. & Siddiqui, S. (2017, June 12). News media, public education and public policy committee. *The Amplifier Magazine*. Retrieved June 29, 2019, from https://div46amplifier.com/2017/06/12/news-media-public-education-and-public-policy-committee/

Fernández-Vara, C. (2011). *Game spaces speak volumes: Indexical storytelling*. Proceedings of DiGRA 2011 Conference: Think Design Play. Tampere: DiGRA.

Fernández-Vara, C. (2019). *Introduction to game analysis* (2nd ed.). London: Routledge.

Feshbach, S., & Singer, R. (1971). *Television and aggression*. San Francisco, CA: Jossey-Bass.

Fine, G.A. (1982/2002). *Shared fantasy: Role-playing games as social worlds*. Chicago, IL: University of Chicago Press.

Flanagan, M. (1999). Mobile identities, digital stars and post-cinematic selves. *Wide Angle: Issue on Digitality and the Memory of Cinema, 21*(3), 77–93.

Flanagan, M. (2003). Une Maison de Poupée Virtuelle Capitaliste? The Sims: Domesticité, Consommation, et Féminité. In D. Desjeux (Ed.), *Consommations et Sociétés: Cahiers Pluridisciplinaire sur la Consommation et l'Interculturel.* Paris: L'Harmattan.

Flanagan, M. (2009). *Critical play: Radical game design.* Boston, MA: The MIT Press.

Foo, C. Y., & Koivisto, E.M.I. (2004). *Defining grief play in MMORPGs: Player and developer perceptions.* Paper presented at the International Conference on Advances in Computer Entertainment Technology (ACE 2004), Singapore.

Forbes. (2014). *Facebook buys Oculus, virtual reality gaming startup, for $2 billion.* Retrieved January 3, 2015, from www.forbes.com/sites/briansolomon/2014/03/25/facebook-buys-oculus-virtual-reality-gaming-startup-for-2-billion/

Frasca, G. (1999). *Ludology meets narratology: Similitude and differences between (Video)games and narrative.* Retrieved March 29, 2004, from www.jacaranda.org/frasca/ludology.htm

Frasca, G. (2001a). *Videogames of the oppressed: Videogames as a means for critical thinking and debate* (Unpublished Master's thesis), Georgia Institute of Technology, Atlanta, GA.

Frasca, G. (2001b). *What is ludology? A provisory definition.* Retrieved March 29, 2003, from http://ludology.org/article.php?story=20010708201200000

Frasca, G. (2003a). *Ideological videogames: Press left button to dissent.* Retrieved August 9, 2004, from www.igda.org/columns/ivorytower/ivory_Nov03.php

Frasca, G. (2003b, November 4–6). *Ludologists love stories, too: Notes from a debate that never took place.* Paper presented at the Level Up—Digital Games Research Conference, Utrecht.

Frasca, G. (2007). *Play the message: Play, game and videogame rhetoric* (PhD thesis), IT University of Copenhagen, Copenhagen.

Frauenheim, E. (2004). No fun for game developers? *C-Net.* Retrieved November 11, 2004, from http://news.cnet.com/8301-10784_3-5449296-7.html

Freedman, J. L. (2001, October 26–27). *Evaluating the research on violent video games.* Paper presented at the Playing by the Rules Conference, Chicago, IL.

Freeman, G., & Wohn, D. (2017, May). *eSports as an emerging research context at CHI: Diverse perspectives on definitions.* CHI EA '17 Proceedings of the 2017 CHI Conference Extended Abstracts on Human Factors in Computing Systems. ACM, pp. 1601–1608.

Freeman, M., & Rampazzo Gambarato, R· (2018). *The Routledge companion to transmedia studies.* New York: Routledge.

Friedman, T. (1995). *Making sense of software: Computer games and interactive textuality.* Retrieved February 8, 2004, from www.duke.edu/~tlove/simcity.htm

Fuchs, M. (2014). Predigital precursors of gamification. In M. Fuchs, S. Fizek, P. Ruffino, & N. Schrape (Eds.), *Rethinking gamification* (pp. 119–140). Lüneburg: Meson Press. Retrieved from http://meson.press/books/rethinking-gamification

Funk, J. B., Baldacci, H. B., Pasold, T., & Baumgardner, J. (2004). Violence exposure in real-life, video games, television, movies, and the internet: Is there desensitization? *Journal of Adolescence, 27*(1), 23–39.

Funk, J., & Buchman, D. (1995). Video game controversies. *Paediatric Annals, 24*(2), 91–94.

Gagne, K. A. (2001). *Moral panics over youth culture and video games.* Unpublished Major Qualifying Project Report, Worcester Polytechnic Institute.

Gagnon, D. (1985). Videogames and spatial skills: An exploratory study. *Educational Communications and Technology Journal, 33*(4), 263–275.

GAMEINFORMER. (2006). The ratings game: The controversy over the ESRB. *GAMEINFORMER.* Retrieved August 3, 2007, from www.gameinformer.com/News/Story/200610/N06.1004.1635.57594.htm?Page=1

Games Press. (2005). Hearts of iron II. *GamesIndustry.biz.* Retrieved August 3, 2007, from www.gamesindustry.biz/content_page.php?aid=6159

GameSpot. (2006). *FTC hot coffee ruling scalds, but doesn't burn take-two.* Retrieved December 11, 2006, from www.gamespot.com/news/6152490.html

GameSpy.com. (2003). *25 most overrated games of all time.* Retrieved July 17, 2007, from http://archive.gamespy.com/articles/september03/25overrated/index.shtml

Garcia, D. (2018). *Gamification in marketing: 16 gamification gurus share their favorite examples & insights.* Retrieved May 4, 2019, from https://surveyanyplace.com/gamification-in-marketing-16-experts/

Gard, T. (2000, June). Building character. *Gamasutra.* Retrieved July 20, 2001, from www.gamasutra.com/features/20000720/gard_pvf.htm

Gardner, P. (2001). Games with a day job: Putting the power of games to work. *Gamasutra.* Retrieved June 1, 2001, from www.gamasutra.com/features/20010601/gardner_02.htm

Gartner. (2011). *Gartner says by 2015, more than 50 percent of organizations that manage innovation processes will gamify those processes.* Gartner press release. Retrieved February 17, 2012, from www.gartner.com/it/page.jsp?id=1629214

Gauntlett, D. (2001). The worrying influence of "media effects" studies. In J. Petley (Ed.), *Ill effects: The media/violence debate.* London: Routledge.

Gee, J. P. (2003). *What video games have to teach us about learning and literacy.* New York: Palgrave Macmillan.

Geen, R. G. (2001). *Human aggression* (2nd ed.). Buckingham: Open University Press.

Gentile, D. (2009). Pathological video-game use among youth ages 8 to 18: A national study. *Psychological Science, 20*(5), 594–602.

Gentile, D. A., Choo, H., Liau, A., Sim, T., Li, D., Fung, D., & Khoo, A. (2011). Pathological video game use among youths: A two-year longitudinal study. *Pediatrics, 127*(2).

Gentile, D. A., Lynch, P. J., Linder, J. R., & Walsh, D. A. (2004). The effects of violent video game habits on adolescent hostility, aggressive behaviors, and school performance. *Journal of Adolescence, 27*(1), 5–22.

Gerbner, G. (1973). Cultural indicators: The third voice. In G. Gerbner, L. P. Gross, & W. H. Melody (Eds.), *Communications technology and social policy*. New York: Wiley.

Gibb, G., Bailey, J., Lambirth, T., & Wilson, W. (1983). Personality differences between high and low electronic video game users. *The Journal of Psychology, 114*, 159–165.

Global e-Sports Report. (2019). *Newzoo*. Retrieved April 14, 2019, from https://newzoo.com/insights/articles/newzoo-global-esports-economy-will-top-1-billion-for-the-first-time-in-2019.

Global Games Market Report. (2018, December). *Newzoo*. Retrieved April 27, 2019, from https://newzoo.com/insights/rankings/top-25-companies-game-revenues/

Gluck, C. (2002, November 22). South Korea's gaming addicts. *BBC News*. Retrieved February 21, 2012, from http://news.bbc.co.uk/2/hi/asia-pacific/2499957.stm

Goldstein, J. (2001, October 27). *Does playing violent video games cause aggressive behavior?* Paper presented at the Playing by the Rules Conference, Chicago, IL.

Good, O., & McWhertor, M. (2011, July). Oslo terrorist used *modern Warfare 2* as training-simulation. *World of Warcraft* as cover. *Kotaku*. Retrieved October 6, 2011, from http://kotaku.com/5824147/oslo-terrorist-anders-behring-breivik-used-modern-warfare-2-as-training+simulation-world-of-warcraft-as-cover

Good, T. L., & Brophy, J. E. (1990). *Educational psychology: A realistic approach* (4th ed.). New York: Longman.

Goodwins, R., & Loney, M. (2002, September 3). In Greece, use a Gameboy, go to jail. *CNET News.com*. Retrieved February 21, 2012, from www.zdnet.co.uk/news/desktop-hardware/2002/09/03/gamers-face-jail-in-greece-2121692

Graetz, J. M. (1981). The origin of *Spacewar! Creative Computing, 8*. Retrieved July 24, 2019, https://www.masswerk.at/spacewar/SpacewarOrigin.html

Green, C. S., & Bavelier, D. (2003). Action video game modifies visual selective attention. *Nature, 423*, 534–537.

Greenblat, C., & Duke, R. E. (1981). *Gaming-simulation: Rationale applications*. London: Sage Publications.

Greenfield, P. (1984). *Mind and media: The effects of television, video games, and computers*. Cambridge, MA: Harvard University Press.

Greenfield, P.M., Brannon, C., & Lohr, D. (1996). Two-dimensional representations of movement through three-dimensional space: The role of video game experience. In P.M. Greenfield & R.R. Cocking (Eds.), *Interacting with video* (pp. 169–185). New Jersey: Ablex Publishing.

Grieb, M. (2002). Run Lara Run. In G. King & T. Krzywinska (Eds.), *ScreenPlay: Cinema/videogames/interfaces*. London: Wallflower Press.

Griffith, J.L., Voloschin, P., Gibb, G.D., & Bailey, J.R. (1983). Differences in eye—hand motor coordination of video-game users and non-users. *Perceptual Motor Skills, 57*, 155–158.

Griffiths, M. (2005). Video games and health. *British Medical Journal, 331*, 122–123.

Griffiths, M.D. (1997). Computer game playing in early adolescence. *Youth and Society, 29*(2), 223–237.

Griffiths, M.D. (1999). Violent video games and aggression: A review of the literature. *Aggression and Violent Behavior, 4*(2), 283–290.

Griffiths, M.D., & Davies, M.N.O. (2005). Videogame addiction: Does it exist? In J. Raessens (Ed.), *Handbook of computer game studies* (pp. 359–373). Boston, MA: MIT Press.

Griffiths, M.D., & Hunt, N. (1998). Dependence on computer games by adolescents. *Psychological Reports, 82*(2), 475–480.

Grossman, D., & DeGaetano, G. (1999). *Stop teaching our kids to kill: A call to action against TV, movie and video game violence*. New York: Crown Books.

Grundy, S. (1991). A computer adventure as a worthwhile educational experience. *Interchange, 22*(4), 41–55.

Hämäläinen, P. (2002). *3D sound rendering and cinematic sound in computer games*. HUT, Telecommunications Software and Multimedia Laboratory.

Hancock, C., & Osterweil, S. (1996). Zoombinis and the art of mathematical play. *Hands On!, 19*(1).

Hanghøj, T., & Brund, C.E. (2011). Teacher roles and positionings in relation to educational games. In S. Egenfeldt-Nielsen, B. Holm Sørensen, & B. Meyer (Eds.), *Serious games in education: In a global perspective*. Aarhus: Aarhus University Press.

Hanus, M.D. & Fox, J. (2015). Assessing the effects of gamification in the classroom: A longitudinal study on intrinsic motivation, social comparison, satisfaction, effort, and academic performance. *Computers & Education 80*, 152–161.

Harmon, A. (2004, January 15). A real-life debate on free expression in a cyberspace city. *New York Times*. Retrieved June 29, 2019, from https://www.nytimes.com/2004/01/15/business/technology-a-real-life-debate-on-free-expression-in-a-cyberspace-city.html

Harris, J. (2001). *The effects of computer games on young children: A review of the research*. RDS Occasional Paper No. 72. London: Home Office.

Hasbro. (2006). *History of the monopoly game.* Retrieved July 9, 2007, from www.hasbro.com/monopoly/default.cfm?page=history

Hawkins, M. (2005). *Go to synesthesia. . . Jake Kazdal's journey through the heart of Rez.* Retrieved June 19, 2007, from www.gamasutra.com/features/20050506/hawkins_01.shtml

Healy, J. M. (1999). *Failure to connect: How computers affect our children's minds.* New York: Touchstone.

Heins, M., Fowles, J., Giroux, H., Goldstein, J., Horwitz, R., Jenkins, H., . . . Greene, D. (2001). *Re: AAP's new policy on media violence.* Retrieved January 20, 2004, from www.fepproject.org/news/aapviolenceltr.html

Herring, R. (1984). *Educational computer games.* Retrieved August 3, 2007, from www.cyberroach.com/analog/an19/edu_games.htm

Herz, J. C. (1997). *Joystick nation: How videogames gobbled our money, won our hearts, and rewired our minds.* London: Abacus.

Hjorth, L. (2011). *Games and gaming: An introduction to new media.* London: Berg.

Holden, S. (2002, March 15). They may be high-tech, but they're still the undead. *New York Times.* Retrieved June 29, 2019, from https://www.nytimes.com/2002/03/15/movies/film-review-they-may-be-high-tech-but-they-re-still-the-undead.html

Holland, J. H. (1998). *Emergence: From chaos to order.* Reading, MA: Addison-Wesley.

Howard, J. (2008). *Quests: Design, theory and history in games and narratives.* Wellesley: A. K. Peters.

Hughes, L. A. (1999). Children's games and gaming. In B. Sutton-Smith, J. Mechling, T. W. Johnson, & F. R. McMahon (Eds.), *Children's folklore.* Logan, UT: Utah State University Press.

Huizinga, J. (2000, first published 1938). *Homo Ludens: A study of the play-element in culture.* London: Routledge.

Hunicke, R., LeBlanc, M., & Zubek, R. (2004). *MDA: A formal approach to game design and game research.* Retrieved August 9, 2004, from www.cs.northwestern.edu/~hunicke/pubs/MDA.pdf

Hunt, L. (2002). "I Know Kung Fu!" The martial arts in the age of digital reproduction. In T. Krzywinska (Ed.), *ScreenPlay: Cinema/videogames/interfaces.* London: Wallflower Press.

Hunter, W. (2000). *The dot eaters—video game history 101.* Retrieved November 23, 2003, from www.emuunlim.com/doteaters/

IDATE. (2004). *Video games: NextGen gaming—on its way and here to stay.* Paris: IDATE.

IDATE. (2010). *Serious games* (2nd ed.). Paris: IDATE.

IDATE. (2014). *Infographics, game summit by digiworld*. Paris: IDATE.

IDATE. (2015, January). *Video games analysis, custom data run*. Paris: IDATE.

IDATE. (2018). *Statistics*. Paris: IDATE.

IDSA. (2003). *Essential facts about the computer and video game industry*. Washington, DC: Interactive Digital Software Association.

IGDA. (undated). *Quality of life*. Retrieved October 13, 2011, from www.igda.org/qol

Iser, W. (1979). *The act of reading: A theory of aesthetic response*. London: The Johns Hopkins University Press.

Iosup, A. & Epema, D. (2014). An Experience Report on Using Gamification in Technical Higher Education. SIGCSE '14 Proceedings of the 45th ACM technical symposium on Computer science education, pp 27–32.

Ivory, J. D. (2001, August). *Video games and the elusive search for their effects on children: An assessment of twenty years of research*. Paper presented at the Association for Education in Journalism and Mass Communication's Annual Convention, Washington, DC.

Jakobsson, M., & Taylor, T. L. (2003). The Sopranos meets Everquest: Social networking in massively multiplayer online games. *FineArt Forum, 17*(8).

Jamison, P. (2010). *FarmVillains*. Retrieved September 8, 2010, from www.sfweekly.com/2010-09-08/news/farmvillains/

Jansz, J., & Martins, R. (2003). The representation of gender and ethnicity in digital interactive games. In J. Raessens (Ed.), *Level up: Digital games research conference proceedings*. Utrecht: Utrecht University Press.

Järvinen, A. (2002). *Gran Stylissimo: The audiovisual elements and styles in computer and video games*. Paper presented at the Computer Games and Digital Cultures Conference, Tampere, Finland.

Järvinen, A. (2008). *Games without frontiers: Theories and methods for game studies and design*. Tampere, Finland: Tampere University Press.

Jenkins, H. (1992). *Textual poachers: Television fans and participatory culture*. New York: Routledge.

Jenkins, H. (2000). *Lessons from Littleton—what congress doesn't want to hear about youth and media*. Retrieved January 13, 2004, from www.nais.org/pubs/ismag.cfm?file_id=1267&ismag_id=14

Jenkins, H. (2001). *From Barbie to Mortal Kombat: Further reflections*. Retrieved May 2004, from http://culturalpolicy.uchicago.edu/conf2001/papers/jenkins.html

Jenkins, H. (2003). Transmedia storytelling. *MIT Technology Review*. Retrieved May 10, 2019, from www.technologyreview.com/s/401760/transmedia-storytelling/

Jenkins, H. (2003a). Game design as narrative architecture. In N. Wardrip-Fruin & P. Harrigan (Eds.), *First person: New media as story, performance, and game*. Cambridge, MA: MIT Press.

Jenkins, H. (2003b, January 15). "Transmedia storytelling" in the "digital renaissance." In *Technology Review*. Boston, MA: The MIT Press.

Jenkins, H. (2005). Games, the new lively art. In J. Raessens & J. Goldstein (Eds.), *Handbook of computer game studies*. Cambridge, MA: The MIT Press.

Jenkins, H. (2007, April 24). *A few thoughts on media violence* . . . Retrieved from http://henryjenkins.org/blog/2007/04/a_few_thoughts_on_media_violen.html

Jensen, J. F. (1997). *"Interactivity": Tracking a new concept in media and communication studies*. Paper presented at the XIII Nordic Conference on Mass Communication Research, Jyväskylä, Finland.

Jenson, J., & Castell, S. de (2010). Gender, simulation, and gaming: Research review and redirections. *Simulation Gaming, 41*, 51.

Jessen, C. (1995). Children's computer culture. *Dansk Paedagogisk Tidsskrift, 5*.

Jessen, C. (1998). *Interpretive communities: The reception of computer games by children and the young*. Retrieved August 9, 2004, from www.carsten-jessen.dk/intercom.html

Jessen, C. (2001). *Børn, leg og computerspil*. Odense: Odense Universitetsforlag.

Jillian, J. D., Upitis, R., Koch, C., & Young, J. (1999). The story of phoenix quest: How girls respond to a prototype language and mathematics computer game. *Gender and Education, 11*(2), 207–223.

Joiner, D. (Talin). (2002). Managing deviant behavior in online worlds. In J. Mulligan & B. Patrovsky (Eds.), *Developing online games: An insider's guide*. Boston, MA: New Riders Publishing.

Johnson, S. (2001). *Emergence: The connected lives of ants, brains, cities, and software*. London: Penguin Books.

Jones, G. (2002). *Killing monsters: Why children need fantasy super heroes, and make-believe violence*. New York: Basic Books.

Jones, R. (2006). From shooting monsters to shooting movies: Machinima and the transformative play of video game fan culture. In K. Hellekson & K. Busse (Eds.), *Fan fiction and fan communities in the age of the internet*. Jefferson, NC: McFarland.

Jung, C. G. (1928). On psychic energy. In C. G. Jung (Ed.), *Collected works 8: The structure and dynamics of psyche*. Princeton, NJ: Princeton University Press.

Juul, J. (2001). Computer games telling stories? A brief note on computer games and narratives. *Gamestudies, 1*(1).

Juul, J. (2002). *The open and the closed: Games of emergence and games of progression.* Paper presented at the Computer Games and Digital Cultures Conference, Tampere, Finland.

Juul, J. (2003a). *Half-real: Video games between real rules and fictional worlds* (Unpublished PhD thesis), IT University of Copenhagen, Copenhagen.

Juul, J. (2003b). *The game, the player, the world: Looking for a heart of gameness.* Paper presented at the Level Up—Digital Games Research Conference, Utrecht.

Juul, J. (2004). Introduction to game time. In N. Wardrip-Fruin & P. Harrigan (Eds.), *First person: New media as story, performance, and game.* Cambridge, MA: The MIT Press.

Juul, J. (2005). *Half-real: Video games between real rules and fictional worlds.* Cambridge, MA: The MIT Press.

Juul, J. (2008). The magic circle and the puzzle piece. In S. Günzel, M. Liebe, & D. Mersch (Eds.), *Conference proceedings of the philosophy of computer games 2008.* Potsdam: Universität Potsdam.

Juul, J. (2010). *A casual revolution: Reinventing video games and their players.* Boston, MA: The MIT Press.

Juul, J. (2011). *Gamification backlash roundup.* Retrieved November 7, 2011, from www.jesperjuul.net/ludologist/gamification-backlash-roundup

Kafai, J. B. (1998). Video game design by girls and boys: Variability and consistency of gender differences. In J. Cassell & H. Jenkins (Eds.), *From Barbie to Mortal Kombat: Gender and computer games.* Cambridge, MA: The MIT Press.

Kafai, Y. (1995). *Minds in play: Computer game design as a context for children's learning.* Hillsdale, NJ: Lawrence Erlbaum Associates.

Kafai, Y. (1996). Software by kids for kids. *Communications of the ACM, 39*(4), 38–40.

Kafai, Y. (2017). Connected gaming: An inclusive perspective for serious gaming. *International Journal of Serious Games, 4*(3).

Kafai, Y. B. (2001). *The educational potential of electronic games: From games-to-teach to games-to-learn.* Paper presented at the Playing by the Rules Conference, Chicago, IL.

Kahn, C. (2004). *Worldwide boxoffice.* Retrieved December 1, 2004, from www.worldwideboxoffice.com

Kain, E. (2014). GamerGate: A closer look at the controversy sweeping video games. *Forbes.* Retrieved February 21, 2015, from www.forbes.com/sites/erikkain/2014/09/04/gamergate-a-closer-look-at-the-controversy-sweeping-video-games/

Kapp, K. M. (2012). *The gamification of learning and instruction: Game-based methods and strategies for training and education.* San Francisco, CA: Wiley.

Karlsson, Ø. N. (2004). *First person politics: Computer games as political communication.* Unpublished manuscript, Copenhagen.

Karsenti, T., Bugmann, J., & Gros, P. P. (2017). *Transforming education with minecraft? Results of an exploratory study conducted with 118 elementary-school students*. Report. Montréal: CRIFPE.

Kennedy, H. (2018). Transmedia games: Aesthetics and politics of profitable play. In M. Freeman & R. Rampazzo Gambarato (Eds.), *The Routledge companion to transmedia studies*. New York: Routledge.

Kennedy, H. W. (2002). Lara Croft: Feminist icon or cyberbimbo? On the limits of textual analysis. *Gamestudies*, 2(2).

Kent, S. L. (2001). *The ultimate history of video games: From Pong to Pokemon, the story behind the craze that touched our lives and changed the world*. New York: Random House.

Kerr, A. (2003). Girls/women just want to have fun: A study of adult female players of digital games. In *Level Up conference proceedings* (pp. 270–285). Utrecht: University of Utrecht.

Kim, A. J. (1998, May 6). Killers have more fun. *Wired*. Retrieved February 21, 2012, from www.wired.com/wired/archive/6.05/ultima.html?topic=gaming& topic_set=newmedia.

Kinder, M. (1991). *Playing with power in movies, television and video games: From Muppet Babies to Teenage Mutant Ninja Turtles*. Berkeley: University of California Press.

King, B., & Borland, J. (2003). *Dungeons and dreamers: The rise of computer game culture from geek to chic*. New York: McGraw-Hill.

King, D., Haagsmab, M., Delfabbroa, P., Gradisarc, M., & Griffiths, M. D. (2013, April). Toward a consensus definition of pathological video-gaming: A systematic review of psychometric assessment tools. *Clinical Psychology Review*, 33(3), 331–342.

King, G. (2002). Die hard/try harder: Narrative, spectacle and beyond from hollywood to videogame. In T. Krzywinska (Ed.), *ScreenPlay: Cinema/videogames/interfaces*. London: Wallflower Press.

King, G., & Krzywinska, T. (2006). *Tomb Raiders and Space Invaders: Videogame forms and contexts*. London: I. B. Tauris.

Kirriemuir, J. (2002). Video gaming, education and digital learning technologies: Relevance and opportunities. *D-Lib Magazine*, 8(2).

Kirsh, S. J. (2003). The effects of violent video games on adolescents: The overlooked influence of development. *Aggression and Violent Behavior*, 8(4), 377–389.

Klabbers, J. (2018). On the architecture of game science. *Simulation and Gaming*, 49(3), 1–39.

Klastrup, L. (2003). *Towards a poetics of virtual worlds: Multiuser textuality and the emergence of story* (PhD thesis), IT University of Copenhagen, Copenhagen. IT-University Copenhagen.

Klastrup, L., & Tosca, S. (2004). *Transmedial worlds—rethinking cyberworld design*. Proceedings International Conference on Cyberworlds 2004, IEEEE Computer Society.

Klastrup, L., & Tosca, S. (2011). When fans become players: LOTRO in a transmedial world perspective. In T. Krzywinska, E. MacCallum-Stewart, & J. Parsler (Eds.), *Ringbearers: The Lord of the Rings Online as intertextual narrative*. Manchester: Manchester University Press.

Klawe, M. M. (1998). *When does the use of computer games and other interactive multimedia software help students learn mathematics?* Unpublished manuscript.

Klawe, M. M., & Phillips, E. (1995). *A classroom study: Electronic games engage children as researchers*. Paper presented at the CSCL Conference, Bloomington, IN.

Klevjer, R. (2002, June 6–8). *In defense of cutscenes*. Paper presented at the Computer Games and Digital Cultures Conference, Tampere, Finland.

Ko, S. (2002). An empirical analysis of children's thinking and learning in a computer game context. *Educational Psychology, 22*(2), 219–233.

Koivisto, J., & Hamari, J. (2016). The rise of motivational information systems: A review of gamification research. *International Journal of Information Management, 45*, 191–210, April 2019.

Koster, R. (2004). *A theory of fun for game design*. Scottsdale, AZ: Paraglyph Press, Inc.

Kotaku. (2014). *How much does it cost to make a big video game?* Retrieved January 3, 2015, from http://kotaku.com/how-much-does-it-cost-to-make-a-big-video-game-1501413649

Krahe, B., & Möller, I. (2010). Longitudinal effects of media violence on aggression and empathy among German adolescents. *Journal of Applied Developmental Psychology, 31*, 401–409.

Krotoski, A. (2004). *Chicks and joysticks: An exploration of women and gaming*. London: ELSPA.

Krzywinska, T. (2002). Hands-on-horror. In T. Krzywinska (Ed.), *ScreenPlay: Cinema/videogames/interfaces*. London: Wallflower Press.

Krzywinska, T. (2009). Arachne challenges minerva: The spinning out of long narrative in world of warcraft and buffy the vampire slayer. In P. Harrigan & N. Wardrip-Fruin (Eds.), *Third person: Authoring and exploring vast narratives*. Boston, MA: The MIT Press.

Kücklich, J. (2001, September). Literary theory and computer games. In *Proceedings of the first conference on computational semiotics for games and new media (COSIGN)*. Stichting Centrum voor Wiskunde en Informatica.

Kücklich, J. (2002). The study of computer games as a second-order cybernetic system. In F. Mayrä (Ed.), *CGDC02 conference proceedings*. Tampere, Finland: Tampere University Press.

Kücklich, J. (2003a). Perspectives on computer game philology. *Game Studies, 3*(1).

Kücklich, J. (2003b). The playability of computer games versus the readability of computer games: Towards a holistic theory of fictionality. In J. Raessens (Ed.), *Level up conference proceedings*. Utrecht: Utrecht University Press.

Kücklich, J. (2004). *Other playings—cheating in computer games.* Paper presented at Other Players: A Conference on Multiplayer Phenomena, Copenhagen.

Kücklich, J. (2005). Precarious playbour: Modders and the digital games industry. *Fibreculture Journal, 5.*

Kühn, S., Kugler, D., Schmalen, K., Weichenberger, M., Witt, C., & Gallinat, J. (2018). Does playing violent video games cause aggression? A longitudinal intervention study. *Molecular Psychiatry, 3*(13).

Kuntz, M. (1999). *SimCity 3000: Teacher's guide. An educational companion for SimCity 3000. For grades 6 and above.* Retrieved April 27, 2019, from https://studylib.net/doc/5921300/simcity-3000-teacher-s-guide

Kuo, A. (2001). *A (very) brief history of cheating.* Retrieved August 23, 2005, from http://shl.stanford.edu/Game_archive/StudentPapers/BySubject/A-I/C/Cheating/Kuo_Andy.pdf

Kushner, D. (2003). *Masters of doom: How two guys created an empire and transformed pop.* London: Piatkus.

Kuss, D. J., & Griffiths, M. D. (2012). Online gaming addiction in children and adolescents: A review of empirical research. *Journal of Behavioral Addictions, 1*(1), 3–22.

Lamb, R., Annetta, L., Firestone, J., & Etopio, E. (2018). A meta-analysis with examination of moderators of student cognition, affect, and learning outcomes while using serious educational games, serious games, and simulations. *Journal Computers in Human Behavior, 80,* 158–167.

Landers, R. N., Auer, E. M., Collmus, A. B., & Armstrong, M. B. (2018). Gamification science, its history and future: Definitions and a research agenda. *Simulation and Gaming, 49*(3), 315–337.

Landow, G. (1992). *Hypertext: The convergence of contemporary critical theory and technology.* Baltimore, MD: Johns Hopkins University Press.

Lane, C., & Yi, S. (2017). Chapter 7 — playing with virtual blocks: Minecraft as a learning environment for practice and research. In F. C. Blumberg & P. Brooks (Eds.), *Cognitive development in digital contexts.* London: Academic Press.

Langway, L. (1981, November 16). Invasion of the video creatures. *Newsweek, 90*–94. Retrieved February 21, 2012, from www.gamearchive.com/General/Articles/ClassicNews/1981/Newsweek11-16-81.htm

Lastowka, G., & Hunter, D. (2004). The laws of the virtual worlds. *California Law Review, 92*(1), 1–73.

Laurel, B. (1991/1993). *Computers as theatre.* Reading, MA: Addison-Wesley.

Lebling, P. D. (1980, December). Zork and the future of computerized fantasy simulations. *Byte.* Retrieved February 21, 2012, from www.csd.uwo.ca/Infocom/Articles/byte.html

Lebowitz, M. (1984). Creating characters in a storytelling universe. *Poetics, 13,* 171–194.

Lederman, L. C., & Fumitoshi, K. (1995). Debriefing the debriefing process: A new look. In K. Arai (Ed.), *Simulation and gaming across disciplines and cultures*. London: Sage Publications.

Lee, J. (1999). Effectiveness of computer-based instructional simulation: A meta-analysis. *International Journal of Instructional Media*, 26(1), 71–85.

Leeson, B. (2005). *Origins of the Kriegsspiel*. Retrieved August 25, 2005, from http://myweb.tiscali.co.uk/kriegsspiel/kriegsspiel/origins.htm

Leino, O. (2009). *On the logic of emotions in play*. Proceedings of ISAGA 2009 conference. Singapore: ISAGA.

Leino, O. (2010). *Emotions in play: On the constitution of emotion in solitary computer game play* (PhD thesis), IT University of Copenhagen, Copenhagen.

Leutner, D. (1993). Guided discovery learning with computer-based simulation games: Effects of adaptive and non-adaptive instructional support. *Learning and Instruction*, 3(2), 113–132.

Leyland, B. (1996). *How can computer games offer deep learning and still be fun?* Paper presented at Ascilite Conference, Adelaide, Australia.

Lieberoth, A. (2014). Shallow gamification: Testing psychological effects of framing an activity as a game. *Games and Culture*, 10(3), 229–248, May 2015.

Lienert, A. (2004, February 15). Video games open new path to market cars: Gamers are influencing new vehicle designs, advertisements. *Detroit News*.

Linderoth, J. (2002, August 19–22). *Making sense of computer games: Learning with new artefacts*. Paper presented at the Toys, Games and Media Conference, London.

Lindley, C. A. (2002). The gameplay Gestalt: Narrative and interactive storytelling. In F. Mayrä (Ed.), *CGDC02 conference proceedings*. Tampere, Finland: Tampere University Press.

Lindstrøm, M. (2003). *Brand games: Your move*. Retrieved August 9, 2004, from www.martinlindstrom.com/index.php?id=writing&archive_id=77

Livingstone, S. (2002). *Young people and new media: Childhood and the changing media environment*. London: Sage.

Loftus, G., & Loftus, E. (1983). *Mind at play: The psychology of video games*. New York: Basic Books.

Lowery, B., & Knirk, F. (1983). Micro-computer video games and spatial visual acquisition. *Journal of Educational Technology Systems*, 11(2), 155–166.

Lowood, H. (2006). High-performance play: The making of machinima. *Journal of Media Practice*, 7(1), 25–42.

Lu, A., & Kharrazi, H. (2018). A state-of-the-art systematic content analysis of games for health. *Games for Health*, 7(1).

Lu, A., Kharrazi, H., Gharghabi, F., & Thompson, D. (2013). A systematic review of health videogames on childhood obesity prevention and intervention. *Games for Health Journal, 2*(3).

Lucasfilm Games. (1990). *Loom manual.* San Francisco, CA: Lucasfilm Games.

Lyman, J. (2003, December 19). Gamer wins lawsuit in Chinese court over stolen virtual winnings. *TechNewsWorld.* Retrieved February 21, 2012, from www.technewsworld.com/story/32441.html

Lynch, P. J., Gentile, D. A., Olson, A. A., & Brederode, T.M.V. (2001, April). *The effects of violent video game habits on adolescent aggressive attitudes and behaviors.* Paper presented at the Biennial Conference of the Society for Research in Child Development, Minneapolis, MN.

MacCallum-Stewart, E., & Parsler, J. (2008). Role-play vs. Gameplay. The difficulties of playing a role in world of warcraft. In H. G. Corneliussen & J. W. Rettberg (Eds.), *Digital culture, play and identity: A World of Warcraft reader.* Boston, MA: The MIT Press.

Magnussen, R., & Misfeldt, M. (2004, December 6–8). *Player transformation of educational multiplayer games.* Paper presented at the Other Players Conference, Copenhagen.

Malaby, T. M. (2007). Beyond play: A new approach to games. *Games and Culture, 2*(2), 95–113.

Malone, T. W. (1980). *What makes things fun to learn? Heuristics for designing instructional computer games.* Paper presented at the Symposium on Small Systems archive, Palo Alto, CA.

Malone, T. W., & Lepper, M. (1987a). Intrinsic motivation and instructional effectiveness in computer-based education. In R. E. Snow & M. J. Farr (Eds.), *Aptitude, learning and instruction.* London: Lawrence Erlbaum Associates.

Malone, T. W., & Lepper, M. (1987b). Making learning fun: A taxonomy of intrinsic motivation for learning. In R. E. Snow & M. J. Farr (Eds.), *Aptitude, learning and instruction.* London: Lawrence Erlbaum Associates.

Mandal, S. (2013, April). Brief introduction of virtual reality & its challenges. *International Journal of Scientific & Engineering Research, 4*(4).

Manovich, L. (2001). *The language of new media.* Cambridge, MA: The MIT Press.

Mateas, M. (2001). A preliminary poetics for interactive drama and games. *Digital Creativity, 12*(3), 140–152.

Mateas, M., & Stern, A. (2003, March). *Façade: An experiment in building a fully realized interactive drama.* Paper presented at the Game Developers Conference, Game Design Track.

Mayer, R. (2001). *Multimedia learning.* New York: Cambridge University Press.

McFarlane, A., Sparrowhawk, A., & Heald, Y. (2002). *Report on the educational use of games.* Cambridge: TEEM (Teachers Evaluating Educational Multimedia).

McGonigal, J. (2003). *A real little game: The performance of belief in pervasive play.* Paper presented at the Level Up—Digital Games Research Conference, Utrecht.

McGonigal, J. (2011). *Reality is broken: Why games make us better and how they can change the world.* London: Jonathan Cape.

McLuhan, M. (1964). *Understanding media: The extensions of man.* New York: The New American Library, Inc.

Mead, G. H. (1934/1967). *Mind, self, and society: From the standpoint of a social behaviorist.* Chicago, IL: The University of Chicago Press.

Meehan, J. R. (1976). *The Metanovel: Writing stories by computer.* New Haven, CT: Yale University Press.

Mencher, M. (2003). *Get in the game! Careers in the game industry.* Boston, MA: New Riders Publishing.

Meretzky, S. (2001, November 20). Building character: An analysis of character creation. *Gamasutra.* Retrieved June 29, 2019, from https://www.gamasutra. com/view/feature/131887building_character_an_analysis_of.php

Meriam-Webster. Retrieved from www.merriam-webster.com/dictionary/gamification

Microsoft Corporation. (2011). *Microsoft earnings release FY12 Q1, key performance indicators.* Retrieved December 8, 2011, from www.microsoft.com/investor/ EarningsAndFinancials/Earnings/Kpi/fy12/Q1/detail.aspx

Microsoft Game Studios. (1982). *Microsoft flight simulator manual.* Redmond, WA: Microsoft Game Studios.

Microsoft. (2014). *Minecraft to join Microsoft.* Retrieved January 3, 2015, from http://news.microsoft.com/2014/09/15/minecraft-to-join-microsoft

MineCraft. (2015). *Statistics.* Retrieved January 3, 2015, from https://minecraft.net/ stats

MMODatanet. (2013). *Total MMORPG subscriptions and active accounts listed on this site.* Retrieved January 3, 2015, from http://users.telenet.be/mmodata/ Charts/TotalSubs.png

Mmogchart.com. (2005). *An analysis of MMOG subscription growth.* Retrieved August 26, 2005, from www.mmogchart.com

MobileDevMemo. (2014). *Why are mobile marketing costs rising?* Retrieved January 3, 2015, from http://mobiledevmemo.com/why-mobile-marketing-costs-rising

MobyGames. (2007a). *Halo 2.* Retrieved June 4, 2007, from www.mobygames.com/ game/xbox/halo-2/credits

MobyGames. (2007b). *SimCity.* Retrieved June 4, 2007, from www.mobygames. com/game/dos/simcity/credits

MobyGames. (2007c). *Call of duty: Modern warfare 2.* Retrieved November 14, 2011, from www.mobygames.com/game/ps3/call-of-duty-modern-warfare-2/credits

Montague, P., & Berns, G. (2002). Neural economics and the biological substrates of valuation. *Neuron, 36,* 265–284.

Mordor Intelligence. (2018). *Gamification market—growth, trends, and forecast (2019–2024).* Retrieved April 16, 2019, from www.mordorintelligence.com/industry-reports/gamification-market

Morningstar, C., & Farmer, F. R. (2003). The lessons of Lucasfilm's habitat. In N. Wardrip-Fruin & N. Montfort (Eds.), *The new media reader.* Cambridge, MA: The MIT Press.

Morris, S. (1999). *Online gaming culture: An examination of emerging forms of production and participation in multiplayer first-person-shooter gaming.* Retrieved from www.game-culture.com/articles/onlinegaming.html

Morrison, M. (2005). *Beginning game programming.* Indianapolis: SAMS.

Mortensen, T. (2007). Mutual fantasy online: Playing with people. In P. Williams & J. H. Smith (Eds.), *The players' realm: Studies on the culture of video games and gaming.* Jefferson, NC: McFarland.

Mortensen, T. (2009). *Perceiving play: The art and study of computer games.* New York: Peter Lang.

Mößle, T., Kliem, S., & Rehbein, F. (2014). Longitudinal effects of violent media usage on aggressive behavior: The significance of empathy. *Societies, 4,* 105–124.

Mouritsen, F. (2003). *Childhood and children's culture.* Portland, OR: International Specialized Book Service Inc.

Mulligan, J., & Patrovsky, B. (2003). *Developing online games: An insider's guide.* Indianapolis: New Riders.

Murray, J. (1997). *Hamlet on the Holodeck: The future of narrative on cyberspace.* Cambridge, MA: The MIT Press.

Nacke, L., & Deterding, S. (2017, June). The maturing of gamification research. *Computers in Human Behavior, 71,* 450–454.

Nacke, L., Ambinder, M., Canossa, A., Mandryk, R., & Stach, T. (2009). Game metrics and biometrics: The future of player experience research. In *Proceedings of futureplay, GDC Canada 2009.* Vancouver: ACM.

New York Times. (2010, August 13). *Down on the social farm.* Retrieved August 14, 2010, from www.nytimes.com/2010/08/14/opinion/14sat4.html?_r=1&partner=rssnyt&emc=rss&pagewanted=all

Newman, J. (2004). *Videogames.* London: Routledge.

Nicholson, S. (2012). A user-centered theoretical framework for meaningful gamification. Paper Presented at Games+Learning+Society 8.0, Madison, WI.

Nieborg, D. B., & Sihvonen, T. (2009, September). *The new gatekeepers: The occupational ideology of game journalism.* DiGRA '09 — Proceedings of the 2009 DiGRA International Conference: Breaking New Ground: Innovation in Games, Play, Practice and Theory. Brunel University, Volume 5. Tampere: DiGRA.

Nietzsche, F. (1891/2005). *Thus Spake Zarathustra*. Abacci Books (online publisher).

Nintendo Co., Ltd. (2011). *Consolidated sales transition by region*. Retrieved December 8, 2011, from www.nintendo.co.jp/ir/library/historical_data/pdf/consolidated_sales_e1109.pdf

Novak, J. (2007). *Game development essentials: An introduction* (2nd ed.). Clifton Park: Thomson, Delmar Learning.

O'Donnell, M. (2002). *Producing audio for Halo*. Retrieved January 23, 2004, from www.gamasutra.com/resource_guide/20020520/odonnell_01.htm

O'Riordan, K. (2001). Playing with Lara in virtual space. In S.R. Munt (Ed.), *Technospaces: Inside the new media*. London: Continuum.

Okagaki, L., & French, P. (1996). Effects of video game playing on measures of spatial performance: Gender effects in late adolescence. In P. Greenfield & R. Cocking (Eds.), *Interacting with video*. NJ: Ablex Publishing.

Okan, Z. (2003). Edutainment: Is learning at risk? *British Journal of Educational Technology, 34*(3), 255–264.

Olson, C.K. (2010). Children's motivations for video game play in the context of normal development. *Review of General Psychology, 14*(2), 180–187.

Papert, S. (1998, June). Does easy do it? Children, games and learning. *Game Developer*, 87–88. Retrieved March 11, 2015, from http://papert.org/articles/Doeseasydoit.html

Parlett, D.S. (1999). *The Oxford history of board games*. Oxford: Oxford University Press.

Pearce, C. (2005). *Theory wars: An argument against arguments in the so-called ludology/narratology debate*. Paper presented at the DiGRA 2005: Changing Views—Worlds in Play Conference, Vancouver.

Pearce, C. (2009). *Communities of play: Emergent cultures in multiplayer games and virtual worlds*. Boston, MA: The MIT Press.

Pellegrini, A.D. (1995). *The future of play theory: A multidisciplinary inquiry into the contributions of Brian Sutton-Smith*. Albany, NY: State University of New York Press.

Pelling, N. (2011). The (short) prehistory of "gamification" *Nanodome*. Retrieved June 29, 2019, from https://nanodome.wordpress.com/2011/08/09/the-short-prehistory-of-gamification.

Perlin, K. (2004). Can there be a form between a game and a story? In N. Wardrip-Fruin & P. Harrigan (Eds.), *First person: New media as story, performance, and game*. Boston, MA: The MIT Press.

Philips, T. (2011, August). Norway stores pull violent video games including *Call of Duty*. *Metro*. Retrieved October 6, 2011, from www.metro.co.uk/tech/games/871121-norway-stores-pull-violent-video-games-including-call-of-duty-after-massacre

Postigo, H. (2003). From pong to planet-quake: Post-industrial transitions from leisure to work. *Information, Communication and Society, 6*(4), 593–607.

Postman, N. (1986). *Amusing ourselves to death: Public discourse in the age of show business*. New York: Penguin Books.

Prensky, M. (2001). *Digital game-based learning*. New York: McGraw-Hill.

Prescott, A., Sargent, J., & Hull, J. (2018, October 2). Metaanalysis of the relationship between violent video game play and physical aggression over time. *PNAS, 115*(40), 9882–9888.

Propp, V. (1969). *Morphology of the folktale*. Austin: University of Texas.

Provenzo, E. F. (1991). *Video kids: Making sense of Nintendo*. Cambridge, MA: Harvard University Press.

Przybylski, A. K., & Weinstein, N. (2019). Violent video game engagement is not associated with adolescents' aggressive behaviour: Evidence from a registered report. *Royal Society Open Science*, 6, 171474. Retrieved from https://royalsocietypublishing.org/doi/pdf/10.1098/rsos.171474.

PwC. (2014). *Global entertainment and media outlook: 2014–2018*. London: PwC.

Raczkowski. (2014). Making points the point: Towards a history of ideas of gamification. In M. Fuchs, S. Fizek, P. Ruffino, & N. Schrape (Eds.), *Rethinking gamification* (pp. 119–140). Lüneburg: Meson Press. Retrieved from http://meson.press/books/rethinking-gamification

Radoff, J. (2011). *Game on: Energize your business with social media games*. Indianapolis: Wiley.

Raessens, J. (2006). Playful identities, or the ludification of culture. *Games and Culture, 1*(1), 52–57.

Ramírez, S. U., Forteza, B. R., Hernando, J. L. O., & Martorell, S. G. (2002). El rol de la figura femenina en los videojuegos. *Edutec. Revista Electrónica de Tecnología Educativa*, 15.

Randel, J. M., Morris, B. A., Wetzel, C. D., & Whitehill, B. V. (1992). The effectiveness of games for educational purposes: A review of recent research. *Simulation & Gaming, 23*(3), 261–276.

Rau, A. (2001, March 1–2). *Reload—yes/no: Clashing times in graphic adventure games*. Paper presented at Computer Games and Digital Textualities Conference, IT University of Copenhagen.

Raymer, R. (2011, September). Gamification: Using game mechanics to enhance eLearning. *eLearn Magazine*. Retrieved November 2011, from http://elearnmag.acm.org/archive.cfm? aid=2031772

Reeves, B., & Read, J. L. (2009). *Total engagement: Using games and virtual worlds to change the way people work and businesses compete*. Boston, MA: Harvard Business School Press.

Rieber, L. P. (1996). Seriously considering play: Designing interactive learning environments based on the blending of microworlds, simulations, and games. *Educational Technology Research and Development, 44*(2), 43–58.

Rimmon Kenan, S. (1983/2002). *Narrative fiction*. London: Routledge.

Robinson, T. N., Wilde, M. L., Navracruz, L. C., Haydel, K. F., & Varady, A. (2001). Effects of reducing children's television and video game use on aggressive behavior: A randomized controlled trial. *Archives of Pediatrics & Adolescent Medicine, 155*(7), 17–23.

Rodgers, Z. (2004, July 28). Chrysler reports big brand lift on advergames. *ClickZ News*. Retrieved February 21, 2012, from www.clickz.com/clickz/news/1715461/chrysler-reports-big-brand-lift-advergames

Rollings, A., & Adams, E. (2003). *Andrew Rollings and Ernest Adams on game design*. Boston, MA: New Riders Publishing.

Rollings, A., & Morris, D. (2000). *Game architecture and design*. Scottsdale: Coriolis.

Rollings, A., & Morris, D. (2004). *Game architecture and design: A new edition*. Boston, MA: New Riders Publishing.

Rothstein, E. (1983, May 8). Reading and writing: Participatory novels. *New York Times Book Review*. Retrieved June 29, 2019, from https://www.nytimes.com/1983/08/07/books/reading-and-writing-recollecting-books.html

Rouse, R. (2001). *Game design: Theory and practice*. Plano, TX: Wordware.

Rutter, J., & Bryce, J. (2006). *Understanding digital games*. London: Sage Publications.

Ryan, M. L. (1991). *Possible worlds, artificial intelligence, and narrative theory*. Bloomington, IN: Indiana University Press.

Ryan, M. L. (2001a). Beyond myth and metaphor: The case of narrative in digital media. *Game Studies*, v1(1).

Ryan, M. L. (2001b). *Narrative as virtual reality: Immersion and interactivity in literature and electronic media*. Baltimore, MD: Johns Hopkins University Press.

Ryan, M. L. (2016). Transmedia narratology and transmedia storytelling. *Artnodes: Revista D'art, Ciència I Tecnologia, Artnodes: Revista d'art, ciència i tecnologia*.

Ryan, M. L., & Thon, J. (2014). *Storyworlds across media, toward a media-conscious narratology*. Lincoln: UNP—Nebraska Paperback.

Ryan, M-L. (2006). Computer games as narrative: The ludology versus narrativism controversy In *Avatars of story* (vol. 1, p. 17). Electronic Mediations Series. University of Minnesota Press.

Ryan, T. (1999a). The anatomy of a design document, part 1: Documentation guidelines for the game concept and proposal. *Gamasutra*. Retrieved October 19, 1999, from www.gamasutra.com/features/19991019/ryan_01.htm

Ryan, T. (1999b). The anatomy of a design document, part 2: Documentation guidelines for the functional and technical specifications. *Gamasutra*. Retrieved December 17, 1999, from www.gamasutra.com/features/19991217/ryan_01.htm

Saegesser, F. (1981). Simulation-gaming in the classroom: Some obstacles and advantages. *Simulation & Gaming, 12*(3), 281–294.

Salen, K., & Zimmerman, E. (2004). *Rules of play: Game design fundamentals.* London: The MIT Press.

Saltzman, M. (2000). *Game design: Secrets of the sages.* Indianapolis: Brady Games.

Schierbeck, L., & Carstens, B. (1999). *Gennemgang af computerspil udgivet i Danmark i 1998.* Copenhagen: The Media Council for Children and Young People.

Schiesel, S. (2007a). P.E. classes turn to video game that works legs. *New York Times.* Retrieved July 17, 2007, from www.nytimes.com/2007/04/30/health/30exer. html?ex=1184817600&en=0d289da4bf2732e9&ei=5070

Schiesel, S. (2007b). Video games conquer retirees. *New York Times.* Retrieved August 3, 2007, from www.nytimes.com/2007/03/30/arts/30seni.html?ex=133 2907200&en=071aee3567f7bb9b&ei=5088&partner=rssnyt&emc=rss

Schiesel, S. (2007c). Genetics gone haywire and predatory children in an undersea metropolis. *New York Times.* Retrieved September 8, 2007, from www.nytimes. com/2007/09/08/arts/television/08shoc.html?pagewanted=all

Schonfeld, E. (2011). *With 250 million downloads Angry Birds moves into magic, cookbooks, and more.* Retrieved June 14, 2011, from http://techcrunch. com/2011/06/14/angry-birds-downloads-250-million-magi/

Schott, G., & Horrell, K. (2000). Girl gamers and their relationship with the gaming culture. *Convergence, 6*(4), 36–54.

Schousboe, I. (1993). Den onde leg—en udvidet synsvinkel på legen og dens funktioner. *Nordisk Psykologi, 45*(2), 97–119.

Scotsman. (2014). *New GTA V release tipped to rake in £1bn in sales.* Retrieved January 3, 2015, from www.scotsman.com/lifestyle/technology/new-gta-v-release-tipped-to-rake-in-1bn-in-sales-1-3081943

Sedighian, K., & Sedighian, A. S. (1996). *Can educational computer games help educators learn about the psychology of learning mathematics in children?* Paper presented at the 18th Annual Meeting of the International Group for the Psychology of Mathematics Education, Florida.

Seldes, G. (1957). *The seven lively arts.* New York: Sagmore Press.

Selling, N. (2011). *The (short) prehistory of "gamification."* Retrieved April 28, 2019, from https://nanodome.wordpress.com/2011/08/09/the-short-prehistory-of-gamification/

Seth, J., Manning, D., Keiper, M., & Olrich, T. (2016). Virtual(ly) athletes: Where eSports fit within the definition of "sport." *Quest, 69,* 1–18.

Shaffer, D. W. (2006). *How computer games help children learn.* New York: Palgrave Macmillan.

Shaw, A. (2010). What is video game culture? Cultural studies and game studies. *Games and Culture, 5*(4), 403–424.

Sheffield, B. (2010). *GDC Europe: Limbo's Carlsen on making players your worst enemy and your best friend*. Retrieved August 16, 2010, from www.gamasutra.com/view/news/29934/GDC_Europe_Limbos_Carlsen_On_Making_Players_Your_Worst_Enemy_And_Your_Best_Friend.php

Sherblom-Woodward, B. (2002). *Hackers, gamers and lamers: The use of l33t in the computer sub-culture* (Unpublished Master's thesis), Swarthmore College, Swarthmore, PA.

Sherry, J. L. (2001). The effects of violent video games on aggression: A meta-analysis. *Human Communication Research, 27*(3), 409–431.

Shippee, M. (2017). *Gaming in the classroom—a classroom guide to civilization IV: Colonization*. Retrieved April 27, 2019, from https://micahshippee.com/2017/02/23/gaming-in-the-classroom-a-classroom-guide-to-civilization-iv-colonization-edchat-gaming-edtech/

Shute, V., & Ke, F. (2015). Games, learning, and assessment. In D. Ifenthaler, D. Eseryel, & X. Ge (Eds.), *Assessment in game-based learning: Foundations, 43 innovations, and perspective*. New York: Springer.

Sicart, M. (2009). *The ethics of computer games*. Boston, MA: The MIT Press.

Silverman, E. (2018, December 28). Not just for kids: Why board games are making a comeback with grown-ups. *The Inquirer*. Retrieved April 16, 2019, from www.philly.com/business/board-games-monopoly-uno-philadelpha-cafe-holiday-20181228.html

Singer, P. (2009). *Video game veterans and the new American politics*. Retrieved February 12, 2012, from www.brookings.edu/opinions/2009/1r117_video_games_singer.aspx

Sitzman, T. (2011, May). A meta-analytic examination of the instructional effectiveness of computer-based simulation games. *Personnel Psychology, 64*(2), 489–528.

Sitzmann, T., & Ely, K. (2010). *A meta-analytic examination of the effectiveness of computer-based simulation games*. ADL Research and Evaluation Team. Alexandria: The Advanced Distributed Learning Initiative.

Smith, H. (2001). *The future of game design: Moving beyond Deus Ex and other dated paradigms*. Retrieved December 16, 2004, from www.igda.org/articles/hsmith_future.php

Smith, J. H. (2000a). The Dragon in the Attic. *Game Research*. Retrieved August 3, 2007, from http://game-research.com/index.php/articles/the-dragon-in-the-attic-on-the-limits-of-interactive-fiction/

Smith, J. H. (2000b). The road not taken: The how's and why's of interactive fiction. *Game Research*. Retrieved August 3, 2007, from http://game-research.com/index.php/articles/the-road-not-taken-the-hows-and-whys-of-interactive-fiction/

Smith, J. H. (2003). Avatars you can trust: A survey on the issue of trust and communication in MMORPGs. *Game Research*. Retrieved August 3, 2007, from http://game-research.com/index.php/articles/avatars-you-can-trust-a-survey-on-the-issue-of-trust-and -communication-in-mmorpgs/

Smith, J. H. (2004). *Playing dirty: Understanding conflicts in multiplayer games.* Paper presented at the 5th annual conference of the Association of Internet Researchers, University of Sussex.

Smith, J. H. (2006a). The games economists play: Implications of economic game theory for the study of computer games. *Game Studies, 6*(1).

Smith, J. H. (2006b). *Plans and purposes: How videogame goals shape player behaviour* (Unpublished PhD thesis), IT University of Copenhagen, Copenhagen.

Sniderman, S. (1999). Unwritten rules. *The Life of Games, 1*(1), 2–7.

Snow, B. (2007). *Wii outsells the mighty PS2 for the same period.* Retrieved July 8, 2007, from www.infendo.com/gamecube/wii-outsells-the-mighty-ps2-for-the-same-period/

Sony Computer Entertainment, Inc. (2011). *PlayStation®3 worldwide hardware unit sales.* Retrieved December 8, 2011, from www.scei.co.jp/corporate/data/bizdataps3_sale_e.html

Sørensen, B. H., & Jessen, C. (2000). It isn't real: Children, computer games, violence and reality. In C. V. Feilitzen & U. Carlsson (Eds.), *Children in the new media landscape: Games, pornography, perceptions.* Göteborg: The UNESCO International Clearinghouse on Children and Violence on the Screen at Nordicom.

Sotamaa, O. (2003). *Computer game modding, intermediality and participatory culture.* Unpublished manuscript.

Squire, K. D. (2004a). *Replaying history* (Unpublished PhD thesis), Indiana University.

Squire, K. D. (2004b). Civilization III as a world history sandbox. In M. Bittanti (Ed.), *Civilization and its discontents: Virtual history. Real fantasies.* Milan, Italy: Ludilogica Press.

Squire, K. D. (2006). From content to context: Videogames as designed experience. *Educational Researcher, 35*(8), 19–29.

Steinkuehler, C. A. (2006). Why game (culture) studies now? *Games and Culture, 1*(1), 97–102.

Stevenson, R., & Berkowitz, B. (2004). Video game industry faces "Crisis of Creativity." *Forbes.com.* Retrieved July 17, 2007, from www.forbes.com/business/newswire/2004/03/26/rtr1313656.html

Strittmatter, E., Kaess, M., Parzer, P., Fischer, G., Carli, V., Hoven, C. W., . . . Wasserman, D. (2015, July). Pathological internet use among adolescents: Comparing gamers and non-gamers. *Psychiatry Research, 228*(1), 128–135.

Subrahmanyam, K., & Greenfield, P. (1996). Effect of video game practice. In P. Greenfield & R. Cocking (Eds.), *Interacting with video.* New Jersey: Ablex Publishing.

Suits, B. (1978). *Grasshopper: Games, life, and Utopia.* Toronto: University of Toronto Press.

Sutton-Smith, B. (1997). *The ambiguity of play.* Cambridge, MA: Harvard University Press.

Sutton-Smith, B., & Kelly-Byrne, D. (1984). The idealization of play. In P. K. Smith (Ed.), *Play in animals and humans.* Oxford: Basil Blackwell.

Swing, E., Gentile, D. A., Anderson, C. A., & Walsh, D. (2010). Television and video game exposure and the development of attention problems. *Pediatrics, 126*(2), 214–221.

Takahashi, D. (2010). *The Sims celebrates 125 million games sold across 10 years.* Retrieved February 3, 2010, from http://venturebeat.com/2010/02/03/the-sims-celebrates-125-million-games-sold-across-10-years/

Taylor, A. (2013, March 28). How to make a video game for the blind: Audio-based games are more than entertainment. They can be a tool to teach blind and visually impaired people how to navigate new environments. *Popular Mechanics.* Retrieved May 12, 2019, from www.popularmechanics.com/culture/gaming/a13065/how-to-mak-a-video-game-for-the-blind-15277536

Taylor, H. (2018). The era of "break-out indie success" is long dead, 11th May 2018. *Gamesindustry.biz.* Retrieved May 12, 2019, from www.gamesindustry.biz/articles/2018-05-11-the-era-of-break-out-indie-success-is-long-dead

Taylor, J. (2003). *Home interactive entertainment market update 2002–2003.* Arcadia Investment Corp.

Taylor, T. L. (2002). Whose avatar is this anyway? Negotiating corporate ownership in a virtual world. In F. Mayrä (Ed.), *CGDC 02 conference proceedings.* Tampere, Finland: Tampere University Press.

Taylor, T. L. (2003a). Multiple pleasures: Women and online gaming. *Convergence, 9*(1), 8–18.

Taylor, T. L. (2003b, November 4–6). *Power gamers just want to have fun? Instrumental play in a MMOG.* Paper presented at the Level Up: Digital Games Research Conference 2003, Utrecht.

Taylor, T. L. (2006). *Play between worlds: Exploring online game culture.* Cambridge, MA: MIT Press.

Thon, J. (2016). *Transmedial narratology and contemporary media culture.* Lincoln, Nebraska, and London: University of Nebraska Press.

Toda, T., Valle, P., & Isotani, S. (2018). The dark side of gamification: An overview of negative effects of gamification in education. In A. Cristea, A. Bittencourt, & F. Lima (Eds.), *Higher education for all: From challenges to novel technology-enhanced solutions.* Switzerland: Springer.

Tønner, U. (2000). *Reklamespil på nettet er effektiv branding.* Retrieved August 9, 2004, from http://design.emu.dk/artik/00/36-branding.html

Tosca, S. P. (2003a). The appeal of cute monkeys. In J. Raessens (Ed.), *Level-up conference proceedings*. Utrecht: Utrecht University Press.

Tosca, S. P. (2003b). The quest problem in computer games. In *TIDSE 03 Proceedings*. Darmstadt: Fraunhofer IRB Verlag.

Tosca, S. P. (2003c). Reading resident evil: Code Veronica X. In *Proceedings of DAC03*. Melbourne: RMIT Press.

Tosca, S. P. (2005). Implanted memories or the illusion of free action. In W. Brooker (Ed.), *The blade runner experience*. London: Wallflower Press.

Tronstad, R. (2001). Semiotic and non-semiotic MUD performance. In *Proceedings of COSIGN 01*. Amsterdam.

Trunnel, D. (2002). *Reality in fantasy: Violence, gender and race in final fantasy IX.* Retrieved from www.communication.ilstu.edu/activities/CSCA2002/Reality_in_Fantasy.pdf

Turkle, S. (1984). *The second self: Computers and the human spirit*. London: Granada.

Turkle, S. (1995). *Life on the screen: Identity in the age of the internet*. London: Phoenix.

Tychsen, A., Hitchens, M., & Brolund, T. (2008). Character play: The use of game characters in multi-player role playing games across platforms. *ACM Computers in Entertainment, 6*(2).

Tychsen, A., Hitchens, M., Brolund, T., McIlwain, D., & Kavakli, M. (2008). Group play: Determining factors on the gaming experience in multi-player role playing games. *ACM Computers in Entertainment, 5*(4).

Valentine, R. Pokemon GO has brought in $1.8 billion since launch, 6th July 2018. *Gamesindustry.biz.* Retrieved April 14, 2019, from www.gamesindustry.biz/articles/2018-07-06-pokemon-go-tops-sales-charts-again-two-years-after-launch

Van Eck, R. (2009). A guide to integrating COTS games in your classroom. In R. Ferdig (Ed.), *Handbook of research on effective electronic gaming in education* (1st ed., pp. 179–199). Hershey, PA: Information Science.

Van Sickle, R. (1986). A quantitative review of research on instructional simulation gaming: A twenty-year perspective. *Theory & Research in Social Education, 14*(3), 245–264.

VentureBeat. (2014). *Online games expected to hit $13B in 2014, with at least $946M from League of Legends alone.* Retrieved January 3, from http://venturebeat.com/2014/10/23/online-games-expected-to-hit-13b-in-2014-with-at-least-946m-from-league-of-legends-alone/

Vera, J., & Terrón, J. (2018, October–December). Following the trail of eSports: The multidisciplinary boom of research on the competitive practice of video games. *International Journal of Gaming and Computer-Mediated Simulations, 10*(4).

Vermeulen, L., Van Looy, J., Courtois, C., & De Grove, F. (2011). Girls will be girls? A study into differences in game design preferences across gender and player types. *Under the mask: Perspectives on the gamer*. Papers presented at the under the mask: Perspectives on the gamer conference.

Video Game Sales Wiki. (2011). *Madden NFL*. Retrieved November 11, 2011, from http://vgsales.wikia.com/wiki/Madden_NFL

Video Game Sales Wiki. (undated). *Video game industry*. Retrieved from http://vgsales.wikia.com/wiki/Video_game_industry

Virtual Reality Society. *History of virtual reality*. Retrieved May 12, 2019, from www.vrs.org.uk/virtual-reality/history.html

Vogel, D., Wright, M. & Bowers, CA (2006). Computer gaming and interactive simulations for learning: A meta-analysis. *Journal of Educational Computing Research*. 34(3):229–243.

Wagner, M. G. (2006). *On the scientific relevance of eSports*. International Conference on Internet Computing, Las Vegas, NV.

Walker, J. (2007). A network of quests in world of warcraft. In P. Harrigan & N. Wardrip-Fruin (Eds.), *Second person: Role-playing and Story in games and playable media*. Cambridge, MA: The MIT Press.

Walton, M. (2010). *Gamespot's guide to 3D gaming*. Retrieved September 20, 2010, from www.gamespot.com/features/6276546/gamespots-guide-to-3d-gaming

Wang, F. (2005, August 3). *China bans minors under 18 from playing online games that allow players to kill other players*. Interfax China.

Ward, M. (2003, September 29). *Does virtual crime need real justice?* Retrieved November 11, 2003, from http://news.bbc.co.uk/1/hi/technology/3138456.stm

Wardrip-Fruin, N. (2009). *Expressive processing: Digital fictions, computer games and software studies*. Boston, MA: The MIT Press.

Wardrip-Fruin, N., & Harrigan, P. (2007). *Second person: Role-playing and story in games and playable media*. Cambridge, MA: The MIT Press.

Waskul, D. D. (2006). The role-playing game and the game of role-playing. In J. P. Williams, S. Q. Hendricks, & W. K. Winkler (Eds.), *Gaming as culture: Essays on reality, identity and experience in fantasy games*. Jefferson, NC: McFarland.

Wastiau, P., Kearney, C., & Van den Berghe, W. (2009). *How are digital games used in school? Complete results of the study*. Retrieved April 4, 2014, from the European Schoolnet website http://games.eun.org/upload/gis-full_report_en.pdf

WCG. (2010). *Hall of fame*. Retrieved from www.worldcybergames.com/6th/history/Halloffame/Hall_main.asp

Weir, P. (2000). *Satisfaction with interaction: Future prospects for interactive audio*. Retrieved January 21, 2004, from www.earcom.net/article_BAFTA.htm

Wentworth, D.R., & Lewis, D.R. (1973). A review of research on instructional games and simulations in social studies education. *Social Education, 37*, 432–440.

Werbach, K., & Hunter, D. (2012). *For the win: How game thinking can revolutionize your business*. Philadelphia: Wharton Digital Press.

Whine, M. (2007). Common Motifs on Jihadi and far right websites. In B. Ganor, K.V. Knop, & C.A.M. Duarte (Eds.), *Hypermedia seduction for terrorist recruiting*. Amsterdam, Netherlands: IOS Press.

White, P.V. (2007). *MMOGData*. Retrieved July 17, 2007, from http://mmogdata. voig.com/Home.html

Whitebread, D. (1997). Developing children's problem-solving: The educational uses of adventure games. In A. McFarlane (Ed.), *Information technology and authentic learning*. London: Routledge.

Williams, D. (2002). Structure and competition in the U.S. home video game industry. *The International Journal on Media Management, 4*(1), 41–54.

Williams, D. (2003a). *Trouble in river city: The social life of video games* (Unpublished PhD thesis), University of Michigan.

Williams, D. (2003b). The videogame lightning rod: Constructions of a new media technology, 1970–2000. *Information, Communication and Society, 6*(4), 524–549.

Williams, D., & Skoric, M. (2005). Internet fantasy violence: A test of aggression in an online game. *Communication Monographs, 22*(2), 217–233.

Williams, P., & Smith, J.H. (2007). *The players' realm: Studies on the culture of video games and gaming*. Jefferson, NC: McFarland.

Williams, P., Hendricks, S.Q., & Winkler, W.K. (Eds.). (2006). *Gaming as culture: Essays on reality, identity and experience in fantasy games*. Jefferson, NC: McFarland.

Willoughby, A., & Good, M. (2012, July). A longitudinal study of the association between violent video game play and aggression among adolescents. *Developmental Psychology, 48*(4), 1044–1057.

Wirman, H. (2009). On productivity and game fandom. *Transformative Works and Cultures, 3*.

Wirman, H. (2010). Playing the Sims 2: Constructing and negotiating woman computer game player identities through the practice of skinning (PhD thesis), University of the West of England, Bristol.

Wittgenstein, L. (1967, first published 1953). *Philosophical investigations*. Oxford: Blackwell.

Wolf, M.J.P. (2001). *The medium of the video game*. Austin: University of Texas Press.

Wong, M. (2004, October 18). *Advertisements insinuated into video games*. Retrieved January 27, 2005, from www.bizreport.com/news/8204

Woodcock, B. S. (2006). *An analysis of MMOG subscription growth—version 21.0.* Retrieved July 17, 2007, from www.mmogchart.com/

Wouters, P., & Oostendorp, H. V. (2013, January). A meta-analytic review of the role of instructional support in game-based learning. *Computers & Education, 60*(1), 412–425.

Wright, T., Boria, E., & Breidenbach, P. (2002). Creative player actions in FPS online video games. *Game Studies, 2*(2).

Yee, N. (2001). *The Norrathian scrolls: A study of EverQuest, version 2.5.* Retrieved from www.nickyee.com/eqt/report.html

Youn, S., Lee, M., & Doyle, K. O. (2003). Lifestyles of online gamers: A psychographic approach. *Journal of Interactive Advertising, 3*(2).

Zichermann, G. (2010, October 26). Fun is the future: Mastering gamification. *Google Tech Talk.*

Zichermann, G., & Cunningham, C. (2011). *Gamification by design: Implementing game mechanics in web and mobile apps.* Sebastobol, CA: O'Reilly Media.

Zichermann, G., & Linder, J. (2010). *Game-based marketing: Inspire customer loyalty through rewards, challenges, and contests.* New York: John Wiley & Sons.

Zichermann, G., & Linder, J. (2013). *The gamification revolution: How leaders leverage game mechanics to crush the competition.* New York: McGraw-Hill.

Zillmann, D. (1979). *Hostility and aggression.* Hillsdale, NJ: Erlbaum.

Zyda, M., Hiles, J., Mayberry, A., Wardynski, C., Capps, M., Osborn, B., . . . Davis, M. (2003). Entertainment R&D for defense. *IEEE Computer Graphics and Applications, 23*(1), 28–36.

Index

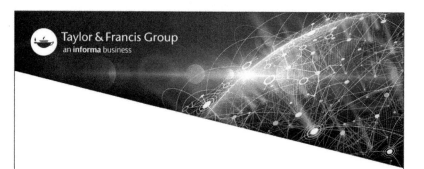